The Patriots' Dilemma

"A stunning achievement. Masterly. Finally, an analysis of slavery and republicanism from the left, not seeking to excuse inhumanity by referring to stale recipes about 'bourgeois democracy.' As the progressive movement in the U.S. begins increasingly to discuss impending fascism, finally we have an account that provides historical foundation for this chilling conception. Brilliant. Insightful."

—Gerald Horne, author, *The Counter-Revolution of 1776: Slave Resistance and the Origins of the USA*

"In explaining the role of self-interest in the abolition work of the founding generation, Timothy Messer-Kruse broadens debates that generally focus on the motives and efforts of those who supported African recolonization to show that the rhetoric attributed to colonizationists permeates the work of early abolitionists in general. Messer-Kruse takes away the illusion of altruism and replaces it with an honest examination of the role of self-interest in the first generation of antislavery."

—Beverly Tomek, author of *Colonization and Its Discontents: Emancipation, Emigration, and Antislavery in Antebellum Pennsylvania*

The Patriots' Dilemma

White Abolitionism and Black Banishment in the Founding of the United States of America

Timothy Messer-Kruse

PLUTO  PRESS

First published 2024 by Pluto Press
New Wing, Somerset House, Strand, London WC2R 1LA
and Pluto Press, Inc.
1930 Village Center Circle, 3-834, Las Vegas, NV 89134

www.plutobooks.com

British Library Cataloguing in Publication Data
A catalogue record for this book is available from the British Library

ISBN 978 0 7453 4967 1   Paperback
ISBN 978 0 7453 4970 1   PDF
ISBN 978 0 7453 4968 8   EPUB

Typeset by Stanford DTP Services, Northampton, England

Simultaneously printed in the United Kingdom and United States of America

Contents

My experience has very much diminished my Faith in the veracity of History.—it has convinced me that many of the most important facts are concealed.—some of the most important characters but imperfectly known—many false facts imposed on historians and the world—and many empty characters displayed in great pomp—All this, I am sure, will happen in our American history.

John Adams*

* *The Adams Papers, Papers of John Adams, vol. 20, June 1789–February 1791*, Sara Georgini, Sara Martin, R.M. Barlow, Gwen Fries, Amanda M. Norton, Neal E. Millikan, and Hobson Woodward, eds. (Cambridge, MA: Harvard University Press, 2020), pp. 104–6.

Introduction

In the summer of 2015, the musical *Hamilton* opened on Broadway. After a short greeting from a voice calling himself "King George the Third," the house lights dimmed, a hip-hop beat drummed out and onto the sparse stage strode a large multiracial cast including actors of color in the roles of Hamilton, Jefferson, Madison, and Washington. *Hamilton's* bold "colorblind casting" was hailed as a subversive refiguring of American heroes who had grown brittle and distant.

Hamilton roared to enduring success both from critics and enthusiastic audiences, quickly becoming what *Rolling Stone* described as "the most unlikely cultural phenomenon in a generation." Whatever concoction made for such popularity is certainly drawn from many ingredients. In part, it rose upon the same hopeful wave of racial reconciliation that carried Barack Obama to the White House. Like America's first black president, *Hamilton* seemed to represent a resolution to America's conflicted feelings about its national heritage. Portraying a Latino Hamilton and a black Washington fighting for liberty made the story of America something that could finally be owned by people of color, as opposed to the reality, which so often refuted the relevance of their part in that saga. Moreover, it granted permission to whites uncertain about the optics of celebrating slave-owners to openly display their patriotism.[1]

It was years before *Hamilton* was the subject of sustained criticism. But in the summer of 2020, in the wake of a nationwide campaign to remove confederate statues from public display and the murder of George Floyd under the knee of Minnesota police officer Derek Chauvin, the play was suddenly criticized for sidelining the issue of slavery. That summer, when *Hamilton* leaped from the stage to the screen on the Disney channel, interviewers pressed playwright, librettist, and composer, Lin Manuel Miranda to explain why *Hamilton* steered clear of the founder's role in perpetuating slavery. Miranda

1

told NPR's Terry Gross that the play's avoidance of slavery mirrored the founders themselves:

... other than calling out Jefferson on his hypocrisy with regards to slavery in Act 2, doesn't really say much else over the course of Act 2. And I think that's actually pretty honest ... He didn't really do much about it after that. None of them did. None of them did enough. And we say that, too, in the final moments of the song. So that hits differently now because we're having a conversation, we're having a real reckoning of how do you uproot an original sin?[2]

Hamilton represented a rare cultural moment of collision between the desire for national heroes and the responsibility for facing squarely the legacies of slavery. Suddenly, the awareness of the hypocritical relationship between the founder's ideals of equality and democracy and the unfathomable cruelty of slavery seemed to trouble most people who gave it a thought. This was a relatively new problem as it couldn't cloud the national mythology as long as whites thought of slavery as a mere footnote and sidebar to the triumphant American story. This creeping knowledge, expanding since the Civil Rights struggles of the 1960s, hollowed out the towering figures of the American pantheon and sullied patriotism itself. How can we celebrate our national founders who were so morally compromised?

While some critics complained that *Hamilton* avoided the issue of slavery, others noted that Miranda's play focused on a group of revolutionary leaders who stood against it. Not long into the first act, Hamilton, played by Miranda, gathers with his buddies, Aaron Burr, John Laurens, and Hercules Mulligan. The words to their rap go this way:

LAURENS: But we'll never be truly free until those in bondage have the same rights as you and me, you and I. Do or die. Wait till I sally in on a stallion with the first black battalion ...

HAMILTON ... Let's hatch a plot blacker than the kettle callin' the pot ... What are the odds the gods would put us all in one spot, poppin' a squat on conventional wisdom, like it or not, a bunch of revolutionary manumission abolitionists? Give me a position, show me where the ammunition is!

Describing these stars of his play as "abolitionists" was quite a stretch. While it's general knowledge that Washington, Jefferson, and Madison were served by many slaves, most of those who have experienced *Hamilton* probably didn't know that every man in this "bunch of revolutionary manumission abolitionists" also owned or trafficked in slaves.[3]

For most *Hamilton* fans, indeed for most Americans, this is one way in which slavery is reconciled with a heroic view of America's founding. Most patriot leaders, like Hamilton and Laurens, expressed their hope that slavery be abolished someday. Their tragedy was not in their hearts but in their lack of action. This solution pushed back against depicting the founders as hypocrites, men like Jefferson who wrote profoundly about liberty and equality and yet refused to grant these ideals to the hundreds of people that were his chattels.

But what did being a "revolutionary manumission abolitionist" mean in 1776? Did it mean, as most modern people would assume, freeing those in bondage and allowing them to direct their own lives? Or did it mean something that is hard for us today to even conceive, let alone sympathize with?

Many people are aware that the first states to abolish slavery did so in a cautiously slow way. George Washington famously supported ending slavery as long as such abolishment was "by slow, sure and imperceptable degrees."[4] Pennsylvania, the first state to enact a law ending slavery, specified in 1780 that those currently in bondage would remain so for the rest of their natural lives while those born of enslaved mothers would remain another's property for twenty-five years.

Such gradual means of ending human bondage are usually understood as being the product of compromise and the politics of what was possible to achieve in the face of the staunch resistance of those invested in slavery. This is an understandable mistake. In fact, in the eighteenth century, even the advocates of abolition recoiled from any suggestion that slavery simply be done away with. Benjamin Franklin signed a public letter for the leading abolitionist society in Pennsylvania that called for ending slavery but warned that "its very extirpation, if not performed with solicitous care, may sometimes open a source of serious evils." Virtually all "abolitionists" at the time of the American Revolution thought of ending slavery not as a means of freeing those in chains to pursue their own lives, but as a process that would require some form of white supervision and control in order to ensure the safety of white citizens. Many opponents of slavery assumed that ending human bondage would necessitate the expulsion of all black people from their states. Only black people themselves raised their voices to argue that freedom meant not only the end of slavery, but their membership in the new republic on an equal basis with white people.[5]

Part of our contemporary difficulty in understanding the founders' attitudes and actions as they operated in their own day is our own assumptions about racism. Today, Americans generally equate racism with bigotry, a category of belief that mixes complicated ideas about human nature with negative emotions of fear, hatred, or repulsion. This understanding of racism is quite modern and is a product of social and political changes that occurred long after the Revolutionary era. In earlier eras, racism was not necessarily charged with emotion, and, when it was, the connotations attached to blackness were not all negative. Eighteenth-century racism could comfortably combine ideas of black inferiority with warm feelings of benevolence and hopefulness.

It is common to place too much credence in patriot and abolitionist pronouncements that to our ears sound like condemnations of racism. Our ears are tuned to sift beliefs into categories of racist and colorblind, exclusion and inclusion, or privilege and equality. But the eighteenth-century mind of white Americans did not parse their world into those same boxes. Racism was not yet a fully formed concept as racial differences were seen as natural and obvious, and the only question was under what conditions would Africans shed their savage ways and whether that process would take an entire lifetime or generations of them. When eighteenth-century revolutionaries declared that "God, who made the world, hath made of one blood all

4

nations of men, and animated them with minds equally rational," they were not making a claim for all races of men to have equal political power for the simple reason that in their time equality of capacities was not linked to an equality of political rights. White men who were poor, itinerant, or of the wrong faith, were routinely denied a say in the governance of their communities and this was not generally seen as a violation of democratic values.[6]

Partisans of both sides of issues that slavery provoked assumed that black people were not equal to whites, though they differed on whether these differences were permanent or temporary, indelible or correctable. Though these complexes of ideas could be quite different, even polar opposites, their implications upon policies of the moment were negligible. Whether one viewed black people as naturally and essentially inferior to whites or one believed they were debased and corrupted by their environment and upbringing, the implication of either belief was that black people should not be turned loose without white supervision or allowed to govern.

In many ways, racism is a concept that lacks usefulness in describing society in the eighteenth century. This is because no white people stood apart from racism; "racist" was at best a spectrum of intensity from hard to soft rather than a label that applied to some patriots and not to others. Fundamentally, all white leaders and activists, even antislavery crusaders, filtered their views through a lens of white interest. As historical sociologist Joe Feagin has argued, white Americans were largely unaware of the extent to which their own "white racial frame" of perception and understanding shaped their attitudes and configured their actions.[7]

To truly understand what ending slavery meant to those we loosely call patriots in the earliest days of the United States of America, we must put aside our tendencies to view the past in terms of heroes and villains. Those who opposed slavery and those who defended it shared more than we imagine. Most defenders of slavery expressed their disapproval, even their hatred of the institution. Most of slavery's opponents expressed their disregard and dislike of black people. Both sides, if we can call them sides, of the slavery question grounded their opinions on what they believed was best for the well-being and future of the white community. Both assumed that the American republic could only function and prosper if black people were disempowered and subject to white rule. Rather than seeing defenders and opponents of slavery as two warring camps, it is more useful to see them as poles of a broad spectrum of opinion all sharing the same principles and assumptions but arriving at different ideas about how best to advance them.[8]

Anxiety about slavery had grown unevenly since the beginning of the 1700s across the Americas, especially at those times when enslaved people took matters into their own hands and attempted to free themselves, either by rebelling on their own or taking advantage of wars between colonizing nations and agreeing to fight for their enslaver's enemies in exchange for their freedom. European nations were able to accommodate both racial slavery and black freedom in their empires by enacting policies that both abolished slavery and limited the growth of black populations in their homelands while strengthening slavery in their far-flung colonies.

Similar policies were not available to the newly independent American colonies because the core of their plantation economy was centered within their homeland. Compounding the Americans' problematic relationship with slavery and black freedom was the simple fact that their own principles seemed to demand that those emancipated should be treated equally and given a share of political power in a democratic republic. Here was the dilemma that America's founders never resolved: how to abolish slavery without overthrowing white rule in a republic where ideally all men enjoy equal rights?

Commonly, both specialists and members of the broader public assume that Americans in the past were politically divided in ways that would also make sense according to the politics of today. Given its complete denial of the humanity of its victims and the totality of its exploitation, slavery seems to offer no middle ground. Thus, it makes sense that if anyone spoke out against slavery in the Revolutionary era then it must have been an issue that demanded that leaders choose sides.

But the complexity of the past exceeds our imaginations. Reading closely into the speeches and writings of the founding generation and documenting their actions reveals that slavery was not nearly as polarizing a question as we imagine it was. Most founders expressed their opposition to it but did little to fight it and often personally labored to keep black men, women, and children in bondage. In expressing their hatred of slavery and their wish to see it eradicated while holding others' chains, the founders were not being hypocritical, because hypocrisy requires a refusal to act on one's principles. In the Revolutionary era, even those most outspoken against slavery balanced their dreams of a future in which slavery no longer existed with what was universally seen as the practical complications of black freedom.

What seems today as clashing camps of opposition to and support for slavery actually shared many presumptions and sprung from the same sources. Both seemingly pro- and antislavery factions based their views on what was best for white Americans. Both agreed that slavery, for all its moral faults, served a vital purpose in controlling and policing what they both agreed was a dangerous and burdensome population. No white Americans, even the most radical white abolitionists of the eighteenth century, were comfortable with the idea of both freeing masses of black people and granting them equal rights as citizens of the young republic.[9]

Historians have generally framed the rhetorical battle over slavery in the years of the American Revolution as one that pitted those who argued that slaves were by nature inferior beings, incapable of rising to the duties of citizenship, against reformers who believed in the universal equality of human nature. A great quantity of quotations can be plucked from tracts and speeches of that era to support breaking the community of patriots into these two camps. But these public controversies can also be read against this grain, identifying as many points of agreement as conflict in this generation's ideas of blackness and slavery. What these debates obscured was a general consensus that slavery was a form of political and moral corruption that needed to end while at the same time, for whatever reason, blacks were presently inferior in character to whites and because of this they could not be easily or safely freed.

There is no better illustration of this dynamic than the famous 1773 Harvard commencement debate between Theodore Parsons and Eliphalet Pearson that scholars have long (and erroneously) highlighted as one of the "clearest expressions" of the conflict between "antislavery writers and defenders of human bondage." In those years Harvard's school year concluded by inviting the top two graduates to present opposing arguments on some moral or philosophical question before an audience of their fellow students, their professors, and often the highest officers of the colony's government. Theodore and Eliphalet were childhood friends whose backgrounds were quite similar, though one's family owned slaves and the other's did not. Most scholars have incorrectly assumed that because Theodore Parsons' family owned slaves, he defended the proslavery side. In fact, it was the opposite— Eliphalet Pearson argued that slavery was "agreeable to the law of nature" while Parsons, who was raised by an enslaved black woman, asserted slavery violated natural law.[10]

Pearson never quite defended slavery itself, but instead attacked the idea of equality, a reasonable position given his audience included the royal governor of the colony. Pearson at one point made this abundantly clear, explaining, "I have only contended, that the notion of equality, in the strict sense, had no foundation in nature." Taking this approach, it mattered not whether Africans' inferior state sprung from nature or their experiences: "For whether the necessity of such subordination arises from natural incapacity, or from any other quarter, it matters not, if this is in fact the case; if the interest of the whole does require it; let the causes or reasons of such requirement be what they may, such subordination is equally justifiable." In the end, Pearsons' clear intention was less to defend slavery than to blast the idea that equality was somehow inherent in natural law.[11]

What is most revealing in Pearson's and Parsons' back and forth were the things that each man presumed the other, and by implication all elite white American men, believed. At one point Pearson turned to the "particular case of Africans in this country" and stated that it was "acknowledged by all" that "it is only in a state of limited subordination … that these people can consistently enjoy a residence among us."

Parsons in supposedly attacking slavery revealed his own very dim view of the character and capacity of African Americans, noting "the unhappy state of degradation into which they are confessedly sunk, they are still some degrees above brutes." He claimed blacks were "extremely unacquainted with the politer arts, and almost wholly ignorant of every thing belonging to science, and consequently strangers to all the pleasures of a scholar and a philosopher." They were "confessedly destitute of an acquaintance with the principles of urbanity." The best Parsons, the supposed abolitionist in this disputation, could say in defense of enslaved African Americans was that though "their condition is allowedly not greatly different from a state of nature," they are "far less savage and barbarous" than most Americans think.

The same year that Parsons and Pearson held their famous disputation, one of America's most prominent physicians and abolitionists, Benjamin Rush, published his attack on slavery, *An Address to the Inhabitants of the British Settlements, on the Slavery of the Negroes in America.* Rush's tract opens by defending the "Intellects of the Negroes, or of their capacities for virtue and happiness" against those who claimed them too naturally inferior to be accepted as political equals. Like many of his Enlightenment generation, and in keeping with Jefferson's aphorism that "all men are created equal," Rush countered that Africans were no less endowed by nature than whites, "Nor let it be said, in the present Age, that their black color ... qualifies them for slavery."

But one does not need to dig very far beneath the surface of these seeming expressions of racial equality to expose the underlying qualifications that diminished black citizenship into an inferior class of rights. Rush quickly conceded that nature could be overcome by habit and environment and that black Americans might be burdened with poor abilities and low characters, "such as Idleness, Treachery, Theft, and the like" due to having lived in the "torpid" tropics or having been stunted by slavery. Africans, Rush said, were "equal to the Europeans, when we allow for the diversity of temper and genius which is occasioned by climate." Rush then concludes his pamphlet by asking the questions that were really on every patriot's mind: "What steps shall we take to remedy this Evil, and what shall we do with those

Slaves we have already in this Country?" Even Rush conceded, "This is indeed a most difficult question." What indeed?

Rush has been portrayed by his biographers as one of the more radical abolitionists of his day, but even he recoiled from the prospect of simply freeing a million enslaved black people into the new white republic.[12] Advocating an end to the slave trade was easy and obvious as this put a cap to the multiplying of the problem of the black presence. As Rush put it, in terms that left open whether he was referring to slavery or blackness as the source of American problems, "let the vessels which bring the slaves to us, be avoided as if they bore in them the Seeds of that forbidden fruit, whose baneful taste destroyed both the natural and moral world." Ultimately, because he feared black people like most of his white countrymen, Rush could not bring himself to support an immediate end to slavery. Rather, he tied ending slavery to some new form of white supervision and policing of black people. His solution was to free only children who could be properly educated and controlled:

> As for the Negroes among us, who, from having acquired all the low vices of slavery, or who from age or infirmities are unfit to be set at liberty, I would propose, for the good of society, that they should continue the property of those with whom they grew old, or from whom they contracted those vices and infirmities. But let the young Negroes be educated in the principles of virtue and religion—let them be taught to read, and write—and afterwards instructed in some business, whereby they may be able to maintain themselves. Let laws be made to limit the time of their servitude, and to entitle them to all the privileges of free-born British subjects.

Rush's denunciation against the evils and sins of slavery did not deter him from purchasing and continuing the enslavement of a man, William Grubber, and keeping him in his confinement for the next twenty years.[13]

In the year that America's new federal government under its rewritten Constitution began functioning, the trustees of the Library Company of Philadelphia announced their plans to build a grand new building for their library. Founded by none other than Benjamin Franklin in 1731, the Library Company's library had been housed in Carpenter's Hall since before the Revolution. William Thornton, the architect who would in a few years design the nation's new capitol, was picked to design the new library.

News of construction of what many expected to be Philadelphia's most grand edifice reached Samuel Jennings in London, a native Philadelphia painter who had recently relocated to England to build his reputation and clientele. Samuel enthusiastically wrote to his father, who was a patriot hero and rising Philadelphia politician, to arrange for him to be asked to contribute "a Painting to the Company that would be applicable to so noble, and useful an Institution." Samuel presumptuously asked his father to send him details of the dimensions of the hall and which direction it would face. He proposed several classical subjects, including Clio, Calliope, or Minerva.

The elder Jennings quickly swung the commission, and a committee of the Library Company directors wrote to Samuel and suggested a different tableau. Though they liked best Samuel's idea of depicting Minerva, they also took "the liberty of suggesting an Idea of Substituting the figure of Liberty (with her Cap and proper Insignia)." Their idea was that Liberty would be best dramatized by showing her in the act of freeing enslaved men and women.

She appears in the attitude of placing on the top of a Pedestal, a pile of Books, lettered with, Agriculture, Commerce, Philosophy & Catalogue of Philadelphia Library. A Broken Chain under her feet, and in the distant back Ground a Groupe of Negroes sitting on the Earth, or in some attitude expressive of Ease & Joy.[14]

It is neither coincidental nor contradictory that the architect of the building in which Samuel Jennings wished to hang his painting, William Thornton, was both a large enslaver, keeping some seventy or eighty people in bondage on his family's West Indian plantation, and an abolitionist who advocated freeing slaves and then shipping them back to Africa. Thornton made plans to purchase land along the African coast where he would resettle his human property and force them to continue to work in servitude until "paying their own Ransom by working or by Commerce, with Interest." Thornton justified this period of contingent slavery as being necessary to impart the steady work habits and elevated morality required to be free. Black colonists, properly Christian and with "their acquired Habits & Customs" would then "bring to Industrious Lives the ignorant & slothful of the warm Country of Africa." Thornton's plans expanded when he made contact with free black communities in Rhode Island and Massachusetts and recruited Samuel Adams to promote the scheme.

Like other abolitionists of his day Thornton believed that emancipation had to be carried out in a manner that protected the safety and convenience of the white community. As he put it in a letter to a French abolitionist, Etienne Claviére, "A total and immediate abolition of Slavery may indeed be pregnant with some Danger to Society, but there can be no inconvenience in a gradual Emancipation to commence as soon as general Safety will permit it." Thornton included in this letter a note from James Madison endorsing his project and justifying its necessity by the impossibility of incorporating freed men and women into America's white society. Madison wrote that "neither the good of the Society, nor the happiness of the individuals restored to freedom is promoted" by simply turning enslaved people loose:

> In order to render this design eligible as well to the Society as to the Slaves, it would be necessary that a compleat incorporation of the latter into the former should result from the act of manumission. This is rendered impossible by the prejudice of the whites, prejudices which proceeding principally from the difference of colour must be considered as permanent and Insuperable. It only remains then that some proper external receptacle be provided for the slaves who obtain their liberty.[15]

The mammoth canvas that Samuel Jennings completed and that still hangs today in the Library Company building (and graces the cover of this book) has been described as the first painting depicting the act of abolition in American history.[16] It depicts the goddess Liberty, represented as a blond white woman, holding the revolutionary symbol of liberty, the workman's cap on a pole, and broken chains at her feet. Nearly a century later, the Statue of Liberty would likewise represent American freedom as a white woman standing amidst severed chains. Opposite the goddess Liberty is a group of black men and women bent in supplication, a posture that was the deferential ideal of white abolitionists. Freed men and women were to gratefully accept their subservient position to either an individual white patron or a white antislavery society that served the same purpose—protecting and tutoring them as they slowly proved they had acquired the "Habits & Customs" that entitled them to live among whites. Further symbolizing this relationship, the goddess Liberty is shown in the act of handing to the benighted blacks heavy tomes of knowledge labeled "Agriculture" and "Philosophy," the former befitting their intended work in the new nation and the later marking their lack of morality and reason.

In the background are ten other black figures, both adults and children, presumably families, seemingly waiting for something. Behind them are three ships. When Thornton beheld this scene for the first time, might he have seen these ships gathering to bear these black families to their new land, far from the white republic? The juxtaposition of Liberty imparting freedom and knowledge to grateful families freed from their bondage and awaiting their transportation perfectly resolves the dilemma that this generation of patriots had long faced. Slavery was corrupting the white republic both from within by promoting luxury, cruelty, and political favoritism and inequality, and from without by encouraging the growth of a dangerous black population. For the young republic to succeed, slavery had to be eradicated, but abolition by unleashing this savage population posed a dire threat to whites. White leaders debated the solution: either free enslaved people and send them out of the country or find some way to police and civilize them while encouraging white immigration to dilute their numbers. This book shows that it was this debate, not some imagined conflict between abolitionist heroes and proslavery villains, that framed how the founders viewed the question of slavery and explains how their plans so colossally failed.

My contention is that the grand conundrum driving American state formation was not the one that would rise up in the nineteenth century and tear the country apart, that between slavery and liberty, but the contradiction between hating slavery and hating the presence of the slave. America's founding generation of leaders struggled their entire lives to devise some means by which they could end slavery and whiten the nation. Their commitment to their own racially defined community (a conception of "whiteness" that was itself a product of these struggles) ran so deep that it usually didn't need to be stated, but its boundaries and content can be inferred from their actions. America's founding leaders may have been a quarrelsome assemblage of men of different economic interests, religious beliefs, and philosophical commitments, but by the mid-1700s they did agree on one thing: they were white and slaves were black and America was to be a white nation. One could not simply set slaves free and achieve that goal.[17]

The traditional narrative of early antislavery leads to some very puzzling outcomes. On its face, the eighteenth-century antislavery movement proved wildly successful. By any standard, the flicker of concern for slaves and the protests against the institution of slavery that sputtered to life at the beginning of the century had by the 1770s become a seeming conflagration of condemnation. In 1772, the highest royal court in London declared slavery unenforceable in England. American revolutionaries declared independence with the words: "We hold these truths to be self-evident, that all men are created equal, that they are endowed by their Creator with certain unalienable Rights ..." All but one of the newly formed American states passed laws prohibiting the international slave trade. Some began considering gradual emancipation laws, others loosened restrictions on the voluntary manumission of one's own slaves. Antislavery rhetoric had migrated from the small religious communities that first spoke of slavery as a sin and passed into the wider society, even into the mouths of some of the largest slaveholders in North America who were busily forming a new American government.

But, paradoxically, all the gains antislavery thinking and rhetoric had made throughout society and culture failed to translate into any diminishment of the power or place of slavery in America. Politically, the successful war for independence forged a federation that was structured to enhance and protect the political power of slave-owners. States that once had no obligation to aid in the capture and return of fugitives from slavery lost that discretion under a new Constitution passed in 1787. Those states that passed schemes of gradual emancipation coupled them with strict new laws limiting the movement, privacy, and civil rights of those eventually to be freed. Most states north of the Chesapeake and Ohio Rivers, actively legislated to bar the entry of black people and limit the growth of their black communities. As Frederick Douglass later famously observed, those northern states had traded personal slavery for collective slavery.

In the South, slavery turned into an even more ruthless engine of exploitation as an internal slave trade flourished, eventually transporting upwards of a million people from the eastern seaboard deep into the interior of a newly conquered western frontier. Although Congress moved to prohibit the international slave trade at the first constitutional opportunity to do so in 1808, no administration was willing to devote any serious effort to enforce it and most actively blocked what little policing was possible under the law. American-made ships continued to drag tens of thousands of Africans across the Middle Passage even into the last year of the Civil War.

All this is hard to square with an antislavery movement supposedly rooted in benevolence that largely achieved its goal of convincing other Americans that slavery was a sin in the eyes of God. For abolitionists to have been as successful in spreading the idea that slavery had to be abolished as claimed, it is puzzling how their goal of ending slavery failed so miserably. One possibility is that white Americans who proclaimed their belief in natural rights and the evil and cruelty of slavery were either insincere in their professions or hypocritical in their actions.

The other possibility is that what appears to us today, 300 years removed, as an altruistic movement to end slavery was actually a self-interested one. Perhaps the white abolitionists' overriding goal was not extending liberty to an oppressed people but protecting their own interests and the well-being of their racially defined group. As difficult such a reorientation of our views of this movement is, it does have the advantage of not picturing them as hypocrites, cynically tossing their principles aside when the going got tough or, worse, selling them off when the price rose. Reconceiving all antislavery expressions as inherently framed by white group interest straightens this history's tortured twists and turns.

Motivation in reform movements matters because it is through the definition of social problems that specific solutions are crafted. Simply opposing slavery does not imply any particular program of reform. Many early evangelicals opposed slavery because they thought it corrupting to themselves or their coreligionists. For the insular community of Quakers, they thought the problem of slavery could be solved by divesting themselves of their human property and shunning slaveholders from their meetings and daily life. Such a solution did not require uprooting slavery elsewhere. As their motivation was particular and their concern extended only to the boundaries of Quaker life, they were generally not interested in fighting slavery throughout their colony.

Others who attacked slavery did so because they viewed slaves as dangerous and savage beings, wholly unsuited to living amongst them except in a relationship of close supervision. To them, slavery and, especially, the international human trafficking it mobilized, were responsible for multiplying the number of such people in their communities. They looked upon their black servants and neighbors as the source of crime, vice, and, more fearfully, the terrifying prospect of a slave uprising or foreign invasion. Additionally, these opponents of slavery saw the rising numbers of black colonists as blocking the immigration of white colonists, thus diminishing their dreams of building a white Christian nation.

In spite of all their occasional exhortations that God "hath made of one Blood all Nations of Men" (Acts 17:26) and color did not forfeit the rights God and nature granted, even the most outspoken and sincere eighteenth-century abolitionists conceived of themselves, and their world, as being fundamentally divided between white and black. Close attention to the language they used in their tracts, letters, and sermons reveals a conceptual gulf between races that could not be bridged. Whites and blacks may both be one in the eyes of God, but they remained two distinct groups whose scope of life, whose role in society, and for whom the meaning of freedom differed.

The distance between conceptions of white life and black life is exposed when antislavery crusaders turned their attention to what freedom meant and what should follow the act of manumission. No white opponent of slavery declared himself or herself in favor of immediate and unconditional emancipation before George Bourne did so to little fanfare in 1816 and William Lloyd Garrison followed to explosive effect a dozen years later. Some proposed programs of gradual freedom, phased in over years; others advocated emancipation coupled with schemes of removing black people back to Africa or deep into the wilderness of the American interior; still others tied freedom to a permanent regime of "education," which in the meaning of this term in the eighteenth century, entailed a strict supervision of behavior as well as religious and moral instruction.[18]

For all these reasons, clear and accurate historical understanding requires that the antislavery movement be understood not only for the evils it perceived and fought, but for the racialized frameworks, motivations, and aspirations underlying their crusade. In the eighteenth century, as will be seen, those campaigning against slavery did so through a lens of racial self-interest.

1

The Religious Roots of White Abolition

Long before any hint of an awakening of a spirit of liberalism was evident in the American colonies, the movement against slavery coalesced as an outgrowth of evangelical Protestantism. In the English-speaking world slavery expanded swiftly throughout the 1600s with nary a squeak of protest (except from the enslaved themselves, of course). Then, at the cusp of the eighteenth century, a handful of zealots began preaching that slavery was dangerous and needed to be contained for both the safety of the community and the salvation of the faithful.[1]

Colonial slavery of the Americas in its most brutal forms was nearly a century old by the time any European spoke out publicly against it. The brutally casual attitude of white Americans toward slavery can be glimpsed in the recollections of John Eliot, who succeeded his father as pastor of Boston's New North Church and lived in a house that Increase Mather had built a century earlier. When asked by a southerner to explain the extent of slavery in the old Bay Colony, Reverend Eliot expressed his opinion that in New England "the slaves were not in hard bondage." But then he paused and added, almost as an afterthought, "yet one thing implies the contrary ... Lovers and friends were separated, and their children given away, with the same indifference as little kittens and young puppies ..."[2]

The history of the first embers of antislavery sentiment brightening among the Quakers in both England and America, and among some of the New Light Congregational dissenters in New England, has been extensively documented and analyzed. Once obscure abolitionist sermons and pamphlets scattered across countless libraries and archives have been collected, anthologized, and digitized. A wide consensus among scholars now holds that the early antislavery movement paved the road that led to the secular antislavery movement that attempted to fulfill the promise of the Independence Declaration's ringing principles of natural and equal rights under a representative government.

Much of this literature has been written in a heroic mode; abolitionists, though flawed, were among the first Europeans to express Christian sympathy toward enslaved Africans. Their ideas progressed slowly from simply urging greater benevolence in the treatment of slaves, to calling for an end to the murderous slave trade, to demanding their congregants divest themselves of slaves, to calling for an end to slavery everywhere. Along each step in this evolution were heroic antislavery leaders like John Woolman, Anthony Benezet, and Benjamin Lay who dedicated themselves to the cause with exceptional commitment and zeal. Every good story needs both heroes and villains and this one naturally had the hard-hearted and selfish slave-owners who put their personal fortunes ahead of humanity and ultimately thwarted this movement. Where the heroic abolitionists fell short, according to such interpretations, was not in their goals, but their inability to overcome the entrenched interests that protected the sinful trade in human souls.

Every social movement is more than the sum of its principles and stated aims. Social movements that attain wide social influence alter not only the terms of formalized public discussion and debate but also deeper cultural meanings and constructions that frame the possibilities and boundaries of change itself. Early abolitionists invented not only the rhetoric with which to attack slavery, they also shaped the categories upon which that rhetoric operated. Over the course of a campaign that in fits and starts spanned more than a century, abolitionists molded the idea of whiteness from a vague term of difference (black/white replacing the older Christian/heathen) into a conception of an ethnic community, a naturalized imagining of belonging and purpose that came to inform the basis of the idea of an "America."

ABOLITIONISM AND THE
ARTICULATION OF WHITENESS

English people began lumping Africans into a single group by their appearance rather than by their nationality, religion, or language early in the 1600s. Prior to then, English practice was to call dark-er-skinned people "Moors" or "Black-a-moors" which were terms that occupied an indeterminate area between nationality and race. But as the slave trade expanded rapidly in the seventeenth century and the utility of defining all Africans by their color rather than their ances-try or culture grew, the term "Negro" was used more frequently.[3] Still, it was several generations before English people thought it necessary to commonly describe themselves as belonging to a group defined by their bodies rather than their language, their nationhood, or their religion.

The term "white" as used to delineate a group of people, rather than merely as an individual description, seems to have first passed into regular usage in the plantation islands of the West Indies in the 1660s. This being so, it is striking that among the early promoters of the term were also the first to publicly criticize the practice of slavery.

For example, one of the earliest Quaker protests against the treat-ment of slaves were the reflections of the sect's founder George Fox on his observations of the practice of slavery in Barbados. His 1676 pamphlet, *Gospel Family-order, Being a Short Discourse Concerning the Ordering of Families, Both of Whites, Blacks, and Indians*, may have been the first English language publication to include the concept of a white people in its title. In the sermons he reproduced in *Gospel Family-order*, Fox preached that Christians needed to show Christian benevolence to their slaves. Fox appealed to "all that have *Negroes* to your Servants, let them have two or three Hours of the Day once in the Week, that Day Friends Meeting is on, or an other Day, to meet together, to wait upon the Lord ..." Fox was particularly concerned that slaves be instructed in the Gospel and that their bondage not lead them into sin. Therefore, masters should allow their slaves to marry and to respect those unions. Similarly, in a letter Fox wrote to his followers while on a mission to Maryland: "And in all your Family Meetings be not negligent among your Whites and Negroes, but do your Diligence and Duty to God and them ..."[4]

Fox's language divided the family of mankind into racial groups, "Whites, Blacks, and Indians." While preaching the unity of mankind, Fox conceived of this unity as consisting in a division of ranks and stations just as the members of a family had different roles in a chain of authority in which children were to obey their parents and wives were to obey their husbands. Indentured servants were to be watched over by their masters and black slaves were subservient to all whites, not just their owners. Thus, inequality was seen as an essential element of unity and harmony within the family, but also the peace and stability of society in general. Fox preached that slaves were part of the spiritual family and thus were both within God's ordained compass of human benevolence and in a lowly, servile role at the same time.

Fox's message to Barbados slave masters was to treat their servants with compassion, to preach to them the Gospel, and, most radically, to release them from service once their years of labor had amply compensated their owners for their investments. In doing so, Fox was not suggesting that slaves and masters, whites and blacks, should have equal rights or standing in society, but that each should be treated humanely, according to the Golden Rule, within their station in life. Indeed, when the island's authorities accused Quaker leaders of fomenting slave insurrections and cracked down by banning Quakers from holding meetings for "Negroes," Fox backpedaled and signaled his racial allegiance by shifting his terminology from "Blacks" and "Negroes" to "Negars." Fox spoke out against the lawmakers for the "Slander and Lye they have cast upon us, is; namely, *That we should teach the* Negars *to Rebel.*"[5]

Quakers were not the only Christians who found biblical inspiration to attack slavery and in doing so brightened the lines between whites and blacks. Morgan Godwyn, an Anglican missionary who was run out of Virginia for proposing that slave-owners allow enslaved people to be brought within the Christian Church, preached that negroes were not "irrational creatures, such as the ape and drill, that do carry some resemblances of men" but were men and therefore "invested … with an equal right to religion." But along the course of his argument, Godwyn accepted and spread the slander that Africans had "unnatural conjunctions" with apes, "though not so as to unpeople that great continent."[6]

Godwyn's argument ultimately hinged on his recognition of the Africans' significant differences from whites combined with a theological argument that these differences did not matter in the eyes of God. "Whereas some may perchance object against my spending Time in this Discourse to prove the Negro's Humanity, and to shew that neither their Complexion nor Bondage, Descent nor Country, can be any impediment thereto." Godwyn drives the logic of this natural and common right to worship the creator toward a more generalized idea that prefigured Jefferson's declaration that "all men are created equal, that they are endowed by their Creator with certain unalienable Rights." Godwyn theorized in 1680 that "as Man alone lays claim to this high *Privilege*, so it is most certainly *every Man's*, there being none so despicable or base, but hath as unquestionable a *Right* thereto ... holding the same equally and *in common* with all others of the like *species* with himself."[7]

Further north, Samuel Sewall, while not a minister himself, was a Puritan judge in Massachusetts who had condemned Salem's witches in 1692. Eight years later he was moved to contemplate the divine cost of holding slaves and in his diary, Sewall expressed his discomfort with the "trade of fetching Negroes from Guinea." Sewall then composed a pamphlet, *The Selling of Joseph*, that made the case that the trade in slaves was sinful.

Sewall, still a sitting jurist on the Massachusetts' Supreme Court, grounded his arguments in the Bible which led him to a unifying vision of mankind, writing that "it is most certain that all Men, as they are the Sons of Adam, are Co-heirs, and have equal Right unto Liberty ..." Finding both Old Testament law against Isrealites selling each other into slavery and the Golden Rule in Matthew 7:12 establishing equality of treatment, Sewall then combined them with the story of Joseph who was sold into slavery by his brothers, as proof of the sin of enslavement.

And seeing GOD hath said, He that Stealeth a Man and Selleth him, or if he be found in his band, he shall surely be put to Death. Exod. 21. 16. This Law being of Everlasting Equity, wherein Man Stealing is ranked amongst the most atrocious of Capital Crimes: What louder cry can there be made of that Celebrated Warning, Caveat Emptor!

Sewell lobbied Massachusetts' legislators during their session of 1705 to soften a bill prohibiting marriage between "White men with Negros or Indians." "I have got the Indians out of the Bill, and some mitigation for them [the Negroes] left in it, and the clause about their Masters not denying their Marriage." Sewell's amendment preserved the rite of marriage among blacks, "And no master shall unreasonably deny marriage to his negro with one of the same nation ..." But in speaking out against a law banning Christian marriage across racial lines, Sewell did not disagree with the fact that these groups existed or should be kept apart, only that the sacrament of marriage should not be violated. As added inducement for slave-owners to consider his proposal, Sewell noted that any man brought up in the doctrines of Christianity were more governable than those "bred in Ignorance and Heathenism ..." As in his other publications, while defending certain of the rights of enslaved people Sewell also underscored that black and white people were fundamentally different groups. Sewell wrote that

> ... some Persons, nay, Nations seem to be born for Slaves; particularly many of the *Barbarians* in *Africa*, who have been such almost from the beginning of the World, and who are in a much better Condition of Life, when Slaves among us, then when at Liberty at Home, to cut Throats and Eat one another, especially when by the Slavery of their Bodies, they are brought to a Capacity of Freeing their Souls from a much more unsupportable Bondage.[8]

While condemning "Man Stealing" and "purchasing Men and Women," Sewell delineated blacks and whites into groups that should be separated: "... there is such a disparity in their Conditions, Color & Hair, that they can never embody with us, and grow up into orderly Families, to the Peopling of the Land: but still remain in our Body Politick as a kind of extravasat Blood."[9]

Sewell was just one among many English writers whose rhetoric served to sharpen the idea that black people belonged to an inherently separate group, but, like other pioneering antislavery writers, his arguments employed the concept of whiteness to define a pan-European people that were the chosen people of America, the people for whom the land was destined. Such arguments, once made, became the terms of discussion and moved far beyond the tracts of abolitionists. Sewell's most famous critic, his fellow judge John Saffin, agreed with Sewell that "white" servants were "conduceth most to the welfare and benefit of this Province" asking "who doubts that?" Saffin attempted to carry his thesis into a *reducto absurdum*:

> But if he could perswade the General Assembly to make an Act, That all that have Negroes, and do set them free, shall be Re-imbursed out of the Publick Treasury, and that there shall be no more Negroes brought into the Country; 'tis probable there would be more of his opinion; yet he would find it a hard task to bring the Country to consent thereto; for then the Negroes must be all sent out of the Country, or else the remedy would be worse than the Disease; and it is to be feared that those Negroes that are free, if there be not some strict course taken with them by Authority, they will be a plague to this Country.[10]

Though he thought he was scoring points on his enemies' argument, Saffin was prefiguring the way that many eighteenth-century antislavery crusaders sliced the Gordian knot of their own making, what they saw as the undeniable problem of abolishing slavery— what to do with the "negroes"?

There may be an even deeper connection between the advent of antislavery thinking, Christian evangelism, and the strengthening of racial categories. Public condemnations of slavery first arose among those Protestant sects who acted on their belief that all men, regardless of their worldly station, should be brought to the sacraments.

Evangelical encouragement to spread Christianity among enslaved people was widespread at the beginning of the eighteenth century. In 1696, the Yearly Meeting of Pennsylvania and New Jersey counseled Friends to have meetings with the people they held as slaves and share the Gospel. About the same time, some ministers of the Church of England across the middle and southern colonies of America began preaching to both enslaved natives and Africans. In New York, Episcopal leaders organized a group of sixteen ministers and a dozen teachers to provide for the religious education and baptism of the city's slaves.[11] In 1711, the Bishop of London formally charged the missionary arm of the Anglican Church, the Society for the Propagating the Gospel, to pay particular emphasis on the instruction of "heathen negroes" in the Christian faith.[12] Even the dour Cotton Mather brooding in New England wrote of his concern for the "precious and immortal souls" of his town's "Negroes."

As Christians began to include their own enslaved communities as objects of their missionary zeal, perhaps the longest-standing point of distinction defining these peoples was thus weakened. Long before English people began referring to themselves as "whites" to mark their difference from those descended from Africa, they commonly referred to themselves simply as "Christians." Once all colonial peoples, both those with English roots and those with African ancestors, could be considered "Christian," this concept was no longer useful as a term of definition. Thus, even though colonial laws clarified that Christian baptism effected no change in a person's status as property or chattel, the obsolescence of terminology left a conceptual vacuum that was soon filled with an obsessive attachment to the body.[13]

Pioneering critics of slavery were not the only English speakers using the terms "negro" and "whites" at the beginning of the eighteenth century, and in this sense to attribute to them the invention of whiteness is to reduce and extend this idea beyond its sources. At the same time, the evidence that antislavery activists contributed to codifying and investing the idea of a white community with some enduring specific qualities is persuasive. Early ministers and colonial leaders who condemned slavery employed arguments and rhetorical strategies that attempted to persuade those involved in slavery less by stressing the equal humanity of the enslaved but instead by tracing slavery's impact upon "whites"—an imagined society that did not include people of color. In this way, the idea of a white community was fashioned, invested with meaning, and its boundaries drawn.

Slavery's early critics crafted an imagined white nation by attempting to convince the owners, traders, and drivers of enslaved people that slavery harmed their own self-interest. Whether this was rhetoric born of deep-seated anxieties or simply a tactic of persuasion is anybody's guess, but in the final analysis this motivation matters little. What has lasting significance in the construction of Americanness and its rooting in whiteness were the particular ways that antislavery appeals fleshed out the meaning of a white community by detailing what threatened it.[14]

In 1688, Francis Daniel Pastorius, Garret Hendericks, Derick op den Graeff, and Abraham op den Graeff, gathered at Thones Kunders' brick townhouse that stood in the center of the only street in the newly founded village of Germantown, Pennsylvania. Their purpose was to compose a letter of protest to their quarterly Quaker meeting. Quakers, for all their egalitarianism, organized their meetings into a clear hierarchy where "Quarterly" meetings advised local meetings and a "Yearly" Meeting in Philadelphia governed the colony and looked to the London Meeting for overall policy.

The two-page letter they drafted that day warned Quakers against the spiritual dangers of the widespread practice of buying and selling slaves. Their letter was presented to the Quarterly Meeting where it was decided that "it being a thing of too great a weight for this meeting to determine." So, it was passed up to Philadelphia's Yearly Meeting where it was deemed disruptive and set aside with the other papers and records of the sect, there to lie unacknowledged until rediscovered by a different generation of abolitionists 156 years later.

This Germantown Protest of 1688 is widely recognized as the first written protest against slavery in early modern European society. Though it wasn't directly influential of subsequent thinking, it contained a number of arguments that would repeatedly crop up in the writings of those critical of slavery over the next century and is therefore universally looked upon as a landmark in the history of abolitionism.[15]

At its core, the Germantown Protest is built on the bedrock of the Golden Rule. "Is there any that would be done or handled at this manner? viz., to be sold or made a slave for all the time of his life?" In striking contrast to a colonial world in which black and white were in the process of becoming absolute markers of status and belonging, the group gathered at Kunders' townhouse proclaimed the equality of men regardless of their race: "There is a saying that we shall doe to all men licke as we will be done ourselves; macking no difference of what generation, descent or Colour they are."[16]

In the seventeenth century, slavery was universally accepted and considered an unremarkable aspect of social life. Even the most passionately religious and moralistic of settlers, such as the Quakers, routinely held and traded slaves. In 1680 there were 58 Quaker families residing on the island of Barbados and all but four held large numbers of slaves. A few years later Quakers in Pennsylvania bought up an entire shipload of 150 Africans. Into the early eighteenth century, Quaker traders in Philadelphia bought and sold enslaved people from abroad and as late as 1757 an elder of Philadelphia's Monthly Meeting purchased a man from the island of Montserrat and resold him in Pennsylvania. At that time, Quakers probably held a higher proportion of Philadelphia's slaves than other religious groups. Tax records reveal that Quakers continued to hold people as property well into the revolutionary crisis of the mid-1770s.[17]

Historians have interpreted the Germantown Protest as marking an awakening to the evils and injustice of slavery. According to this view, slavery first came to be criticized by those who could not reconcile their religious precepts with the inherent inhumanity, sinfulness, and, in the case of the Quakers, the violence, of slavery. Spread by a handful of zealots like Anthony Benezet and Benjamin Lay, these ideas slowly trickled out from the meeting houses and sectarian churches where they were born and solidified into an antislavery discourse (a system of standard ideas, metaphors, and images) that by the latter half of the eighteenth century informed a growing secular opposition to slavery.[18]

There is some truth to this explanation of the rise of antislavery. There can be no doubt that an increasing chorus of voices speaking in the language of Christian benevolence were raised against slavery as the eighteenth century progressed. But alongside many, if not most, of the antislavery statements written in the mode of religious humanitarianism there were also criticisms of slavery expressed in the logic of racial self-interest. Frequently in the very same pamphlet or sermon an antislavery leader would offer both altruistic and moralistic arguments against slavery as well as practical ones that highlighted the dangers of slavery to his own congregation, his fellow European colonists, his English nation, or white people in general.

The Germantown Protest of 1688 is a perfect example of this confusing juxtaposition. Following its Golden Rule principle, it rhetorically asks that, if it is wrong for Turks to seize Christians as slaves, isn't it also wrong for Christians to bring "negers ... against their will & consent" to Pennsylvania? It expresses an equality of rights between whites and blacks: "Now tho they are black, we can not conceive there is more liberty to have them slaves, as it is to have other white ones." But then it pivots and makes a practical and immediate argument against slavery, that it deters Europeans from immigrating to Pennyslvania: "This mackes an ill report in all those Countries of Europe, where they hear off, that ye Quackers doe here handel men licke they handel there ye Cattle. and for that reason some have no mind or inclination to come hither."

An even greater danger to the colony's future than a dwindling supply of white settlers was the prospect of a slave revolt. "If once these slaves (wch they say are so wicked and stubbern men) should joint themselves, fight for their freedom and handel their masters & mastrisses, as they did it, handel them before; will these masters & mastrisses tacke the sword at hand and warr against these poor slaves?" This argument simultaneously invoked moral principles and racial group interest, for while taking up the sword and warring against slaves was a clear violation of one of the cardinal principles of Quaker pacifism, the ever-present danger of slave uprisings was a threat to the white community in general.[19]

The Germantown Protest letter was typical in its mixing of Christian principles of equality and benevolence with racial appeals to the interests of white society. Such rhetoric, whether fundamentally benevolent or self-interested, served to form and clarify the idea of a white community itself and invest it with specific meanings. In proposing that Africans' color did not justify their enslavement, Germantown Quakers were implicitly inviting their slaveholding neighbors to imagine other grounds upon which slavery could be defended. When they argued that slavery should be restricted because it deterred more desirable immigrants from "all those Countries of Europe," they were also communicating the concept of a pan-European identity as the right and proper basis of their colony. The Germantown Quakers did not refute the common notion that black slaves were "wicked and stubbern men" but simply added this to the reasons why slaves were a dangerous presence in their land. In the end, such rhetoric, though ornamented with the moral filigree of human equality served mainly to sharpen the meaning of black and white and accustom free colonists to think of themselves as white.[20]

FIGHTING SLAVERY TO ABOLISH WHITE SIN

When white abolitionists expressed their concerns about slavery, they crafted arguments that centered on the impact of slavery on the white community. Such arguments were some of the earliest writings to consider blacks not only as dangerous due to their justified desire to rebel against their bondage, but as threats to the morality of whites as well. They worried that slavery itself posed a moral hazard to the white community. Slavery, by generating great wealth, insidiously spread the evils of luxury, pride, and sloth. In addition to being deadly sins when the fate of one's immortal soul was judged after death, these vices slowly corrupted white society here on earth.[21]

Most expressions of concern for the enslaved that appear to modern eyes as sympathetic were at bottom worries about fellow white masters. Historian Margaret Abruzzo pointed out that early abolitionists were not moved or motivated by the suffering of the enslaved, writing that abolitionist "objections to cruelty grew out of concern for slaveholders' salvation, not enslaved people's pain." This was because physical pain was not viewed in the early modern world as intrinsically repulsive or immoral. Rather, many instances of suffering were necessary, even virtuous if endured in pursuit of eternal salvation. Few people before the Victorian age of sentimentalism worried that those living in bondage experienced pain, exhaustion, or despair. Their only concern with the pain inflicted upon the slave by the lash or the manacle was that such acts could slide from necessity to cruelty and cruelty besmirched the soul of the master.[22]

The chorus of voices raised against slavery stressed not the debasement of the slave but the evils of sin and their toll on white morality and character. Such concerns were expressed by London's leading Quakers who warned all Friends in their annual epistle for 1758 to "be careful to avoid being any Way concerned, in reaping the unrighteous Profits arising from that iniquitous Practice of Dealing in Negroes" because this "most unnatural Traffick ... hath often been observed, to fill their Possessors with Haughtiness, Tyranny, Luxury and Barbarity, corrupting the Minds, and debasing the Morals of their Children ..."[23]

Likewise, many of the most famous and influential of early eighteenth-century antislavery writers expressed their concern for the way slavery fostered vices among the master race. Alongside the sympathy Anthony Benezet expressed for Africans ("innocent People ... brought under the greatest Anxiety and Suffering, by being violently rent from their Native Country, in the most cruel Manner, and brought to our Colonies"), he worried that slavery debased the enslaver by estranging him from God, "How miserable must be our Condition, if, for filthy Lucre, we should continue to act so contrary to the Nature of this Divine Call ..." Benezet dedicated his *Short Account of That Part of Africa Inhabited by the Negroes*

> in Hopes it may be some Inducement to those who are not defiled therewith to keep themselves clear; and to lay before such as have unwarily engaged in it, their Danger of totally losing that tender Sensibility to the Sufferings of their Fellow Creatures, the Want whereof sets Men beneath the Brute Creation ... May the Almighty preserve the Inhabitants of Pennsylvania from being further defiled by a trade, which is entered upon from such sensual motives, and carried on by such devilish means.[24]

Benezet and other white abolitionists also argued that slavery's corrosive effects weakened and debased white society. Benezet at times thought this the most serious problem with slavery, writing "... the worst Effects [of slavery] naturally flow to the Religion and Morals of the People where it prevails."[25]

That slavery's greatest threat was spiritual in nature, and, moreover, a threat to the master class, was also stressed by Benezet in his personal letters to friends and family. "Books treating of Negroes are, I believe, not much in fashion amongst you, yet certain it is that all Persons, but more especially of youth, ought to know by what wicked & corrupt views & methods of Trade is carried on & the curse that will attend those who, for selfish ends, engage in it."[26] As late as 1771, Benezet was writing to his friends about the urgency of publishing pamphlets against the slave trade "for the information of the rising generation ... if thro' the divine blessing we may prove instrumental to keep them from being defiled with this mighty evil."[27]

Benezet's writings were among the more empathetic examples of this trope in that they cast blacks as agents and slavery as the ultimate cause of the moral pollution of the white community. But however intentioned, such formulations still served to divide blacks and whites into separate moral frameworks. Blacks, whether the carriers of immorality or corruptors themselves, remained untouchable and equally excludable from white society. Even in its most benevolent form, such rhetoric created a hierarchy of concern and value: preserving the morals of whites was obviously of greater importance than saving black people.

John Woolman, revered as a pioneering evangelist and antislavery crusader in the mid-eighteenth century, revealed in his memoirs a complicated mixture of motivations in explaining why he embarked on his crusade against bondage. Slavery's corrupting influence on white people was one of Woolman's deepest concerns. After preaching from Perquimans, North Carolina, through Virginia and around the Chesapeake towns of Maryland, Woolman observed that where "masters bore a good Share of the Burthen, and lived frugally, so that their Servants were well provided for, and their Labour moderate ..." Woolman "felt more easy" around these communities where the ennobling effect of labor was valued. But in other places he found the masters "lived in a costly Way" and consequently "laid heavy Burthens on their Slaves" and in these places Woolman was troubled, "the white People and their Children so generally living without much Labour, was frequently the Subject of my serious Thoughts." In these places Woolman scolded his hosts: "I frequently had Conversation with them, in private, concerning it."

For Woolman, it wasn't the slaves' lack of liberty that most troubled him, but the deleterious effect of the lazy luxury that slavery afforded whites. Woolman saw this wealthy indolence as not just a personal moral failing, but as a dire threat to the entire white nation. "I saw in these southern Provinces so many Vices and Corruptions, increased by this Trade and this Way of Life, that it appeared to me as a Gloom over the Land; and though now many willingly run into it, yet, in future, the Consequence will be grievous to Posterity ..."[28]

Woolman came to center many of his antislavery arguments on the damage slavery did to the character of white enslavers. Slavery was sinful because its luxuries and indolence led white Christians away from God: "they, who in the Midst of high Favours, remain ungrateful, and under all the Advantages that a Christian can desire, are selfish, earthly, and sensual, do miss the true Foundation of Happiness, and wander in a Maze of dark Anxiety."[29]

Abner Woolman, John Woolman's brother, first wrote of the "cause" of the "negroes" in his journal in 1768 when "the present sufferings and oppression of the negroes under us was often in my mind." Abner's fixation was not on the plight of slaves alone, but also on the connection between their poverty and the luxury of their masters, a connection that threatened the white masters' eternal soul.

> Now if a true history of the oppression of the negroes, together with an account of the costly apparel, household furniture, and high living of many amongst us, were published, how evidently would it appear that there is a grievous backsliding and degenerary, from that uprightness and simplicity which in time past appeared amongst friends.[30]

Similarly, Quaker Thomas Nicholson who freed several of the people he enslaved in North Carolina (most of whom were seized and resold) wrote an open letter to other Friends advocating they distance themselves from the sin of slavery. Nicholson wrote that he was "fully believing that they prove a Snare to Friend's Children, by being

32

made use of as Nurseries to pride, Idleness, and a Lording Spirit over our Fellow Creatures ..."[31]

THE ANTISLAVERY JEREMIAD
AND WHITE SELF-INTEREST

Those who were the first to raise their voices in opposition to slavery have been misunderstood by those who have uncritically imagined that the people of these long past times shared their own social vocabulary. Some of the words and phrases expressed in these sources exuded a Christian benevolence mixed with moral condemnation that seemed unmistakably like a call to end the slave system and recognize the humanity, even the equality, of those traded as property.

But self or group interest is often disguised as altruism. Seeming expressions of benevolence are especially hard to see as being self-interested when the object of benevolence is worldly and the selfish concern is metaphysical. Such is the case with many of the earliest condemnations of slavery which are read as moral protests against human bondage but are actually motivated by dread of divine judgment and damnation.[32]

It is especially difficult for modern readers of late seventeenth-century and early eighteenth-century writings to connect consequences in the spiritual world with actions in the material one. This is because modern secular consciousness distinctly separates life and the hereafter into two realms while the premodern outlook saw them as interpenetrating and co-existing. While modern readers easily see how buying and keeping slaves could be self-interested, as owners profit in various ways from exploiting labor and bodies, the self-interest involved in freeing one's slaves is less apparent and tangible.

When an early eighteenth-century evangelical Christian determined that an action was a violation of God's law, the consequences for violation transcended time and place. God's wrath was visited upon the sinner both in this world, through pestilence, famine, plague, and war, and in the next, through damnation. For someone whose daily experience of life was one filled with signs, omens, and interactions with an unseen spiritual world, the penalty or the payoff for following or falling off the narrow path of righteousness was not put off to a distant future, but experienced in the present.

Around the end of the 1600s, many preachers began to draw from Old Testament passages to label various aspects of slavery as sinful and, more importantly, to warn their parishioners of the impending wrath of the Lord. This form of sermonizing assumed a set form known as the jeremiad. The jeremiad had three essential parts: it began with the identification of sinful actions, it reminded the faithful that God's justice is served both on earth and in the hereafter, and it thunderously concludes with the possibility that repentance of the highlighted sin might avert God's avenging hand or save the sinner's eternal soul. Sect or denomination did not matter—Congregational, Baptist, Quaker, Methodist—all had their share of clerics fired with evangelicalism and a fear of God's judgment.[33]

A highly distilled example of this logic of white salvation through slave reform is glimpsed in the preaching of George Fox, the Quaker founder who was one of the first to preach that masters should allow their slaves to marry and to respect those unions. Fox preached against dividing enslaved families, not for their own sake, but for that of their masters, for promoting such immorality "may bring the Judgments of God upon you …" For Fox, and other founding Quakers who worried about the spiritual consequences of slavery, the purpose of benevolence and closely supervising the morality of one's slaves was to avoid "the Judgments of God" and to "shew that you are Disciples of Christ."[34]

Many religiously driven crusaders turned away from slavery out of concern for their own salvation. To many Friends, slavery was evil not primarily because it injured and confined the slave but because it violated the central Quaker doctrine of pacifism. Even those masters who worked out some sort of arrangements with the people they owned so that they did not wield the lash, found they could not completely distance themselves from a system that ultimately rested on violence. Moreover, ministers frequently cautioned their parishioners against the worldly temptations and vices that the owning of others cultivated. But the generally held solution to these spiritual concerns was not to campaign to end the institution in general, but to simply divest themselves of their human chattel.

For example, in 1696, a Friend in Merion, Pennsylvania, Cadwalader Morgan, wrote to his Yearly Meeting with thoughts that came to him when considering buying a slave. At first he thought it a good idea as "It would be some help to me and that I could with more ease Leave my calling to go to Meeting," but then he thought, what

> If I should have a bad one of them, that must be corrected, or would Run away, or when I went from home, & leave him with a woman or maid, and he should desire or seek to comitt wickedness, if such a thing happened that it would be more Loss and Trouble to me, than any outward gain could countervail.

Asking others what he should do ("Some advised me to buy and others to forbear"), Morgan searched his heart for the Lord's will and he realized that God did wish him to be so concerned "as to worldly things." While having "nothing in my heart" against anyone who bought slaves, Morgan thought he should share his revelation with other meetings: "I would have them Consider this thing before the Lord to know his will therein."[35]

Anthony Benezet, easily the most prolific of all antislavery writers in the eighteenth century, often employed the threat of divine retribution to condemn slavery. Benezet encouraged Christians to release from bondage the people they held (though only those who "have sufficiently paid, by their Labour, for their Purchase or bringing up") so as to avoid the retribution of a just God, or as Benezet put it, "the best Means to avert the Judgments of God, which it is to be feared will fall on Families and Countries, in Proportion as they have, more or less, defiled themselves with this iniquitous Traffick."[36]

Like earlier white abolitionists, Benezet's criticisms of slavery grew seamlessly from both morality and fear of Holy retribution against white society.[37] As he told his London friend Joseph Phipps, slavery needed to be combated by all "concerned for the civil, as well as religious welfare of their Country, and desirous to avert those judgments which evils of so deep a dye must necessarily sooner or later bring upon every People who are deffiled thereby."[38]

Likewise, another early Quaker antislavery crusader, John Woolman, in his 1754 tract, *Some Considerations on the Keeping of Negroes*, prophesied that keeping slaves might anger a just God: "When a People dwell under the liberal distribution of Favours from Heaven, it behoves them carefully to inspect their Ways, and consider the Purposes for which those Favours were bestowed, lest, through Forgetfulness of God, and Misusing of his Gifts, they incur his heavy Displeasure ..."[39]

Writing to a generation still fired with the idea of Puritans as fulfilling the holy mission of the Isrealites and the New World as promised land and fulfillment of Gospel prophesy, Samuel Sewall warned not only of God's judgment on sinners, but the failure of their New Jerusalem. Sewall wrote that if slavery was allowed to grow, "the Sons and Daughters of New England would become more like Jacob, and Rachel," the discontented parents of Joseph who led their people not to Jerusalem but to Egypt. He ends by exhorting his readers that treating slaves with "Respect agreeable" would attract signs of God's blessing: "for men obstinately to persist in holding their Neighbours and Brethren under the Rigor of perpetual Bondage, seems to be no proper way of gaining Assurance that God has given them Spiritual Freedom."[40]

More particular concerns roiled the conscience of even so stout a defender of slavery as Jonathan Edwards, that most famous of Calvinist divines who displayed no compunction against purchasing enslaved men and women at an open air slave market in Newport, Rhode Island. Reverend Edwards quietly wrote in 1741 that he had decided the African slave trade was immoral, because it vastly complicated the task of spreading the Gospel to that benighted continent.[41]

Edwards inspired many of his acolytes to preach against slavery because it was sin in the eyes of an angry God. Nathaniel Niles preached a brimstone sermon to his Connecticut congregation in 1774 that veered into the lurid detail of God's vengeance: "God gave us liberty, and we have enslaved our fellow-men. May we not fear that the law or retaliation is about to be executed on us? ... happy shall he be that taketh and dasheth thy little ones against the stones."[42]

John Wesley, founder of Methodism, anchored his condemnation of slavery on the toll it took on men's souls. Wesley had been influenced by Anthony Benezet's writings on Guinea and penned his own *Thoughts upon Slavery* in 1774. Wesley cautioned that a just God punishes sinners, either in this world or the next. Wesley was confident that "there must be a state of retribution: a state wherein the just God will reward every man according to his works." Addressing slave-owners generally, Wesley predicted that when the "measure of your iniquities is full" then "will the great God deal with you, as you have dealt with them, and require all their blood at your hands."[43]

By the time of the American Revolution, the antislavery jeremiad had become a common element of religious condemnations of slavery and a means of exhorting patriots to fight for their own liberty from England. In 1772, John Allen, a young Baptist minister, thundered from a Boston pulpit, "This unlawful, in human practice is a sure way for mankind to ruin America, and for Christians to bring their children, and their children's children to a morsel of bread." In a following sermon and pamphlet, Allen put his jeremiad warning more bluntly, "with what face can you look up to the Almighty ... and beg of him his aid and assistance in our political affairs, while we are oppressing our *African* brethren ten thousand times as much ...?"[44]

Philadelphian Richard Wells took an even more strident stance against slavery in his essay *A Few Political Reflections* published in 1774, but even Wells grounded his opposition in what was best for white republican America and the fear of an offended God. Wells worried that the sheer hypocrisy of Americans decrying slavery and demanding liberty while holding the neck chains of millions could invite ridicule to their cause. "In vain shall we contend for liberty, as an 'essential in our constitution,' till this barbarous inhuman practice is driven from our borders." Wells too pointed out that England had the upper hand in arguments of consistency and morality: "by what right do we support slavery?—the instant a slave sets his foot in England he claims the protection of the laws, and puts his master at defiance."[45]

A divine logic was inescapable for Wells and many other Americans raised to believe in a present and judgmental God. Slavery was contrary to the Bible and God's laws; therefore America could never prevail against England unless it should "expel this horrid demon from our lands." Only then would the "intervening arm of Providence to be extended in our favour." So, while Wells personally expressed a disgust and moral revulsion against slavery, his primary arguments to his fellow Americans were to their own self-interest.[46]

While appearing to be a fierce attack on the institution of slavery, the antislavery jeremiad was less an effort to abolish that institution than it was a call for Christians to distance themselves from it. It is this distinction that has long confused accounts of early antislavery movements and led to their misinterpretation as being more radical and sweeping in their intent than they were. Antislavery jeremiads were first and foremost part of a theological worldview that held that the wages of sin were to be paid twice, both on earth and in heaven. In other words, this line of attack on slavery depended on a vengeful Old Testament God weighing every worldly action against His laws and ultimately served the interests of faithful whites.

As such, the antislavery jeremiad only served as an engine of antislavery thought and action when the fear of an Old Testament God and the fires of damnation loomed as a present danger. When believers cleansed themselves of the sin of slavery, either by not buying slaves, divesting themselves of those they owned, or expelling from their churches those that failed to do either, their Christian duty was complete. Just as God spared those in Jerusalem who lamented the "abominations" in their city, within the logic of the jeremiad it was enough for most Christians to condemn slavery and not actually take any actions to oppose it. For those lacking such faith, the arguments and threats of the jeremiad failed completely.

Warner Mifflin, one of the leading Quaker abolitionists in the days of the American Revolution, went about manumitting his slaves and advocating that other Quakers follow his example. Again, Mifflin's efforts to free himself and his fellow Friends from the sin of slavery remained primarily motivated by the terror of damnation and the corrupting effects of slavery on the master class. In a letter urging

Congress to restrict the slave trade as much as the Constitution would allow, he condemned the trade as "barbarous and inhuman" but rested his primary argument on the inevitability of God's judgment:

> ... the great Author of our existence will, in displeasure, take cognizance of the neglect, if, by the want of this discountenance, multitudes of our unoffending fellow men, should be brought from their native land into barbarous slavery ... "He who rules over men, must be just, ruling in the fear of God" ... That "vengeance is mine, I will repay, saith the Lord."[47]

Unlike others, Mifflin's motivations and inclinations in advocating an end to the slave trade or for Christians to shun the sin of slaveholding need not be inferred from a close reading of his speeches or a study of his actions. In Mifflin's case, he bared his racial allegiance in a letter to a friend, John Dickenson, author of the important revolutionary pamphlet, *Letters from a Farmer in Pennsylvania*, who freed the first half dozen of his sixty-five slaves in 1781. Mifflin wrote:

> It gave me satisfaction when I heard that thee had recorded a manumission for thy blacks more on thy account than theirs, for however people may think I favour black people I think I am more in the white interest than the other when laboring to have them freed from oppression, which if rightly done is certainly in my view of more advantage to the master than slave.[48]

Likewise, Mifflin reassured a friend that his coming to visit him would not "corrupt thy servants." Rather, Mifflin promised, "this I would with carefully to guard against, not to make them restless or dissatisfied in their condition." Expressing his solidarity and sympathy with this enslaver, he recounted that he had owned slaves and that he "never would have given up mine ... if I could have conceived I might have got to heaven, (as I believe there is such a place) and have kept them." He then explained that:

> I uniformly recommend to them wherever occasion occurs, to submit in patience to their situation, resigning their cause to God

Almighty, that he may do with and for them according to his will. On this principle I have prevailed on some to return to their masters, when I have seen them near an hundred miles off. They have returned with a letter from me, and I have received the thanks of their masters therefor.[49]

Delaware Quaker leader, David Ferris, campaigned against slave-holding in his Wilmington Meeting in the 1760s using the "usual" arguments that had become the substance of protest against slavery. Ferris pointed out slavery's violation of the Golden Rule through its cruelty toward black Africans, denied that the Bible condoned the practice, and then warned enslavers that they jeopardized their souls by the many sins slavery dragged along in its train. Here, as in other eighteenth-century jeremiads, speaking of the slaveholder's eternal spirit, Ferris' priority of whiteness is evident.

In a letter to "Samuel Field and Wife," a couple he had known for "many years," Ferris asked them "seriously to consider the law that was given forth under the present dispensation," namely, the Golden Rule, and how slavery was an obvious violation of this principle. While expressing his view that the "poor Blacks have the same right to freedom that we have," in the end, Ferris urged the Fields to free their slaves not for the slaves' benefit but for theirs, out of Ferris' "desires for your present and eternal welfare ...":

My desire for you is, that you may so act as to stand clear, and be acquitted in the day of account. I pity the slaveholder far more than I pity his slaves, because I believe him to be in a worse condition than they. I should choose rather to be the slave than his master or mistress.[50]

Slaves may have been in physical bondage, but slave masters, bound in their souls, were in "much greater bondage than their poor Negroes." Like Warner Mifflin, Ferris confessed to his white friend that his main concern was for the salvation of white slave-owners: "My motive is thy well being: slave-holding is a sin and Christ said if men die in their sins where he is gone they cannot come." While

Ferris said he was "somewhat concerned for the deliverance of the poor Negro captives," he was "more especially for the freedom of all my Friends, who are in any measure entangled with slave keeping."[51]

Ferris expressed the same sentiments in 1774 in a letter to Robert Pleasants, worrying that slavery was harmful to the master: "I fear that to hold them in a state of slavery, deprived of their natural right, may be a means of depriving thee of thy own freedom, and not only prevent thee from being so serviceable in thy day, as otherwise thou might be, but be a bar in the way of thy peace here, and hereafter."[52]

As Ferris made the rounds of recalcitrant Friends, cajoling and arguing with them to steer away from the sin of slavery and rid themselves of their chattel, he made clear that the priority of manumission was the master's soul while the enslaved person's freedom was secondary. Ferris urged a slave-owner toward the light by writing "If thee lays aside pecuniary interest, become fully resigned, willing to part with all for Truth's sake, a way will be made for thy escape and for the safety of the negroes also."[53]

Such arguments easily passed from religious to secular language as they were embraced by the rising generation of American revolutionaries, fired by Enlightenment philosophy but no less concerned about the moral fiber of the new nation. When James Otis digressed from discussing *The Rights of the British Colonists* to discussing the philosophical problem with slavery in his 1764 pamphlet, he also foregrounded the peril slavery posed not to black people, but to white ones. Otis followed the well-worn pattern of declaring the natural rights of all men "white or black" and the absurdity of enslaving one part of mankind because they had "short curl'd hair like wool" and "a flat nose." The "cruel slavery exercised over the poor Ethiopians," Otis proclaimed, "threatens one day to reduce both Europe and America to the ignorance and barbarity of the darkest ages." This was because of the corrosive effect of slavery upon white men's moral fiber. "It is a clear truth that those who every day barter away other men's liberty will soon care little for their own." Republics cannot rest upon such unstable firmament, so slavery tended to produce tyrranical governments and therefore was a direct threat to white liberty.[54]

While some southerners warned against the damage slavery did to masters' morals, it was usually Yankees who expressed the most moral disgust at the behavior of their fellow slaveholding Americans. Josiah Quincy had never traveled far from his native Boston and so when the twenty-nine-year-old Harvard graduate, lawyer, and leader of the Sons of Liberty traveled to the South in 1773, it was a trip full of surprising first impressions. He was shocked at the immorality on display in the deep plantation South when he visited South Carolina in 1773. "The enjoyment of a negro or mulatto woman is spoken of as quite a common thing: no reluctance, delicacy or shame is made about the matter. It is far from being uncommon to see a gentleman at dinner, and his reputed offspring a slave to the master of the table. I myself saw two instances of this ... The fathers neither of them blushed or seem(ed) disconcerted."[55]

By the time of the American Revolution, jeremiad sermonizing had seamlessly blended with natural rights philosophizing to produce a potent spur to action. A typical example of this tone is a letter published under the pen name Eumenes (likely this was the Reverend Jacob Green of Morris county, New Jersey) entitled "On Liberty." Eumenes warns his fellow patriots not to lose the liberty they had gained in their hard fight against tyranny by falling into the chasm of vice. Vice is the primary instrument of oppression because "it provokes God to withhold his protection, and punish a sinning people by permitting usurpers and tyrants to seize on their natural rights, and reduce them to a state of bondage." Eumenes then extended his logic to the debts already incurred to God:

At present I observe, that we are infinitely indebted to divine Providence for all the privileges we enjoy; and especially for that state of freedom that we are, or hope soon, to be in the fullest possession of. By divine Providence our ancestors were led into this land as an asylum; by the same benign power, their posterity have been preserved and increased to what they are now; by the same gracious God we have hitherto been helped in the present war, for to him we have appealed in the present contest. It would be wicked, it would be very ungrateful, it would be shameful, for us to forget, or give up our privileges. What less can we do in return for the divine benignity, than to maintain the practice of virtue, use all proper means to preserve our freedom, and cast an eye of pity on the negro slaves among us, who are groaning under a bondage which *we* think worse than death.[56]

Virginia's Arthur Lee sparked much controversy when he published his "Address on Slavery" in the *Virginia Gazette* in 1767. Addressing the Virginia House of Burgesses, Lee expressed his concern for the safety and virtue of the white community. While confessing that upon "Long and serious Reflection upon the nature & Consequences of Slavery" had convinced him that "it is a Violation both of Justice and Religion," Lee seemed just as worried that slavery was "dangerous to the safety of the Community in which it prevails; that it is destructive to the growth of arts & Sciences; and lastly, that it produces a numerous & very fatal train of Vices, both in the Slave and in his Master."

Like the more religiously inclined Quakers of an earlier time, Lee followed the jeremiad form and warned of that "awfull day, when your Saviour shall pronounce judgment upon you ..." After a long passage counting the myriad ways slavery violated both God's law and natural rights, Lee returned to the question of the safety of the white colonists, cautioning against a repeat of the bloody uprisings in Jamaica:

to imagine that we shall be forever exempted from this Calamity, which experience teaches us to be inseprable from slavery ... is an infatuation as astonishing as it will be surely fatal. On us, or on our posterity, the inevitable blow, must, one day, fall; and probably with the most irresistable vengeance the longer it is protracted. Since time, as it adds strength and experience to the slaves, will sink us into perfect security and indolence, which debillitating our minds, and enervating our bodies, will render us an easy conquest to the feeblest foe.[57]

As protest movements against British taxes ripened into insurrection against British authority, a number of antislavery writers linked the continuing sin of slavery to the onrushing prospect of a bloody civil war. In 1772, David Cooper completed his first antislavery pamphlet, "A Mite into the Treasury, or Considerations on Slavery." Typically, in describing his conversion to the antislavery cause, Cooper began by framing slavery as a moral problem for the slaveholder: "As I have at times," he writes, "for many years past, felt my mind warmly affected with a sense of the cruelty and wickedness of slavery, and its inconsistency with Christianity ..."[58] But, following the form of the jeremiad, Cooper warned that slavery posed a dire threat to the white community from the wrath of a just God. America's sin of slavery was only compounded by its hypocrisy in condemning the tyranny of the British empire.

> Our rulers have appointed days for humiliation, and offering up of prayer to our common Father, to deliver us from our oppressors, when sighs and groans are piercing his holy ears from oppressions which we commit, a thousand fold more grievous; pouring forth blood and treasure, year after year, in defence of our own rights; exerting the most assiduous attention and care to secure them by laws and sanctions, while the poor Africans are continued in chains of slavery, as creatures unworthy of notice in these high concerns, and left subject to laws disgraceful to humanity, and opposite to every principle of christianity.[59]

In an address to the Continental Congress in 1776, Reverend Samuel Hopkins, the pastor of First Congregational Church in Newport, Rhode Island, began in the conventionally general form of the jeremiad: "If the slavery in which we hold the blacks is wrong, it is a very great and public sin, and, therefore, a sin which God is now testifying against in the calamities he has brought upon us; consequently, must be reformed before we can reasonably expert deliverance, or even sincerely ask for it ..."[60] But Hopkins was not satisfied to speak of vague calamities and an abstract God. Instead Hopkins pointed out that the British invaders were clearly God's instrument as their goal was the mirror of the patriot's own wrongs: "our distresses are come upon us in such a way, and the occasion of the present war is such, as in the most clear and striking manner to point out the sin of holding our blacks in slavery, and admonish us to reform, and render us shockingly inconsistent with ourselves, and amazingly guilty if we refuse."[61]

Likewise, Pennsylvania's patriot leaders urged adoption of a gradual manumission bill on the grounds that it would acknowledge God's blessings in freeing the state from British occupation. "In divesting the State of Slaves you will equally serve the cause of humanity & policy, & offer to God one of the most proper & best returns of Gratitude for his great deliverance of us & our posterity from Thraldom."[62] President Joseph Reed of the Executive Council cautioned that in fulfilling this Holy duty, the legislature should not forget that their primary duty was to benefit the interests and well-being of whites. Slavery needed to go because it was "disgraceful ... to those who have been contending in the great cause of liberty themselves, and upon whom Providence has bestowed such eminent marks of its favour and protection." Patriots were "called on to evince our gratitude, in making our fellow-men joint heirs with us of the same inestimable blessings, under such restrictions and regulations as will not injure the community," by which, of course, Reed meant the white community.[63]

Pennsylvania's original "Act for the Gradual Abolition of Slavery" began with a preamble that justified the novel measure by the damage slavery did to the white community. It drew a line through history between "the natives of Africa and their descendants" and "Christians" and claimed that white people, those "who contend for their own freedom" had an obligation "to promote the liberty of others as far as the same is practicable and lawful." In keeping with long-standing white abolitionist rhetoric that tied antislavery to white salvation, the preamble reminded patriots of God's hand in saving their state from British invasion and what they owed Him in return: "whereas the most remarkable deliverance from thraldom, which God, the great disposer of all events, had graciously vouchsafed to grant to Pennsylvania, in common with the other free united states of North America, calleth for suitable returns of gratitude to the author of all salvation."[64]

When the clerk of the assembly, Thomas Paine, finally read out the bill in March of 1780, its preamble had been rewritten and except for dropping criminal penalties for miscegenation that were in the original, the bill was in substance largely the same and passed thirty-four to twenty-one. The abolition law's new preamble leaned more heavily on gratitude and obligation to the Supreme Being and largely dropped references to white safety.

In 1794 abolitionists from half the states gathered in the same Philadelphia Hall in which a few years before state delegates had drafted the nation's Constitution. One of the first tasks of the inaugural American Convention for Promoting the Abolition of Slavery and Improving the Condition of the African Race was to hammer out a joint statement to the citizens of all the states of the union expressing their shared beliefs and values regarding slavery. They began by listing their reasons for opposing the institution of slavery, the first five of which all centered on the needs, aspirations, and safety of the white community.

At the top of their list of concerns was the old charge that slavery was incompatible with democracy because slavery corrupted the slave-owners. Slavery, the members of this convention declared, was "inconsistent with the safety of the liberties of the United States" because the experience of mastering slaves "unfits men for discharging the public and private duties of citizens of the republic." So important was the corrosive effect of slavery on the republic that the drafters of this manifesto repeated this same charge as their fourth point, saying that "In vain has the tyranny of kings been rejected, while we permit in our country a domestic despotism, which involves, in its nature, most of the vices and miseries that we have endeavoured to avoid."

Next followed the deeply held white fear that the people they kept in bondage might one day rise up and free themselves in a similarly bloody manner that was then being witnessed in "one of the richest islands in the West Indies," by which they meant Haiti.

The third reason for opposing slavery was novel but drew on Puritan traditions of seeing America as a "city on a hill" or a "beacon of liberty" to the world. Slavery, these reformers asserted, was "unfriendly to the present exertions of the inhabitants of Europe, in favour of liberty." They then added, rhetorically, "What people will advocate freedom … while they view the purest republic in the world tolerating in its bosom a body of slaves?" (It is worthwhile to linger a moment on this wording and note how the evil that is tolerated is both slavery and slaves themselves.)

Their next concern centered on the way in which slavery debased all white men by association, and not just those who kept other men in bondage. "It is degrading to our rank as men in the scale of being." While this point was worded in secular language, it rested on Christian notions of creation, sin, and divine retribution as it warned that if Americans should continue to misuse the "reason and social affections for the purposes for which they were given" they may as well "cease to boast a preeminence over animals, that are unpolluted with our crimes."

After listing half a dozen reasons for opposing slavery, all of them tightly centered on the well-being of white people and the betterment of the white republic, the authors of this public address were suddenly self-aware that they had not yet condemned slavery on any grounds having to do with the welfare or rights of the people chained in perpetual servitude, and so they observe: "But higher motives to justice and humanity towards our fellow-creaturs remain yet to be mentioned."

Nevertheless, though this glimmer of self-consciousness breaks through their self-interested complaints, this opening quickly clouds over, and the text regains its focus on the white community. Its very next paragraph notes that slavery "is repugnant to the principles of Christianity" but the problem with such a violation is that it invites God's wrath:

The crimes of nations, as well as of individuals, are often designated in their punishments; and we conceive it to be no forced construction, of some of the calamities which now distress or impend our country, to believe that they are the measure of evils, which we have meted to others.

The ravages committed upon many of our fellow-citizens by the Indians, and the depredations upon the liberty and commerce of others of the citizens of the United States by the Algerines, both unite in proclaiming to us, in the most forcible language, "to loose the bands of wickedness, to break every yoke, to undo the heavy burthens, and to let the oppressed go free."[65]

To arouse the sympathy of their fellow Americans, these wordsmiths illustrated how the sin of slavery was being paid for by white citizens who were themselves made slaves by Africans or murdered by Indians. Such language would have been familiar to the white abolitionists who invented it a century earlier.

SELFISH MANUMISSION

During slavery's first century in America, there were few restrictions on the rights of masters to free the people they enslaved. Partly this was the result of the monopoly of political power in the hands of landed elites who owned the bulk of slaves, partly it was the result of the autonomy granted to property in the British legal tradition, and partly it was the result of a paradigm of government in which the state rested on private patriarchs who were expected to rule their "families," a term which in the eighteenth century embraced not only people related by birth and marriage, but servants, slaves, and various children who were under the patriarch's authority. As a writer described in *The Virginia Gazette* in 1775, "Private families are petty kingdoms ... The prejudicial effects of severity how often have we seen in those smaller societies! ... Neither is it less fatal in public Administrations than it is in private families."[66] In such an age when many of the modern functions of the state were privatized and domesticated, lawmakers were reluctant to usurp the "natural" authority of patriarchs.

As the number of slaves in America rose quickly in the eighteenth century and with it the numbers of "free" African Americans, a backlash against the blackening of the population began pressuring legislatures to consider restraining the growth of the free black population by restricting the ability of slave-owners to free their slaves.

Tellingly, the first colonies to formally restrict an owners' ability to free his or her slaves were those in New England. Connecticut pioneered such measures by passing a law in 1702 making slave-owners financially responsible for any persons they freed until the end of their natural lifetimes. This law reveals that the states' interest in restricting manumission was not only to curtail the growth of the free black community but to govern and discipline black people by their continuing legal ties to their former masters and heirs. Connecticut's lawmakers justified this law as a means of preventing "slaves not being able to provide necessaries for themselves may become a charge and burthen to the towns where they have served."[67]

Massachusetts Bay Colony went further the next year and specified not only a master's perpetual liability for released slaves, but required a stiff bond to be paid to the town court; "a valuable sum, not less than fifty pounds, to secure and indemnify the town or place from all charge for or about such mulatto or negro, to be manumitted and set at liberty, in case he or she by sickness, lameness or otherwise, be rendered uncapable to support him or herself." Moreover, Massachusetts' act made it clear that failure to abide by the specified terms of manumission negated a person's freedom:

> no mulatto or negro hereafter manumitted shall be deemed or accounted free, for whom security shall not be given as aforesaid, but shall be the proper charge of their respective masters or mistresses, in case they stand in need of relief and support, notwithstanding any manumission or instrument of freedom to them made or given; and shall also be liable at all times to be put forth to service by the selectmen of the town.[68]

In 1728, the colony of Rhode Island banned all manumissions except upon pledging securities worth at least £100 to the local township. The law did not authorize anyone to claim the improperly released person as their own property, as in southern colonies, but instead enslaved the illegally freed person to the community at large:

> no mulatto or negro hereafter manumitted, shall be deemed or accounted free, for whom security shall not be given as aforesaid … notwithstanding any manumission or instrument of freedom to them made … and shall be liable at all times to be put forth to service by the justices of the peace, or wardens of the town.[69]

Viewed systematically, such manumission laws can be seen to act in two additional ways other than simply narrowing the opportunities for elective manumission. They established an administrative system for recording, authorizing, and verifying an individual's passage from the status of slave to free person. Such was in keeping with the overall slow consolidation of the modern bureaucratic state. Additionally, and importantly, they also implicitly defined the meaning of freedom for African Americans. Through these terms freedom became a provisional and perpetually probationary status for people of color, subject to revocation by either a public entity such as a town council or continuing through the extenuated private rule of one's former master.

At the other extreme, South Carolina placed no barriers in the way of a master's desire to free their own slaves other than the requirement that freed persons vacate the colony. South Carolina's slave codes of 1712 and 1735 required that all freed slaves leave the colony within six months of manumission. Failure to quit the state as required fell back upon former masters who could be forced to pay passage to a foreign port. These laws were in effect throughout the eighteenth century. In effect, like Massachusetts' manumission law of 1703, South Carolina was also defining the meaning of freedom for African Americans, though their definition was far simpler—freedom should legally only exist beyond the colony's borders. South Carolina recorded only 379 manumissions between 1737 and 1785.[70]

Pennsylvania began restricting manumissions in its session that lasted from the fall of 1725 to the summer of 1726. It required all masters before setting free "any Negroe" to deposit a suretie of £30 "to secure and indemnify the City, Township or County where he resides, from any Charge or Incumbrance they may bring upon the same, in case such Negroe, by Sickness or otherwise, be rendered incapable to support him or herself; but until such Recognizance be given, such Negroes shall not be deemed free."[71] These requirements must have been widely known in the Quaker community as it was a Friend and member of the Philadelphia Meeting, Anthony Morris, who wrote them.[72]

New York and New Jersey dramatically narrowed the ability of masters to release their human property in the wake of the great slave insurrection panic of 1712. New York required two bonds of £200 each and New Jersey £20 per year for each slave freed for life. New York ended the requirement of annual support of manumitted slaves by their masters a few years later as slave-owners complained that by nearly completely extinguishing the already small but flickering hope of freedom, the law may "excite" rebellions and "very much Discourage and Dishearten" slaves from their duties.[73] New Jersey held on to its slave annuity system until 1769. (In 1775, the New Jersey Assembly considered petitions both for and against easing the restrictions on manumissions in that state and voted not to take up the issue.[74])

Remarking that "And forasmuch as great inconveniences may happen to this country by the setting of negroes and mulattoes free, by their either entertaining negro slaves from their masters service, or receiveing stolen goods, or being grown old bringing a charge upon the country; for prevention thereof …" Virginia's legislature first regulated the manumission of slaves by requiring slave-owners to pay to transport emancipated people out of the colony, or to pay a fine of £10 sterling that would be applied to "cause the said negro or mulatto to be transported out of the countrey, and the remainder of the said money to imploy to the use of the poor of the parish."[75] Then, in 1723, the door to manumission was closed further and no Virginia slaves could be legally freed without permission of the governor. The only grounds for granting such a petition was "some meritorious service." Any slave freed without such permission was considered "derelict" property, available to be seized and sold at public auction. Very few individuals asked for the governor's permission. It was ten years before the first petition was sent. A second was received two years later. The Virginia legislature renewed and reenacted these restrictions in an updated slave law of 1748.[76]

Thus, by the mid-eighteenth century, the ability of slave-owners to divest themselves of their living property was strictly curtailed by law. Moreover, these laws were designed to be self-enforcing by recognizing the legal right of any private citizen to uphold them by claiming improperly freed people as their own property. Nevertheless, Quakers in several colonies, worried about living in a state of sin that put their eternal souls at risk or pressured by their fellow congregants to divest themselves of their chattel or risk excommunication, began renouncing their property interest in the people they legally owned. Despite the uncertain future that enslaved people set loose in this way faced, the push for all Quakers who held people in slavery to conduct irregular manumission became a movement that impacted untold numbers of enslaved families.

While living in New Jersey in 1756, John Woolman advised a dying neighbor to free a young slave rather than will her to an heir. At the time, New Jersey required masters to post bonds amounting to two times the market value of such a young slave and pledge to contribute £20 per year toward their support in perpetuity in order for that manumission to be recognized by the state. The law was effective at preventing manumissions as there is no record of any such manumissions being recorded by the state of New Jersey prior to the revocation of this bond requirement in 1786.

Quakers in New York state debated the godliness and spiritual danger of slavery after John Woolman traveled around the state in 1760. Prior to this time the meridian of their concern was for masters to not mistreat their slaves. But after Woolman's visit, several members, particularly in New York City, publicly renounced the ownership of human beings. Samuel Underhill reconsidered his previous involvement in the slave importing business and told his fellow Friends, "Sorry I ever had any Concern in that Trade." By 1767, New York City's Meeting was enforcing a rule against the buying and selling of slaves. Following the lead of the Philadelphia Yearly Meeting, New York City's Quakers formed a visiting committee in 1775 to urge Friends to free their slaves. Within a year, the committee happily reported that their efforts had influenced a "considerable number" to "sett them free" and reported that "some few have already complied with the advice given and Executed Manumissions for that purpose." New York's Yearly Meeting issued a "Minute," or religious mandate, that all members grant manumissions to their slaves in 1777. The next time the investigating committee reported to the Yearly Meeting, it included the names of the recalcitrant members who stood in jeopardy of being disowned.[77]

As in other parts of the country, Quakers in New York disregarded the established legal procedures for granting freedom to slaves. During the year in which the great majority of Quaker slaves were released, New York state required in addition to the manumission being approved by a local magistrate, the posting of a bond of £200 in guarantee of the support of the freed person.[78]

Quakers proved by their actions to be far less concerned with the fate of the enslaved men, women, and children they "freed" than the cleansing effect their morally distancing themselves from slavery would have on their souls. A growing faction of Quakers began campaigning among neighbors and fellow Friends to free their slaves even though at that time many states prohibited manumission without legislative approval and others imposed prohibitive bonds, fees, and other legal obstacles that few could afford.[79]

While the stated policy of all the meetings was for Friends to set free their slaves, some chose to sell their human property. William Cox, a Maryland Quaker, was visited by a committee of his Monthly Meeting and he complied by selling the five people he owned. There is no record that Cox was disciplined, or that his action was a matter of controversy in his community.[80]

During the roughly nineteen years from when the purchasing or selling of slaves was first prohibited to the time when this policy was expanded to ban all slave-owning in 1776, Pennsylvania's Meeting disciplined a total of 162 members for infractions having to do with the business of slavery. Of this total, more than three-fifths of these disciplinary actions occurred in the first seven years. According to a careful study of Quaker manumission records for Pennsylvania, of the 443 slaves held by Friends in that state, all but one-fifth were freed before 1780, the year manumissions were legalized, thus leaving them technically outlaws and fugitives.[81]

The fate of those turned out by slaveholders without court-approved manumission papers was well known. Delaware preacher David Ferris himself detailed the right way and the wrong way to free slaves in 1767 when urging a slave-owner to save his eternal soul:

Set them all free *now*, whilst it is in your power. Give them a full discharge in writing; and by a bond secure to the minors their freedom, when they shall arrive at age. Let the manumissions be legally drawn and executed, so that neither you nor your children, nor any other person, may take them again into bondage. Let these instruments of writing be duly and safely recorded.[82]

But even knowing this, the unhappy fate of the illegally turned-out slave, Ferris still urged masters to divest themselves of their slaves for their own sakes. In 1774, Ferris urged Robert Pleasants to free his slaves regardless of the law and the likelihood that they would suffer being sold back into slavery because once freed they were no longer the master's moral responsibility, and their fate was up to God:

I beseech thee not to dally, or put it off any longer. Do justice without delay. Don't hesitate about the value of thy slaves, neither boggle at the law, saying "if I set them free the public will take them, and sell them into worse slavery, and it will be hard that the poor negroes should suffer by my act." I fully believe if thou could see the *danger* of thy present state, and could lay aside the influence of *pecuniary interest*, so as to be fully resigned, and willing to part with all for the Truth's sake, a way would be made for thy escape and for the safety of the negroes also. If the Lord requires thee to set thy slave free, obey him promptly, and leave the result to him, and peace shall be within thy borders.[83]

As early as 1772, North Carolina Quakers were well aware of their legal limitations to simply declare their slaves free as they informed London that

there is an act of Assembly in this province which prohibits any person from setting a negro free except for meritorious services to be judged of by the County court—under penalty of said negro being seized and sold to the highest bidder, for the benefit of the parish—such Friends as desire to liberate their slaves from principles of justice and christianity are under great difficulty on that account.[84]

Thomas Newby of Perquimans Monthly Meeting was particularly troubled by his ownership of other humans and asked his meeting's Standing Committee for guidance in 1774. They responded that "all Friends finding themselves under a burden and uneasiness on account of keeping slaves, may set them at liberty by applying to the monthly meeting."

Newby then released ten of his fourteen enslaved people in March of 1776. Newby's self-drawn manumission proclamation, a document having no legal force in North Carolina, conditioned these ten persons' freedom on their making annual payments to Newby for the privilege of their liberty.

[I] most freely Set at Liberty Six negro men on their paying me or my heirs the Sum of twenty shillings a year and on the terms of good behaviour ... Also four Negro Women and their Increase that they may hereafter have but in case they or Either of them Should behave bad or not pay their Leveys in due time then they he or She so offending to be Sold by me or my heirs for as Long a time as will make full Satisfaction for the offence Committed and all Charges that may arise thereon.[85]

Newby was aware of the state's legal requirements for manumission because a few months later he attempted to follow the law in releasing another of the women he held, a midwife named Hannah. Hannah stood out because she could arguably meet the legal standard of having performed "meritorious" service by having been "an Excellent Midwife called on Every hand turn to Both White Women & Black." Newby considered Hannah too old to be profitable to keep: "She being Grown ould And Can be Very little Service to me, as to any Hard Work or Drudgery." Hannah still lived with her husband of forty years, though her children were all scattered, having been distributed among Newby's relatives when his father died.

Newby's county court declined his petition, effectively concluding that Newby was attempting to evade his responsibility for maintaining a slave who could no longer support herself. In spite of this ruling,

Newby sent Hannah packing and she was seized by a sheriff and auctioned into some other person's possession.[86]

Another of the men Thomas Newby freed in 1776 was James. James took to sea and during the Revolutionary war was twice captured by the British and twice managed to escape and find his way back to his wife and children in North Carolina. He then signed on with an American warship, though the details and duration of his tour are lost. James was subsequently seized by North Carolina authorities and Newby and other Quakers petitioned for his freedom.[87]

In 1775, at the urging of the Western Monthly Meeting, the North Carolina Yearly Meeting discussed prohibiting members from any involvement with slavery and concluded that "Friends in unity shall neither buy or sell a negro without the consent of the monthly meeting to which they belong." The Eastern Quakers were not quite ready to go that far and urged reconsideration, whereupon the Yearly Meeting advised that slaveholding members "be earnestly and affectionately advised to clear their hands of them as soon as they possibly can." Visiting committees were organized and pressure applied to free enslaved people. Within two years the visiting committee reported "that they found a great willingness, even beyond their expectation, to promote the work."[88]

But of the slaves these Quakers released at least forty were seized and resold in 1777. Others took the tactic of binding their slaves as servants for life, though this was frowned upon by the various meeting leaderships as it left heirs in a morally compromised position if the master died before the servant. Quakers employed lawyers to represent the people they freed at a cost of £64 and justified their actions to the public in terms of God's judgment and quoted the book of Isaiah:

> We have endeavored to be clear from the least stain of guilt in the blood shed on the earth—when that awful day shall come in which "The earth shall disclose her blood and no more cover her slain."—Isaiah xxvi, 21,—fully believing that the trade in slaves and souls of men is justly chargeable with a large share therein, and that those who do remain partakers with murderers and manstealers will be involved in their guilt. And therefore whatever ignorance

may surmise to the contrary, having through divine assistance, done what we believe was our duty to do in liberating our slaves if men shall be permitted to reduce them to a state of bondage and slavery, the guilt will lie at the door of those that are the cause thereof, and we shall appeal to Him who judgeth righteously without respect of persons.[89]

In 1778, the Friends redoubled their attempts to litigate the freedom of their former slaves now owned by others and raised £600 for legal fees. According to a Quaker historian, "The suit was attended to, and an order obtained for the freedom of the negroes. But the spirit of oppression has an hundred grasping hands. Another act was passed to reduce them again to bondage."[90]

A group of a dozen men in Perquimans County, North Carolina, petitioned their local court pleading for a Peter, who one of them had illegally freed, to "remain freed & unmolested as long as he behaves himself." Peter, the son of a native woman and a black father, was, they said, "an orderly servant" who had never been "accused of any Villany." Rather, Peter had "done several Meritorious Actions in Destroying Vermin such as Bears, Wolves, Wild Cats ..."[91] Its not clear what became of Peter.

In October of 1788, a black man named Dick was seized and taken to jail on presumption he had been illegally freed by a Quaker. A friend of Dick's complained to the local county court that Dick was indeed free, that his grandmother Betty had been an Indian and "a free woman by the laws of nature."[92]

Among the slaves Thomas Nicholson freed were four members of one family who took the Nicholson name. Jupiter Nicholson and his brother Jacob, along with their mother and father (whose names are lost to history), were soon pursued. Jupiter recounted how his family like "several hundreds under our circumstance," were "hunted day and night, like beasts of the forest, by armed men with dogs, and made prey of as free and lawful plunder." Jupiter's mother and father and brother were all captured and reenslaved, however, he and his wife escaped. First, they fled to Portsmouth, Virginia, where Jupiter had once visited as a seaman, and he found work as a sawyer. From there they then fled to Philadelphia.

Job Albert, lived with his free wife in a house given to them by a former master. Bounty hunters broke into his house and stole their meager possessions, then hunted Job who was caught soon after. His wife was sheltered by her former master in his attic. Job was tied and led to Hartford jail where he was held for four weeks before he escaped and after paying $3 for a conveyance in a covered wagon, made his way to Portsmouth, Virginia, with his wife. Job worked with Jacob in sawing for about four years before also fleeing north to Philadelphia. He then learned his mother and sister were reenslaved, "both taken up and sold into slavery."

Thomas Pritchet was manumitted by his master and given a plot of land which he cleared and upon which he built his own house. But in his third year, just before harvesting what would have been his bumper crop of corn, the widow of his former master remarried and her new husband demanded that Pritchet was his slave. He gave him the option of working for him or being sold to the West Indies. "being thus in jeopardy, I left my little farm with my small stock and utensils, and my corn standing, and escaped by night into Virginia." There he left his wife and children and shipped to Boston in search of work, but only made it as far as New York, where Pritchet worked as a waiter for nearly a year and half. Pritchet had saved some money and returned to Norfolk to see his family but when he arrived found advertisements offering a $20 bounty on his capture. Pritchet was forced to leave without seeing them and moved to Philadelphia where he resumed work as a waiter. Ultimately, Nicholson, Albert, and Pritchet were all seized by bounty hunters and dragged back into North Carolina slavery.[93]

A few slaveholders who wished to cleanse their hands of slavery went to great lengths to ensure that those they released did not fall back into bondage. Robert Pleasants was a Virginian and Quaker elder who owned extensive lands and at least eighty people. Pleasants first experimented with manumission in 1772 when he determined to free a child named James. Knowing that James' manumission would not be recognized in Virginia, Pleasants attempted to provide some legal cover by recording a "deed of manumission" with his meeting and specifying that he exchanged James' freedom "in consideration of the sum of five shillings lawful money," probably figuring that some future court might look more favorably on a manumission based on the sale of human property rather than one based on religious scruples.[94] It is unclear from the records what happened to James but his fate was probably similar to that of Betty, a seven-year-old girl who Pleasants "freed" by drafting another of these extralegal manumission papers but was seized by the sheriff and sold at auction five years later.[95]

Such failures prompted Pleasants to take a different tack, settling a number of the people he owned on some of his fallow lands.[96] It may have been Pleasants' activities that Thomas Jefferson referred to when he wrote to a friend complaining of planters who pretended to have "tenants" who were actually their slaves. Jefferson thought even this halfway form of freedom was wrong because "to abandon persons whose habits have been formed in slavery is like abandoning children." Jefferson then repeated what he had heard of this experiment, that the "tenants" refused to work and their "landlord" was "obliged to plan their crops for them, to direct all their operations during every season and according to the weather, but, what is more afflicting, he was obliged to watch them daily and almost constantly to make them work, and even to whip them." Such slanderous rumors were probably born of the need to justify slavery in the face of the insistent appeals to equality and liberty aired by patriots among landholding Virginians. Jefferson told his friend that these "slaves chose to steal from their neighbors rather than work" and "became public nuisances, and in most instances were reduced to slavery again." Here the elements of racist stereotypes that would not fully coalesce until the early nineteenth century can be recognized in their early formulation. Many of these tropes would be evident in Jefferson's *Notes on Virginia*.[97]

In 1790, petitioners in North Carolina's Perquimans County complained that "great numbers of negroes have been taken up in that county and sold and the monies arising from such Sales have been paid into the Treasury." They complained that "nearly one third of the time of the Court is taken up in the Tryals of those negroes to the great hardship and inconvenience of the people ..." These petitioners asked the state to pass a law "authorizing the Sheriff to pay to the Wardens of the Poor of this county such a sum of money arising from the Sales of such liberated negroes for the purpose of building a House for the reception of the Poor ..."

A committee charged with reporting on this petition found the charges accurate.

> ... it appears that a number of People call'd Quakers ... have at sundry times liberated their slaves and that many of the said slaves have been seized and sold and the monies arising from such sale hath been paid into the public treasury of this State. It also further appears that it is the wish of a great number of the Quakers and others ... that so much of the monies arising from the sales of those liberated slaves as should be thought sufficient to erect a House for the reception of the Poor of said County should be appropriated ...

The committee, however, recommended against granting the petitioners' wishes. The following year, 134 people who had been "freed" by North Carolinian enslavers were auctioned back into slavery by state officials.[98]

In 1795, Quakers in North Carolina complained that

> divers of the members of our Religious Society [have been moved] ... to Emancipate their Negroes but many so Liberated in this particular State have since been taken and reduced to abject Slavery under Sanction of several acts of assembly, in the prosecution of which (beside other distressing circumstances) the Cruel and Unnatural parting of Man and Wife, and Parents and Children have been perpetrated.

They humbly requested that the legislature pass an act "whereby such who are conscientiously scrupulous of holding their fellow Creatures in a State of Slavery may have liberty to emancipate them, and that those who are or may be so liberated be protected by Law under such Restrictions as to you in Wisdom may appear Just and Reasonable."[99]

It was not until the 1780s that Virginia's Quakers began sending petitions to the state legislature praying for a relaxation of the prohibitions on manumission. Their appeals began by declaring their interest in ending slavery was rooted in their loyalty to the white community: "… your Petitioners have long been convinced, not only of the Injustice but also of the pernicious and dangerous tendency of Slavery …" Because of this,

> Many among us as a People from a full and clear conviction thereof, and that Freedom is the natural Right of all Mankind, could not continue their Fellow-Men in Slavery … they therefore Manumitted and set them Free by Wills, or other instruments of writing, which we apprehend to be quite consistent with the Principles of the present Constitution …"[100]

Virginia's Quaker petitioners recounted how they struggled with slavery. At first, they thought they might lessen the burdens of their slaves by allowing "them a certain portion of Time to work for themselves" or paying wages. But "upon a weighty, disinterested Consideration" they concluded this did not protect enslaved people in the long term. What happened, Quaker masters wondered, if they died and their estate was sold for debts or divided among heirs who didn't share their Christian concern?

The Virginia Assembly relaxed its prohibitions on manumitting enslaved people in 1782, though it refused to grandfather into freedom those who had been illegally released prior to the law's passage. In 1806, this law was amended to require that all people freed had to leave the state within one calendar year.[101]

Nevertheless, Quaker attempts to divest themselves of their human property were frequently thwarted. "Yet, notwithstanding such particular Care, some who have been manumitted under Hand and Seal, are detained in Bondage by Executors as part of the Estate of the deceased. And others have been sold by the Executors as Slaves …"[102] Still others, they explained in a subsequent petition, "the Officers in different Counties have seized several negroes who were emancipated, and after being informed of their situation, sold them as Slaves …"[103]

The informal and therefore unenforceable Quaker manumissions became a problem in northern states as well. Eventually the New York legislature passed a special act in 1798 to deal with the problem it described in its preamble:

Whereas the people composing a society commonly called Quakers ... did a considerable time past manumit their slaves, and in several instances not in strict conformity with the statutes in such case and ... whereby doubts have arisen whether the slaves so manumitted and their offspring are legally free: Therefore ... such manumissions shall from the time thereof be valid to all intents and purposes.[104]

Decades later Moses Sheppard, by then an old Quaker who had worked in the antislavery movement for more than fifty years, wrote to a friend about his disgust with other abolitionists. Sheppard complained that he found a surprising lack of interest in emancipating any enslaved people among his fellow reformers. Sheppard described how he had compiled a list of all the prospective manumissions pending in Maryland and had planned to use this information to push each county Sheriff "to attend to the discharge of the slave" by furnishing an official certificate of freedom to the Colonization board office. But after Sheppard left the board "no attention is paid to these cases, the slave is told you are not free yet, and they are sold as slaves frequently."

Sheppard was particularly disturbed by the case of a mother of six who had legally been free nine years but was still enslaved by her master. The woman sought out his assistance while traveling through Baltimore with the man who claimed her as his property and Sheppard thought her case was one "among a number in which the authority of the state board might have been availingly exerted in the cause of Justice and freedom." Instead, Sheppard supposed that her master would sell her to cover his tracks: "today I expect she might be found in one of the slave marts."[105]

Many Quakers opposed slavery because they thought it corrupting to themselves or their coreligionists. To them, this problem could be solved by purging slaveholders from their meetings and shunning them in daily life and this did not also require uprooting slavery elsewhere. As their motivation was particular and their concern extended only to the boundaries of Quaker life, they were not interested in fighting slavery throughout their colony.

Most historians who have studied the early antislavery movement have painted it as heroic, humanitarian, and even antiracist. Even when scholars have perceived that antislavery arguments were framed in a manner that conceived of slavery as a practical threat to the well-being and future of the white community, they have discounted this orientation as being of lesser importance than the benevolence and altruism also contained in these texts.[106]

Historians' casual exaggerations of the altruism of antislavery voices in the eighteenth century is illustrated by Sean Wilentz's determination to bathe America's founders in the rosiest light. Wilentz writes: "As early as the 1760s, spokesmen for what would become the patriot cause, notably James Otis, began linking resistance to Britain to calls for, in the words of a Boston town meeting petition in 1766, 'the total abolishing of slavery among us.'" To support his sweeping observation, Wilentz cites a like-minded scholar, Richard D. Brown's *Self-Evident Truths*, who writes: "Boston, too, instructed its delegates not merely to prohibit further importation of slaves but to pursue 'the total abolishing of slavery among us.'" Here it is suddenly apparent that these Bostonians were calling upon its representatives to both prohibit the further importation of slaves and for the "total abolishing of slavery among us" and that Wilentz chose to drop any reference to the slave trade.[107]

This might seem like a picky point, but tracking the trail of historical references further to their roots uncovers an entirely different meaning of the Boston Town Meeting's resolution. Neither Wilentz nor Brown followed the chain of citations back to their original sources, even though Wilentz' important claim, had it been as he presented it, would have been the first instance of any white American lobbying for the "total abolition of slavery" before George Bourne did so in his book, *The Book and Slavery Irreconcilable*, in 1816.

Brown, too, relied on another historian's narrative, namely, George H. Moore's 1866 *Notes on the History of Slavery in Massachusetts.*

There we find that what Wilentz depicts as the end of the sentence was actually a dependent clause as Moore reveals a little more of the original source: "And for the total abolishing of slavery among us, that you move for a law to prohibit the importation and the purchasing of slaves for the future." Seeing here the full sentence for the first time it becomes clear that the Boston Meeting was not making two separate demands, one for ending the slave trade and one for the abolition of slavery but that the reference to the "total abolishing of slavery" was actually not a demand but an argument for the actual ask, namely, to end the slave trade.

Moore drew his quote from an earlier history compiled by the clerk of the Massachusetts' state legislature that is commonly referred to as "Lyman's Report, 1822." Lyman's Report makes clear that Bostonians were not "petitioning" to end slavery, rather they were reiterating their support for a bill pending in the General Assembly to prohibit the importation of slaves into Massachusetts. The record of the Boston Town Meeting for Monday, March 16, 1767, shows that this outburst of opposition to slavery came after a long list of things the town fathers wanted their representatives to "take particular care" to do, and followed a sentence that indicated that their concern about slavery was grounded in their question of their rights and well-being. The surviving original description of that town meeting describes how the assembled addressed their lawmakers and wished "that you be very watchful over our Just rights, liberties and privileges And give us notice whenever you apprehend them in danger; and for the total abolishing of slavery from among us; that you move for a law, to prohibit the importation and purchasing of slaves for the future." So, what was actually simply another demand to prevent more black people being brought into their community, a quite common concern among white Americans during the entirety of the eighteenth century, is twisted into evidence of white altruism and commitment to abolishing slavery.

Antislavery texts should be read as both statements of principle and as framed by self-interest. Certainly, their practical arguments, when spread beyond their communities of coreligionists, had a larger impact on the public discourse than did their moralizing. This transfer of ideas can be traced through the progress of the movement to restrict the importation of slaves, a movement that appeared first in religious communities then grew rapidly throughout British North America. By the time of the American Revolution, it was nearly unanimously regarded as a sound policy by Americans.

2

Abolishing Slavery by Abolishing the Slave

It is not for the good of the Negroes, but for that of the whites, that measures are taken to abolish slavery in the United States. —Alexis de Tocqueville[1]

Looking backward from the present day, through the prisms of modern sensibilities, most people assume that those who fought against slavery did so as they would, out of moral revulsion at the institution and empathy for people denied the most basic human rights. Similarly, our present values lead us to associate slavery and racism as being closely connected, thus prejudging that those who opposed slavery did so out of concern for those shackled, whipped, and trafficked. But the reality of the eighteenth century was that the outlooks of those opposed to slavery and those defending it over-lapped where they both agreed that the numbers of Africans and the descendants of Africans had grown too large and needed to be dramatically shrunk. Eighteenth-century abolitionists hoped that ending slavery itself would accomplish this. Even many slave-owners looked in the short term to ending the international slave trade and in the long run to encouraging the mass immigration of whites which they expected would drive slavery gradually into its natural grave. In the meantime, both poles of this political spectrum agreed that any black people who were freed, needed to be more completely policed and disciplined.

From the first stirrings of their movement, antislavery activists targeted the slave trade as the keystone of slavery's evil. This focus on the trade in slaves rather than the owning of them was not simply due to the cruelty of the slave trade being the most visible aspect of slavery's many inhumanities. Rather, ending the slave trade was the highest priority of the movement because it was responsible for the steadily rising black population in their midst.[2]

By the turn of the eighteenth century, Quaker leaders were expressing concern about the growing numbers of "Negroes" and counseled that white slave-owners had a responsibility to protect the white community by more effectively overseeing and controlling the black people they owned.[3] Philadelphia's Yearly Meeting warned Friends about participation in the slave trade many decades before they warned of involvement in owning slaves and did so on the basis of their growth in numbers. The minutes for the meeting in July of 1696 noted that "several Papers have been Read ... Relating to the Keeping and bringing in of Negroes" and the delegates responded by advising

> that Friends be careful not to Encourage the bringing in of anymore Negroes, & that such that have Negroes be careful of them, bring them to meetings, or have meetings with them in their Families, & Restrain from loose & lewd living as much as in them lies, & from Rambling abroad on First Days or other Times.[4]

Two years later the Philadelphia Meeting repeated these warnings in a letter sent to Friends in Barbados, in which they wrote,

> It haveng been the sence of our yearly meeting that many negroes in these parts may prove prejudissial several wayes to us and our posterety, it was agreed that endevors should be used to put a stop to the importing of them, and in order they run to that those friends that have correspondencies in ye West Indeis should discuredg ye sending any more hither ...[5]

A generation later, though still debating slavery, Pennsylvania Quakers were certain that the growing number of "negroes" in the colony was a pressing problem that needed to be addressed. A letter from the Chester, Pennsylvania, Meeting, to the larger body was read that expressed their concern over "the great Quantity of Negroes fetch't and imported into this Country" and suggesting that Friends should be "restricted from buying them when imported." Though not yet prepared to condemn slavery itself, the Philadelphia Yearly Meeting referred the Chester Quakers' letter to all other meetings "who are desired to consider it."[6]

In response, the Bucks County Meeting reported they had "deeply considered" the proposition to restrict the buying of imported slaves but "could not so far agree as to come to any Result about it." Burlington followed a chain of logic: "it is not agreeable to our Discipline, to be actually concerned in the importing of Negroes into these Countreys, So consequently it cannot be agreeable to buy them when imported, because it has a manifest Tendency to incourage the Importation of Them." But though Burlington linked the buying of a slave to the importation of them generally, they did not think restrictions should "extend Further than Advice and Counsell" and certainly not include "Censure."

Glouster & Salem Meetings endorsed restricting members "from purchasing of Negroes, as well as from importing Them" and Quakers in Shrewsberry agreed, writing that "the Practice of buying Negroes is wrong and therefore they Desire Friends may be restricted from purchasing of them for the Future." In the end the Quaker leaders in Philadelphia chose the softer path of instructing Friends "to be very Cautious of making any such Purchases for the Future, It being Disagreeable to the Sense of this Meeting" but going no further than offenders being "admonished and caution'd."[7]

When the influential Yearly Meeting in Philadelphia was finally moved to take a stand against trading in slaves in 1754, its concerns were primarily for the spiritual health of white Christians combined with the worldly danger of a growing black population. In the letter the meeting distributed entitled *An Epistle of Caution and Advice Concerning the Buying and Keeping of Slaves* that was reputedly written by John Woolman with the editorial assistance of Anthony Benezet, the congregation expressed its "Uneasiness and Disunity, with the Importation and purchasing of Negroes and other Slaves" and urged all Friends to "press those that bear our Name, to guard, as much as possible, against, being in any Respect, concerned in promoting the Bondage of such unhappy People."

Why was this step now being taken after years of tolerating slavery? The Philadelphia Yearly Meeting could not have been clearer, saying its concern with slaves was that there were too many of them: "as we have with Sorrow to observe, that their Number is of late increased amongst us, we have thought Proper to make our Advice and Judgment more public." Quickly hedging this mortal concern with spiritual ones, the letter goes on to observe that slavery violates the Golden Rule (what they termed the "Royal Rule"), and that all slaves were ultimately brought to their condition by violence, a violence that true Christians could not condone. But like most early antislavery expressions, the charges against slavery were mostly ones having to do with endangering the spiritual interests of the white community. The powerful Yearly Meeting explained,

> To live in Ease and Plenty by the Toil of those whom Violence and Cruelty have put in our power, is neither consistent with Christianity, nor common Justice; and we have good reason to believe, draws down the Displeasure of Heaven, it being a melancholy but true Reflection, That, where Slave keeping prevails, pure Religion and Sobriety decline, as it evidently tends to harden the Heart ...

Even when the *Epistle* appears to express sympathy for the sufferings of enslaved people themselves—"it's obvious that the future Welfare of those poor Slaves, who are now in Bondage is generally too much disregarded by those who keep them"—its empathy is firmly tethered to the priority of elevating white souls. "How fearful then ought we to be," they warned, "of engaging in what hath so natural a Tendency to lessen our humanity, and of Suffering ourselves to be enured to the Exercise of hard and cruel Measures, lest thereby we in any degree, leave our tender and feeling Sense of the Miseries of our Fellow Creatures and become worse than those who have not believed?"[8]

Religiously motivated rejection of the slave trade that was percolating in various colonies was a minor current in a larger stream of opposition to the importing of slaves that was not rooted in any moral objection to trafficking humans. Many colonial leaders demanded restrictions on human importations out of concern for the safety of the white community, the economic impact of free trade in people, or a desire to attract larger numbers of white immigrants. Moralistic reformers were happily swamped by this larger effort to regulate the numbers of Africans brought to America and their protests were relatively insignificant compared with the wealthy and powerful interests that moved in the same direction but for entirely different reasons. The danger of looking back on these parallel movements is mistaking the latter for the former.

Policymakers who debated whether to restrict or allow the Atlantic trade in Africans displayed no hint of concern for the morality of the trafficking of humans in the early part of the eighteenth century. When the royal Commissioners of Trade and Plantations, who reviewed all bills passed by the colonies that impacted imperial commerce, deliberated over a sheaf of bills imposing tariffs intended to deter the importation of slaves sent to them from the American colonies, they invited a representative of Maryland to defend their proposed law. Colonel Hart, a former governor of Maryland, appeared before them and was asked: "what particular motives induced the Assembly to lay the duties ... on negroes." Hart responded that "the reason given for it by the people of Maryland, though he could not approve it himself, was that they had too much tobacco, which was thereby lowered in value ..." The commissioners then issued a general instruction to all the colonial governors to find "other duties" that "may be substituted in lieu of those on negroes imported, in as much as the said duties on negroes do in some measure enhance the price of labour, and consequently the price of several commodities produced in the Plantations, wherein our neighbours rival us in foreign markets."[9]

Nevertheless, various proposals to discourage the slave trade by levying duties on the importation of slaves cropped up periodically throughout the eighteenth century. These measures were driven by popular factions who saw them as a way of shifting the tax burden onto the colony's wealthiest class, and even some members of the plantation-owning class themselves who recognized that the rapidly growing slave population generated an overproduction of staple crops that pushed down prices and profits for everyone. Thus, these political conflicts over the slave trade were mostly fought out on the ground of conflicting white economic interests, not the morality of kidnapping and transporting Africans to America.

For example, Virginia's first 20s duty on imported enslaved people of 1699 was justified by the need to rebuild the state capitol. When renewed and increased six years later (to £5 for Africans, though Indians taken from the frontier were allowed at the old lower rate), the legislature thought it important to note that "no better expedient can be found to lessen the levy by the poll or to defray the charge of any publick design than impositions of that nature."[10]

When Virginia Governor Spotswood objected to the bill because he said he feared that it "May be Interpreted as a prohibition of That Trade Which her Majesty is graciously pleased to Countenance," the assembly refused to alter their bill, replying, "The way we have Taken for Raising of Mony by Laying a Duty on slaves And Liquors, is what this house and former Assemblys have long Since thought Least Burthensome to The people ..." Governor Spotswood then revealed to London's Board of Trade his secret suspicions about the House of Burgesses' intentions:

> I soon perceived that the laying so high a duty on negros was intended to discourage the importation ... they [Virginia's legslators] urged what is really true, that the Country is already ruined by the great numbers of negros imported of late years; that it will be impossible for them in many years to discharge the debts already contracted for the purchase of those negros if fresh supplys be still poured in upon them while their tobacco continues so little valuable, but that the people will run more more and more in debt.[11]

Though it was contrary to his royal instructions, Governor Spotswood himself approved the act, hoping that it would give Virginia time to "pay off the debts already contracted." Spotswood was eventually overruled, and the law disallowed by the King's Council at St. James.[12]

Virginia's House of Burgesses repassed the act in 1728 clarifying that it would not be effective until royal assent was granted and that it was for the purpose of "recompensing the Owners of Slaves condemn'd for capital offences" and paying public salaries and maintaining public buildings. It was swiftly disallowed a second time. Following Governor Gooch's recommendations, the Burgesses passed a duty bill a third time, this time not stipulating a specific sum as a duty, but a percentage of the sale price.[13]

Struggles over the taxing of the slave trade were also class struggles within the white community. As London merchants complaining of these duties to the Board of Trade pointed out,

> this act is Calculated for preventing the Increase of the Growth of Tobacco and to discourage all small Freeholders who have but few hands, from Furnishing themselves with more, that being the Interest of the great Planters who have passed this Law, so as thereby the Less Tobacco being made by the former, that which is made by the Latter who are well furnished with Hands would sell so much the Dearer at Markett. A Bristol merchant added at a subsequent hearing that such duties "would chiefly tend to the Ruin of the Poorer planters."[14]

No one exemplified these attitudes more than William Byrd, one of Virginia's most prosperous tidewater planters and member of the Governor's Council. In 1736 Byrd wrote to the royal president of Georgia's board of trustees praising the wisdom of that colony's prohibition of slaves and wishing something could be done about their burgeoning numbers in his area:

> They import so many Negros hither, that I fear this Colony will some time or other be confirmed by the Name of New Guinea. I am sensible of many bad consequences of multiplying these Ethiopians amongst us. They blow up the pride, and ruin the Industry of our White People, who seing a Rank of poor Creatures below them, detest work for fear it shoud make them look like Slaves. Then that poverty which will ever attend upon Idleness, disposes them as much to pilfer as it dos the Portuguese, who account it much more like a Gentleman to steal, than to dirty their hands with Labour of any kind.

Another unhappy Effect of Many Negros is the necessity of being severe. Numbers make them insolent, and then foul Means must do what fair will not ... these base Tempers require to be rid with a tort Rein, or they will be apt to throw their Rider. Yet even this is terrible to a good nature Man, who must submit to be either a Fool or a Fury. And this will be more our unhappy case, the more Negros are increast amongst us.

But these private mischeifs are nothing if compard to the publick danger. We have already at least 10,000 Men of these descendents of Ham fit to bear Arms, and their Numbers increase every day as well by birth as Importation. And in case there shoud arise a Man of desperate courage amongst us, exasperated by a desperate fortune, he might with more advantage than a Cataline kindle a Servile War ... and tinge our Rivers as wide as they are with blood ...[15]

Byrd suggested to Lord Egmont that it might be "worth the consideration" of Parliament "to put an end to this unchristian Traffick of makeing Merchandize of Our Fellow Creatures." The only ones who would object to such a scheme would be "a few ravenous Traders" who would "freely sell their Fathers, their Elder Brothers, and even the Wives of their bosomes, if they coud black their faces and get anything by them."

Byrd failed to mention how he and his fellow tidewater planters would profit by such a suspension, as then the price of the humans who grew up on their properties and that they sold away from their family and friends would steadily rise along with the value of the crops they raised as their backcountry competitors stagnated. That the politics of taxing the slave trade revolved around intramural conflicts among whites was well known at the time. Even Virginia Governor Fauquier felt compelled to tell the London Board of Trade that "the true foundation of the Squabble" was

the contest ... between the old Settlers, who have bred great quantity of Slaves, and would make a Monopoly of them by a duty which they hoped would amount to a prohibition; and the rising Generation who want Slaves, and don't care to pay the Monopolists for them at the price they have lately bore ...[16]

When Virginia's legislature again raised the duty by an additional 10 percent in 1769, a petition of Liverpool merchants accused the colony's policymakers of pursuing their own selfish class interests.

That your Petitioners are fully satisfied that that Act passed with no general view to the Public good but to the Private Emolument only of the Law makers whose Estates (the most considerable in that Country) would rise in value for the present in proportion as the number of Negroes is diminished which must inevitably be the case was this Bill to pass into a Law.[17]

Thus, by the beginning of the eighteenth century the slave trade was a focus of colonial regulation because it was an engine of revenue that shifted the burden of taxation to the purchasers of humans (who presumably were among the wealthiest members of colonial society). But because slave trading companies sold their living commodities on long-term credit, deferring payment for up to a year in many cases, the plantation economy was periodically on the brink of seizing up with too much debt in too many hands. Colonial legislatures demanded the right to tax the slave trade even to the point of suspending it when circumstances dictated. While the theory of the empire was that the regulation of intercolonial commerce was solely the privilege of the Crown and its ministers, colonials had come to understand, through direct experience, that such regulation impacted not just its foreign trade, but reverberated through every financial circuit of the colonial community.

While colonial legislatures at first demanded the right to restrict the importation of enslaved Africans as a means of economic regulation, they soon expanded their arguments to include the danger of increasing numbers of "unseasoned" slaves posed to the safety of the white community. A steady growth in the black population not only grated on racist nerves but was widely believed to pose distinct perils to the colony. All colonists believed that there was some point at which the growing proportion of enslaved people exceeded the bounds of safety and sound economy. Slavery was, after all, maintained not only by private acts of oppression and cruelty but the provision of costly public services such as slave patrols, militias, armories, public slave pens, and numerous officials from inspectors of ships to local magistrates. Moreover, Africans were blamed for being the vectors of disease and the periodic epidemics that swept through colonial towns were often attributed to upticks in slave importations. Slave trader Henry Laurens wrote to a partner in 1773, "I have a foreboding of several troublesome Events. In the first place there will probably be a superabundant Importation of Negroes. Charles Town will be thereby in danger of Contagious Distempers which alone are very dreadful."[18]

Propagandists against human bondage and human trafficking innovated the argument that a rising black population retarded the growth of the white one and thereby dimmed the prospect of creating the white nation all assumed America was destined to be. As slavery predominated in a colony, prospective white immigrants viewed it as a less desirable destination, and they chose other frontiers to settle. Slave labor was presumed to be cheaper than labor indentured for a few years, or hired in wages by the day or season, or even recruited on crop shares. Thus, it was widely believed that slavery drove "free" settlers out of the labor market and immiserated those who persisted in competing with it.

Boston's town council approved a resolution in 1701 that tied a desire to end slavery with a desire to increase the white population. That resolution expressed the councilmen's "desire to promote the encouraging of white servants, and to put a period to Negroes being slaves."[19]

Philadelphia Quaker Ralph Sandiford in 1729 listed among spiritual arguments against slavery that it "promotes Idleness in the Rich, being furnished with Slaves, that it hinders the Poor from Bread ..."[20] John Hepburn, a New Jersey tailor and Quaker, writing as "a Native of America," published a series of tracts against slavery in 1714–15. Being a tradesman himself, Hepburn noted the ill effects of black competition upon white workers: "When the Country grows full of People, and also abounds which (sic) negros, poor People will want Imploy, and must either *beg* or *steal* for their Living …"[21]

Both sides of the slavery debate aimed at increasing the numbers of whites in the colonies. In 1738 when Georgia colonists petitioned the Crown to relax the prohibition against slavery that was written into that colony's charter, they argued that doing so would "induce great Numbers of White People to come here …" A group of Scottish settlers in Darien, Georgia, responded with their own plea to retain the slave ban on the same grounds. "We, therefore, for our own sakes, our Wives and Children, and our Posterity, beg your Consideration, and intreat, that instead of introducing Slaves, you'll put us in the way to get us some of our Countrymen …"[22]

In 1734, New York's governor, William Crosby, lectured the state council on the dangers caused by its filling up with black laborers. "I See with Concern that whilst the neighbouring provinces are filled with honest usefull & laborious white people," Crosby intoned,

the truest riches and Surest Strength of a Country; this province seems regardless of the vast advantage which Such acquisitions might bring them and of the disadvantages that attend the too great Importation of Negroes and Convicts. These things are worthy of your Consideration and require your Speedy attention, as the greatest good is to be expected from one, and the greatest evil to be apprehended from the other.[23]

One of Anthony Benezet's antislavery pamphlets reprinted on both sides of the Atlantic in the 1760s synthesized many of these arguments by pointing out that slavery takes the jobs of whites, lowers wages generally, and spreads poverty across the land. The "Discouragement also given by this [slave] Trade to many poor people," Benezet wrote, "if not prevented, on Account of the great Number of Negroes, would be likely to come over into the Colonies where they might, with Ease, procure to themselves a more comfortable Living than at Home."[24] Similarly, Reverend Samuel Cooke in his widely published 1770 sermon delivered before the governor and assembly of Massachusetts briefly mentioned the need for the colony to take the "lead in the cause of the oppressed" slave, not for their own sake, but for the betterment of the white community, because slavery had "dishonored the christian name" and when "God ariseth, and when he visiteth, what shall we answer!" Reforms had to be made to "avert the impending vengeance of heaven." As for those currently enslaved, the pastor thought it best to leave them in chains: "Difficulties insuperable, I apprehend, prevent an adequate remedy for what is past." However, he did hope to "propose the pursuit of some effectual measures, at least, to prevent the future importation" of more of them.[25]

Benjamin Lay, the ex-communicated Quaker hermit, reminded his rich readers that "you came to live sober lives, and by your industry, the Almighty favouring, some attained to very large possessions here, being a large Country and few People ..." But now, because of slavery, the country has filled up with "Negro-Slaves" making it difficult for the next generation to repeat their success. Those who prospered in earlier times should remember that "for had this Land been covered with 'em as it is now in some Places, and too much here already, how would you have come to this greatness ..." Lay prophesied that their children would come to curse their slave-owning parents for leaving them with their slaves and then appropriated Samuel Sewall's passage as his own:

And all things considered, it would conduce more to the Welfare of the Province, to have White Servants for a Term of Years, than to have Slaves for Life. Few can endure to hear of a Negro's being made free; and indeed they can seldom use their Freedom well; yet their continual aspiring after their forbidden Liberty, renders them Unwilling Servants. And there is such a disparity in their Conditions, Colour and Hair, that they can never embody with us, & grow up in orderly Families, to the Peopling of the Land ...[26]

Early white abolitionist complaints and warnings about the growth of the black population were realized in the first half of the eighteenth century. The black proportion of Virginia's population quadrupled from fewer than one in ten of the totals at the beginning of the century to four in ten by the time independence was declared. In those early decades many colonists, including large slaveholders, called for restrictions to be placed on the slave trade to reverse this trend. Some of those demanding policies to restrain black population growth tied prohibitions on the slave trade with measures to promote the immigration of whites. A Virginia colonist calling himself or herself "Philo-Bombastia" argued in a letter to the *Virginia Gazette* in 1752 that the colony should disestablish the Anglican Church and radically expand religious toleration as a means of attracting white settlers. Ireland, Philo-Bombastia pointed out, is full of "laborious people" who "groan under the Burden of exorbitant Tithes and Decimations, in their native Country" and Virginia "has Room enough to spare for an Inundation of them." "Free-Thinkers, Infidels, Jacobites, and Convicts ... but also Roman man Catholicks themselves ... will help to fill up the vacant Places of the Colony, upon Missisippi." Twenty years later, Virginia passed a religious toleration act granting "Protestant Subjects dissenting from the Church of England" their "full and free Exercise of their Religion."[27]

A few influential thinkers posed the same concerns in an entirely secular framework. Benjamin Franklin, though an enslaver himself, grew to be a critic of slavery and composed one of the most influential arguments against slavery that was not rooted in religious fears of divine retribution. In 1754, Franklin had published his essay, "Observations Concerning the Increase of Mankind," in which he associated slavery with a stagnant population and white immigrants with a growing one. His argument was that slavery, because it relieved whites of the burden of work, rendered them "enfeebled, and therefore not so generally prolific." Worse, the luxury of living on the labor of others corrupts the character of the master and his family: "Slaves also pejorate the Families that use them; the white Children become proud, disgusted with Labour, and being educated in Idleness, are rendered unfit to get a Living by Industry."

Franklin innovated the argument that slavery was less economically efficient than wage laborers. This was because slavery carried with it many extraneous costs beyond the initial purchase price, such as "the Insurance or Risque on his Life, his Cloathing and Diet, Expences in his Sickness and Loss of Time … Expence of a Driver to keep him at Work," among others. Moreover, the enslaved person, by being entirely disincentivized to be productive because all his efforts go to his owner's benefit produced less. Franklin observed that "Neglect is natural to the Man who is not to be benefited by his own Care or Diligence" and that "pilfering" is endemic as "almost every Slave being by Nature a Thief." (Franklin changed this wording to "from the nature of slavery" to indicate he more clearly was not locating thievery in the slave's race but in his circumstances in the 1769 edition of his essay.)[28]

Famously concluding "Observations" with an open and conscious appeal to racial prejudices, the upshot of Franklin's essay was to provide a powerful secular argument for an end to slave importations, if not to slavery itself. Franklin continued to connect the abolition of the slave trade to the whitening of his beloved colonies: "The Duty on Negroes I could wish large enough to obstruct their Importation, as they every where prevent the Increase of Whites," he wrote to Richard Jackson, with whom he originally shared his then unpublished essay.[29]

It is hard to overestimate the later influence of Franklin's "Observations" in spurring American white antislavery sentiment. It was widely reprinted, appearing in the *Gentleman's Magazine*, the *Scots Magazine*, and the *London Chronicle* a few years after its initial publication. Franklin included it in several of his most popular books, including *Interest of Great Britain Considered* (1760), and his *Experiments and Observations on Electricity* (1769). Franklin's arguments that slavery was unproductive and retarded the growth of the American economy even influenced his friend Adam Smith's views who later made similar statements in the *Wealth of Nations* and other works.[30]

Franklin's concerns illustrate well that many of the voices that were raised in mid-century advocating a prohibition on slave importation have been misinterpreted as protests against the institution of slavery generally. Rather, they were equally outcries against a growing black population. Likewise, in 1765, George Mason argued that the practice of farming with slaves reduced the immigration of free (white) people:

The Policy of encouraging the Importation of free People & discouraging that of Slaves has never been duly considered in this Colony, or we shou'd not at this Day see one Half of our best Lands in most Parts of the Country remain unsetled, & the other cultivated with Slaves; not to mention the ill Effect such a Practice has upon the Morals & manners of our People. That the Custom of leasing Lands is more beneficial to the Community than that of setling them with Slaves is a Maxim that will hardly be denied in any free Country.[31]

Mason's antislavery sentiments were expressed at the same time that he was actively involved in using violence and terror to maintain authority over the people he claimed as his property. In 1767, four of George Mason's slaves were accused of plotting to poison their overseer and they were swiftly executed, and their severed heads were lashed to the four chimneys of the Fairfax county courthouse.[32]

Deep concerns about how slavery increased the black population and deterred white settlers sometimes emerged in other contexts. In 1756 the Pennsylvania Assembly petitioned the royal governor to use his influence to prevent British recruiting officers from dragooning white indentured servants into the army and navy. So great have been the forced enlistments, the colonial representatives complained, that the property in servants had been "render'd precarious," making "People driven to the Necessity of providing themselves with Negro Slaves, as the Property in them and their Service seems at present more secure." Were this to occur, the whole complexion of Pennsylvania would shift: "Thus the Growth of the Country by Increase of white Inhabitants will be prevented, the Province weakened rather than strengthened (as every Slave may be reckoned a domestic Enemy) one great and constant Source of Recruits be in a great Measure cut off ..."[33]

By the time of the American Revolution, such arguments had taken on an increasingly economic cast. Boston merchant James Swan's 1772 pamphlet, "A Disuasion to Great Britain and the Colonies from the Slave Trade," began with religious arguments that making slaves of Africans was against the revealed laws of God and against the laws of nature. But Swan, being a Boston merchant, noted how the slave trade inhibited the production of commodities in Africa and disrupted their commerce with Europe, making for uncounted losses on all sides. If the slave trade could be replaced by a normal commerce between the contintents, then Africa would be better Christianized and Europeans would more effectively "introduce their customs among the natives" including getting them to wear "European dress."

Swan then extended his keen economic arguments to America and pivoted to the trade's "disadvantages" to the English territories: Swan began plainly by promising "To shew the disadvantages to the British Plantations in *America, &c.* in bringing Black people into them." Swan made the obvious point that "these numerous Black People" were "very poor ... not having a penny to command" so that America and the island colonies "are filled with these necessitous Black People, and must be put upon the townships to which they belong, in case this enslaving them be ever abolished ..." Why, Swan asked, "do they fill their Plantations with Black People, so unnatural to the Whites ... when it seems no way difficult to obtain White People to serve free in their stead?"[34]

Swan circled back to the importance of attracting white settlers to the colonies in his conclusion, addressing himself to colonial governors:

I ... may not have occasion to remind you of the same again, but that you will punish with equity all those who import Negroes; there being hundreds of poor *Europeans* that would be glad to come and serve in any of the British Plantations, [thcy] ... will come nigh if not full as cheap as buying and keeping Negroes; and it will be attended with this advantage, that these White people when they have served some years in the lowest capacities turn out upon the waste land, marry, and in a few years we see a town well settled ... by this means the country will fill up and we become respectable and secure from an enemy, and furnished with every conveniency of life.[35]

Massachusetts' patriot and member of the Committees of Correspondence, Nathaniel Appleton, recounted the sufferings of slaves, the injustice of their treatment, the false justifications for their enslavement and trafficking, and then pivoted to the threat slavery posed to a vision of a republic of liberty because it will "blacken these fair northern climates." Appleton warned that "By the importation of black slaves, we prevent the importation of white servants."

The slave trade, Appleton argued, might be profitable to the importer, but this gain comes at dear cost to the white community by requiring imports of items that might otherwise be produced by white labor, and reducing the number of white citizens "interested in the welfare of the community." Slavery reduced the white poor to a lower level:

> having black slaves [is] ... the greatest inconvenience our poorer sort of People are put to by this means, who would gladly serve us for a support, but then they must be upon a level with negro slaves; they being born free, can't think of such a disgrace as they esteem it, and so often spend their youth in idleness, and for want of proper employ and government then, become ever after poor vagrants.

In his next letter, Appleton wrote that ending the slave trade was the highest priority. "Without all doubt, it will be thought necessary immediately to prohibit any future importation of slaves, which, as Dr. Franklin says, has already blackened half America."[36]

In 1801, 366 citizens of Delaware signed a petition to their legislature urging the abolition of slavery. Beyond their moral arguments, the petitioners observed that slaves blocked white settlement, noting the dramatic rise of New York's white population in contrast to that of Virginia. "The experience of our sister states proves to us that the abolition of slavery is every where followed by a more rapid increase of the white population; of improvements of every kind; and by a permanent rise in the value of real property."[37]

In 1805, Tom Paine wrote to Jefferson with praise and advice for the vast new territory of Louisiana purchased from France. Paine was most concerned with who would "people" and "settle" the continent.

In Paine's view, which he probably knew was shared by most other white Americans, policies should be adopted to keep the region free of black people.

> I know not if in Virginia they are much acquainted with importation of German redemptioners, that is, servants indented for a term of years. The best farmers in Pennsylvania are those who came over in this manner or the descendants of them ... These would be the best people; of foreigners, to bring into Louisana, because they would grow to be Citizens. Whereas bringing poor Negroes to work the lands in a state of slavery and wretchedness is, besides the immorality of it, the certain way of preventing population and consequently of preventing revenue. I question if the revenue arising from ten Negroes in the consumption of imported articles is equal to that of one white citizen ... the country would become strong by the encrease of Citizens; but it would be weakened by the encrease of Negroes ... This appears to me to be the best and quickest Method of peopling Cultivating and settling Louisana and we shall gain by it a usefull industrious set of Citizens.[38]

As these examples illustrate, the pioneer crusaders fighting slavery both sharpened the rhetorical borders between conceptions of white and black and invested these categories with new ideas of difference. In addition to offering reasons to abandon the trafficking and holding of humans as chattel, these fuller conceptions of difference added new and powerful reasons for white colonists to desire the eradication of the black presence entirely from their now narrowly defined community. Such rhetorical arguments as the idea that slavery debases white morals or retards the natural growth of the white population wear their white priority and antiblack anxieties on their surface. But an even more pervasive pattern of antislavery rhetoric contained within it a logic of white priority and ethnic particularism that also constructed America as an imagined white community.[39]

South Carolina's first levy upon imported slaves that passed in 1714 was justified as a means of keeping the white and black populations in better proportion: "whereas, the number of negroes do extremely increase in this Province, and through the afflicting providence of God, the white persons do not proportionately multiply, by reason whereof, the safety of the said Province is greatly endangered ..." This levy was modest, just £1 sterling, and was to be used partly as a means of providing a bounty for the importation of white servants.[40] London's Board of Trade eventually got around to disallowing it.

South Carolina's legislature again worried about its own racial imbalance in 1751 and again imposed an import tax on slaves to establish a fund to encourage the immigration of whites. It was allowed to expire after a few years. When the business of South Carolina slave merchants boomed in 1765 and they increased the colony's enslaved population by 10 percent in a single year, the colony imposed a three-year moratorium on imports (enforced by a prohibitory tax of £100) again in the hopes of better balancing the white and black population.[41] By the time of the American Revolution, all patriots seemed to agree that taking steps to augment the white population was an absolute priority of government. One South Carolina legislature summed up the problem this way, "it had been said ... that negroes should be considered as the riches of a country, but ... [t]hey might indeed constitute the strength of it, but its riches should be estimated by the number of its white inhabitants, for it was upon them that our commerce, our agriculture, and manufacture depended ..." (p. 482).

A direct relationship between restricting the importation of slaves and the value of slaves born in the colonies had long been understood but rarely discussed openly. In 1766 the Virginia House of Burgesses petitioned the Crown to allow an increase in the duty levied on each human dragooned into the colony. Liverpool's merchants immediately objected and sent the Lords of Trades and Plantations a petition of their own that accused Virginia's legislators of passing their import tax "with no general view to the Public good but to the Private Emolument only of the Law makers whose estates (the most considerable in that Country) would rise in value for the present in proportion as the number of Negroes is diminished." Supporting a bill prohibiting slave imports to South Carolina in the 1770s, one legislator, as a final kicker to his argument, spoke out loud a fact that few thought appropriate to air publicly. As a way of distancing himself from his own selfishness, he said he heard it from a friend: "An honorable friend of his had said, that to stop the importation of negroes would greatly enhance the value of those in the state ..." Two years later when the legislature again took up a similar bill, such expressions were more common: "Commodore Gillon had another reason against the importation, which was, that negroes would rise in value, and the debtor who sold slaves had a better chance of satisfying his creditors."[42]

Such laws were not viewed as blows against the institution of slavery or to alleviate the suffering of those transported across the murderous Middle Passage. Typical was the complaint against the imperial policymakers that blocked prohibitive legislation that Peter Fontaine sent to his brother in 1757: "our Assembly, forseeing the ill consequences of importing such numbers [of slaves] amongst us, hath often attempted to lay a duty upon them which would amount to a prohibition ... but no Governor dare pass such a law ... By this means they are forced upon us, whether we will or will not." Because of all the large importation of slaves "this is the reason we have no merchants, traders, or artificers of any sort but what become planters in a short time." Fontaine then swings from complaining of how many "negroes" are filling up Virginia to a different complaint; common laborers were too expensive and even a "bungling carpenter" cost 2s a day and "a lazy fellow to get wood water" nearly £20 per year! Therefore to "live in Virginia without slaves is morally impossible." Fontaine had no objections to slavery per se, just the poor management of it.[43]

New Jersey passed a succession of tariffs on the importation of slaves in the 1760s, all justified on the need to shift the balance of population more in favor of whites. In 1762 the state's legislature began its bill with the statement:

WHEREAS the Provinces of New-York and Pennsylvania, have each laid Duties on the Importation of Negroes, and this Province being situate between both, and there being no Duty here, exposes this Government to many Inconveniences, and prevents industrious People from our Mother Country, and Foreigners, to settle among us; which calls aloud for a Remedy:[44]

85

Five years later it published a new act with the preamble:

> WHEREAS Duties on the Importation of Negroes, in several of the neighbouring Colonies, hath, on Experience, been found beneficial in the Introduction of sober industrious Foreigners to settle under His Majesty's Allegiance, and the Promoting a Spirit of Industry among the Inhabitants in general: In order therefore to promote the same good Designs in this Government, and that such as choose to purchase Slaves may contribute some equitable Proportion of the publick Burthens.[45]

When a committee of South Carolina's House protested the Stamp Act, it also took the occasion to petition for a suspension of the slave trade, a measure that the legislature described as "absolutely necessary to the safety and welfare of the province, as well to guard against the danger to be apprehended from too great a disproportion of slaves to white inhabitants ...[46]

Prohibitive duties were never intended to outlaw the business of human trafficking for all time, but merely to bring the supply and demand for slaves into market balance. When one of South Carolina's temporary prohibitive duties on slave imports expired in 1769, it was business as usual for many merchants. Henry Laurens, one of the colonies leading importers, enthused to his business partner, "The high duty upon Negroes expires with the present year and I make no doubt that this will be the best Market for Africans all the next, of any in America."[47]

When a South Carolina merchants committee protesting British taxes declared a boycott on British goods in 1769, slaves were among the "items" listed. But given the experience of South Carolina's three-year suspension of the trade, where merchants like Laurens reaped a windfall from the pent-up demand at the period's end, Americans involved in the trade knew they would likely make up in the future what they sacrificed in short-term sales. In Charleston alone, 142 importers pledged themselves to the non-importation movement, a move that certainly carried no abolitionist intentions. Three years later, just like the last pause in the trade, the market reopened, and a rush of importations resulted, one Charleston agent reporting, "their has been a Great many negroes imported here this Summer and many more Expected ..." Prices for enslaved men and women reached new highs.[48]

Despite the political tensions driving a wedge between royal governors and the colonial assemblies with which they were forced to consult, many governors and legislatures continued to work together toward the common goal of restricting the importation of enslaved Africans. In 1772 Lord Dunmore, Governor of Virginia, forwarded to London a draft law passed by the House of Burgesses that attempted to increase the duties on the landing of enslaved people to prohibitive levels. Dunmore urged the laws' approval, saying it was needed to "restrain the introduction of people, the Number of whom, already in the Colony, gives them [Virginians] Just cause to apprehend the most dangerous Consequence therefrom, and therefore makes it necessary that they should fall upon means, not only of preventing their increase, but also of lessening their number ..." Dunmore noted that the rising black population was requiring extraordinary efforts to keep a restive people in chains. Only by "unremitted observance of their conduct, a rigorous exertion of the Laws relating to them, and the most examplary punishment of all the refractory (a lamentable necessity for a Country to be under) they might so far Suceed as ever to prevent any insurrection from being Contrived among them ..." But "the great addition of new imported ones every year, is Sufficient to allarm not only this Colony, but all the Colonies of America ..." Every Virginian realized that their peace and security could at any moment be overturned by circumstances beyond their control: "in case of a War (which may probably oftten happen) with Spain, or indeed any other power ..." Dunmore mused:

> the people, with great reason, tremble at the facility that an enemy would find in procuring such a body of men; attached by no tye to their Masters or to the Country, on the contrary it is natural to Suppose their Condition must inspire them with an aversion to both, and therefore are ready to join the first that would encourage them to revenge themselves ...

Dunmore prefigured later northern antislavery concerns when he wondered if the "interest of the Country would Manifestly require the total expulsion of them." Ironically, it would be Dunmore himself who would employ this tactic of turning the patriots' slaves against them just a few years later.[49]

In their preamble to the law Dunmore urged his superiors to accept, the House of Burgesses called the importation of slaves "a Trade of great Inhumanity" that would "endanger the very Existence of your Majesty's American Dominions." While never explaining the nature of this inhumanity to the slaves, the preamble does detail the many ways that it harms white Virginians, drawing on the, by then, standard arguments borrowed from the white abolitionists who pioneered them decades earlier. The slave trade "retards the Settlement of the Colonies with more useful Inhabitants," it threatens the "Security and Happiness" of his Majesty's loyal subjects. (The King's Privy Council not only disallowed the new law, it issued a specific instruction barring the "enacting of any measure by which the Importation of Slaves shall be in any respect prohibited or obstructed.")[50]

By the time of the American Revolution, the spiritual and practical arguments against the slave trade had intertwined into a common set of arguments. In 1772, the Quaker Yearly Meeting moved to restrict all trading in slaves only among "friend(s) in unity," except to prevent the separation of man and wife, or parent and child. They also strengthened their stand on the slave trade, issuing a Minute that blended concern for the enslaved with the corrosive effect of the slave trade on the white community:

Being fully convinced in our minds and judgments beyond a doubt or scruple, of the great evil and abomination of the importation of negroes from Africa, by which iniquitous practice, great numbers of our fellow creatures with their posterity are doomed to perpetual and cruel bondage without any regard to their natural right to liberty and freedom which they have not forfeited through any act of their own or consent thereto, but by mere force and cruelty— we are impressed with abhorence and detestation against such a practice in a christian community; for experience makes it fully manifest that instead of their embracing true religion and virtue in exchange for their natural liberty, they have become nurseries of pride and idleness to our youth—in such a manner that morality and true piety are much wounded where slavekeeping abounds, to the great grief of true christian minds.[51]

Quakers in Salem County, New Jersey, petitioned their Crown representative in 1774 to end the slave trade and allow slave-owners to more easily free the people they owned. Salem's Quakers too expressed concern for the spiritual stain the practice left on their souls as well as the problems it caused for the good order of society: "the Toleration of personal Slavery, among a free People, is not only inimical and destructive to the Constitution, but, in its Consequences, greatly pernicious to the Morals of the People among whom it prevails, and utterly inconsistent with the Spirit and whole Tenor of the Christian Religion." Hanging over all such petitions was the mounting problem of a growing black population which the Salem petitioners called a "complicated Evil" and begged to find some means "most effectual" to prohibit "the further Importation of the Natives of Africa into this Province." Notably in this last phrase Salem's Quaker leaders departed from the terminology of slavery and instead referred to "Natives of Africa," making clear that this "complicated Evil" was vexing because it involved not just the status of being enslaved, but the bodies and presence of Africans themselves.[52]

Revolutionary ferment carried over from protest against taxation to opposition to the slave trade but only as human trafficking was seen as endangering the white community. In the summer of 1774 at various places across the South, meetings of residents gathered in protest against the continuing slave trade and they worded their complaints identically. In June a group in Prince George's County, Virginia, resolved that "the African Trade is injurious to this Colony, obstructs the population of it by freemen, prevents manufacturers and other useful emigrants from Europe from settling amongst us, and occasions an annual increase of the balance of trade against this Colony." The "Freeholders and other Inhabitants" in nearby Culpepper County, Virginia, passed nearly the identical resolutions, opposing the slave trade generally, but excluding from their boycott list "negroes, clothes, salt, saltpetre, powder, lead, nails, and paper." They too opposed the slave trade on the grounds that it limited the growth of the white population: "That the importing slaves and convict servants, is injurious to this Colony, as it obstructs the population of it with freemen and useful manufactures, and that we will not buy any such slave or convict servant hereafter to be imported."[53] In August, a meeting in Rowan County, North Carolina, passed the same resolution expressing how they were upset at the growing black population and what they perceived as its economic costs.[54]

Blocking the importation of slaves was not always an act of mercy or of opposition to slavery but sometimes nearly the reverse. In the summer of 1775, a slave ship named *Viz* arrived in Savannah after a long middle passage from Senegal. Its cargo of 204 chained humans was refused permission to dock by the Patriot Committee of Safety. Georgia's Governor Wright, nearly powerless to enforce his own laws, wrote to Lord Dartmouth,

> the Captain is Compelled to proceed to Sea just at the Equinox, which may be the loss of the lives of numbers of them as we often have very Tempestuous weather at this Season, and indeed the Vessel and Cargoe may Probably be lost, and all Perish, and if not the Poor Creatures are so dispirited at the thoughts of being carried to sea again that they are growing sickly and many of them will certainly dye before they can get into another Port.

The *Viz* immediately encountered bad weather and unfavorable winds to reach its next destination of St. Augustine and was forced to turn back, and again requested to land. A couple of days later the Committee of Safety issued a permit and instructed "their Officer to let the Negroes be brought up." "Several had Dyed in the mean time, and many Were then unable to Stir, and the Cargo in General I Suppose one third less in value than when the Vessell arrived ..."[55]

Thomas Jefferson had the occasion to write the first draft of a slave trade ban for Virginia's revolutionary independent government in 1777. The first line of this bill, that it was meant to "To prevent more effectually the practice of holding persons in Slavery" was scratched from the final law. A tough import penalty of £1000 was added and all language dealing with voluntary manumission was dropped.[56] The act that Virginia's revolutionary government finally passed banned the importation of slaves (excepting migrants bringing their human property from other states or visitors passing through), but it did so without any moralizing preamble or statement of purpose. Rather, it simply began with the phrase "For preventing the farther importation of slaves into this Commonwealth."[57]

In August of 1778, in the midst of war, Pennsylvania's Executive Council called the state assembly to session several weeks early to consider some bills that it considered too vital to delay till the fall. One of these was a bill to prohibit the importation of slaves which the Executive Council explained was too obvious a necessity to even justify: "The mischiefs arising from the importation of slaves are too well understood in Pennsylvania, to permit reasons to be given for an increase of the duty, or a prohibition." State leaders connected restricting the inflow of Africans to the whitening of the state: "It is reasonable to expect that the present scarcity of Labourers will be soon relieved, in a far preferable manner, by a flow of new comers from Europe."[58]

That this was not seen as a step toward abolition was evident in the fact that the Executive Council had just a few months before requested that the assembly consider amending criminal laws so that slave masters would not have to pay any costs of prosecution, as the current practice of trying enslaved people by a "Jury of the Country" incurred "fees, sometimes payable by innocent masters, [that] were double the fees in the Quarter Sessions." Urging reform, the Executive Council noted that "experience prooves that Negroe Servants are with difficulty brought to Justice because of the expense hereby brought upon their Owners." Therefore, they proposed that in order to speed prosecution the legislature should consider "whether the master ought in any case to pay Costs of prosecution."[59]

As opposition to the transatlantic slave trade united both opponents and defenders of slavery, by the early years of the republic under the Constitution a national consensus against the slave trade was evident to most observers. The *Gazette of the United States*, the semi-official Federalist newspaper, reprinted portions of a letter received from a correspondent in Boston, dated March 14, 1790, who observed, "that there is no sentiment that can be mentioned, in which the citizens of the United States, are so generally *united*, as in this— that the abolition of the Slave Trade is a duty of humanity, justice and sound policy." That same year, America's leading abolitionist, Warner Mifflin, expressed his belief that "nine-tenths of the citizens of America reprobate ... the infamous slave trade."[60]

Only South Carolina and Georgia, states that had lost a large proportion of their enslaved laborers and where the market for purchasing more was still growing, remained outliers and exerted their political power to retain their ability to import enslaved people from Africa. But even there, enslavers' self-interest mobilized some opposition to continuing importations of people in bondage. A committee of residents of Charleston, South Carolina, led by Colonel Jacob Read, the speaker of the South Carolina House of Representatives, agreed on a set of resolutions that they publicly distributed in the summer of 1792 condemning the importation of slaves from other states. They were concerned that slaves guilty of crimes were being sold off in South Carolina, which was, they said, "a practice [that] cannot fail to be productive of pernicious effects to this state." This group of citizens threatened to boycott and shun any traders, buyers, or shippers of slaves from other states.[61]

Colonel Read was no opponent of slavery. As leader of South Carolina's lower house, he staunchly defended the interests of the low country planter class against the rising power of western settlers who were less invested in slavery. It was Read who broke a stalemate by voting against granting the upcountry counties more representation in the gerrymandered legislature that heavily favored plantation owners.[62]

Though frequently couched in the language of benevolence and morality, broad public opposition to the slave trade was driven by three ideas, all of them centered on limiting the growth of the black population or the well-being of the white community. They were that slavery imperiled the white community with rebellion or invasion, slavery undermined the morals of white society, and slavery blocked the natural emigration of white settlers.

While none of these ideas constituted a theory of the inherent character of Africans, their constant repetition and attachment to black people created an association that developed into a powerful image of the black character. Antislavery advocates' early depiction of the black character was not primarily based in an essentialist conception as some scientists and naturalists were brewing at this time. Rather, black character was seen as being shaped by the peculiar circumstances of slavery itself. Black people were seen as treacherous and rebellious because all men chafed against their chains and dreamed of liberty. Slaves were considered promiscuous because they lived under the constant threat of separation from loved ones. Slaves were prone to thievery due to their enforced poverty and idleness because the fruits of their labor were denied to them.

While originally formulated as a critique of slavery, the constant association of these behaviors with African people cemented them as character traits in the minds of most white people. These traits came to be seen as just as essential and certain as the harsh biological theories of difference and new racially exclusionary theories of government were just emerging.

Eighteenth-century white abolitionists had limited success in fighting against the growth of slavery despite their success in formulating and spreading a spiritual and worldly disdain for treating humans like chattels throughout the British empire and particularly in North America. By the time of the American Revolution, white abolitionists had succeeded in weakening the institution of slavery by stoking ancient religious fears of Divine wrath with the newfound sin of slavery. At the same time these same white abolitionists developed and propagated ideas of how slavery was dangerous and corrupt, ideas that fully entangled black people with these warnings. Though successful in forcing masses of people to question slavery as something unnatural and apart from the rest of society, so also did they promote looking upon people of color through this frame of suspicion. The harshly racist culture that emerged as the century of Enlightenment and Liberal Revolutions drove on was not uniquely the product of religious ideas, just as it wasn't the simple consequence of liberal ones. But together these newly invented set of ideas about black people posed a set of irresolvable questions.

By the time of the American Revolution, most white Americans were caught in a cruel dilemma. They believed that slavery, because it increased the dangerous black presence and provoked God's disfavor, must be ended. They also believed that the danger that enslaved people posed to white society was vastly increased when they were set at liberty. Americans had come to regard slavery as having only one virtue, namely, that it was an effective means of controlling a restive mass of black people. Once these beliefs had chemically bonded to what was popularly understood as common sense, they became the fuel of history.

Americans from that time forward fought not between conceptions of slavery and liberty, but over how to control or eliminate the black presence from white society. Because of the relatively small numbers of African Americans north of the Chesapeake, northerners could avoid this dilemma by expelling black people and prohibiting their emigration. They crafted emancipation policies that pushed freed people beyond their borders and left those that remained under strict surveillance and discipline. Southerners enjoyed no such advantages and felt forced to defend slavery as the best means of containment of the black threat because outright banishment proved either too expensive or compromised their dreams of a Continental empire. Americans could agree on only one thing: the descendants of Africans (and native peoples) had no place in this newly independent nation.

3
White Liberty vs. Freedom's Anarchy

For most of the years Americans protested British trade and tax policies they enjoyed standing upon the moral high ground afforded by the happy harmony of their colonial interests and their abolitionism. As Parliament levied new taxes on sugar, then on legal documents, and then on tea and a panoply of other imported goods, Americans boycotted English imports, including African people. Colonials, especially those in the declining tobacco tidewater region of the Chesapeake, had long been frustrated by London's vetoes of their attempts to curtail a slave trade that depressed the value of their human chattel and increased the need for slave patrols, white militias, and demonstrative punishments. In this moment planter elites could think themselves principled while also pursuing their narrow self-interest.[1]

But this alignment of ideals and interests suddenly and dramatically reversed as a movement focused on protesting English goods broke into open conflict with English soldiers. As Crown forces provoked war by occupying Boston and attempting to disarm the irregular militias known as "Minutemen," patriot leaders for the first time faced the hollowness of their own claim that they were enlightened opponents of slavery. Circumstances had thrust upon them an inescapable choice: to weaken slavery to win their independence, or to cling to it and risk defeat.

A long and uncertain war presented such a choice to American leaders numerous times in various guises. At each juncture the founders chose human bondage over liberty. With each decision that compromised their professed hatred of slavery, their resolve to ever directly act against it weakened and their self-justifications for clinging to it were made more polished and skillful. The true impact upon slavery of the war for independence is that it confirmed for patriots that slavery should never be ended by simply releasing people from bondage. In war the founders faced their true dilemma: how could they divest themselves of slavery without also bequeathing to their posterity a multiracial society?

To most American leaders, English moves to mobilize enslaved men and women against them could not be countered in kind without contemplating the possibility of setting many enslaved people free and thereby, in their view, unleashing anarchy.

In June of 1775, a remarkable but sadly anonymous letter, posted from somewhere in Virginia, was opened by John Adams. It outlined a plan for the patriots to recruit slaves to fight the British in exchange for their freedom and a colony of their own to be established somewhere far away in Canada.

To proclaim instant Freedom to all the Servants that will join in the Defence of America, is a Measure to be handled with great Delicacy, as so great, so immediate a Sacrafice of Property, may possibly draw off many of the Americans themselves from the common Cause.

But is not such a Measure absolutely necessary? And might not a proper Equivalent be made to the Masters, out of the Large Sums of Money which at all Events must be struck, in the present Emergency?

If America should neglect to do this, will not Great Britain engage these Servants to espouse her Interest, by proclaiming Freedom to them, without giving any Equivalent to the Masters? To give Freedom to the Slaves is a more dangerous, but equally necessary Measure.

Is it not incompatible with the glorious Struggle America is making for her own Liberty, to hold in absolute Slavery a Number of Wretches, who will be urged by Despair on one Side, and the most flattering Promises on the other, to become the most inveterate Enemies to their present Masters?[2]

Adams held in his hand the key to patriotic victory. The letter writer's strategic sense was clear and seemingly sound. Were the American revolutionaries willing to relent on their keeping of men and women in bondage they would unchain a force that England could not resist. Looking over Adams' voluminous correspondence it appears he never mentioned this letter to anyone. Rather, as the war began to deepen, Adams expressed concern that too many black soldiers were somehow filtering into the patriots' ranks and, later, in negotiating the terms of peace, demanded the return of all the thousands of people who had run away from patriot enslavers and been given sanctuary by the British.[3]

This letter uncovers the fact that the strategic importance of slavery was well known as the Revolutionary war began and that patriot leaders did not blindly blunder into fighting on two fronts: fighting the British and their own enslaved people at the same time but chose to risk their independence rather than realize the feared consequences of a general emancipation.

The anonymous letter writer who advised Adams was not the only person thinking along these lines. Adams himself recounted how he had heard similar sentiments from a pair of Georgians around the same time:

In the Evening Mr. Bullock and Mr. Houstoun, two Gentlemen from Georgia, came into our Room and smoked and chatted, the whole Evening ... These Gentlemen give a mancholly Account of the State of Georgia and S. Carolina. They say that if 1000 regular Troops should land in Georgia and their commander be provided with Arms and Cloaths enough, and proclaim Freedom to all the Negroes who would join his Camp, 20,000 Negroes would join it from the two Provinces in a fortnight.[4]

Likewise, in early 1775 William Lee of Virginia's famous and powerful Lee family, shared with relatives and friends in America what he had heard around London of Governor Dunmore's plan to emancipate Virginia's slaves and turn them into a royal army to suppress the American rebels:

I am informed by unquestionable authority, that he, Lord Dunmore, has wrote to the ministry that the negroes have a notion the King intends to make them all free, and that the Associations, Congress and Conventions are all contrivances of their masters to prevent the King's good intentions towards them and keep them still slaves; that from this circumstance, it is probable they will rise and give their masters employment enough to keep them from opposing the ministerial measures ... The folly of this plan is only to be equalled by its wickedness, since a proper execution of the patrol law will entirely defeat it, and I have no doubt you will take care that this law shall be properly executed through the colony.[5]

In addition to crushing such a rebellion with Virginia's militia, Lee offered another possibility,

Perhaps the best method of defeating so dreadful a scheme as is planning against you, would be to emancipate all the negroes yourself by act of Assembly, and instead of their being slaves, make them your tenants. This I acknowledge is a bold idea, but still I am convinced the more you think of it [the better you will like it].

Lee also shared the same idea with his older brother Richard Henry Lee in Virginia and urged him to consider his "plan for emancipating the Negroes and abolishing every kind of Slavery in America" as a means of securing independence from Great Britain.[6] However, such proposals as Lee's, or that sent to Adams, were never aired publicly.

The American response to one parliamentary overture to avoid a full-on war with its colonies starkly illustrates the patriots' refusal to consider a future for their society that included African Americans. On December 7, 1775, the House of Commons considered a series of motions from David Hartley, member from Kingston upon Hull, to end the rebellion through conciliation. Hartley's plan involved allowing Massachusetts to restore its Assembly and Council; to pardon and indemnify the rebels; for the King to rely on a system of requisitions rather than specific taxes for the colonies; and generally, "to establish a permanent Reconciliation between Great Britain and its Dependencies in North America, and to restore His Majesty's Subjects in North America to that happy and free Condition, and to that Peace and Prosperity, which they enjoyed in their constitutional Dependance on Great Britain before the present unhappy Troubles."[7]

Hartley, a longtime advocate of reconciliation with the Americans, suggested that while peace and unity within the empire could be achieved, it had to come at a cost. It would not be wise to simply hand the Americans all that they asked for without asking for something in return. Hartley then suggested that this could be the abolition of slavery.

> The object of the act of parliament to be proposed to America, may be perhaps in the event the abolition, but at present can only be considered as the first step to correct a vice, which has spread through the continent of North America, contrary to the laws of God and man, and to the fundamental principles of the British constitution. That vice is slavery.

Having raised what was an idea of such radicalism, Hartley stepped back to a more pragmatic stance:

> It would be infinitely absurd to send over to America an act to abolish slavery at one word, because however repugnant the practice may be to the laws of morality or policy, yet to expel an evil which has spread so far, and which has been suffered for such a length of time, requires information of facts and circumstances, and the greatest discretion to root it out; and moreover, the necessary length of settling such a point, would defeat the end of its being proposed as an act of compromise to settle the present troubles ...

Realizing he could not realistically call upon Parliament to offer the Americans peace in exchange for giving up their slaves, Hartley proposed a modest first step, what he called "an auspicious beginning to lay the first stone of universal liberty to mankind." A symbolic act that would indicate that the Americans were acting in good faith to gradually end slavery, one slow step at a time, namely, that "every slave in North America should be entitled to his trial by jury in all criminal cases."

Hartley, out of touch with what was transpiring across the pond, thought Americans could not "refuse to accept and to enroll such an act as this, and thereby to re-establish peace and harmony with the parent state." His mistake was grounded in taking American republican rhetoric at face value and believing that "those who seek justice and liberty for themselves [would gladly] give that justice and liberty to their fellow- creatures." To this end, Hartley submitted a motion to extend civil rights to American slaves: "That Leave be given to bring in a Bill to establish the Right of Trial by Jury in all Criminal Cases to all Slaves in North America, and to annul all Laws of any Province repugnant thereto, and to require the registering of the same by the respective Assemblies of each Colony in North America."

Hartley's motion was seconded by George Savile, who rose and said he was "ambitious of seconding ... lightening the chains of slavery in America, recommended by my honourable friend." Then Lord North spoke against the motion because of its "unseasonableness." Edmund Burke supported it in his usual elliptical manner, "the very reason assigned why the present motion should not be agreed to, was the best reason for agreeing to it ..." Lord John Cavendish supported it, but "despaired of success." In the end, none of Hartley's motions for reconciliation passed.[8]

Hartley's bill, though rejected by the House of Commons, only provoked patriot animosity against Parliament as it came from the supposed friends of America. News of Hartley's plan took months to make its way to the American colonies, but when it did it attracted only public condemnation.

The first reference to it may have been in the *Philadelphia Gazette* for February 28, 1776, which avoided mentioning its most important detail, namely, the extension of the protections of juries to the enslaved.

Mr. Hartley made a motion, the purport of which was, to address his Majesty, that he would be graciously pleased to withdraw his troops from Boston; that the colonists should be restored to their constitutional right of trial by jury, and that all the grievances which they complain of, on the score of taxation, should be redressed; at

the same time he proposed a plan for establishing the supremacy of
the legislature of Great-Britain in all other cases ...

This was clearly cribbed from any of a number of London newspapers.[9] The nearly exact wording was in the item carried in the
competing Philadelphia paper, *The Pennsylvania Packet* and the *Maryland Gazette* a few days later.[10]

The full text of the Hartley Plan was published in the *Pennsylvania Ledger.* Hartley's speech was also printed in the *Parliamentary
Register*, number 14, which was a monthly compendium of the most
important business of the government.[11] The *Maryland Gazette* of
Annapolis printed Lord Savile's speech in support of Hartley's plan
in the first column of its front page on June 13, 1776. This speech
included Savile describing Hartley's motion as "lightening the chains
of slavery in America, recommended by my honourable friend" and
urging its necessity as proof of America's sincerity and loyalty, a "test
of living obedience." Americans had to accept "an enrolling a British
act of parliament; to which, I hope it will not be a capital objection, that it is not OPPRESSIVE, that it is not UNREASONABLE;
and has MORALITY, HUMANITY, and the RIGHTS of a part of
mankind, for its OBJECT and FOUNDATION."[12]

Few responses to news of Hartley's plan were published, but those
that were printed were all hostile to the idea. *The Pennsylvania Gazette*
published a letter from an American to a correspondent in London
dated March 24, 1776:

Mr. Hartley's plan ... bill respecting "slaves" is undoubtedly upon
humane principles, but he has slipped into the error which *Englishmen*, under immediate subjection to Parliament, find it very
difficult to avoid: he should consider that the Americans cannot
consent to the operation of the *wisest* and *best* act that a British
Parliament could frame, if it meddles with internal matters ... The
only acts which can ever bind America must respect foreign trade,
and this must be handled with the utmost caution and judgment. If
he had proposed a law to discourage the *slave-trade*, to be binding

on the African traders in *England*, it would be a noble object, and worthy of the humanity of a Hartley …[13]

In the end, Hartley's scheme was viewed by white patriots as part of a broader English plot to emancipate slaves and extend greater legal protections to freed people.

Those far-sighted patriots who urged the raising of a free black army were few. One of these notable visionaries was Silas Deane, former member of the Continental Congress from Connecticut who was sent to Paris as the newly independent country's secret envoy to the French government. Deane wrote to Congress' "Committee of Secret Correspondence" in October of 1776 urging them to open a new front in the war. Deane, considered a military strategist of the first rank, having helped American generals plan the successful attack on Fort Ticonderoga, relayed a plan to foment uprisings of enslaved people throughout the English Caribbean.

Employment must be found for the forces of Great Britain out of the United States of North America. The Caribs in St Vincent, if set agoing, may be supplied through Martinique with stores. The Mountain negroes in Jamaica may employ a great number of their forces. This is not employing slaves, which, however, the example of our enemy authorises. Should there arise troubles in these two Islands, which a very little money would effect, the consequence would be, that Great Britain, which can by no means think of giving them up, would be so far from being able to increase her force on the continent, that she must withdraw a large part to defend her Islands.

Deane took care to distinguish between urging islanders to rise up against the English and leading them directly, a difference of sufficient substance to allow patriots to claim they were not stooping to Dunmore's level. Nevertheless, Deane's plan was the exact equivalent of English actions toward native peoples on their frontier that patriots regularly pointed to in justification of their revolution. Congress immediately tabled Deane's suggestion without discussion.[14]

After Congress took no action on his plan, Deane went about his secret mission, accumulating and dispatching to the Continental army an arsenal of 200 cannon, 30 mortars, 200 tons of powder and ball, and muskets, tents, and uniforms sufficient to outfit an army of 30,000 soldiers. Deane negotiated loans from the King of Prussia and received offers of any number of German and Swiss troops. Still, Deane thought his Caribbean plan demanded action and wrote privately to John Jay, "*Omnia tentanda* [everything possible] is my motto, therefore I hint the playing of their own game on them, by spiriting up the Caribs in St Vincents, and the Negroes in Jamaica, to revolt." Along these lines, Deane also proposed stirring up "troubles" in Ireland by "sending from hence a few priests, a little money, and plenty of arms."[15]

Clearly, at a very early point in the war for independence, many, if not most, patriot leaders understood that recruiting enslaved men with the promise of freedom was a powerful weapon they could wield to defeat the enemy. Nevertheless, they overwhelmingly refused to do so, not because they were determined to preserve the institution of slavery at all costs but because to them simply releasing people from bondage would result in anarchy, the opposite of their carefully designed schemes of emancipation premised on white safety by either pushing freed people out of the nation or subordinating them to the status of a disempowered caste.

By understanding that patriot antislavery was fueled by a deep desire for the elevation and improvement of the white community and thereby the building of their republic upon a firmer racial foundation, the refusal to form slave regiments was partially driven by a fear of producing free black veterans with a claim to citizenship. In other words, the visionaries who fought the war for independence were committed to fighting it in a way that built the society they envisioned, and this society was free both of slavery and of black people.

While patriots chose not to pursue any policies that would result in the sudden freeing of slaves, the circumstances of the war itself continually created the conditions where enslaved people could seize their own liberty. To them, sudden, unregulated emancipation was the opposite of liberty as it would lead to anarchy, which was merely

103

the rule of the strong over the weak. Ruminating on what would happen if there was a general release of slaves, the *Pennsylvania Journal* observed:

> Most of the free states in the world have been formed by men just emerged from a state of slavery. No wonder, therefore, they have been liable to disorders, and a speedy dissolution. What sort of government would the negroes in the southern colonies form, if they were suddenly set at liberty?[16]

As the Revolutionary war dragged on (a pace dictated by the choice of not recruiting slaves with the promise of freedom) white patriots faced the prospect of an anarchic emancipation made possible by the conflict's disruption of the customary means of policing and repression. As the number of people who successfully fled their bondage mounted, the patriots were confronted with a stark choice that could not be deferred or diverted: they had either to redouble their efforts to contain enslaved people, even at the cost of losing the war, or accept that the institution of slavery might abruptly end.

Patriots reacted to the growing threat of their slaves running away or rebelling by redoubling their efforts to police them. Such efforts were just as vigorous in the North as they were in the South. In March 1775, farmers in Ulster County, New York, believed they had uncovered a plot of their slaves to rise up and burn down their houses. One farmer said he had overheard York, a man he enslaved, talking with Joe, a man owned by another family member, and thought he heard them talking about "powder" and making a plan to "set fire to the houses, and stand at the doors and the windows to receive the people as they come out." York and Joe were swiftly thrown in the local jail along with seventeen or eighteen others, and many of the black men in the area were questioned, but no further details could be uncovered, if there were in fact any at all.[17]

Fears of English instigation of slave insurrections spread across the colonies, and patriots north and south took measures to more effectively police people of color. The Pitt County Committee of Safety was one of the first to organize in North Carolina and its earliest actions were to raise funds for the relief of Bostonians suffering from the British closure of their port and to form a slave patrol authorized to shoot "resisting negroes." Likewise, one of the first action of Wilmington's patriots was to establish patrols "for control of negroes."[18]

The Committee of Correspondence in Newburgh, New York, met at the house of Martin Wyganh on May 15, 1775, and noted the danger produced by the potential loss of the area's young men to the newly forming Continental army. To meet this threat, they passed several security regulations, ordering that "any Negroes [who] shall be found absent" after sundown "shall be apprehended by any person or persons' whatsoever, and brought forthwith before any two or more of this Committee, who shall cause them to receive thirty five lashes, or any number less, as the said Committee shall judge proper."[19]

New York's patriot patrols were extra vigilant in policing the city's black community. A squad of patriots broke up a gathering of "thirty negroes dancing in Mr. Walton's house in the square." Then a few nights later nervous patriots burst in upon another gathering of African Americans, or as Captain Johnson of the Committee of Safety put it, "a large company of negroes dancing in a small house of Davan's in the East ward near the East river." Johnson was particularly alarmed that an enslaved man named Will possessed "a drum with the King's arms on it." Johnson did not believe Will's explanation that patriot general William Heath had given him the drum and dragged him off to a jail, clearly suspecting that Will had collaborated with the British.[20]

In August of 1775, New York's Provincial Congress passed a Militia Bill that established uniform standards for all patriot volunteers. This document revealed that from the beginning of the conflict, one of the main concerns of the patriot resistance was securing their slaves.

That in case of an alarm or invasion, the officer commanding in each district shall leave a proper detachment of his company to guard against the insurrection of slaves, or if judged more expedient and safe may take the slaves or part of them with him, and employ them in carrying baggage, drawing cannon, or the like.[21]

New Yorkers' fears of slave disloyalty were heightened a few months later when the Provincial Congress received affidavits from various commanders of patriot militias reporting that loyalists in Queens County were "enlisting negroes."[22]

Sometime in May of 1776, Connecticut patriots grew suspicious when they heard that the colony's black community had elected a new "governour," John Anderson, who happened to be a man enslaved by Philip Skene, the Tory officer then under patriot house arrest. Hartford's black community had for many years celebrated a spring holiday of "Lection Day" in which they named a community leader and bestowed on him the title of "governour." On this Lection Day, John Anderson threw a "treat" that he said cost him the significant sum of $25, an amount he had saved while serving as a sailor "upon the lakes." Cuff, the man who had previously served as governor, engaged the services of a sergeant in the British garrison to draft his letter officially transferring his duties to Anderson. The soldier scribe later said he agreed to write the letter "as a piece of fun," which apparently included referring to Anderson in the letter as "niegor-man to Governour Skene" and Cuff as "Governour over the Niegors in Connecticut."[23]

A committee was charged with conducting a full investigation, which they did, interviewing dozens of witnesses and making a thorough armed search of Skene's house for incriminating papers. In the end, they found no clear evidence of a loyalist plot, yet in their report they did not vindicate either Skene or Anderson, leaving the suspicions to linger.[24]

Soon after independence was declared, a patriot leader in Bucks County Pennsylvania wrote to his counterpart in the Committee of Safety in Philadelphia that the "people in my Neighborhood have been somewhat alarmed with fears about Negroes & disaffected people injuring their families" and asked him to send a quarter cask of powder to "quiet their minds."[25]

On the first Fourth of July 1776, George Washington sat working in his command tent, receiving messages and sending orders to better arrange his beleaguered army. One of the letters brought to him had been sent early that morning by a committee of Essex County, New

Jersey. They requested that the great general release some of his militia to guard their countryside, not from General Howe who they didn't think was moving anytime soon from his shelter on Staten Island, but from "the Tories and negroes in the midst of us." Washington, working by candlelight later that night, issued an order to General Mercer to send some of the New Jersey militia home, and to realign his other forces for the purpose of "quieting the apprehensions of the inhabitants of Newark by stationing some troops there."[26]

The day after the Continental Congress approved a draft of the Declaration of Independence, the Provincial Congress of New Jersey met and discussed the problem of keeping captured British soldiers in public places where they were "continually plotting with the negroes, discouraging persons from enlisting in the Continental service, ridiculing the Congress, &c."[27] That same day, Samuel Tucker, president of the Congress of New Jersey, wrote to the Continental President John Hancock, complaining of the difficulty of keeping militias in his state while reports of slave plots swirled. Tucker told Hancock that the "story of the negroes ... arming and attempting to form themselves" was reliable. As a result, "Our Militia are gone off in such numbers that we have hardly men or arms left in those parts which are best affected to the cause."[28]

Over the next month New Jersey's Provincial Congress made preparations for a fuller mobilization of the patriot militia, but they made sure to hold back some troops to secure the state's slave population:

> Resolved, That the commanding officer of the militia in the counties of Orange, Dutchess and Ulster, be immediately ordered to hold their whole militia in readiness to march with 5 days' provisions on the earliest notice, and that when they march they leave a sufficient guard to prevent insurrections of slaves, and to guard the prisoners in the respective Counties.[29]

When General Washington sent requests for several counties in New York to mobilize their militia and send them as reinforcements that September, the Provincial Congress of New York refused, claiming that the dispatch of their militias would make it difficult to guard their slaves: "our enemies would not scruple to stir up our slaves to bear arms against us, it would be extremely hazardous to the internal peace of the said counties to draw out at present any more of their militia."[30] Instead, New Yorkers insisted that the Continental army dispatch some of its units to assist in patrolling their slaves. General Horatio Gates, Washington's sub-commander for the North, was asked by the Committee of Safety in Tryon County, New York, in November of 1777, to station troops near the hamlet of Unadilla, because

Unadilla is a receptacle for all deserters from the army, runaway negroes, and other bad people. We therefore judge it extremely necessary to have that nest entirely eradicated; and until that is done, we never can enjoy our possessions in peace, for those villains carry off all the cattle they can find, besides robbing the well affected inhabitants.[31]

The difficulty of maintaining slavery while fighting an invasion force was most acute in the South. Southern states diverted a significant portion of their manpower to keeping people enslaved. Virginia amended its militia law in the summer of 1777 to dedicate more soldiers to policing enslaved people. Each county's chief militia officer was required to form additional slave patrols consisting of an officer and up to four men who were assigned to "visit all negro quarters and other places suspecte of entertaining unlawful assemblies of slaves" and to interdict slaves "strolling about from one plantation to another, without a pass." In thickly populated areas where "one company of patrollers shall not be sufficient" militia officers were empowered to "order more companies for the same service."[32]

General Thomas Johnson complained to the Maryland Council of Safety that he and General Dent faced difficulty in assembling the needed number of militia to campaign southward against Governor Dunmore's forces "as a good many of the men, notwithstanding their desire to go on the service, very reluctantly leave their own neighbourhoods, unhappily full of negroes, who might, it is likely on any misfortuned to our Militia, become very dangerous."[33]

Soon after independence was declared, Georgia's rebel legislature charged a committee with assessing Georgia's strategic situation, and it reported that the state's position was untenable due to the need to repress enslaved people.

> ... the vast number of negroes we have, perhaps of themselves [are] sufficient to subdue us. In point of numbers, the blacks exceed the whites, and the ready channel and secure retreat which Saint Augustine affords, render them much to be dreaded ... Under all these circumstances, it must certainly appear indispensably necessary that measures be immediately taken for the defence and security of that Province. But the low situation, in point of means or ability, of its inhabitants, puts it out of their power to do it of themselves ...[34]

The committee composed of seasoned military officers estimated that Georgia's defense required at least six battalions of troops, but because "we do not conceive any of these men can be recruited in Georgia" (as they were too preoccupied patrolling slaves and Indians to fight the British), the needed soldiers should be enlisted from northern states and paid by the Continental Congress.

Likewise, South Carolina charged a committee with forming a plan for the defense of the colony and its report stressed the importance of keeping "negroes" well away from British positions. Indeed, much of the military effort of defending South Carolina would be expended in this way according to the committee's plan "by which all communication will be cut off between the enemy in the town, and the negroes in the country."[35] Accordingly, as the war turned southward in earnest in 1781, Governor Rutledge of South Carolina ordered his bushwacking general Francis Marion to summarily kill all blacks found aiding the British, "who carry any provisions of any kind, aid or assist or carry any intelligence for the enemy."[36]

Southerners continued to demand that Washington send troops southward and the general finally asked his war council to study the issue and advise him on whether to do so. General Henry Knox summarized the council's thinking, acknowledging that the South was a weak link in the chain of defense: "An addition of continental troops to the southward, would certainly be a matter devoutly to be wish'd. The great number of negroes, and disafected people, in North, & South Carolina, will always render the conquest of that Country, comparatively easy." Yet Knox and the other generals were reluctant to commit more Continental troops to shield the South. Part of the generals' hesitation was their awareness of the difficulties of fighting the British and guarding the enslaved at the same time.[37]

While chronically short of recruits due to the need to police enslaved communities, southern states diverted what few resources they had to missions also aimed at securing slavery. The Georgia Council of Safety urged General Lee to place the invasion of East Florida at the top of his priorities. "The Council ... are clearly of opinion that an irruption into the Province of *East Florida* will be attended by the most salutary of consequences to this Province, and of course render service to the whole Continent." Why was invading what one British resident called that "weak and infant Province" such a priority? It was because "... the driving of our enemies so far from our country will be of infinite advantage in this, that it will be a means of preventing the loss of negroes, either by desertion or otherwise by land."[38]

At the end of August 1776, General Lee informed his Board of War and Ordinance that he was planning to organize a fleet of armed galleys to patrol the inland rivers of Georgia. "They will secure the rivers against the predatory incursions of the enemy, prevent the desertion of negroes, sweep the coasts clear of tenders; but, above all, facilitate the means of the different States mutually assisting each other ..." Each galley would be crewed by a compliment of thirty soldiers and Lee had begun by outfitting three of them. This fleet would require the establishment of forts and redoubts along the inland rivers and these would have the added benefit to "enable us to make incursions from time to time, when circumstances require it, into East-Florida ..."[39]

In the fall of 1779, the war in the South turned badly against the rebels as the British pressed on toward Charleston and the patriots' southern army withered away for lack of reinforcements and provisioning. With a cold eye to the facts, General Benjamin Lincoln analyzed for Washington why their forces were so diminished. There was little stomach among the people of the deep South for leaving their homes and joining the army: "we have no reason to expect that their number will be much augmented, considering the aversion the people have for the service here—or that any permanent force will be brought by them into the field ..." Though Lincoln does not say it, it is likely that the deeper source of this aversion was the reluctance of white Carolinians to leave the people they held in slavery unpatrolled. To enslavers, leaving one's home under such circumstances was to invite either rebellion or flight from those held down by the constant threat of force and violence.

Lincoln went on to observe that the state of South Carolina was in no mood to force its enslaving citizens to risk their slave property or insurgency by drafting white men into an army: "after solemn debate in the House of Assembly they resolved that the Militia should not be draughted to fill up the continental battalions, and that the militia when in the field should not be under the continental articles of war ..." Unwilling to risk leaving their daily enslaving duties to fight the British, Carolinians were also not about to consider upending the entire slave system by recruiting a slave army under promise of eventual freedom. Lincoln also reported that the South Carolinian legislature "refused on the recommendation of Congress to raise any Black Corps ..."[40]

John Laurens observed the disinterest of his fellow Carolinians in serving in the militia or arming black troops in the legislature and his disgust reached new heights around this same time:

> The Governor ... intends to propose the completing our Continental batts. by drafts from the militia; this measure I am told is so exceedingly unpopular that there is no hope of succeeding in it— either this must be adopted, or the black levies, or the state may fall a victim to the supineness and improvidence of its inhabitants ... [41]

Out of necessity, Lincoln realigned his forces to allow the state militias to guard the western frontier: "I mean to collect the continental troops to a point, and to leave the well affected Militia to cover

111

the back part of the country—they will render more service there than in Garrison ..." Lincoln does not explain why by doing this the militias would be more effective, but this makes sense if the militiamen's first motivation was guarding their homes and human property. The backcountry was where they could defend against Indian attacks while also sealing one escape route of runaway slaves.

RECRUITING SLAVE SOLDIERS

While wintering at Valley Forge in early 1778, George Washington's aide-de-camp, Lt. Col. John Laurens, the dashing son of South Carolina's powerful politician Henry Laurens, who was at that time serving in the Continental Congress, began pushing his commander to consider raising a regiment of slave soldiers to protect the deep South. Laurens' plan for raising a black regiment to fight the British was not a humanitarian gesture but a plan crafted out of the dire necessity of the dwindling numbers of white recruits. In fact, Laurens actually had a rather dim view of black soldiers in general. Laurens at other times expressed disgust for black troops, describing the British forces in Savannah as: "their number about 3000. exclusive of Negroes & other rubbage."[42]

Nevertheless, Laurens pursued his plans and excitedly wrote to his father that his cajoling was taking effect, and Washington "is convinced that the numerous tribes of blacks in the Southern parts of the Continent offer a resource to us that should not be neglected ..." However, he also noted that Washington still had reservations, particularly what effect such recruitment would have on their owners, "with respect to my particular Plan, he only objects to it with the arguments of Pity, for a man who would be less rich than he might be ..."[43] Clearly Washington's hesitancy prevailed for nothing was done to put Laurens' plan in motion through the next year of the war.

Washington understood that the largest pool of available labor to drive the army were the enslaved people of the South, but he also doubted their loyalties. Washington understood that without offering enslaved men a genuine prospect of liberty, their loyalty would always be in doubt as it was well known that the enemy extended the offer of emancipation on their side of the front line. Washington discussed this in another context, when he was thinking through how to handle a shortage of teamsters for his wagons:

> The difficulty of getting waggoners and the enormous wages given them would tempt one to try any expedient to answer the end on easier and cheaper terms. Among others, it has occurred to me, whether it would not be eligible to hire negroes in Carolina, Virginia and Maryland for the purpose. They ought however to be freemen, for slaves could not be sufficiently depended on. It is to be apprehended they would too frequently desert to the enemy to obtain their liberty; and for the profit of it, or to conciliate a more favorable reception, would carry off their waggon-horses with them.[44]

Washington may have been correct. Much evidence points to the conclusion that most African Americans placed little faith in the patriot promises of eventual freedom and viewed the British as their best hope for liberty. British commanders noted in their correspondence that black Americans were reluctant to fight for the rebel army even when promised their eventual freedom.[45]

In March of 1779, John Laurens decided to go around his commander and asked his father to push his "black project" in the Congress. Congress passed such a resolution a few weeks later. Most significantly, Congress envisioned this black regiment, made up of slaves commanded by white officers, to be recruited based on the men being given their emancipation upon completion of their service, along with a freedom bonus of $50. Henry Laurens wrote to Washington soon after the vote that South Carolina was in desperate need of troops:

> the Country is greatly distressed & will be more so, unless further reinforcements are sent to its relief. had we Arms for 3000. such black Men as I could select in Carolina I should have no doubt of success in driving the British out of Georgia & subduing East Florida before the end of July.[46]

113

British spies included in their coded dispatches summarizing American troop movements their swift assessment that Congress' plan to raise a black regiment in the deep South had no chance of success. One informant reported "The Congress are damned openly in taverns at Philadelphia. Their order to take 3,000 negroes into their service gives great disgust to the Southern Colonies."[47]

Alexander Hamilton wrote to John Jay supporting the idea of a black battalion on the basis of military exigency.

> It appears to me, that an expedient of this kind, in the present state of Southern affairs, is the most rational, that can be adopted, and promises very important advantages. Indeed, I hardly see how a sufficient force can be collected in that quarter without it; and the enemy's operations there are growing infinitely serious and formidable.

Hamilton also used the occasion to offer his views on the native abilities of African Americans:

> I have not the least doubt, that the negroes will make very excellent soldiers, with proper management ... I frequently hear it objected to the scheme of embodying negroes that they are too stupid to make soldiers. This is so far from appearing to me a valid objection that I think their want of cultivation (for their natural faculties are probably as good as ours) joined to that habit of subordination which they acquire from a life of servitude, will make them sooner became soldiers than our White inhabitants. Let officers be men of sense and sentiment, and the nearer the soldiers approach to machines perhaps the better.[48]

Hamilton did not think Laurens' "black project" was going to be easily sold to Americans. In fact, his assessment of how this proposal would probably be received was entirely accurate as it was never seriously considered by the southern legislative bodies that were needed to implement it. Hamilton wrote, "this project will have to combat much opposition from prejudice and self-interest." The plan would run up against the "contempt we have been taught to entertain for the blacks." But Hamilton recognized that strategically the measure was necessary, arguing "it should be considered, that if we do not make use of them in this way, the enemy probably will; and that the best way to counteract the temptations they will hold out will be to offer them ourselves."

Counseling Laurens directly, Hamilton cautioned him that he was likely to be disappointed because of the selfishness and narrow-mindedness of his fellow Americans. "I think your black scheme would be the best resource the situation of your country will admit. I wish its success, but my hopes are very feeble. Prejudice and private interest will be antagonists too powerful for public spirit and public good."[49]

After Congress had approved Laurens' plan, Washington moved to squash the idea because it would spread a hope of liberty among the enslaved. He wrote to Laurens that such a plan would only serve to weaken the hold on other slaves in the country because it would "render Slavery more irksome to those who remain in it—Most of the good and evil things of this life are judged of by comparison, and I fear comparison in this Case will be productive of Much discontent in those who are held in servitude ..."

Washington also expressed his fear that if the Americans began arming slaves, the British would as well, thus setting off a competition for who could arm more.

The policy of our arming Slaves is in my opinion a moot point, unless the enemy set the example, for should we begin to form Battalions of them I have not the smallest doubt (if the war is to be prosecuted) of their following us in it, and justifying the measure upon our own ground. The upshot then must be who can Arm fastest ...

Of course, Washington knew full well that the British had already armed and fielded regiments of escaped American slaves and continued to welcome runaways into their camps, the only break on their policy being that the human property of loyalists was respected and protected. In fact, in the letter from Laurens to which Washington was responding, Laurens had included extracts from letters from commanders in South Carolina who reported that many slaves had fled to the British, including at least 200 from a single plantation.

Washington, the man who never told a lie, then insincerely pretended that this idea was so radical that he had never thought of it, "but as this is a subject that has never employed much of my thoughts, these are no more than the first crude Ideas that have struck me upon the occasion."[50]

John Laurens returned to South Carolina and took a seat in the state legislature where he lobbied for his "plan of black levies." But despite his efforts, and the looming threat of a new British campaign against the South's withering force of regulars, he made no headway.[51] Instead, Laurens and his fellow South Carolina legislators offered enslaved men, women, and children who had been confiscated from loyalist estates as bounties to white men who volunteered to enlist. About the same time, Washington was informed that the British general Henry Clinton had issued orders that any enslaved soldier captured while fighting for the Americans would be sold at auction, the proceeds given to his captor as a bounty. Any other enslaved people who wished to join British ranks were guaranteed freedom and "full Security to follow within these Lines, any Occupation which he shall think proper."[52]

Laurens' plan's failure was followed by several states crafting plans that expanded slavery rather than risking increasing the free black population. Virginia filled its quota to the Revolutionary Army by recruiting white men on the promise of giving them their own slaves. In late 1780, the Virginia Assembly confronted the problem of diminishing numbers of army recruits by formulating a plan to induce Americans to enlist by promising them land and slaves as bounties for their service.

The plan as originally formulated was to offer each recruit "a Negro not younger than ten or older than 40 years." These human bounties would be requisitioned from the largest American enslavers. For every twenty slaves they owned, they would have to sell one to the nation in exchange for an eight-year bond that paid 5 percent interest and began paying, in specie, on the fifth year. In the end this plan was changed to offer every recruit either £60 or a slave between £10 and £30, and to pay for the exorbitant cost of purchasing thousands of slaves by a general property tax.[53]

James Madison privately opposed this plan on ethical grounds: "would it not be as well to liberate and make soldiers at once of the blacks themselves as to make them instruments for enlisting white Soldiers? It wd. certainly be more consonant to the principles of liberty which ought never to be lost sight of in a contest for liberty..." Yet while arguing that offering slave soldiers their freedom was a sounder plan, Madison judged it so because he did not think it threatened to liberate others. Madison did not think emancipating black soldiers would have the feared effect of loosening the bonds of those remaining in chains:

> ... with white officers & a majority of white soldrs. no imaginable danger could be feared from themselves, as there certainly could be none from the effect of the example on those who should remain in bondage: experience having shown that a freedman immediately loses all attachment & sympathy with his former fellow slaves.[54]

Joseph Jones, a representative in the Virginia Assembly, who proposed confiscating slaves from the largest property owners and offering them as bounties for poor whites who enlisted, nevertheless still considered himself a steadfast opponent of slavery.

> The freedom of these people is a great and desirable object. To have a clear view of it would be happy for Virginia; but whenever it is attempted, it must be I conceive by some gradual course, allowing time as they go off for labourers to take their places, or we shall suffer exceedingly under the sudden revolution which perhaps arming them would produce.[55]

Jones expressed what most patriot leaders were thinking—that slavery was a corrosive, corrupting system that was dangerous to the delicate balance of powers required by a democratic republic. But even more threatening to white interests and a future white republic would be any sudden freeing of America's slaves.

Patriots' strategies and conduct of their war for independence have been misconstrued as an expression of their simple desire to protect and secure the institution of slavery. When patriots chose to risk defeat rather than recruit slaves into their armies, or expended precious specie to compensate owners for slaves the state executed, or diverted already stretched military resources to patrol against runaways, or reacted with murderous swiftness to destroy maroon communities, they were not necessarily doing these things because they wished slavery to remain their fundamental institution, but because all their dreams of a slavery-free republic rested on banishing freed people to some land far from white communities or firmly controlling free black communities. Any action, policy, or event that could lead to a sudden freeing of enslaved people was viewed as a dire threat to the safety and peace of the white community. All white patriots, from the most invested apologist for slavery to the most passionate critic of it, agreed that simply releasing people from their bondage was tantamount to an intolerable anarchy.

4

Patriot Dreams of Black Banishment

Arthur Lee was the youngest son of what was arguably Virginia's first family. Lee's family owned vast swaths of Virginia's best lands and kept hundreds of people in slavery to cultivate them. Arthur grew up in the company of the children his family enslaved but never saw them as anything other than an alien presence in his beloved country.

As the youngest son, Arthur was sent off to England for his education, and as a Lee he was matriculated to Eton for his primary schooling and then on to Edinburgh to study medicine. Caught up in the rising tide of patriot protest, Lee served the American cause as a diplomat to France and Spain before returning to America in 1781 and taking up his virtually hereditary seat in the Continental Congress.

Before leaping into the great pamphlet wars of the late 1760s and excoriating Parliament for its oppressive attempts to squeeze taxes out of the colonies, Arthur Lee sharpened his quill to condemn the institution that had provided all his privileges. While still a medical student in Edinburgh in 1764, Arthur Lee rehearsed in a pamphlet entitled *Essay in Vindication of the Continental Colonies of America* all the arguments against slavery that had been pioneered by white abolitionists.

Lee explained that his odd choice of subject matter was driven by the need to defend his beloved Virginia against the insults of Adam Smith, whose *Theory of Moral Sentiments* had condemned American slavery where Africans with "a degree of magnanimity which the soul of his sordid master is too often scarce capable of conceiving" were held in bondage by "the refuse of the jails of Europe, of wretches who possess the virtues neither of the countries which they go to, nor of those which they come from …"[1] Lee's strategy to refute Smith was to first give an "authentic account of the African slaves, who are the

119

objects of [Smith's] ... praise and compassion" and then to correct his depiction of the "American colonists."

Lee's description of the character of Africans could hardly have located them lower on the scale of humanity. He missed no opportunity to paint them as wild and subhuman, writing that they were "savage," "prone to lying," "without either discipline or courage." Africans broke their agreements, disrespected marriage, committed cruel murders, consumed food like beasts, and worshipped the Devil. Lee concludes that "negroes" were "a race the most detestable and vile that ever the earth produced."[2]

From tracing the barbarous nature of the African, Lee then moved to assure his readers that Americans treat their slaves in the most fair and benevolent manner. "I am sensible that it is a common creed, that the negro slaves here are very barbarously treated: A creed that takes its rise from the reports of wretches, who frame falsehoods to catch the ear of vulgar credulity ..." Compared to the shanties of Scotland and Ireland, "the habitations of the negroes are palaces" and compared to "the peasants of either of these countries" America's slaves enjoy a life that is "luxurious."[3]

Lee then switched gears and proceeded to offer philosophical, moral, and practical arguments against slavery. Lee drew heavily upon Montesquieu's *Spirit of the Laws* to distinguish between the equality of rights in humanity's primitive state, the necessary creation of laws and governments, and the distinction between just and unjust laws. Like Montesquieu, Lee could find little legal justification for slavery, rejecting even the commonly held belief in the ancient right of conquest.

Following Montesquieu, Lee chalked up the imbecility of slaves not to nature but to the environment of slavery that smothers all thought: "... there can be no question that the slavery of which we are treating must be injurious to science; since the minds of our slaves are never cultivated." And following Montesquieu again, Lee argues that slavery debased both the slave and the master; the slave for obvious reasons and masters because it "may deprave the minds of the freemen; steeling their hearts against the laudable feelings of virtue and humanity." As an afterthought, Lee appended a touch of benevolence toward the enslaved person at the end of his rehearsal of the reasons for curtailing slavery: "Need I add to these, what every heart, which is not callous to all tender feelings, will readily suggest; that it [slavery] is shocking to humanity, violative of every generous sentiment, abhorrent utterly from the Christian religion ..."[4]

The answer to slavery, because the problem was not just the system of slavery but the presence of black people themselves, thought Lee, was to import more white people. "I observe ... that the colonies might be more advantageously peopled from Europe; and that it would be for the interest of the Europeans, to abolish the slave-trade."[5]

Once back in America, Arthur Lee resumed his campaign against slavery by publishing a specific plan of emancipation that would, with a single blow, smash slavery and expel the menacing black presence from Virginia. Writing under the pseudonym Philanthropos, Lee called for the Virginia legislature to end all slave importations with a prohibitively expensive import duty. Proceeds from the tariff would then be used to purchase slaves and resell them in the West Indies. Virginians would then be encouraged to use the funds they derived from the sale of their slaves to import white indentured servants. Lee reveled in the cleverness of a self-funded plan that would over time end slavery, augment the white population, and drain away all the slaves.

Lee callously acknowledged that the men, women, and children shipped off to the Caribbean faced a worse fate because it was well known that slaves were "used with more barbarity" there than in Virginia, but he thought the moral balance was about even because "this sacrifice of themselves will put a quicker period to a miserable life."[6]

Lee's thoughts on America, slavery, and black banishment were emblematic of the thinking of Virginia's patriot elites. Scholars have long recognized that Virginia's wealthiest and most powerful planters regularly expressed their desire to be rid of slavery in the Revolutionary era.[7] But such desires were often paired with proposals to reduce the black population generally by barring the importation of additional black slaves and finding some means of expelling the people who were to be emancipated.[8]

121

Patriotic dreams of a republican America, condemnations of slavery, and a desire to whiten the nation by expelling blacks were not separate ideas but different facets of the same mindset spied from different angles. All of these were manifestations of a complex of values, identities, and aspirations (such as civic virtue, corruption, and national character) that informed the meaning of such key concepts as "independence," "slavery," "citizenship," and "liberty." As already shown, some of the elements of this cultural complex were most powerfully formulated by those who first raised their voices in objection to slavery out of concern for their own souls and the wrath of divine providence. Others were shaped and sharpened in the propaganda skirmishes provoked by each twist and turn of British policy.[9]

But there is yet another source of patriot fear and loathing of the black presence and the slavery that built it, hidden within the monuments of Enlightenment philosophy that are usually hailed as cornerstones of abolition thought.

The philosopher Charles W. Mills has unpacked centuries of liberal ideology and exposed how they were fundamentally based on a racial division of the world. Rousseau's "social contract" was conceived as the epochal dividing line between civil society and savagery—a civilization available to white men and a savagery of the "darker" regions of the world. Citizenship, in the depths of its conceptual premises, is a means of drawing that line between the civil and the savage and effectively represents what Mills renames as a "racial contract." Thus coiled within the apparently universal values of the Enlightenment were specific mechanisms by which people of color, particularly those being expropriated or enslaved, were excluded from the blessings of liberty, citizenship, and civil rights.

The basis for such exclusion was the theorized basis of civilized society that rested on the "social contract." In this way, society was conceived of as an agreement among rational beings, but non-whites, savage and locked in a permanent state of nature, were deemed ineligible to participate in this contract that constituted society. The thrust of natural rights moralizing, Mills pointed out, followed an exclusionary logic: as republics depended on the loyalty of their citizens, as civil society rested on the unity of its people, and as democracies derived their character from that of their citizens, those lacking loyalty, cultural similarity, or dependable character must be excluded from the body politic.[10]

Rousseau never directly addressed the question of the sort of slavery that was common in America, chattel slavery, treating humans as property. Rather, when Rousseau made pronouncements such as "Man is born free, and everywhere he is in chains" he was referring to other white men whose liberties were crushed under the heel of monarchs.[11] For this reason, the rising generation of American patriots looked elsewhere for guidance on how to solve the dilemma slavery posed. They looked mostly to one philosopher for advice and intellectual inspiration, Charles Louis de Secondat, Baron de La Brède et de Montesquieu.

Montesquieu's *Spirit of the Laws* was arguably the most influential book for patriot leaders. In *Spirit of the Laws* Montesquieu not only systematically analyzes the existing legal justifications for slavery, but smashes, one by one, the facile arguments that slaves may be justly taken in war, or purchased from their monarchs, or are by nature fitted for chains. But in the end, he too allows the possibility that slavery could be justified by colonial, meaning white men's, necessity. In chapter seven of his first book, he notes that there are some places too hot for white men to toil: "There are countries where the excess of heat enervates the body, and renders men so slothful and dispirited that nothing but the fear of chastisement can oblige them to perform any laborious duty: slavery is there more reconcileable to reason." Dividing the world in this way drew a moral line across the tropics, a line which when crossed transposed the arguments against slavery into their opposites:

> But, as all men are born equal, slavery must be accounted unnatural, though, in some countries, it be founded on natural reason; and a wide difference ought to be made betwixt such countries and those in which even natural reason rejects it, as in Europe, where it has been so happily abolished ... NATURAL slavery, then, is to be limited to some particular parts of the world. In all other countries, even the most servile drudgeries may be performed by freemen.[12]

123

Montesquieu ventures even further down this road in chapter 12, which he titles "Danger from the Multitude of Slaves." In it, the great philosopher warned that slaves posed a unique danger to the stability of liberal governments. Slavery posed no problems for a "despotic" government, for in effect all the citizens of such a regime were already oppressed by a system of "civil slavery." No, slavery was truly only a threat to governments that cherished liberty: "Nothing more assimilates a man to a beast than living among freemen, himself a slave. Such people as these are natural enemies of the society; and their number must be dangerous."

In his next chapter, Montesquieu observed that while monarchies with their standing troops and armed aristocrats are little troubled by a rebellion now and then, republics can easily fall before their fury. America's patriots paid attention as Montequieu advised not to arm slaves in time of war for "the pacific members of a republic would have a hard task to quell a set of men, who, having offensive weapons in their hands, would find themselves a match for the citizens."

Much of Montesquieu's arguments against slavery turned not on the deleterious impact upon those in bondage but fretted over the effect of the institution on the morals and behavior of the white enslavers. "The state of slavery is in its own nature bad. It is neither useful to the master nor to the slave ... to the master, because by having an unlimited authority over his slaves he insensibly accustoms himself to the want of all moral virtues, and thence becomes fierce, hasty, severe, choleric, voluptuous, and cruel." Thomas Jefferson copied these words into his journal nearly word for word.[13]

Beyond the threat of the enslaved as a disloyal and rebellious mass, Montesquieu anticipated the political conundrum freed men posed to American patriots' desire to construct a white republic. How can the enslaved be freed without handing over to them the reigns of power? Montesquieu stated succinctly what most patriots assumed: "in a popular government, the power ought not to fall into the hands of the vulgar." To highlight this danger, Montesquieu recalled the history of the Volscian people who lived in Etruria in ancient Italy. When the Romans freed the Volscians and granted them suffrage, the Volscian men voted for a law giving themselves seignorial rights to rape newly married brides. Of course, in raising this example in the mid-eighteenth century when slavery was entirely racialized Montesquieu was trucking in colonizers' fears of miscegenation and the difficulty of maintaining the consistency of the physical marks of denoting enslaved status. These were warnings that surely resonated deeply with white Americans.

Montesquieu detailed for his republican readers how to navigate around these rocks. Naturally, first, a "considerable number of freedmen ought not suddenly to be made by a general law." Rather, they should be introduced slowly, their numbers limited by either forcing them to purchase their liberty, or specifying that they serve some intermediate term of service before being accepted as citizens. "It is easy to enfranchise, every year, a certain number of those slaves, who, by their age, health, or industry, are capable of getting a subsistence," Montesquieu advised. Even better, what Montesquieu called curing "the evil … in its root" was to take some of the employments of slaves "for example, commerce or navigation" and "divide [them] amongst the free born." This, Montesquieu observed cryptically, would result in "diminishing the number of slaves." To follow this logic, however, requires that one assume that those slaves thrown out of those employments would somehow migrate or be removed to some far-away land.

Montesquieu found examples in the ancient world of how freed men could be both accepted as citizens and rendered irrelevant. He thought the best model was Republican Rome, "where they had so many freed-men, the political laws, with regard to them, were admirable." The Romans "gave them very little, and excluded them almost from nothing: they had even a share in the legislature; but the resolutions they were capable of taking were almost of no weight." Moreover, things could be rigged so that their voting power was limited. "They might bear a part in the public offices … but this privilege was in some sort rendered useless, by the disadvantages they had to encounter in the elections." Montesquieu extrapolated from these examples a general rule for the construction of white power: "It is certain, that their [freed men] condition should be more favoured in the civil than in the political state."[14]

But by the eve of the war for independence, the idea that a free and republican America needed to be rid of both slavery and black people was rising toward its peak currency.[15]

THE ROOTS OF BLACK BANISHMENT

Colonizing blacks to some frontier or foreign land was paired to emancipation in some of the earliest writings of white abolitionists. John Hepburn, the New Jersey Quaker tailor who wrote under the pen name "a Native of America," tied emancipation to the removal of black people from America in 1715. Hepburn advanced beyond a Christian condemnation of slavery to look to the future and what might actually be done to abolish such a sinful practice. "Proposal 1. That Subscriptions be taken of all Masters that will set their Negroes free, and of the Number of Negroes so to be set free, that they may be sent to their own country."

Hepburn could not imagine his society as containing free black residents; according to his "proposal," the only black people to remain were those that agreed to continue their own enslavement: "That such Negroes as had rather serve their Masters, then go home, may be kept still (it being their *Free Act*, and not being safe to have them free in this country)."[16]

When they imagined the perfected nation they dreamed of creating, America's patriot leaders conceived of a land purged of its black people. This is well illustrated in "The Paradise of Negro Slaves," a piece Benjamin Rush first published in Mathew Carey's *Columbian Magazine* the same year the Constitution was written. In it, Rush relates a dream in which he finds himself "conducted to a country, which in point of cultivation and scenery, far surpassed any thing I had ever heard, or read of in my life." To his surprise, Rush found that this beautiful country "was inhabited only by negroes." As Rush approaches a group engaged in prayer, they "panic," which a "venerable looking man" explained was caused by the appearance of a white man among people "once dragged by the men of your colour from their native country." It is then revealed that this is a land in the afterlife and all the people in it were former slaves. The venerable man then explained, "The place we now occupy, is called the *paradise of negro slaves*." One after another deceased men and women relate the torments of their slave lives and, for most, their deaths at the hands of their owners. Rush's dream ends when another stooped white man limps toward the group and he is greeted warmly because he is the great liberator, Anthony Benezet.[17]

Rush's dream reveals in a literary form the same patterns of thinking that motivated many white abolitionists to view their national prospects in terms of racial separation. Even in Rush's vision of the beyond, black people are colonized away from the other saints.[18]

Colonization desires and schemes proliferated as the patriot resistance to taxation heated into outright rebellion. By the 1770s, calls to curtail slavery and to export people of color were clearly interrelated and becoming ever more widespread. The French traveler M. Brissot de Warville noted that Virginians claimed to be in favor of emancipating their slaves but simply were stymied by having no place to send them to. Warville wrote that there was one "objection which you will hear repeated every where against the idea of freeing them," namely, that the

> Virginians are persuaded of the impossibility of cultivating tobacco without slavery; they fear, that if the blacks become free, they will cause trouble; on rendering them free, they know not what rank to assign them in society; whether they shall establish them in a seperate district, or send them out of the country.[19]

The degree to which the patriots' desire for abolition and for the racial cleansing of the nation become entangled is evident by the tactics adopted by a group of enslaved people in Massachusetts in 1773 to argue for their own liberty. In a letter addressed to their colonial legislature that had just debated a measure to end slavery but failed to agree on its terms, these men appealed for white sympathy and support by promising to leave the country. "The efforts made by the Legislative of this province in their last sessions to free themselves from *Slavery*, gave us, who are in that deplorable state, a high degree of satisfaction." (Note how these authors began by framing slavery

127

as a problem and oppression for whites rather than people of color.) "We expect great things from men who have made such a noble stand against the designs of their *fellow-men* to enslave them. We cannot but with hope, Sir, that you will have the same grand object, we mean civil and religious *Liberty*, in view in your next session …"

Their letter was crafted to appeal to the prejudices and presumptions of readers who held absolute power over the authors' lives. Carefully interwoven underneath their tone of servility was a calculated attempt to play on whites' anxiety about the cost of slavery and their desire to rid the nation of a black presence.

> We are very sensible that it would be highly detrimental to our present Masters, if we were allowed to demand all that of *right* belongs to us for past services; this we disclaim … We are willing to submit to such regulations and laws, as may be made relative to us, until we leave the province, which we determine to do as soon as we can from our joynt labours procure money to transport ourselves to some part of the coast of *Africa*, where we propose a settlement.[20]

The idea of banishing black people not only survived the "contagion of liberty" that supposedly flourished during the Revolutionary war but seemed to thrive upon it.[21] "Impartial," who contributed a lengthy discussion of the pros and cons of ending slavery to the *New Jersey Gazette* at the start of 1781, asked rhetorically what many others in both the North and South had come to question.

> If the freemen of the country find it difficult to support themselves and families at the present time, is it reasonable to suppose that our slaves, naturally indolent, unaccustomed to self-government, destitute of mechanical knowledge, unacquainted with letters, with a peculiar propensity to spirituous liquors, destitute of property, and without credit, would pay their taxes and provide for themselves, in the path of integrity, the necessaries and comforts of life?

For "Impartial" and certainly many others, wartime rigors had only increased their desire to push people of color out of their communities.

"Impartial" then posed the central dilemma facing the founders: "Should our slaves be freed, they must either continue with us or inhabit some territory by themselves." The answer was foregone, but "Impartial," like many other white abolitionists, dressed it up so as to seem an act of benevolence rather than white intolerance:

> Our state of war forbids their removal to any exterior part of the country, not only in regard of safety, but also in other respects. Whenever they shall be emancipated, on mature deliberation, perhaps it will be thought that small settlements of them, in different parts of the continent, under proper regulations, will be most compatible with our safety and their felicity. They may thus become useful members of the body politic, enjoy the sunshine of freedom, together with the cheering rays of the light of the gospel. Some compensation will this be for their servitude![22]

Reverend Samuel Hopkins was one of the most influential Congregational theologians of his generation and one of the leaders of the religious revival of the early eighteenth century known as the "Great Awakening." Hopkins lived in the epicenter of the American corner of the slave trade, Newport, Rhode Island, and like most of the better-off class of that city he owned his domestic servants. One of the people he owned was a woman named Chloe who was taken from Africa and suffered the Middle Passage. Sometime after the British invaded and occupied Newport in December of 1776, Hopkins was visited by a man from North Carolina who offered to purchase the woman and Hopkins was eager to make the trade as his circumstances under occupation were difficult.

It wasn't long before Hopkins began to regret selling Chloe and when asked by his wife why he was so glum, he reputedly responded:

> I have a heavy burden lying upon my soul. It is the sin—the sin of slavery in which we have partaken, for which I am cast down. True, we needed the money, for my living is all cut off by the war; but I fear that that money will be no better to us than the thirty pieces of silver were to Judas, for which he sold his Saviour. I have made

merchandise of a fellow mortal; yes, of a fellow Christian—for we thought her pious. It is like selling my Saviour: for He regards our treatment *of one of the least of these that believe in Him* as the index and exponent of our treatment of Himself. I am brother to Judas Iscariot. The iron has entered into my soul. Can I ever be forgiven? I shall carry a wounded spirit with me to my grave.[23]

Later Hopkins wondered if he had condemned the woman, despite the kindly promises of her buyer, "to labor in the field, beneath the lash and a burning sun," but his first and foremost worry was for his own soul and his own redemption. This experience led him in 1776 to preach his first sermon against slavery which tied condemnations of slavery to a vision of removing black people from the young nation:

The slaves who are become unprofitable to their masters by the present calamitous state of our country, will be with the less reluctance set at liberty, it is hoped; and if no public provision be made for them that they may be transported to Africa, where they might probably live better than in any other country, or be removed into those places in this land where they may have profitable business and are wanted ...[24]

Hopkins embraced the idea of colonization in greater detail as he moved from simply preaching against slavery to organizing politically as one of the founders of the Providence Society for Promoting the Abolition of Slavery, for the Relief of Persons unlawfully held in Bondage, and for Improving the Condition of the African Race. (Jonathon Edwards was also an early member.) In 1789 he told fellow abolitionist Moses Brown that "if a way should be opened for their settling in Africa, and the society should, in any time hereafter, be able to promote and assist them in such a design, it would be desirable that it might be done ..."

Hopkins had raised with Brown the idea of colonizing America's free black people to Africa as early as 1784. "There has been a proposal on foot some time, that a number of blacks should return to Africa, and settle there ..."[25] Hopkins wrote to Granville Sharpe, organizer of the colonization of freed British slaves to Sierra Leone, a few years later explaining the bright prospects for building a similar colonization movement in America:

> In Massachusetts, all the Africans are made free by their Constitu-
> tion, and many have obtained their freedom in this State. But their
> circumstances are, in many respects, unhappy, while they live here
> among the whites; the latter looking down upon them, and being
> disposed to treat them as underlings, and denying them the advan-
> tages of education and employment, &c., which tends to depress
> their minds and prevent their obtaining a comfortable living, &c.
> This and other considerations have led many of them to desire to
> return to Africa, and settle there among their brethren, and in a
> country and climate more natural to them than this ...[26]

Hopkins and other New England divines envisioned colonization as a means of proselytizing Africa, but even more than that, they saw it as a means for their own national redemption. From the pulpit, Hopkins expressed the joy of this vision: if Africa could be Christian-ized and brought up out of its barbarism, then, perhaps, all the sin and suffering of the slave trade was all part of God's greater plan all along! "Thus all this past and present evil, which the Africans have suffered by the slave trade and the slavery to which so many of them have been reduced, may be the occasion of an overbalancing good ..."[27]

Colonization was not just for the talented and industrious, but for all people of color, because America offered them nothing but con-tinuing oppression and misery. In a pamphlet that Hopkins circulated widely, he promoted his plan to have the states finance the removal of all black people to Africa and frankly promoted his scheme based on the self-interest of whites.

> And even selfishness will be pleased with such a plan as this, and
> excite to exertions to carry it into effect, when the advantages of it
> to the public and to individuals are well considered and realized.
> This will gradually draw off all the blacks in New England, and
> even in the Middle and Southern States, as fast as they can be set

free, by which this nation will be delivered from that which, in the view of every discerning man, is a great calamity, and inconsistent with the good of society; and is now really a great injury to most of the white inhabitants, especially in the Southern States.[28]

Samuel Hopkins' fellow famous minister, Jonathan Edwards, of New Haven, Connecticut, also both spoke out against slavery and offered some novel solutions to the question of what to do with the people of color eventually liberated. Addressing the newly formed Connecticut Society for the Promotion of Freedom, and for the Relief of Persons Unlawfully Holden in Bondage in 1791, Edwards reviewed the many ways that slavery injured the white community. Its "destructive tendency to the moral and political interests of any country," how it "discourages industry," how it "produces indolence in the white people," and breeds "intemperance, lewdness and prodigality" and it decreases the white birthrate. Edwards was very concerned with the sexual mixing slavery afforded, describing how a "planter with his hundred wenches about him is in some respects at least like the Sultan in his seraglio ..."

This was rather standard white abolitionist rhetoric by this time, but as he wrapped up his speech, Edwards cleverly reversed the usual arguments for banishment or colonization. Edwards ended by warning that with the slave trade cut off, and even slow steps taken to emancipate slaves, that black people will eventually interbreed with whites and thereby "raising their colour to a partial whiteness," creating "a mungrel breed," a prospect he described as "mortifying." Better, Edwards wondered, if a reverse process of colonization would be preferred whereby whites left the South to their former chattels.

If therefore our southern brethren and the inhabitants of the West-Indies would balance their accounts with their Negro slaves, at the cheapest possible rate, they will doubtless judge it prudent, to leave the country with all their houses, lands and improvements to their quiet possession and dominion; as otherwise Providence will compel them to much dearer settlement, and one attended with a circumstance inconceivably more mortifying, than the loss of all their real estates, I mean the mixture of their blood with that of the Negroes into one common posterity.

Conveniently, Edwards pointed out that Yankees like themselves need not adopt the same drastic policy, they need not leave their estates to their former slaves, for in the North their numbers were so few that they could afford to let them loose, even at the risk of some intermixing:

> It is not to be doubted, but that the Negroes in these northern states also will, in time, mix with the common mass of the people. But we have this consolation, that as they are so small a proportion of the inhabitants, when mixed with the rest, they will not produce any very sensible diversity of colour.[29]

Similarly, a Philadelphia printer published a tract of Jacques-Pierre Brissot, founder of the first abolitionist society in revolutionary France who also endorsed an African colonization scheme as a means of preventing interracial mixing of white and black families in 1788. Brissot's essay was a salvo in a pamphlet war against the Marquis de Chatellux, one of the victorious French generals of Yorktown, who had just published a travelogue of a tour through America. Chatellux excused the slavery he witnessed in Virginia as being far less brutal than what was practiced in the sugar islands of the West Indies on the grounds of the savage nature and imbecility of enslaved people themselves.

Brissot blasted Chatellux's blind prejudices and proclaimed all men of all colors brothers, and championed abolition, though of the typically white-centric variety. Brissot appreciated the difficulty of the question of abolition, "the danger which might attend a general emancipation of the Negroes ..." Brissot agreed that "the Negroes will never be our friends, will never be men, until they are possessed of all our rights, until we are upon an equality ... If we would make the Negroes worthy of us, we must raise them to our level by giving them this liberty."

Brissot, however, saw only three potential outcomes of ending slavery. Were slaves to merely be set loose they would "remain a distinct species, a distinct and dangerous body" that would lead to "torrents of blood spilt and the earth disputed between the whites and blacks, as America was between the Europeans and Savages." Such a grim future could be avoided if "we intermix with them, and boldly efface every distinction." Even from Brissot's Parisian perspective he really couldn't have meant this as a serious proposal, especially in English translation addressing Americans, and so he offered a third course of action that was like the plans championed by Samuel Hopkins. "Perhaps, and it is no extravagant idea," Brissot mused, "perhaps it might be more prudent, more humane, to send the blacks back again to their native country, settle them there, encourage their industry, and assist them to form connections with Europe and America."[30]

White abolitionists formulated the idea of cleansing America of its black population because they were primarily interested in abolishing slavery. But once they promoted this idea, once they turned it loose into the patriot wilds, it found the means to survive both with and without the cause of emancipation. Where white abolitionists saw colonization as a tool for emancipation, other white Americans saw it as a worthy and necessary solution to their ongoing dilemma of building a white republic on the back of black slavery. Many white Americans prioritized colonization and viewed general emancipation as a means of achieving it. The urgency of racially purifying the white republic increased once the war was won and the seeming endless possibilities opened by independence excited patriot imaginations.

The anonymous author of a 1785 tract entitled *The Golden Age* recounted his ecstatic vision of America's future, a golden age in which every race lived apart and in peace. Recounted as the dream of an old soldier of the war for independence, this story appealed to Americans who suddenly felt that they could remake the world. It opens with an old veteran named Celadon resting against a tree, looking up at a serene blue sky, and seeing a vision of an angel descending to greet him. The angel reassures him that the country he had fought for had a glorious future.

Celadon.

And what is to be done with the poor Negroes? Nothing! There are vast crouds of them in some States.—And is not their rigorous servitude an odious blot in our scutcheon of honor?—Wretched creatures! Must they alone remain in irrevocable bondage? I hope not.

Angel.

No, they too, shall in the proper season be set at liberty.—A tract of land will be allowed them.—They shall be furnished with implements of husbandry, and every thing necessary to begin the world with.—They will by degrees form a State of their own.—And at length also, prove a rich, a religious, and useful people. But there must be time for their manumission. It cannot be done at once.

This exchange is revealing of what were clearly the anxieties of a generation of post-revolutionary white men. Note that Celadon expresses concern with the "poor Negroes" but then immediately complains of how many there are, "vast crouds" of them, and only then notes, as an afterthought, that some continue to labor in "irrevocable bondage." But the angel has a solution, they will slowly be set at liberty and banished to a nation of their own.

The angel then led Celadon to the top of a mystical mountain where he could miraculously see across the expanse of the continent. The angel pointed out the four corners of the land. To the southwest lay one lone timbered valley that was to be "Savagenia" which she indicated was to be "the future habitation of your now troublesome Indians." To the northwest was another valley with clean air which was to be "Nigrania … allotted for the Negroes to dwell there." The "vast spaces westward" where the soil was richer and the rivers larger were for the whites from the "sundry foreign nations" of Europe. All of these people were apart, but Celadon imagined them "united in brotherly affection" and in that togetherness "form the most potent empire on the face of the earth."[31]

Such dreams excited even men who owned vast plantations worked by hundreds of enslaved men and women. Ferdinando Fairfax, whose

Virginia plantation abutted some of Washington's properties, published his "Plan for liberating the negroes within the United States" which was a plan for ridding America of both slavery and slaves. Appearing in Mathew Carey's influential *The American Museum*, Fairfax spoke for many elite Virginians who wished to remake their state as a white republic. Fairfax began by noting that the "unhappy race" had "natural right and justice" on their side, while whites "opposes a general emancipation, on account of the inconveniences which would result to the community and to the slaves themselves," as well as the "legislative interference ... in private property" that emancipation would require. Significantly, Fairfax reported that among whites it "is equally agreed, that, if they be emancipated, it would never do to allow them *all* the privilege of citizens" because there was "something very repugnant to the general feelings ... of their being allowed that free intercourse, and the privilege of intermarriage with the white inhabitants ..." As free blacks "endanger the peace of society" there is a "necessity of removing them to a distance from the country."

Fairfax believed that "there are many who would willingly emancipate their slaves, if there should appear a probability of their being so disposed of ..." Fairfax proposed having Congress set aside funds for such a colony and to "appoint the proper officers for the government of the colony ... until the colonists should themselves become competent to that business." Of course, Africa was the "most suitable" place for such a colony as it was "their native climate."[32]

Other prominent slaveholding Virginians echoed Fairfax's advocacy of removing black Americans to the western frontier. George Tucker, who was related by marriage to both the powerful Byrd and Washington families, and who served in both Virginia's House of Delegates and was elected to three terms in the U.S. Congress was so threatened by the planned insurrection of the enslaved known as Gabriel's Rebellion, that he wrote an open letter urging black colonization before the "danger arising from domestic slavery" leads to the inevitable conflagration of rebellion. Tucker's *Letter to a Member of the General Assembly of Virginia on the Subject of the Late Conspiracy of the Slaves* was a hit and was rushed through a second edition a couple of months after its first printing.[33]

In contrast to many white abolitionists who stressed the need for colonization because slavery had debased the character of the slave and left them vicious and unable to provide for themselves, Tucker, who owned slaves all through his long life (until he was poetically killed by a falling cotton bale), praised the "advancement of knowledge among the negroes of this country." Tucker observed that "every year adds to the number of those who can read and write; and he who has made any proficiency in letters, becomes a little centre of instruction to others." This, however, was not necessarily a public good: "This increase of knowledge is the principal agent in evolving the spirit we have to fear." If there was some way to keep enslaved people in ignorance and fear that would probably be worth considering, Tucker thought, but "of the multitude of causes which tend to enlighten the blacks, I know not one of whose operation we can materially check." [34]

Tucker's pamphlet continued through the usual white abolitionist complaints about slavery's injuries to white people: that it made "idleness … the prerogative of a white skin" and made "labour be thought unworthy of a free man." Slavery was unproductive, as "a slave does but half the work of a free man; and consequently … no country can attain a great height in manufactures, in commerce, or in agriculture, where one half of the community labours unwillingly." Of course, it also fostered immorality among whites, which undermined the "truest principles of republicanism." Slavery's inherent dangers to the white community were multiplied by the scheming of foreign powers and the steady growth of the black population. Ultimately, the only solution was black "transportation." Sending the entire black population of Virginia to Africa, Tucker calculated, would cost upwards of a million dollars, a sum "beyond the resources of the state." They could be sent to the West Indies, but only by being forced into such a "cruel exile." That left only somewhere on the American continent itself, and Tucker recommended either purchasing some lands west of the Mississippi from Spain, or lands in Georgia from the Indians.

The core of Tucker's plan was a scheme to reengineer Virginia's demography by replacing black slaves with white laborers, or as Tucker phrased it: "a sketch of a plan … for ridding the country of an evil ... that deforms one of the fairest portions of the globe." It was intended to be gradual, for as Tucker observed, "a rapid decrease of the class, which constitutes the productive labour of the country, is not desirable." Rather, as African Americans were drawn out of Virginia, "emigrants from the northern states, and from Europe, would as gradually fill the places they would leave." Slow colonization was to be financed with a tax on Virginia slaves. It was also designed to lower the black birthrate by pairing a tax on young black women "above the age of puberty" with a bounty for the voluntary "exportation" of any black female to a western black colony. This would strongly encourage the exportation of prepubescent girls, which by Tucker's accounting, "when a girl under fourteen or fifteen is sent out of the country, six or eight unborn negroes are probably sent with her."[35]

Support for ending slavery by shipping off America's slaves came just as loudly from the North as from the South. New Hampshire's Moses Fisk, whose Puritan ancestors were members of Cotton Mather's congregation, and who trained as a minister and taught at Dartmouth College, wrote his plan for colonization of blacks in 1795 as the pamphlet *Tyrannical Libertymen: A Discourse upon Negro-Slavery in the United States*. Fisk condemned slavery in the conventional fire and brimstone method of threatening enslavers' souls and Gods' angry withholding of his blessings upon the white community. But in the end, he faced the question, "What can be done? ... But suppose the negroes prepared for freedom, are they then to settle *among* us?" Fisk thought not.

Rather, different groups of African Americans should go to different destinations. "I do not know, but *some* should be returned to Africa." One who is "worn out with age and sore travail" should not be "cast helpless into the highways" but should remain supported by his master. "Give him food from your own table, and beg him to pray for your avaricious soul." But the "great body of the negroes" should be "sent to colonize" some "new territory ... assigned for the purpose."

Such a new black colony would be completely under the control of white "guardians." "They must have wagons and cattle, provisions and rament ... and overseers." America would eventually have to send "missionaries and teachers to the land of the negroes" and in case a neighboring power should invade, they must be "defended" and "if they should rebel" they needed to be "awed by soldiery."

Soon after publishing *Tyrannical Libertymen*, Fisk departed New England and settled in Tennessee where he refused to own slaves.[36]

William Thornton, the physician, lexicographer, inventor, and architect whose plans for the nation's first capitol building were approved by Congress in 1792, did more than advocate colonization but attempted to organize a mass exodus of New England's black community to Africa. Thornton, a close friend of George Washington, and owner of "seventy or eighty slaves" on the island of Tortola, tried to enlist the governments of Massachusetts and Rhode Island in his scheme.

In 1787, Thornton resolved to free and resettle his own slaves in Sierra Leone and encouraged other African Americans in Newport and Boston to join his expedition. Thornton enlisted Samuel Adams to endorse his scheme and boasted of having several hundred free black Americans ready to sail. While waiting to see how the initial British efforts at colonizing Africa proceeded, Thornton drafted a letter sharing his colonization plans with Paris' Les Amis de Noirs which he asked James Madison to read. He had gotten to know Madison quite well when both men lodged at Mary House's boarding house in Philadelphia. Madison gushed over Thornton's plan, saying it "might prove a great encouragement to manumission in the Southern parts of the U. S. and even afford the best hope yet presented of putting an end to the slavery in which not less than 600,000 unhappy negroes are now involved." Madison thought colonization the only possible means of freeing slaves because the "prejudices of the Whites" and the "vices and habits" and other "ill effects" of slavery they possessed made them dangerous to the "good of the Society," by which, of course, he meant white society. While there certainly was land enough in the west to accommodate them, Madison thought that black people's character and white people's prejudices dimmed the hopes that such a black colony could survive:

The interior wilderness of America, and the Coast of Africa seem to present the most obvious alternative. The former is liable to great if not invincible objections. If the settlement were attempted at a considerable distance from the White frontier, it would be destroyed by the Savages who have a peculiar antipathy to the blacks: If the attempt were made in the neighbourhood of the White Settlements, peace would not long be expected to remain between Societies, distinguished by such characteristic marks, and retaining the feelings inspired by their former relation of oppressors & oppressed. The result then is that an experiment for providing such an external establishment for the blacks as might induce the humanity of Masters, and by degrees both the humanity & policy of the Governments, to forward the abolition of slavery in America, ought to be pursued on the Coast of Africa or in some other foreign situation.[37]

When Thornton then lobbied members of the Massachusetts' Assembly for funds to pay for the transportation of black Bostonians "out of the Country" he found legislators eager to help. Thornton reported that "I had no doubt from the ardour with which the proposal of taking them away entirely, was advocated, that the Legislature would have furnished then [sic] with Ships, with provisions, Tools &c. and many of the members promised that every requisite would cheerfully be granted." However, the Bay State politicians tried to steer Thornton from taking Boston's African Americans to Sierra Leone, but instead thought it better if "a Settlement to be made in the most southern part of the back Country between the whites & Indians" be created instead. Shrewdly, these Yankee leaders wished to not only rid themselves of their African American population, but to use them to secure the frontier for the growth of the American empire.

When word that the black colony at Sierra Leone had struggled and floundered, Thornton cast about for a new home for America's enslaved and ex-enslaved and thought he had found it in Spanish Puerto Rico. Even though his African plans had dimmed, Thornton enthusiastically drafted a memorial to Congress that noted that the "same Causes that induced the Inhabitants of Boston to desire a place of settlement for the Blacks still exist ..." and urged the government to purchase the island.[38]

David Lummis, a Philadelphian who struck out for the west to survey lands and earned a footnote in history by sailing the first vessel from Lake Erie to his native city, a journey of nearly a thousand miles, twenty-nine of which were overland, shared his solution to America's slavery problem with President Jefferson in 1802. Lummis began by stating that he was purposely not a member of "the Abolition Society" that free slaves without "considering the injustice they have done the owner by depriving him of his property." Nevertheless, Lummis was against slavery, as he presumed all patriots were. "Where is the American who adores the virtue of Our Constitution, and does not blush at the idea of holding Slaves?" Lummis asked.

Lummis, who was probably a member of what people at the time termed the "middling sort," condemned slavery on grounds that many other patriots would have agreed with. Slavery was cruel to be sure, and Lummis objected to the "impropriety of Republicans holding slaves" but he was most perturbed by the "many other inconveniencies attending it":

> If the planter who lives in affluence on the labor of his negroes will but look around he may observe multitudes of poor White inhabitants in his neighborhood who are in want of the daily necessaries of life, and who have no means in their power to provide for the sustenance of their families ... How many usefull Citizens are thus lost to the public? ... But could we suitably dispose of our slaves, this custom would be reversed, immedeate encouragement would be given to the white laborer, and the planter would in a few years find his plantation to produce as much, yes more, than when it was covered with negroes.

Lummis then shared with Jefferson his idea of abolishing slavery and shipping all those freed to "the French West India islands."[39]

Dreams of whitening the republic by pushing African Americans out of the nation were not partisan. Though historians have generally saddled Jefferson's Democratic-Republican faction with a racist desire for ethnic cleansing this is largely due to the prominence of *Notes on Virginia*. Hugh Henry Brackenridge was still in his twenties when he edited and published the influential *United States Magazine*, one of the only American monthly compendiums to appear during the Revolutionary war. Brackenridge, who counted as former school-mates from the College of New Jersey, luminaries James Madison and patriot poet Philip Freneau, served as a chaplain in Washington's army and later lent his editorial skills to support of the Federalist faction and stood for election to Congress on the Federalist ticket. Brackenridge's *United States Magazine* attracted submissions from many of the most celebrated patriotic (and mostly Federalist) authors, including John Jay, David Ramsay, John Witherspoon (president of Breckenridge's former alma mater), and William Livingston, the governor of New Jersey.[40]

Brackenridge's magazine was eclectic but like Freneau's poetry, spread-eagled patriotic, which included envisioning a future without slavery. In an essay entitled, "Thoughts Upon the Enfranchisement of the Negroes" that appeared in his final issue, Brackenridge followed Montequieu and condemned slavery as incompatible with republican ideals but also premised abolition on banishing emancipated people far from white society.

> Shall they be set immediately at liberty amongst ourselves? No; for my part I am for the plan to colonize them ... Thus would I have these black people led out by some generous mind, and colonized, perhaps beyond the Ohio, or the Misissippi River, in that country forfeited by the native Indians ...[41]

The *United States Magazine* was second only to John Fenno's *Gazette of the United States* in loyalty to the emerging Federalist Party. Soon after Washington was inaugurated as president in New York, Fenno ingratiated himself with Hamilton and other Federalist leaders and won printing contracts with the Treasury Department that kept his paper afloat. That spring, Fenno ran a series of six letters written anonymously by "Rusticus" that condemned slavery, proposed that Africans were inferior in both body and character to Europeans, and proposed a plan for the "gradual abolition of slavery, and the happiness of the African free negroes, living now among us."

Rusticus (who was, in all likelihood, William Duer, Hamilton's assistant secretary), advocated that Congress give "every free negro man, or family," or any slave manumitted by his or her master, a grant of land in what is today the upper peninsula of Michigan, and be "transplanted there at the expense of the Commonwealth." Black colonists would be governed by "a governor, judges, white citizens" who would be appointed to "direct the colony in its infant state." Additionally, churches and Sunday Schools would be established "to teach the young Negro slave, reading, religion, and morals."

Though expressing his hatred of slavery, Rusticus was not motivated out of benevolence for those enslaved as one part of his plan was to allow owners to "sell their slaves for misbehavior, under warrant of a Judge, in the West-India islands." This would provide the stick along with the carrot of colonization that would improve the African race. "The benefits of such measures would be, that as reward, punishment, and instruction, go hand in hand, the slave will become trusty, less troublesome, and more profitable to his master; the fear of being sent to the Islands will mend his conduct; the hopes of freedom and wealth will excite him to deserve them." As the productivity of enslaved people increased because of these threats of punishment or reward, owners of slaves would profit, compensating them for manumission, and allowing "the Augean stable will be cleaned without loss of property."[42]

Such themes resonated over the next decade as evidenced by the outpouring of antislavery writings of Thomas Branagan, a young Irish immigrant who had worked as a hand on slave trading ships and as an overseer on an Antiguan plantation. It was in the West Indies that Branagan abandoned Catholicism, embraced evangelical Protestantism, and began preaching against slavery and other social evils. Choosing Philadelphia as his home, largely because it was the capital of a state that had passed a law for gradual emancipation, Branagan befriended both Benjamin Rush, leader of the city's white abolitionists, and the Reverend Richard Allen, a leader of the African American community.[43]

In his book that some historians have labeled his work of antislavery apostasy, Branagan viewed himself as part of the antislavery movement and dedicated the work "To all the true friends of Liberty ... who by their distinguished exertions in advocating the rights of man, have done immortal honor to themselves."[44] Branagan called himself a "penitential tyrant," having participated in both the slave trade and slavery, whose mission was to "expose the complicated guilt of tyrannical slave traders, as well as the deleterious evils resulting from the impolitic commerce and slavery of the human species." His "primary object" was the "happiness" of the "independent citizens of America" and "the political emansipation of the African race" and his opposition was to "the tyrants of the South" who have gained "an ascendency over the citizens of the North ... as they enslave and subjugate the inoffensive, the exiled sons of Africa."[45]

Branagan's colonization plan was for Congress to allocate individual tracts of land to black homesteaders in some new western settlement. Unlike most other schemes of black colonization, Branagan's plan was founded on the principle of black autonomy and black rule. The free black colony would be administered by a governor and judges appointed by the president, just as was then the case in the territory of New Orleans, the only caveat being that such appointments were only open to members of the "African race" so that "such white persons as wish to emigrate and associate with the blacks, may likewise be under their control and governed by them." Uniquely, Branagan called for "making them free and independent citizens of America, in a separate state of their own..."[46]

While he assumed that most all African Americans would "think proper" to take up this offer and leave voluntarily, Branagan was not against forcing the recalcitrant to emigrate. "This would not be infringing the laws of hospitality, or philanthropy, for every reasonable person must allow that it is better for the blacks themselves to be accomodated domestically, and settled politically independent by themselves, than associate with the whites with whom they never can enjoy reciprocal rights, and political privileges." Branagan never doubted the capacity of black colonists to not only suceed but flourish if given a chance: "There is no doubt with me, but that on such an event, the land which is now and will be a wilderness for hundreds of years, would be metamorphised to a terrestrial paradise; for the slaves of the South, would do more work for themselves and their families in one day, than for their tyrants in three."[47]

Another Philadelphia Quaker, John Parrish, followed his standard rehearsal of the arguments against slavery with his own colonization scheme. Parish argued against slavery on the grounds it would "draw down Divine displeasure." Like other white abolitionists, Parrish opposed simply freeing those in bondage out of concern for the safety of whites, "The immediate liberation of all the slaves, may be attended with some difficulty; but surely something towards it may now be done." Such concerns when mixed concocted the idea of colonization. Parrish asked, "Would it not be of more importance to devise means for the removal of a national evil, of so much magnitude, and on which the welfare of the United States so much depends, than the acquisition of unbounded territory?"[48]

Like his fellow Philadelphian, Thomas Branagan, Parrish thought colonization the best remedy because by distancing blacks from whites it reduced the possibility of intermixture of the races: "instead of promoting those unnatural connexions, it would be in a good degree effectual to preserve the distinctions of nation and colour." Parrish added a religious dimension to his sexual segregation, "Divine Providence, as if in order to perpetuate the distinction of colour, has not only placed those different nations at great distances from each other, but a natural aversion and disgust seems to be implanted in the breast of each."[49]

Parrish, Branagan, Benezet, Brissot, Lee, Hopkins, Edwards, and many others formulated white abolitionist plans for black expulsion years before Jefferson's more famous call to remove black people from America that he published in *Notes on Virginia* in 1787. In that work, Jefferson famously compares America's situation to ancient Rome's: "Among the Romans emancipation required but one effort. The slave, when made free, might mix with, without staining the blood of his master. But with us a second is necessary, unknown to history. When freed, he is to be removed beyond the reach of mixture."[50]

This passage from Jefferson's *Notes* is generally considered the watershed moment when colonization schemes began to proliferate. But such a periodization insulates the Revolutionary era from the embarrassment of patriot plans for black banishment. Instead, it posits colonization schemes as evidence of the failure of the sincere patriot efforts for abolition. In this way, the 'Contagion of Liberty' thesis is preserved as the great men of the Revolution stood by their principles until conditions shifted beneath their feet, and they were no longer able to stand upon such ground.[51] The evidence simply fails to support such a timeline.

Notes on Virginia did not mark Jefferson's inauguration of proposals for black colonization, but rather the failure of one of his schemes to whiten his beloved Virginia, and his pivoting to another. By the time Jefferson published his hope that black Virginians "be removed beyond the reach of mixture" he had already devoted nearly a decade to attempting to alter Virginia law to gradually evict black people from Virginia.

JEFFERSON'S MASTER PLAN OF GRADUAL BANISHMENT

Early in 1776, Thomas Paine fired the imaginations of patriot leaders when he wrote that "We have it in our power to begin the world over again." One young patriot who would soon emerge as the Revolution's foremost philosopher, the thirty-three-year-old Thomas Jefferson, seized the moment to remake the world. But his most sweeping attempt to do so has gone unrecognized, overshadowed by his more famous role in penning the first draft of the Declaration of Independence and serving as the new nation's third president. Jefferson's audacious plan to redesign America from its foundations has been overlooked because it evenly rested upon the seemingly opposite pillars of antislavery and white supremacy.

It took Jefferson some time after the Revolution began to find the clay he wished to mold. According to John Adams, he had to be persuaded to author the Declaration of Independence. Adams, the only Yankee on the committee, cajoled him into doing so by telling him "You are a Virginian, and Virginia ought to appear at the head of this business."[52] While later that summer Jefferson dutifully took notes and followed closely the contentious debates that hammered out the

146

outline of the Articles of Confederation, the nation's first constitution, he chose to leave Congress at the first opportunity, taking up a seat in the Virginia legislature that he had last warmed seven years before.

Rare is it for a young, ambitious politician to step back from a national office to take a seat representing a county in a state legislature. Jefferson in his *Autobiography*, plainly stated that though his place in Congress had been renewed for the coming year, he thought he could do more important work back home, "I knew that our legislation under the regal government had many very vicious points which urgently required reformation, and I thought I could be of more use in forwarding that work." What legislative issues were so urgent that they drew Jefferson away from the largest city in America, back to sleepy Williamsburg, and kept him there even when offered the ambassadorship to France?

Less than a month into Virginia's legislative session of 1776, Jefferson revealed the true scope of his ambition, the project that he perceived as giving him the largest scope of action, the greatest possibility of doing what every philosopher dreamed, reforming not just one law or policy, but them all:

> When I left Congress, in 76 it was in the persuasion that our whole code must be reviewed, adapted to our republican form of government, and, now that we had no negatives of Councils, Governors & Kings to restrain us from doing right, that it should be corrected, in all it's parts, with a single eye to reason, & the good of those for whose government it was framed.

Historians have tended to overlook how eager Jefferson was to be the architect of a new comprehensive legal code. Jefferson is described as simply "being appointed" to the Committee of Revisors charged with this task. In fact, Jefferson introduced the legislation to create the committee, ensuring that when it passed, he would sit upon it. Knowing that his fellow lawmakers would balk at empowering him to redesign 169 years of the basic laws of Virginia from scratch, Jefferson obscured what he planned and claimed that the committee's charge was just to reorganize the existing laws from their present haphazard chronological arrangement into an organized "digest" of the law.

As chief "revisor," Jefferson was able to draft more legislative bills in his three-year term than any other member of the General Assembly, but he often hid his authorship by having colleagues introduce bills or inserting them within other pieces of pending legislation when they were in committee. In this way, Jefferson concealed the way in which he was designing a complete structure of some 128 new laws and not just smoothing out the rougher corners of the legal code. Unlike some other famous legal revisions, because Jefferson, and later his collaborators, never submitted the full revision as a single piece of legislation, his accomplishment was not appreciated until a few scholars in the mid-twentieth century endeavored to collect everything Jefferson ever wrote or read. The editor of Jefferson's voluminous papers at one point realized the true scale of Jefferson's work on Virginia's laws: "In the variety of subjects touched upon, in the quantity of bills drafted, and in the unity of purpose behind all this legislative activity, his accomplishment in this period was astounding. He was in himself a veritable legislative drafting bureau."[53]

A decade after Jefferson had begun remaking the world of Virginia, many laws he had authored years before still knocked around the Virginia Assembly. Jefferson still camouflaged his work as mere legal housekeeping, writing to a curious Dutchman who asked about his legal project,

> It contains not more than three or four laws which could strike the attention of a foreigner ... The only merit of this work is that it may remove from our book shelves about twenty folio volumes of statutes, retaining all the parts of them which either their own merit or the established system of laws required.[54]

Jefferson contributed to ongoing misunderstanding of his project by highlighting a few notable pieces of the whole in his *Notes on Virginia* rather than revealing the way in which many of the laws worked together to refashion society. Historians rightly point to his

Act for Establishing Religious Freedom, or his bills reforming the system of education or eliminating aristocratic systems of inheritance and land rents as landmarks in the establishment of republican institutions. Some fragments of the language Jefferson used in his early legal revisions circuitously made their way into other charters, such as the Constitution's Bill of Rights, an unsurprising traverse given that George Mason was probably Jefferson's closest co-worker on the revisor's committee.[55]

Besides purging Virginia's laws of monarchical remnants, the way the revised legal code constituted a set of gears working together to engineer a new social order is most clearly seen in Jefferson's attempt to phase out what he saw as the towering evils of his nation: slavery and the black presence in America.[56]

Connecting the dots in the bills Jefferson and the other revisors wrote, a master plan for both ending slavery and whitening Virginia emerges from the haze of legalisms. Decades later in his *Autobiography*, Jefferson insincerely claimed that the laws dealing with slavery that he authored during Virginia's revision did not constitute a system. "The bill on the subject of slaves was a mere digest of the existing laws respecting them, without any intimation of a plan for a future & general emancipation."[57] Actually, when all the pieces of Jefferson's legal revisions are gathered, they can be seen to form an interlocking whole that followed a consistent strategy. Laws dealing with the slave trade, migration of free people of color into the state, punishments for petty crimes, and procedures for manumission, all worked seamlessly together to achieve a common purpose—weakening slavery and diminishing the black population.

To fully appreciate Jefferson's blueprint for eradicating both slavery and black people from Virginia, it is important first to understand that his changes to the existing slave code made the immediate conditions of slavery more harsh and crueler. While historians mistakenly speak of Jefferson's changes to the slave code as constituting "reform," they actually reversed several decades of progress that Virginia's lawmakers had made toward treating those enslaved as people and not chattels. Particularly in the last decade of imperial rule of the colony, the commonwealth's House of Burgesses, with the approval of the royal governor and ultimately the King and Council, had undertaken a liberalization of the harsh laws governing slaves and free people of color.

For example, the standing "Act for the Better Government of Servants," passed in 1754, punished white women who bore children with free black men by condemning their children to be bound out to servitude until the age of thirty-one. Finding this law of an "unreasonable severity towards such children" the royal government lowered it to the same terms as any other destitute children were generally treated, boys until they were twenty-one, girls to the age of eighteen.[58]

Jefferson himself played a role in these earlier royal reforms. Jefferson was a twenty-six-year-old lawyer when he took his seat in the capitol in May of 1769. On his second day, a petition was read "of the People called Mulattoes and free Negroes, whose Names are there unto subscribed, was presented to the House, and read, praying that the Wives and Daughters of the Petitioners may be exempt from the Payment of Levies." The petition was sent to the large forty-seven-member committee of Propositions and Grievances that Jefferson was a member of, and two days later it promptly reported that it found "it is the Opinion of this Committee, that the Petition of the Mulattoes and free Negroes, praying that their Wives and Daughters may be exempted from the Payment of Levies, is reasonable."[59] The law that emerged from these deliberations declared that charging head taxes on the wives and daughters of free black men "is found very burthensome to such negroes, mulattoes, and Indians." In a dramatic statement, the Burgesses declared that taxing such people "is moreover derogatory of the rights of free-born subjects." Presumably, this tax was "derogatory" because "free negroes" were not eligible to vote or hold office or were treated differently by many dimensions of the laws. But whatever the source of their derogation, the governing body of the colony with assent of the King and Council included free people of color within the scope of "free-born subjects."[60]

Jefferson's first session in the legislature came to an abrupt end just ten days after it began when the assemblymen adopted a resolution supporting Massachusetts in its defiance of the Townsend Acts under threat of being dismissed by Governor Botetourt. Botetourt carried through with his threat and the legislature was dissolved, not to meet again until November. In the meantime, Jefferson returned to his affairs in Monticello, in September he placed an ad in the *Virginia Gazette* offering a reward to anyone who apprehended and returned to him Sandy, a thirty-five-year-old shoemaker, carpenter, and jockey, and the white horse Sandy made off with. Though Jefferson depicted Sandy as a disreputable person: "he is greatly addicted to drink, and when drunk is insolent and disorderly, in his conversation he swears much, and his behaviour is artful and knavish," Sandy's skills had earned for Jefferson £18 per year, making the maximum reward Jefferson offered, £10, a bargain. Sandy was found and returned, and Jefferson sold him for £100 a few years later.[61]

When the assembly finally reconvened in November, one large committee of forty-seven members that included Jefferson was charged with considering revisions to the old law that allowed county courts to order the dismemberment of slaves who "are notoriously guilty of going abroad in the Night, or running away, and laying out, and who cannot be reclaimed by the common Methods of Punishment."[62] A bill limiting the infliction of the punishment of castration to "an attempt to ravish a white woman" was also passed during that session.[63]

The Burgesses lessened the punishments for minor crimes committed by slaves. A slave "who shall break into any house in the night time" was not automatically subject to capital punishment but could be sentenced to a lesser punishment as long as the break-in was not an actual burglary. The process of sentencing a slave to death was taken out of the hands of a lone judge and now required four members of a court to concur. The standing system was abolished by which justices could issue writs against fugitive slaves that authorized anyone to kill them and then the state would compensate the owner for the value of their "condemned property." Going forward, justices of the peace would have to establish that such slaves were "outlying and doing mischief."[64]

This group of legislators who looked favorably on measures to ameliorate the burdens of slaves and free people of color were a different group from the patriots who would compose the new rival revolutionary legislature that called itself the House of Delegates in 1776. Only one-third of the members of the House of Burgesses who had met in 1773 were members of the new state House of Delegates when it convened in 1776.[65]

Jefferson's master plan for racially cleansing Virginia first required modernizing the categories of race that all else depended upon. By the 1770s, monarchical law, based as it was on the accumulation of precedents, edicts, favors, and exceptions, had rendered race ill-defined and difficult to enforce in court. It was assumed that the terms "negro" and "white" did not need legal definition. Some effort was put forth to categorize those who seemed to fall between recognized categories. In 1705, lawmakers tried to clear "all manner of doubts which hereafter may happen to arise upon … who shall be accounted a mulatto" and defined a mulatto as "the child of an Indian and the child, grand child, or great grand child, of a negro," leaving the racial status of the children or grandchildren, or great grandchildren of those called "white" or "negro" hanging in limbo.[66]

Jefferson simplified this racial system by tying definition to African ancestry alone. Thus, courts had only half the definitional burden, namely, of deciding who was a "negro" rather than judging all racial identities involved. He then solidified racial categories by reducing the scope of ancestry required to be labeled. Jefferson also lowered the required black blood quantum from an eighth to a quarter ("every person, who shall have one fourth part or more of negro blood") which in an age when birth records were haphazard and far flung across parishes patched several holes in the wall between races.[67]

Jefferson then employed the same strategy of simplification that he had used to solidify the boundaries between races to clarify who was a slave and who was not. Though Virginia had in practice associated race and slave status, its laws did not. Virginia's slave law of 1753 did not equate status and appearance or ancestry. Slaves were defined as people who had been brought to Virginia but were "not christians in their native country, except Turks and Moors in amity with his majesty" and their offspring following the status of their mothers. A further exception was made for anyone who could prove they were free in England "or any other christian country" prior to arriving in

Virginia and their descendants.[68] In this way, the existing legal code provided several narrow exceptions through which a small number of people held as slaves could struggle through to freedom. Jefferson closed and locked these escape hatches by the plain and clever wording that "no persons shall, henceforth, be slaves within this commonwealth, except such as were so on the first day of this present session of Assembly, and the descendants of the females of them."

Jefferson's system depended on shoring up the bulwarks of race and basing the law on a theory of government that withdrew the protection of government from unfavored groups. But its aim was not simply to construct a segregationist state, one in which the descendants of Africans and slaves would exist as a permanent subordinate caste, but, rather, to use these powers and distinctions to purge people of color entirely from society. Jefferson's preferred tool for accomplishing this was the ancient legal device of banishment and he set about to incorporate it throughout the legal code of Virginia, adding it to laws banning the importation of slaves, laws governing the migration of free people of color, laws of interracial bastardy, criminal statutes, manumission, and ultimately, slavery itself.

The Sage of Monticello's preoccupation with banishment was not without precedent. Virginia had once before in its past attempted to curtail its rising black population by ordering freed people to leave the colony. As early as 1691, legislators grew alarmed at the rising numbers of free people of color, proclaiming, that "great inconveniences may happen to this country by the setting of negroes and mulattoes service free, by their either entertaining negro slaves from their masters service, or receiveing stolen goods, or being grown old bringing a charge upon the country." Lawmakers then limited manumissions by requiring that masters transport manumitted persons out of the colony within six months or pay a fine of £10. The requirement that manumitted women and men be banished from the colony was rescinded in 1748 and replaced by a ban on all manumissions unless permission was granted by the governor and council and then, only upon grounds of "some meritorious services."[69]

Early in the eighteenth century banishment was also set as the penalty for any white man or woman intermarrying with a "negroe, mulatto, or Indian man or woman bond or free." However, in such cases, it was the white person who was exiled, not the person of color.[70] A revision of this law in 1753 eliminated the punishment of exile and substituted jailing for six months and a fine of £10 for the white offender.[71] But by the time Jefferson himself sat in the House of Burgesses in 1769, such policies were a receding memory and no laws expelled free or enslaved black people from the colony.

Jefferson's new legal code revived the banishment of any white woman who had a child with a black or mixed-race man from the state (though black women who bore the children of white men were exempt because their offspring were the property of their white fathers). But unlike the ancient precedent Jefferson copied, his measure was aimed more at policing the borders of race than morality, for his proposed law exiled both mother and her free mixed-parent-age child. In those earlier times when the upholding of public morals was a higher concern and the having of children between whites and people of color was always fornication and bastardy because interracial marriage itself was illegal, it was a crime punishable by whipping (with harsher beatings prescribed for the darker-skinned partner). Jefferson, obviously not one to be troubled by such rules of conduct, exploited this crime of morality to achieve his larger goal of diminishing the black population.

More directly, Jefferson's proposed law to choke off the international trafficking of slaves shifted from a traditional reliance on tariffs and stiff fines for violators to a simplified ban on bringing into the state any people of color on a permanent basis. This law can be (and has been) mistakenly read as one encouraging the freeing of slaves by its language that apparently encourages freedom: "Negroes and mulattoes which shall hereafter be brought into this commonwealth and kept therein one whole year, together, or so long at different times as shall amount to one year, shall be free." But what appears on its surface to be a measure freeing illegally imported slaves is just a means of enforcing a much broader ban on the importation or migration of any people of color, free or enslaved. This is made abundantly clear in the succeeding passage that requires any people freed in this way to either leave the state or become outlaws: "But if they shall not depart the commonwealth within one year thereafter they shall be out of the protection of the laws."[72]

The phrase "out of the protection of the laws" had serious but different implications for slave masters, slaves, and free people of color. For slave merchants, the sanction of rendering their human chattel unprotected by the state's legal code and courts essentially destroyed its value as property. For enslaved people, being "out of the protection of the laws" legally entitled any Virginian to seize, beat, maim, or kill them with abandon. Free people of color "out of the protection of the laws" could be killed, or they could be seized and claimed as property.

As this law referred not to "slaves" but to "Negroes and mulattoes" it served as a prohibition on the entry into Virginia of any free person of color. This feature of the law was made clear in a subsequent passage that made an exception for black "seafaring persons," who were commonly not enslaved, and were allowed one day in port before subject to being seized and claimed by any Virginian as their legal property.

Having closed off the avenues of entry of black people, Jefferson turned his attention to finding other parts of the legal code that could be turned to expel black Virginians from their home. Buried away in a different bill was a provision whose intent was to continually push people of color out of the state. Any slave who committed an offense "punishable ... by labor," which in the jargon of the day meant serious felonies such as manslaughter, arson, robbery, horse-stealing but also lesser offenses such as housebreaking and larceny, were to be "transported to such parts in the West Indies, S. America or Africa, as the Governor shall direct, there to be continued in slavery."[73]

Slavery itself was attacked by easing restrictions on manumission, which technically was not simply setting someone free, but was the complicated legal ability of a slave-owner to convey his ownership of a person to the person themself. Manumissions under Jefferson's system were encouraged by eliminating the long-standing requirement that only an act of the assembly could legally transform an enslaved person into a free one. The catch, and it was a catch upon which rested much of Jefferson's racial architecture, was that all manumitted persons were required to leave Virginia forever, or face reenslavement.

In the end, Jefferson's racial architecture for his native state proved incomplete because he failed to mortise in the keystone of his plan. Since he first sat in the colonial House of Burgesses in 1769, Jefferson had been eager to introduce a plan for the gradual ending of slavery.[74] Older and more politically astute colleagues convinced him to shelve his ideas then and decades later, being more experienced and politically savvy himself, he felt even more headwinds and never offered his plan for gradual emancipation to the legislative docket. Tellingly, no text of it survives and only the barest outline exists in Jefferson's *Notes on Virginia*. There, in introducing his lengthy section detailing the racial differences of blacks, whites, and Indians, Jefferson recounted the features of the bill he regretted not seeing the light of day:

> To emancipate all slaves born after passing the act … and further directing, that they should continue with their parents to a certain age, then be brought up, at the public expence, to tillage, arts or sciences, according to their geniuses, till the females should be eighteen, and the males twenty-one years of age, when they should be colonized to such place as the circumstances of the time should render most proper, sending them out with arms, implements of household and of the handicraft arts, seeds, pairs of the useful domestic animals, &c. to declare them a free and independent people, and extend to them our alliance and protection, till they have acquired strength; and to send vessels at the same time to other parts of the world for an equal number of white inhabitants; to induce whom to migrate hither, proper encouragements were to be proposed.

Later, as he parsed out the elements of his comprehensive plan to end slavery and diminish the black presence in his state, Jefferson again contemplated introducing a gradual emancipation act to the assembly, but was dissuaded, again, by his estimation that he could not garner enough support to pass such a bill.[75]

In discussing this episode in his *Autobiography*, Jefferson reveals much about how his opposition to slavery and his opposition to the presence of black people were intertwined. He connected his plan of emancipation to his belief, stated even more robustly in *Notes on Virginia*, that white and black people could not possibly live together in a single republican nation. Moreover, in discussing what should happen to freed men and women, Jefferson does not use the term "colonization" that had the benevolent connotations of aiding people to be self-sufficient and to flourish on their own, but the term "deportation" which not only was legally a form of punishment but identified those "deported" as not being members of the body politic in any way. Only those who were not included within the community of citizens could be "deported":

> The principles of the amendment however were agreed on, that is to say, the freedom of all born after a certain day, and deportation at a proper age. But it was found that the public mind would not yet bear the proposition, nor will it bear it even at this day. Yet the day is not distant when it must bear and adopt it, or worse will follow. Nothing is more certainly written in the book of fate than that these people are to be free. Nor is it less certain that the two races, equally free, cannot live in the same government. Nature, habit, opinion has drawn indelible lines of distinction between them. It is still in our power to direct the process of emancipation and deportation peaceably and in such slow degree as that the evil will wear off insensibly, and their place be pari passu filled up by free white laborers.[76]

Though he felt the bill for general emancipation was politically premature, Jefferson did author a bill to quicken the pace of white immigration and replace people of color. Jefferson's fellow revisor Edmund Pendleton sketched out a first draft of a law that encouraged immigration and naturalization of Protestants, even titling the bill, "Bill for the Naturalization of Foreign Protestts." The bill offered easy terms of naturalization, a $20 payment "for the purpose of defraying his passage hither over sea" and a bounty of "fifty acres of unappropriated lands wherever he shall chuse." Jefferson edited Pendeleton's draft, excising all references to Protestants, thereby broadening the potential pool of white foreigners that might be enticed to immigrate.

This version of the bill did not contain the qualifier "white," though this seems to have been generally seen as implied. The bill was read out twice by the assembly, debated and further amended and Jefferson took cryptic notes of this exchange that echo the arguments he makes in *Notes on Virginia* about the racial supremacy of whites in general:

Physical advantages
Consumption
Labor
Procreation

...

Moral
Honesty—Veracity[77]

Ultimately, this bill to encourage immigration was deemed a less pressing matter as the war cut off the flow of transatlantic settlement and was tabled. When revived several years later, its emphasis was less on stimulating immigration than codifying whiteness as the basis of citizenship.

Jefferson's master plan to end slavery and remove all black people from Virginia was never fully implemented. His fellow legislators, most of whom were slave-owners themselves, chose not to restrict their own freedom to dispose of their human property as they saw fit and in 1782 passed a manumission law without Jefferson's requirement that freed men and women be banished. But when this law was revised in 1806, Jefferson's original requirement that all freed men and women leave Virginia within one year or face reenslavement "for the benefit of the poor" was restored.[78]

Jefferson's last effort to revive his vision of a Virginia without slavery or black people came in 1783 as he was preparing to return to Congress. That year he sent to James Madison, who was just then about to make the opposite journey from Congress back to Virginia, a confidential draft Constitution for the state. Jefferson included in his charter a deceptively brief antislavery clause that barred the state's legislature "to permit the introduction of any more slaves to reside in this state, or the continuance of slavery beyond the generation which shall be living on the 31st. day of December 1800; all persons born after that day being hereby declared free."[79] Though it didn't pass, it proved influential to Madison and others who a few years later would hammer out a new constitution for both Virginia and the United States.

As some historians have pointed out, the fifteen- or sixteen-year gap between when this Constitution could have been ratified and the deadline for freedom in 1800 would have stimulated a vast outflow of slaves as masters sold slaves to eager buyers in other states, territories, and countries. Absent some sort of prohibition on such sales, this simple device of setting a future date for emancipation would have worked to achieve both of Jefferson's long-standing goals— the ending of slavery and the expulsion of all people of color from the state.[80]

Jefferson's friend and long-standing colleague in Virginia governing circles, St. George Tucker, was critical of Jefferson's plan. Tucker noted that Jefferson's draft bill for gradual emancipation in Virginia required that all adults had to be expelled from the state and colonized somewhere else and he saw many practical (though apparently not principled) problems with this plan:

> To establish such a colony in the territory of the United States, would probably lay the foundation of intestine wars, which would terminate only in their extirpation, or final expulsion. To attempt it in any other quarter of the globe would be attended with the utmost cruelty to the colonists, themselves, and the destruction of their whole race ...[81]

Though Virginia's slaveholding elites refused to go along with Jefferson's full program for ethnic cleansing the state of people of color, Jefferson clung to his vision of a whitened nation and remained fascinated with colonization schemes. His chance to facilitate ethnic cleansing on an even larger scale presented itself soon after he was inaugurated as the nation's third president.

Virginia legislators considered new proposals for black expulsion in the panic that followed the enslaved people's attempted insurrection known as Gabriel's Rebellion that was discovered and drowned in blood in the summer of 1800.[82] Initially, lawmakers sought a way to limit the mounting costs of executing the many enslaved people who were accused of plotting rebellion (state law required that owners be fully compensated from the state treasury for the market value of condemned slaves). But they also thought to keep the option open of using frontier territory as a means of ethnically cleansing the state of people of color altogether. Lawmakers drafted a resolution instructing the state's governor, James Monroe, to ask President Jefferson for a grant of land somewhere out in the frontier with language that kept open all their options for a more general black banishment. They instructed Monroe to correspond with the president to obtain "lands without the limits of this State, to which persons obnoxious to the laws or dangerous to the peace of society may be removed."[83]

In his letter to Jefferson, Governor Monroe highlighted that this territory of black exile could be either for the transportation of condemned rebels, or for black people more generally. He noted that the legislative pressure for such a territory "was produced by the conspiracy of the slaves which took place in this city [Richmond] and neighborhood last year" and that it was in that regard "applicable to that description of persons only." But Monroe notes that the legislature worded its resolution more generally and could be interpreted to imply a more sweeping plan of black expulsion, a prospect that clearly had captured his imagination:

> As soon as the mind emerges, in contemplating the subject, beyond the contracted scale of providing a mode of punishment for offenders, vast and interesting objects present themselves to view. It is impossible not to revolve in it the condition of those people, the embarrassment they have already occasioned us, and are still likely to subject us to. We perceive an existing evil, which commenced under our colonial system, with which we are not properly chargeable, or, if at all, not in the present degree; and we acknowledge the extreme difficulty of remedying it ... Under this view of the subject,

I shall be happy to be advised by you whether a tract of land in the western territory of the United States can be procured for this purpose ...[84]

Monroe ended by calling the idea of banishment "a subject of great delicacy and importance"—delicate by which he probably meant that it would not be wise to let several hundred thousand people know plans were being discussed to dump them outside the limits of the nation into what was widely thought to be the wastes of the "Great American Desert." (Jefferson thought likewise as in his answer he noted that "some circumstances connected with the subject, and necessarily presenting themselves to view, would be improper but for yours and the legislative ear. Their publication might have an ill effect in more than one quarter."[85]) The plan was obviously important, as Monroe pointed out, because it "involves the future peace, tranquillity, and happiness of the good people of this commonwealth," or, in other words, the best interests of white folks.

Virginia's legislators thought that Jefferson would be sympathetic to their plan as it was originally his plan, part of his proposed code revisions of 1777 that read "Slaves guilty of any offence punishable in others by labor in the public works, shall be transported to such parts in the West Indies, S. America or Africa, as the Governor shall direct, there to be continued in slavery." Monroe even told Jefferson that he knew he would look sympathetically on their plan because he had "confidence that you will take that interest in it which we are taught to expect from your conduct through life."

Jefferson responded by embracing the "enlarged construction of the resolution" that Monroe pointed toward, a more general ethnic cleansing rather than a destination for a few convicted rebels. "Common malefactors, I presume, make no part of that resolution. Neither their numbers nor the nature of their offences seem to require any provisions beyond those practised heretofore ... many perhaps contemplated, and one expression of the resolution might comprehend, a much larger scope." He then turned to the problems and practicality of implementing a large-scale black expulsion.

The president discussed the possibility of simply purchasing some of the "very great extent of country north of the Ohio [that] has been laid off into townships." But Jefferson pointed out, this option would probably prove too expensive and, more importantly, "Questions would also arise whether the establishment of such a colony, within our limits, and to become a part of our Union, would be desirable to the State of Virginia itself, or to the other States, especially those who would be in its vicinity." In other words, why go to the trouble of exiling an entire people only to have them remain as a presence within the nation? Rather, Jefferson thought it better to "procure lands, beyond the limits of the United States, to form a receptacle for these people" but the question was where?

Over America's northern border was British land, British subjects, and several Indian nations. None of them, Jefferson thought, would be interested in welcoming a mass emigration of black people. "It is hardly to be believed that either Great Britain or the Indian proprietors have so disinterested a regard for us as to be willing to relieve us by receiving such a colony themselves." (Jefferson's language of America needing to be relieved by finding a receptacle to dump people of color should end all academic debates over the altruism of colonizationists.) As a renowned naturalist, Jefferson could add that an additional problem with a northern receptacle was that it was "much to be doubted whether that race of men could long exist in so rigorous a climate."

Another alternative was the "immense country" beyond America's western and southern frontiers. Virginians had dreamed of dumping freed black people deep into the western frontier for decades, but as early as 1766 future patriot leader Patrick Henry bemoaned that to "re-export them is now impracticable." Henry, in his fragmentary pamphlet on religious toleration, posed the question on every patriot's mind: "Our country will be peopled. The question is, shall it be with Europeans or Africans?" America's future growth, prosperity, and security all depended on attracting sturdy and industrious European immigrants instead of relying on unproductive and dangerous slaves. Pennsylvania was a more prosperous colony than Virginia because a "Dutch, Irish, or Scotch emigrant" prefers to settle there.

Henry's hope lay in "scattering" the "present stock" of slaves and "their descendants ... through the immense deserts of the West," a vision of colonizing African Americans to the far west that would dazzle the imaginations of generations of patriots.[86]

One of these patriots, Reverend David Rice, was a delegate to the Kentucky Constitutional Convention who famously campaigned to prohibit slavery in the new state. Typically, Rice condemned slavery as both ill-founded in law and morally unjust to other men. But he seemed equally, if not more motivated by the corrosive effects of slavery on whites, the danger of "the anger of heaven" and "the inconsistency of slavery with good policy" because it threatens "our prosperity and happiness." (Note the use of "our" in this context only refers to white Kentuckians.) Slavery endangers the safety of the white community ("Can it be in our interest ... to nourish within our bowels such an injured inveterate foe? ... What havock would a handful of savages, in conjunction with this domestic enemy, make in our country!"), it innervates white men ("Slavery produces idleness; and idleness is the nurse of vice"), it destroys understandings of justice among whites ("If I have no sense of obligation to do justice to a black man, I can have little to do justice to a white man"), it destroys the value of chastity putting "an end to domestic tranquility," it corrupts democratic government ("Slavery naturally tends to sap the foundations of moral, and consequently of political virtue"), and it deters industrious poor white immigrants from settling in Kentucky. Rice proposed that Kentucky immediately ban the importation of more slaves, and free those born after some future date who are deemed "qualified by proper education to make useful citizens." A few years later Rice added to this plan "to lay off a state in the western lands for the use of the blacks."[87]

Samuel Stanhope Smith, president of the College of New Jersey, is widely remembered today for propounding theories that Africans were physically and mentally inferior but that this black inferiority was not an essential aspect of Africans' natural inheritance. Rather, black inferiority was acquired through their environment and the degrading experiences they suffered by being wrenched from their native Africa and thrust into American bondage. Smith was, like most patriots of his day, highly critical of slavery, repeating Montesquieu's demolition of the legal arguments supporting human bondage in a prominent speech. "Men deceive themselves continually by false pretenses, in order to justify the slavery which is convenient for them," Smith concluded.[88]

Faced with his conclusion that slavery was immoral, inhumane, unsupported by law, and falsely defended, Professor Smith nevertheless found a way to steer around the solution of simply freeing those in bondage. Cleverly, Smith cleaved the moral arguments against slavery from the practical considerations of its continuation. "Is that slavery which was unjust in its origin" (and Smith here admits that "our enquiries must receive a new direction"), is it also "equally unjust in its continuance?" Smith's answers are worth a close investigation because they seem to elaborate in systematic detail the thinking of many of his generation of educated white men, including and especially those that have been hailed as leaders of early abolitionism.[89]

Smith thought extending liberty to those in bondage "worthy a humane legislation" but warned that "generous feelings" should not propel legislators to "rush too precipitately to their end" and "render their emancipation a worse evil than their servitude." The threat to the white community was too great: there was nothing "more dangerous to a community than the sudden introduction into it of a vast multitudes of persons, free in their condition, but without property, and possessing only the habits and vices of slavery." People freed suddenly from their bondage would resort to "theft, plunder, and violence" because their "servile principles would take off the shame of the basest action." Without the "former restraints" that kept them at labor, "they would become idle and profligate" and "we should soon see property every where invaded, public safety disturbed, and even domestic peace and security constantly endangered." This is what the Quakers had done, "to throw on society a multitude of idle dependents, with a mass of servile vices, which no citizen has a right to do, either for the mistaken relief of his conscience, or the display of his vanity."

It was not unusual that the full compass of Smith's moral focus when considering emancipation circled just the welfare and well-being of the white community. This is the key to understanding both the rise of the movement against slavery and to all early programs to end it. There was probably no white opponent of slavery in America who would have disagreed with Smith's conclusion, that "the emancipation of the African race in the United States, if it ever be accomplished, must necessarily be the slow and gradual work of time." When Smith did for a moment consider the welfare of black people themselves, he thought a slow and cautious plan of gradual emancipation was best as slavery "did not press with the same severity" upon the current generation of enslaved people as it did their forebearers because "the habits and ideas of these people" had been "accommodated to it from their infancy."

Perhaps more than any other abolitionist, Smith systematically analyzed the problems and possibilities of the actual process of emancipation. In reexamining Smith's arguments can be seen an important, but often unstated reason for crafting plans for ending slavery that extended the process of granting liberties far into the future. This was so that enslavers could be compensated for the property the state effectively confiscated and the enslaved could be freed only once they had "qualified themselves by good moral and industrious habits." In other words, those who had profited from slavery had to be granted restitution and those who had been exploited had to leave their freedom in the hands of supervising whites. Smith here said aloud what all the self-proclaimed abolitionists of this period really believed.

Smith recognized that in a republic of laws property could not simply be taken away without compensation. Legally, states "could not equitably compel them [enslavers] to make a sacrifice of so great value, to the convenience and comfort of any class of men." Morally, "neither justice nor humanity requires that the master, who has become the innocent possessor of that property, should impoverish himself for the benefit of his slave."

One common solution to this dilemma was to declare an end to slavery but to make "an equitable estimate of the value of his labor for a year" and to then "bind these slaves to their present masters ... for a term of years, to be calculated from the preceding estimates." In other words, to compensate masters for the property but to draw this "recompence" entirely from the labor of those freed. Smith thought this approach false and discriminatory as it treated human property differently from other forms of property.

Another version of this solution was to grant to each slave a *peculium*, a small plot of land that they could cultivate and "bring into the market the product of his industry" so that "in a course of years ... a revenue, adequate to the purchase of his own freedom" could be accumulated. The beauty of this plan was that it solved both the problem of compensating those who were forced to give up their human property as well as freed only those who demonstrated their "good habits" and "proper disposition to labor."

Smith recognized that even these schemes did not go far enough to ensure domestic peace. Like Jefferson, Smith thought that freed people would need to be segregated away from white society because even freedom obtained in these gradual ways would not eradicate the "prejudices which exist against a union of the whites with the blacks." Following his own environmentalist theories, Smith understood that these measured plans of emancipation which emancipated some but not all would leave freed people in the company of those yet enslaved. Smith believed this would be "injurious to both" because such an association would "impair the motives which should prompt the freeman to aspire to respectability" and "corrupt the submissive duty of the slave." Smith's solution, in fact the only answer, or as Smith put it, the one "provision [that] alone occurs to me to prevent this evil," was to exile the emancipated to that blank spot on maps of the continent often labeled the "Great American Desert." To assign

> a large district out of the unappropriated lands of the United States, in which each black freedman, or freed woman, shall receive a certain portion of land ... together which such privileges as would induce them to prefer a settlement in the new territory to remaining in the vicinity of their former servitude.

In other words, to make their liberty dependent on their leaving.[90]

Smith departs from the consistency of his own theories of environmentalism in imagining how this distant black territory might develop over time. He thought it might be necessary to encourage the marriage of whites and blacks, perhaps by giving white men or women who marry a black person a double share of land, in order "to obliterate those wide distinctions which are now created by a diversity of complexion." (Note as property was held by men, Smith's scheme would have enriched white men, not their female partners. Smith apparently didn't want to grant the same double shares to black men who marry white women.) Revealingly, Smith did not envision giving black people political power even in their own colony, as his plan called for "the magistrates, for a considerable period, ought to be appointed from the white nation." Notably, Smith's language here reveals a certain uneasiness with the racial amalgamation he envisioned for the black territory. Amalgamation was best restricted to the black colony and shouldn't flow in the other direction, for if it did Smith would no longer be able to describe it as "the white nation."

The dream of employing the vastness of the continent as a dumping ground for emancipated African Americans even captured the imagination of patriots who had publicly expressed their opposition to African colonization. Jefferson's friend and legal advisor, St. George Tucker, who had declared he was opposed to "banishment" also wrote that "There is an immense unsettled territory on this continent more congenial to their natural constitutions than ours, where they may perhaps be received upon more favorable terms than we can permit them to remain with us." Tucker then references in a footnote that there exists the "immense territory of Louisiana ... would probably afford a ready asylum for such as might choose to become Spanish subjects ... The climate is undoubtedly more favourable to the African constitution than ours, and from this cause, it is not improbable that emigrations from these states would in time be very considerable."[91]

Similarly, Robert Pleasants, founder of the Virginia Society for Promoting the Abolition of Slavery, and the Relief of Free Negroes, and Others, who opposed "forced" colonization, still toyed with ideas of tying emancipation to western relocation. Pleasants stood apart in that he allowed that emancipation would mean joining black and white people into some sort of shared community. He criticized a fellow antislavery writer because "he objects to the admission of negroes to the priviledges of Citizens" and he opposed schemes of

African colonization for their "injustice & cruelty." However, even Pleasants thought differently about the possibility of some sort of frontier colony, writing:

> would it not be bad policy to deprive the country of so great a number of Labourers, who have generally been looked upon by wise legislatures, as the most sure source of power and opulence: especially too, as we have so much uncultivated land in this state and an extensive territory to the westward uninhabited?[92]

A southerner calling himself "Citizen free born" sent a letter to the president a few months later in which he shared his plan for "gradial liberation" by sending African Americans out west. This anonymous writer claimed to have much experience with slavery, "I have Known many tied & stript And a hundred hard Lashes laid on the Naked Backs." Citizen Free Born expressed his sympathy with Jefferson's difficult task, "I know that it is hard for you to Emancipate them And you'l find many of those Barbarous Wretches that Will Oppose you, But fear not, you have Justice on your Side & thousand of Friends to Support you in so laudable An Undertaking." Many people wished for an end to slavery because they believed the "Safety to these states" hung in the balance. Citizen Free Born feared that "while we ruleing them with a rod of Iron and they themselves Uneasy, should some Dareing, bold Massanello, or Some Great BOANAPARTE, stand at their heads … What miserable Destruction would be made, Amongst our Wives, our Sons & our Daughters." But Citizen Free Born worried that most white patriots would not see past the problem of what happened once the slaves were freed.

> One thing more that appears to hurt the minds of the People they say it will never do to set them free & let them stay amongst us Send them clear off & I should be glad they were gone But for my Part I am not of that way of thinking they would greatly Contribute to the Union But I would have them Set on Some Large plat of Land (As we have in the United States such a vast Quantity of Unlocked Lands, And Claimed by Different Indians tribes that

never do these states any Service, but are very hurtful to them in holding the Lands) Let a spot on the Missippi be Laid out; And as the Creatures are Liberated, let them immegrate themselves thither within one year after they are set free ...[93]

Likewise, Michael Walton, "a fellow citizen," wrote to Jefferson in 1809 with his advice for how to bring "Lawyers, Bank Directors, British Importers, Justices of the Peace, Bailiffs & Tavern Keepers" (who he called "turbulent & ambitious Men") to the same "level with the peaceable Farmer [and] the Mechanick." His list of reforms included:

Let the Negro be well clothed fed & receive his Liberty at such an Age if his past conduct merits it—If not, let him be transported to an other Country & sold to pay the Expence—if after he receives his Liberty, he is found guilty of crimes, let him be either sold again as a Slave, or transported & sold[94]

Even Thomas Paine tried to nudge Jefferson to consider Louisiana as a possible site for black relocation. He reminded Jefferson that he had once confided in him a plan to convert slaves to share-croppers. Paine thought this an excellent suggestion as long as it was done on the far reaches of the American frontier:

I recollect when in France that you spoke of a plan of making the Negroes tenants on a plantaion, that is, alotting each Negroe family a quantity of land for which they were to pay to the owner a certain quantity of produce. I think that Numbers of our free Negroes might be provided for in this manner in Louisana. The best way that occurs to me is for Congress to give them their passage to New Orleans, then for them to hire themselves out to the planters for one or two years; they would by this means learn plantation business, after which to place them on a tract of land as before mentioned. A great many good things may now be done; and I please myself with the Idea of suggesting my thoughts to you.[95]

Jefferson, apparently, didn't encourage further discussion of Paine's ideas for colonization and there the discussion ended. From this point on, Jefferson worked to reserve the western territories for whites alone, partly out of fear that a black population on the nation's frontier would render slavery insecure in the states bordering Louisiana. When America's secretary of state, Robert Livingston excitedly wrote to his fellow New Yorker, Rufus King, about his triumph in persuading Talleyrand to sell all of Louisiana in the spring of 1803, one reason for buying the entire territory was his fear that France may "have sent their black troops and upon any dispute have found a great occasion of slaughter in our southern slaves."[96]

Jefferson in his second inaugural speech in 1805 alluded to the importance of the west being white, "is it not better that the opposite bank of the Mississippi should be settled by our own brethren and children, than by strangers of another family?" The racial meaning of such language of brethren, strangers, and family was not lost on his fellow Americans who viewed the world through starkly racial categories.[97]

While receiving this steady current of appeals to free and colonize black Americans, Jefferson's own views of the issue broadened. Looking out from the president's desk, Jefferson no longer saw black settlement in the western territories as a desirable, or even achievable option. Like Britain, Jefferson thought it "very questionable, indeed, whether the Indians would sell; whether Spain would be willing to receive these people; and nearly certain that she would not alienate the sovereignty." But even if Spain could be induced to cede lands, would it be in America's interest to have a black nation on its border, or as Jefferson put it "… should we be willing to have such a colony in contact with us?"

In response to Monroe and the Virginia legislature, Jefferson emphasized the practical problems of securing territory from hostile or indifferent neighbors, but these were not his only concerns. Part of his deeper reluctance to endorse the idea of a western "receptacle" for Virginia's people of color was that a black colony would have been an obstacle to Jefferson's grand dream of white Americans marching across the continent and occupying these same lands.

[I]t is impossible not to look forward to distant times, when our rapid multiplication will expand itself beyond those limits, and cover the whole northern, if not the southern continent with a people speaking the same language, governed in similar forms and by similar laws. Nor can we contemplate with satisfaction either blot or mixture on that surface.

Heading off this "blot" on his vision of the west, Jefferson redirected the Virginians' attention to other possibilities. "The West Indies offer a more probable & practicable retreat for them. Inhabited already by a people of their own race & colour; climates congenial with their natural constitution." The most promising of all these islands was, of course, St. Domingo, "where the blacks are established into a sovereignty de facto, & have organised themselves under regular laws & government." Anticipating the argument that sending more black people to Haiti could be a danger to the safety of the United States because "these exiles might stimulate & conduct vindictive or predatory descents on our coasts, & facilitate concert with their brethren remaining here," Jefferson pointed out that the danger is slight, given America's "relative strength" that grows ever more disproportional. More importantly, the benefit of removing the black population offshore outweighed by far the dangers it might produce: such dangers are "over-weighed by the humanity of the measures proposed, & the advantages of disembarrassing ourselves of such dangerous characters." In the end, Jefferson remained an enthusiastic booster of Virginia's proposal for ethnic cleansing and promised to "execute their wishes with fidelity & zeal."[98]

Monroe and his colleagues in the Virginia House guarded their discussions of their expanded plan for mass black exile. When the day came to present Jefferson's letter to the legislature, spectators and reporters were ordered out of the gallery and the capitol lobby and the chamber doors were shut. Jefferson's towering authority in Virginia swayed the lawmakers and in their next resolution dropped the suggestion of dumping freed men and women in the west and thought instead to send them to the West Indies or Africa.[99]

Dutifully, Jefferson referred the Virginia legislature's request to his ambassador to England, Rufus King, to explore the possibility of joining the already established colony of Sierra Leone. Jefferson saw much potential in creating "one large colony" on the African coast:

> The consequences of permitting emancipations to become extensive, unless a condition of emigration be annexed to them, furnish also matter of solicitude to the legislature of Virginia, as you will percieve by their resolution inclosed to you. Altho provision for the settlement of emancipated negroes might perhaps be obtainable nearer home than Africa, yet it is desirable that we should be free to expatriate this description of people also to the colony of Sierra Leone, if considerations respecting either themselves or us should render it more expedient. I will pray you therefore to get the same permission extended to the reception of these as well as those first mentioned. nor will these be a selection of bad subjects; the emancipations for the most part being either of the whole slaves of the master, or of such individuals as have particularly deserved well. The latter is most frequent.[100]

Even after leaving office, Jefferson's dreams of colonizing American blacks somewhere far from the white republic remained strong. Like many of his fellow white patriots, Jefferson began to consider the newly independent nation of Haiti as a potential destination for African Americans. Jefferson's son-in-law, Thomas Mann Randolph, Jr., laid plans for manumitting and expatriating people in Virginia when he became governor of that state in 1820. Randolph extolled the advantage of shipping black Americans to an island, because it was "sufficiently near us to admit of emigration at little cost, and yet separated by a sufficient space of sea, to render the interdiction of return an effective measure."[101]

In the spring of 1819, a Philadelphia Quaker merchant named Robert J. Evans began publishing his plan for the gradual emancipation of slavery and asked the living founding fathers their opinions on the matter. He sent Adams, Jefferson, and Madison nearly identical letters begging them for their advice, "Knowing your devotedness to the best interests of your country I solicit the favour of such practical hints on the subject, as may have occurred to you in the course of your reflections ..."[102]

All three men graciously responded to Evans. Jefferson managed just a short note of apology for taking months to reply and not responding in full: "I am just now recovering from the third long & dangerous illness which I have had within the last 12. Months." Adams sympathized with Evans' desire for the "eventual total extirpation of Slavery" but noted that it would be inhumane to free slaves just to leave them at "the necessity of roberry plunder Assassanition and Massacre to preserve their Lives" and, moreover, that "the same humanity requires that we should not by any rash and violent measures expose the Lives and property of those of our fellow Citizens who are so unfortunate as to be surrounded with these fellow Creatures ... "[103] Likewise, Madison too cautioned that emancipation required the removal of blacks to some distant land, but also discussed the legal and constitutional dimensions of ending slavery.

In characteristic fashion, Madison considered Evans' plan in the light of what was constitutional. From that angle, the only scheme Madison thought possible was fully compensated voluntary manumission because the Constitution, recognizing that slaves were property, did not allow for anything else: "To be equitable & satisfactory, the consent of both the Master & the slave should be obtained. That of the Master will require a provision in the plan for compensating a loss of what he has held as property guaranteed by the laws, and recognized by the constitution."[104]

While Jefferson, Madison, and other national leaders expressed their hatred of slavery without aligning themselves with abolitionist societies, their fantasies of black banishment were not all that far from the thinking of organized white abolitionists. By the end of the eighteenth century, colonization advocates were not viewed as opponents or adversaries by the white activists working for manumission or gradual emancipation. Some of the most outspoken champions of banishing black Americans abroad like Mathew Carey and Elliott Cresson were both members of the Pennsylvania Abolition Society (PAS). Beverly Tomek brilliantly analyzes the relationship between these strands of antislavery thought and found that they shared more than they differed, bonding on their shared "desire to control the state's free black population and prepare them for productive citizenship." Even with the formation of the American Colonization Society (ACS) in 1817, usually considered the landmark of the divergence of white antislavery reformers into two distinct movements, Tomek found that the PAS and the ACS had friendly relations with each other and viewed each other as "fellow advocates for black liberty."[105]

Indeed, at the national convention of abolition societies the year before the founding of the ACS, this body, the American Convention for Promoting the Abolition of Slavery, drafted a memorial to Congress "to set apart a portion of the wide extended territory owned by the United States, for the colonization of legally emancipated blacks, or to adopt some other measure calculated, as well to prevent the injury of the mixture of too large a proportion of such persons amongst the white people of our country."[106]

Between that convention and its next, a rival and much larger organization formed whose stated purpose was "elevating, from a low and hopeless condition, a numerous and rapidly increasing race of men." Its plan of achieving such a goal was summed up in its name, the American Society for Colonizing the Free People of Color of the United States (later commonly known as the American Colonization Society, or ACS). Organized in the Davis Hotel in Washington on December 21, 1816, by a diverse collection of powerful men, including clergymen and evangelists, Philadelphia bankers, wealthy planters from Virginia, and members of Congress including Henry Clay of Kentucky and Daniel Webster of New Hampshire.[107]

Though many of its organizers had been outspoken critics of slavery and campaigners for gradual emancipation, Henry Clay warned at their first meeting that "it constituted no part of the object of this meeting to touch or agitate, in the slightest degree … or consider at all, any question of emancipation." Congressman John Randolph echoed Clay's admonition and added his hope that "this meeting does not in any wise affect the question of negro slavery, but, as far as it goes, must materially tend to secure the property of every master in the United States over his slaves." Randolph predicted, however, that by establishing a colony abroad to send freed people, "hundreds, nay thousands of citizens" would begin "manumitting their slaves."[108]

Clay and Randolph's addresses were the public face of the ACS and really the only formal declaration of its principles over its first year of organizing. At this moment the ACS was openly hostile to all forms of emancipation. Before the ACS had gathered for its first annual meeting at which antislavery activists managed to introduce "gradual emancipation" as a goal, the American Convention for Promoting the Abolition of Slavery held its annual convention and hammered out a statement regarding its upstart rival that was remarkably uncritical of these purposes. It began with the curiously generous observation that "many of the advocates of humanity, of the protectors of persons of colour, and of the holders of slaves, appear to have united their views, and concentrated their powers for the attainment of one great object," namely, some "project for colonization." It then praised the newly formed "society, whose declared purpose at present, is the colonizing of the free people of colour on the coast of Africa" as uniting "a large portion of talent and virtue" and having "dignified and benevolent intentions." Its only reservation, what the abolitionists called "their unqualified wish" was that "no plan of colonization -... go into effect, without an immutable pledge from the slave holding states of a just and wise system of gradual emancipation." A formal resolution expressing the sense of the convention was then passed stating that "the gradual and total emancipation of all persons of colour, and their literary and moral education, should precede their colonization."[109]

Clearly, colonization was an idea that continued to hold white abolitionists spellbound as they were unable to condemn an organization whose spokesperson had declared its goal of reinforcing slavery in southern states. In the meantime, a special meeting of the abolitionist societies was held in December of 1818 and colonization was at the top of the list of concerns, as its president's circular announcing the meeting described the "operations of a society established at the seat of government for accomplishing the design" for the "establishment of a colony of free people of colour" was viewed with "anxious interest by the friends of African emancipation." At the special meeting, the question was to be resolved, will "such colonization ... subserve the interests of humanity" or will it "have the effect to perpetuate slavery in the United States?"[110]

When the delegates assembled, they deemed the subject of colonization so important they made it the only one of six topics to be dealt with by the convention as a whole rather than being delegated to a committee. However, after some discussion and debate that was not recorded in their minutes they could not come to agreement and shunted the question to a committee. Over the next day the convention heard talks from two black leaders of Philadelphia, James Forten spoke on the "condition of the people of colour in Philadelphia" and Prince Saunders presented "an interesting memoir on the present state of Hayti." Neither man, nor any black person, was actually a delegate of the convention.

A couple of days later the committee on colonization reported that it had gathered all the relevant documents it could and could not "discern, in the constitution and proceedings of the American Colonization Society, or in the avowed sentiments of its members, any thing friendly to the abolition of slavery in the United States." The committee concluded that schemes of colonizing Africa were doomed to failure, not only for their expense, but due to the harsh realities of securing clear title to land, climate, and native resistance, and not least the opposition to being removed on the part of people of color themselves. Worse, any plan of colonization unconnected with the goal of abolition would only strengthen the bonds of human bondage.

The full convention then modified this report into a portion of their omnibus "Circular Address" to the public. Most of the committee's reservations were preserved, but the delegates left the door to colonization open a crack, stating that they remained "confirmed in the opinion" expressed in the petition they had sent to Congress two years earlier, that colonization was an "interesting subject" but that "the gradual and total emancipation of all persons of colour, and their literary and moral education, should precede their colonization."

At its next regular convention, the abolitionists backpedaled and embraced the idea of establishing a colony in the American west instead of Africa. The Kentucky Abolition Society got the ball rolling by submitting a statement that in light of the "degraded situation of the free coloured inhabitants of these United States, we cannot but have favourable views and thoughts of the subject of colonization, if a suitable colony could be obtained." Then the committee that established the agenda for the convention resolved for the convention to consider the "practicability of establishing settlements of free persons of colour, within the lands belonging to the United States, or of procuring for them a safe and liberal reception in the island of Hayti." A committee charged with investigating these possibilities concluded African colonization was both impractical, "hazardous" to the health and lives of the emigrants, and costly to the United States because "the labour of those who may be removed to Africa, would be entirely lost to this country." Haiti, however, was a possible destination and recommended corresponding with its president. The best option, they thought, was "removal into the interior of our country," preferably "west of the Missouri ... beyond the line of white settlement."

What is most revealing in their carefully detailed plan is that the white abolitionists were more concerned with the impact of a black colony within or neighboring the United States of America than the welfare of the black settlers. White abolitionism had always presumed that whatever "advancement," "elevation," or "uplifting" they accomplished for their black clients would never lead to their actual wielding of political power within the white republic. Even when criticizing the African colonization proposals of the ACS, the white abolitionists presumed that the colony would be administered and governed by white officers. Likewise, in imagining how a western black colony would develop their minds went to great lengths to formulate ways of blocking any self-government or political autonomy. They worried about the "danger of erecting an independent power, which might hereafter prove formidable; if not to the United States generally, at least to the white settlements in the neighborhood."

For the white abolitionists at this convention, white power and control was presumed and white political rule was non-negotiable. The most "alarming prospect" of the plan for a western black colony was "the foundation would be laid of an independent power, which can never be admitted, on equal terms, into our confederacy" because they feared it "may hereafter become a dangerous enemy, or a doubtful friend." After all, if their plan succeeds, "Is there reason to apprehend that they will become too numerous and too powerful for our general safety?" With nearly an audible sigh of relief, these white reformers found the solution to this dilemma right in front of them; the black colonists could be treated just as the Indians are, as they "are not contemplated as future members of our political confederacy" either.[111]

For all the talk of ridding the young republic of the presence of people of color, such patriot dreams never were realized. Partly this was due to the resistance of slaveholders whose riches depended on the forced labor of African Americans. More importantly, the patriots' failure to implement their programs of mass racial banishment was attributable to the resistance of African Americans themselves, who struck a powerful blow against this nascent white supremacy by finding ways to survive in a nation that didn't want them. But the vision of an all-white American republic proved powerful enough to refresh and reinvent new schemes of black expatriation, one after the other, for generations to come.

5

The Invention of White Citizenship

Thomas Jefferson did not want to be in Philadelphia that fateful summer of 1776. He arrived late to the session of Congress and had asked friends to finagle him a seat back in the Virginia Assembly where what he thought was the important business of drafting a state constitution was just beginning. As the summer heat and humidity descended on the city, Jefferson had the servants he owned drag a high-backed chair and his desk to the second floor of his rented townhouse where there was some breeze through the windows. It was at this desk, over the course of just a day or two, that Jefferson composed and recomposed at least three drafts of the Declaration of Independence.

At the time Jefferson couldn't know how this document would eventually come to be enshrined in the national imaginary as the nation's philosophical charter. Nevertheless, he reworked the text, striving for moral and logical clarity.

In Jefferson's first attempt at composing a list of the reasons that America was breaking away from King George and the English empire, he made the following charge: that King George had abandoned his duty to protect Americans "by inciting insurrections of our fellow subjects with the allurements of forfeiture & confiscation." Sometime after, Jefferson reconsidered his first draft and scratched out the word "subject" and wrote above it a word rarely used in political speech at the time. A word that must have sounded arcane and crimped for the heavy work it was being drafted to do. Jefferson replaced the word "subject" with "citizen," a small change with huge, even epochal, implications. By substituting "citizen" for "subject" Jefferson signaled a fundamental shift in the philosophy of the relationship between people and their government.

American revolutionaries cast off the notion of subjecthood, of dependence and protection, for a theory of government in which people established representative government to uphold their collective interests. Government was thereby not organically rooted in place, nor to a particular group of people. Instead of recognizing preexisting subjects, the state now constructed citizens. American revolutionaries reconstructed their society based on this new concept, citizenship, that operated to distinguish between two fundamental social groups: those eligible for representation, equal rights and the equal protection of the laws, and those excluded from them, indeed from civic life itself.[1]

THE COLOR OF SUBJECTHOOD

Prior to the Revolution, American colonial jurists, like lawyers throughout the British empire, based their understanding of the technical relationship between their government and its people on the case that settled the extent and rightfulness of the reign of King James I at the dawn of the seventeenth century. Robert Colville was born in Scotland in 1603, the same year that King of Scots James VI assumed the throne of England as King James I, thereby uniting the two warring kingdoms in his royal person. For the infant Robert Calvin, this union raised the question of whether he was entitled to the protection of the laws of England, rather than those of Scotland, a question that determined his ability to inherit lands in Haggerston and Bishopsgate in England. Relatives attempting to dispossess wee Robert from his freeholds argued in court that he was an alien and therefore not entitled to sue them in an English court.[2]

Lord Chief Justice Edward Coke was one of fourteen justices involved in rendering a decision in *Calvin's Case* (Robert's last name was broken on the English wheel into Calvin) but published a commentary on the case that would be read for centuries. Coke reported that the justices reached back to ancient feudal precedents and combined them with notions of "natural allegiance" derived from the God-given mutual obligations of king and subject to assert that Calvin (nee Colville) was by right of birth able to enjoy the full rights of all

180

other English subjects.[3] At the heart of his decision which contained more than the usual share of obiter dictum and rambling commentary, Sir Coke thundered that all people born within the realm of the monarch were his natural subjects, entitled to the protection of his laws and owing the sovereign their allegiance in turn. Thereby, Coke elevated the idea of subjecthood to an inviolable principle of natural law. It mirrored the natural bond between a parent and child and did not require positive law for its existence.

American patriots were acutely aware of these principles as they repeatedly cited *Calvin's Case* in defense of their claim to owe loyalty only to the King, not to Parliament (which conveniently rendered Parliament incompetent to legislate over their own colonies). Virginia's charter predated Coke's ruling in *Calvin's Case* but the same principle was declared in the charter issued by King James I in 1606 that granted Virginians the right to "have and enjoy all Liberties, Franchises, and Immunities ... to all Intents and Purposes, as if they had been abiding and born, within this our Realm of England."[4]

The words "citizen" and "citizenship" certainly existed prior to 1776, but they were not used to define the fundamental character of the people of a nation. Blackstone, the great codifier of the English common law, in his *Commentaries*, rarely employed the term "citizen" and then used it only in its classic sense to refer to persons having certain legal privileges or disabilities as a result of living in towns and cities.[5] Rather, aristocratic governmental systems rested on a concept of subjecthood which differed from the idea of citizenship because it was a social compact not among subjects but between subjects and their sovereign. While the patriots' idea of "We the People" is one that can be shaped and trimmed by limiting who counts as a person, monarchy's idea of the subject tied people, land, and state into a single complicated relationship of dependence. A monarch was the ruler of all her or his subjects and while this did not impose a burden of treating all subjects equally, it did encompass all in the exchange of loyalty for protection.

William Blackstone, whose legal commentaries were the most influential source of legal precedent in the English-speaking world, described birthright as the foundation of subjecthood. In his tenth chapter, titled "Of the People, Whether Aliens, Denizens, or Natives," Blackstone begins by observing that the foundation of the law was the membership of all those born in the realm to the body politic.

> The first and most obvious division of the people is into aliens and natural-born subjects. Natural-born subjects are such as are born within the dominions of the crown of England; that is, within the ligeance, or as it is generally called, the allegiance of the king: and aliens, such as are born out of it. Allegiance is the tie, or ligamen, which binds the subject to the king, in return for that protection which the king affords the subject.

This tie works in both directions and is perpetual. Subjects owe the sovereign their loyalty and "therefore the prince is always under a constant tie to protect his natural-born subjects, at all times and in all countries, for this reason their allegiance due to him is equally universal and permanent."[6]

While all natural-born persons were included under the broad umbrella of subjecthood, this did not imply any equality of their standing or condition:

> This allegiance then, both express and implied, is the duty of all the king's subjects ... Their rights are also distinguishable by the same criterions of time and locality; natural-born subjects having a great variety of rights, which they acquire by being born within the king's ligeance, and can never forfeit by any distance of place or time, but only by their own misbehaviour ...[7]

Nevertheless, there are clear indications that the concept of shared subjecthood provided more opportunity for the non-observance of color than citizenship later would. When Bishop Fleetwood proclaimed it an Anglican duty to spread Christianity among "negroes," he based this obligation on the spiritual unity of mankind. But in 1711, the Bishop, operating within a framework of subjecthood, also expressed a conception of the worldly political order that lacked a clear boundary between white and black:

... the souls for which I am now pleading, have a more particular claim to our regard, as they are truly a part of our own nation, and live under the same government with ourselves, and which is more, contribute much by their labor to the support of our government, and the increase of the trade and wealth of this kingdom.[8]

In 1790, royal lawyers advised that a British settlement in Honduras could not exclude "free persons of colour" from the customary rights and privileges of British subjects.[9]

English law excluded no natural-born persons from membership in subjecthood. Blackstone celebrates this fact, noting that even the "children of aliens, born here in England, are, generally speaking, natural-born subjects, and entitled to all the privileges of such. In which the constitution of France differs from ours; for there, by their jus albinatus, if a child be born of foreign parents, it is an alien." Blackstone also observes that disfavored groups, such as Jews, if born on English soil, are equally embraced within the category of subjecthood.[10] Before any protest movements against English rule occurred, Boston's James Otis, Jr., who would a few years later begin penning protests against British policy toward America, expressed confidently that "black and white, born here, are free born British subjects, and entitled to all the essential civil rights of such."[11]

American notions of citizenship did not evolve from earlier legal understandings of subjecthood but were a rupture of its basic principles. There was, however, one earlier analog of the exclusive and selective nature of citizenship in the British experience, and that was the status of being recognized as a "freeman" by the governing council of a large city. Only certain residents of London were recognized as "freemen" and these had to "claim the freedom of the city" in a proscribed manner. While birth was one manner by which a person could claim the freedom of the city, others could do so by completing an apprenticeship and by being accepted into membership of the governing guild of their trade. Moreover, a process that would later be akin to naturalization was open to those foreign tradesmen and merchants who could afford to find citizens willing to post various bonds on their behalf and pay steep fees for their privileges.[12]

Crucially, these procedures for gaining urban citizenship did not recognize citizenship as a right, but a status conferred or withheld by the governing authority of the city. Ideas of city citizenship were then carried to America in the seventeenth century, appearing first in New York City after its capture from the Dutch.

Such distinctions between the ancient and universal status of "subject" and the new exclusive rights of "citizens" were formally recognized in the Treaty of Paris that ended the war for independence in 1783. In describing the shared rights of navigation on the Mississippi, that document stated, "The navigation of the river Mississippi.. shall forever remain free and open to the subjects of Great Britain and the citizens of the United States."[13]

Importantly, the boundaries of royal subjecthood were not drawn as narrowly as that of republican citizenship. English subjecthood was seen as a continuum of degrees, rather than something possessed or not. When legislating that free "negro women" were to be subject to the tax on tithables unlike white women, Virginia's lawmakers still recognized that they existed within the scope of English subjectness: "It is declared by this grand assembly that negro women, though permitted enjoy their freedome yet ought not in all respects to be admitted to a full fruition of the exemptions and impunities of the English, and are still lyable to payment of taxes."[14]

North Carolina was the first colony to specifically declare that "no negro, mullatto or Indians shall be capable of voting for members of the Assembly" in 1715. At the suggestion of the Crown council, the colony repealed this provision twenty years later. In 1743 North Carolina legislators enacted a law that specifically enfranchised all "freemen," though in 1760 that colony's assembly revoked it again.

Voting on the part of people of color was known to have occurred in South Carolina, as petitions were sent to London complaining that "free Negroes were received and taken for as good Electors as the best freeholders in the province." Not until 1716 did South Carolina restrict the franchise to "white" freemen.[15]

Similarly, the rights of men to participate in Virginia's elections was not limited by color prior to 1723. Criteria for voting for Burgesses was established in 1654 and included none that defined rights by color or ancestry: "That all house keepers whether freeholders, lease holders, or other wise tenants, shall onely be capeable to elect Burgesses …" Though women, boys under twenty-one, and convicts were formally disenfranchised in 1699, "negroes and mulattoes" were not.[16]

When Virginia's lawmakers moved to restrict suffrage in their session from 1722 to 1723 and declared that "no free negro, mulatto, or Indian whatsoever shall have any vote at … any election whatsoever," this effort to disenfranchise on the basis of race caused disagreement and consternation in London. Initially the counselor of the Commissioners of Trade and Plantations, Richard West (later Lord Chancellor of Ireland), rejected the bill, writing: "I cannot see why one freeman should be used worse than another, merely on account of his complexion … It cannot be right to strip all free persons of a black complexion from those rights which are so justly valuable to any freeman." Though approving the bill, London's colonial council directed that a letter be sent to the governor of Virginia requiring him to detail "what effect the act … by which free negroes are deprived of voting in all elections had." Though the commissioners ultimately approved the law, their attorney's objections reveal a widespread understanding that free subjects of the Crown could be any color. Though they lost the right to participate in elections, Virginia's free black men remained within the category of "freeman."[17] At London's urging, this article too was repealed around 1733, only to be reenacted by Virginians in 1762, about the same time Georgia enacted its first racial bar to voting. Most powerfully, the Undersecretary of State for the American Department throughout the Revolutionary era, William Knox, argued that slaves were royal subjects and therefore had a right to an "impartial dispensation of the laws." Knox was not alone in high levels of government to hold such views.[18]

Two things stand out from this brief history of voting: first, that during the colonial period it was felt necessary to specifically name those racial and ethnic groups to be excluded from political participation and that these exclusions were frowned upon by royal authority. Such exclusions vastly expanded in the post-Revolutionary era in the opposite manner—rather than specifying what rights "negroes and mullattos" were to be denied, patriots simply defined citizenship as being reserved to "whites" or "freemen," the latter term employed loosely as a synonym for white.

States founded on the principle of subjecthood, like England, viewed the extent of their territories as defining the people they governed. Sovereign, soil, and subjects were all organically connected. Americans' novel idea of citizenship severed these connections and treated each of these things as unique individual elements. America's state structure was unique and revolutionary in that it claimed the right to select which inhabitants of its territory were part of the body politic, leaving others outside the social compact and the protection of the law and the benefits of government.[19]

That American patriots drew the line between citizens and mere inhabitants on the fictional basis of race may have been arbitrary, but it wasn't unprecedented. In fact, the earliest democracy, that of Athens in the classical period of Greece, also defined citizenship based on a mythic identity. Ancient Athenians innovated the idea of a citizen as they instituted democratic government and simultaneously invented justifications for restricting participation in it. Aristotle understood "citizen" to mean those men qualified to deliberate and vote in the affairs of the city-state. It mattered not to these learned philosophers that the criterion for citizenship rested on a fairytale. Only those who could trace their lineage far back into the shrouded past, back to the first day when the original men emerged bodily from Athenian ground, were citizens.[20]

It was only in the American Revolution's first days, in the flush of independence and the yawning future that seemed overfull of possibility, that patriots faced the question of whether black people had a place in the new republic. After George Mason submitted his draft of a Bill of Rights to the Virginia Assembly in 1776, its universal language provoked concern that it could empower and protect slaves and other non-whites, as well as proper white Virginians. Edmund Randolph, the governor at the time, later recalled what transpired:

The declaration in the first article in the bill of rights, that all men are by nature equally free and independent, was opposed by Robert Carter Nicholas, as being the forerunner of pretext or civil convulsion. It was answered, perhaps with too great an indifference to futurity, and not without inconsistency, that with arms in our hands, asserting the general rights of man, we ought not to be too nice and too much restricted in the delineation of them; but that slaves not being constituent members of our society could never pretend to any benefit from such a maxim.[21]

Aside from this kerfuffle, rarely did the architects of American government ever discuss the relationship of African Americans to citizenship. This curious omission is not due to any gap in historical sources but is itself powerful evidence of the founders' utter exclusion of people of color from the nation they constructed. Patriot leaders never debated whether free black people were citizens under either national or state law because most agreed that they were not. Like their conventional free interchange of the terms "negro" and "slave," the founders never assumed that Americans with African ancestry were encompassed within the phrase "We the People."

When the Virginia Assembly undertook the task of defining just what a "citizen" was it simply built its definition upon the bedrock of whiteness. One has only to read the order of qualifications the committee charged with revising the basic legal code established for what a citizen was to appreciate that whiteness was of paramount importance. "Be it enacted ... that all white persons born within the territory of this commonwealth ... shall be deemed citizens of this commonwealth ... And all others ... shall be deemed aliens." All subsequent clauses setting forth various requirements for citizenship rested upon this foundation of "all white persons" by beginning, "and all"; "and all who have resided therein two years" or "and all who shall hereafter migrate into the same" or "and all infants wheresoever born." Additionally, comity and equality with the citizens of other states was also expressed in terms of whiteness: "The free white inhabitants of every of the states, parties to the American confederation ... shall be entitled to all rights, privileges, and immunities of free citizens in this commonwealth ..."[22]

Jefferson's wording as it was recorded in the Committee of Revisions report was adopted largely without alteration in 1779. (In later revisions of 1783 and 1786, the word "white" was changed to "free.") However, growing anger at the English for providing sanctuary to the fugitive slaves and their families who had served under their colors during the war led to it being revised in 1783 to bar naturalization of any American who bore arms against the republic (including those who owned shares in pirate ships acting under British letters of marque) and, tellingly, any person who served on the "Board of Refugee Commissioners at New-York," the English agency that assisted freed people to leave the United States. Its language would reappear again in the first act of the new U.S. Congress seated under the Constitution, the Naturalization Act of 1790 that limited citizenship to "any Alien being a free white person, who shall have resided within the limits and under the jurisdiction of the United States for the term of two years."

After Virginia declared that only white persons born on its soil were citizens, South Carolina followed suit and specified that only "free white persons" were citizens in 1784. The following year Georgia specified that only "free white persons" could be naturalized.[23] Likewise, Georgia specifically bestowed the elective franchise to "white" men when they drafted their first constitution in 1777. Thus, the three states with the highest proportion of African American population, Virginia, Georgia, and South Carolina, where three-fifths of all African Americans lived, felt the need to specifically include the word "white" in their definitions of citizenship. Did this mean that those other eleven states meant to include their black inhabitants within the compass of citizenship?

Some historians have pointed to the absence of specific racial exclusions to voting, like Georgia's, in other southern states' legal codes as evidence of a powerful spirit of equality. But the absence of laws prohibiting people of color from certain civil rights was not evidence that patriots were willing to construct a multiracial electorate, but quite the opposite. In many of these places, patriots were so certain in their assumptions that non-whites had no place in their republic that they felt little need to codify this in law. In 1795, a Pennsylvania court ruled that the state's statutes, though they did not qualify voters by race or color, nevertheless debarred blacks from voting.[24] During Virginia's constitutional debates in 1835, several delegates explained the absence of a specific racial bar to voting in that state by noting that blacks were never considered citizens and therefore weren't thought to be eligible.[25]

As conceived by American patriots, citizenship was the reversal of the relationship between the state and the people. Pennsylvania's "An act obliging the male white inhabitants of this state to give assurances of allegiance to the same and for other purposes therein mentioned," passed in June of 1777, and revived and expanded in 1778, redefined the state from having an ancient and unalterable position of protector to its people into one that chose the people it governed. Pennsylvania's law claimed to be a "test of allegiance" but it actually operated as a means of winnowing who qualified as a citizen because only "male white inhabitants" were allowed to demonstrate their allegiance. Soon in its official correspondence, the state legislature would refer to "the citizens and inhabitants of Pennsylvania," marking a clear distinction between those included in the protection, privileges, and representation of the state and those who were not.[26]

Famed Virginia jurist, patriot, and law professor, St. George Tucker, codified these new notions of citizenship by arguing that a state's ability to pick and choose its citizens was consistent with natural rights: "But have not men when they enter into a state of society, a right to admit, or exclude any description of persons, as they think proper?" Tucker continued,

> If it be true, as Mr. Jefferson seems to suppose, that the Africans are really an inferior race of mankind, will not sound policy advise their exclusion from a society in which they have not yet been admitted to participate in civil rights; and even to guard against such admission, at any future period, since it may eventually depreciate the whole national character?[27]

Congress in December of 1775 resolved to evenly distribute the burden of raising $3 million to prepare for war among all the colonies. It issued a letter to all the colonial congresses and committees to compute a census of their population. The way this mandate was phrased reveals the degree to which their understanding of society was divided between white colonists and black others. "That the proportion or quota of each respective Colony be determined according to the number of inhabitants of all ages, including negroes and mulattoes in each Colony." Likewise in March of 1776 as the patriot militias built fortifications to defend New York City, the New York Provincial Congress ordered the patriot committees of Kings County to assist Col. Ward in their construction so as "thereby turning out for the service as many of the male inhabitants, negroes included, every day to work at the fortifications in that county." The presumption was, that unless specifically included, "negroes and mulattoes" would not be presumed to count as "inhabitants" of the colony.

When the Virginia Assembly gathered in Williamsburg on May 6, 1776, to ratify a constitution for the new state government, they began their charter with a list of grievances against King George, including the charge that he has been "prompting our negroes to rise in arms among us, those very negroes whom, by an inhuman use of his negative, he hath refused us permission to exclude by law." Tellingly, these patriots did not use the term "slave" or some euphemism of slave, but wrote "negroes," indicating that the fact of being black placed a person outside the realm of the new state and its proper circle of citizenry.[28]

America's first great historian of its Revolution, David Ramsay, who had the benefit of watching events unfold from his seat in the Continental Congress, understood the tectonic shift that redefining Americans from being subjects to being citizens represented. In 1789, Ramsay observed that this switch "radically changed" the "principle of government" and noted that this was not just a semantic change but that the "difference is immense." Ramsay thought this immense difference arose from subjects being "under the power of another," namely, their sovereign, while citizens were "a mass of free people" who were sovereign in themselves.

Ramsay went on to explain that a citizen was someone who surrendered a portion of his natural sovereignty to the nation, to what he called the "collective," but in doing so reserved the right to participate in his government, either by making laws or voting for his representative who legislated. Such was the function of all the oath-taking conducted during the war for independence as British subjects publicly renounced their former allegiance and adopted the character of an American citizen. Naturally, all children born under the new American republic were citizens by birthright as they were never subjects of England. Others could be naturalized according to the procedures specified by state and federal laws.

However, there was one glaring exception to these principles, which Ramsay made a feeble attempt to justify. Ramsay observed that "Negroes are inhabitants, but not citizens." Following the practice of the founding generation that equated slaves and "negroes," Ramsay did not justify the exclusion of black people from American citizenship on the basis of their being property or servants but argued that as a class "negroes" were simply "residents" of the nation. He then attempted to clarify what was clearly a distinction without any difference but race:

The precise difference may be thus stated: The citizen of a free state is so united to it as to possess an individual's proportion of the common sovereignty; but he who is no more than an inhabitant, or resident, has no farther connection with the state in which he resides, than such as gives him security for his person and property, agreeably to fixed laws, without any participation in its government.

By this formulation, African Americans were merely "inhabitants" and "residents" of the United States because they could not be "united" to the nation. Ramsay does not need to explain to his patriot readers why black people could not be included within the "collective sovereignty." Ultimately his argument, like all discussions of citizenship in this era, could stand inconsistent and incomplete because of the pervasive white assumption that blacks were a dangerous presence within the body politic, ever ready to be the tools of foreign manipulation, political corruption, or the agents of insurrection.[29]

CEREMONIES OF CITIZENSHIP

Defining the people as a community of white citizens was not limited to southern states with their large, enslaved populations. Northern states too treated people of color as unsuitable and ineligible for full citizenship but did so without enshrining these restrictions in statute law. In New England, states relied on the informal but powerful enforcement of community standards to govern color bars to the rights of citizenship.[30] One example of how this worked can be glimpsed in the ceremonies organized to "test" loyalty to the newly formed nation.

In the spring of 1776, the Continental Congress ordered every Committee of Safety across the colonies to "immediately to cause all Persons to be disarmed, within their Respective Colonies, who are notoriously disaffected to the cause of AMERICA, or who have not associated, and refuse to associate, to defend by ARMs, the United Colonies, against the Hostile attempts of the British Fleets." It was left up to individual states to organize these oath-taking and loyalty tests and some states used them as a public display of who were deemed citizens and who were not.

The Committee of Safety and the General Assembly of New Hampshire set about to uphold this directive by administering an "Association Test" which consisted of requiring people to publicly sign or affirm a declaration that "they solemnly engaged and promised that they would, to the utmost of their power and at the risk of their Lives and Fortunes, with ARMs, oppose the Hostile Proceedings of the British Fleets and Armies, against the United American Colonies." Such oaths, however, were not to be given to everyone, only "all Males above Twenty one years of age (Lunaticks, Idiots, and Negroes excepted)."

There are few records of how this "Association Test" was conducted throughout New Hampshire, though it is known that it was administered to 8972 white men, 773 of whom refused to sign and were presumably disarmed. By enacting such a public ceremony of loyalty, the soon-to-be independent revolutionary state was laying the basis for the modern and exclusive notion of citizenship. In this new understanding of the relationship between the government and the governed, the state was able to choose who among its people it would represent and then require of those a visible sign and affirmation of loyalty in order to qualify for its protection.[31]

Pennsylvania, long considered a beacon of antislavery activism, plunged headlong into establishing their state as a government of whites alone. In addition to defining citizens as white men, in 1777 the state assembly gave all white men one year to participate and enact their citizenship by taking an oath of loyalty to the state. The president of the state Executive Council, Thomas Wharton, ordered that state militia commanders "make Returns of all the Male white inhabitants" in their district.[32] Pennsylvania's 1777 militia law described militia service as "the indispensable duty of the freemen of this commonwealth" and then restricted this duty to white men.[33]

Across the state groups of white men gathered to publicly demonstrate their membership in the new state and thereby physically display to all who was and who was not entitled to the state's protection and equal rights. These ceremonies of speech were powerful actions that cemented the sense of belonging among white men as well as powerfully excluding people of color who could only watch from the fringes of the crowd.

When the window for oath-taking expired, Pennsylvania's lawmakers worried that some white men may have been unable to participate: "divers faithful subjects of this state and well affected to the liberty and independence thereof, from sickness, absence, want of information, and other unavoidable causes have omitted to take the said oath within the limited times" and extended the deadline.

That this new construction of national identity differed fundamentally from those that came before was demonstrated by the treatment of a group of Philadelphia Quakers and others who "uniformly manifested in their general character & conversation, a disposition highly inimical to the cause of America." As the city was then barricading and preparing to be invaded, the state's leaders, in consultation with Congress, decided to exile those who refused to take the pledge of allegiance out of the state. Several dozen were locked into the Mason's Lodge to await transportation to a permanent detention camp and ultimate exile.

One of those locked up was Reverend Coombe, an assistant Episcopalian minister in Philadelphia. A letter appealing for his parole from a group of his church wardens shows that not all Americans understood the true nature of this new concept of citizenship. In asking for Reverend Coombe's release, the petitioners appealed to his "undoubted Birth Right, to an hearing in the Face of his Country" which was precisely the antiquated construction of national belonging being upended by citizenship.[34]

Like Coombe and his Church of England supporters, the Quakers confined to the Mason's Lodge also seemed to have missed the point of all this oath-taking and swearing allegiance. In their "Remonstrance and Protest" the Mason's Lodge prisoners wrote that their confinement was "… contrary to the inherent Rights of mankind" and that the American revolutionaries "condemn us to Banishment unheard." From their protests, the Quakers seemed to think that the oaths were something outside of citizenship, which was inalienable: "The Tests you proposed we were by no Law bound to subscribe, and notwithstanding our refusing them, we are still justly & lawfully entitled to all the Rights of Citizenship, of which you are attempting to deprive us."[35]

Worried about the political fallout if "these people mean to publish and raise a ferment," Pennsylvania's leaders wondered if "perhaps be worth consideration whether the removal of those persons might not be relaxed as to such as would yet swear, or affirm, allegiance to this state." Pennsylvania's Executive Council relented and allowed that "such of the persons now confined in the lodge as shall take & subscribe an oath, or affirmation, of allegiance … shall be discharged." Rather than requiring them to "swear" an oath, the council allowed them to state that they "affirm" it.[36]

As the Quakers discovered, oath-taking could be a means of excluding groups from citizenship and thereby the right of permanent residency, but they were not the primary targets of this discrimination. Rather, oath-taking requirements were generally used to exclude people of color from the privileges and rights of citizenship in the Keystone State. Ultimately Pennsylvania passed six laws requiring public declarations of loyalty to the revolutionary government in order to vote or hold any office or serve on juries in the state. Each of these acts specified that only "male white inhabitants" be allowed to stand and declare their allegiance, thereby relegating free African Americans to an inferior and uncertain status.[37]

NATIONAL RACIAL CITIZENSHIP

One year after declaring independence, the Continental Congress began debating the structure of a national government but in doing so the question of the place of black people in the new nation remained undebated and assumed. Legal scholars and historians have generally viewed the Articles of Confederation as an expression of the patriots' universal ideals of equality because most of its drafters kept the word "white" out of those clauses relating to citizenship. The word "white" appears only once in this charter of national government, in Article Nine that enumerated the powers of the Congress. In a clause granting the power to requisition recruits for the army from each state, Congress may "make requisitions from each state for its quota, in proportion to the number of white inhabitants in such state."

Congress' inclusion of the racial qualifier "white" has been the focus of scholarly analysis of the racial meanings and intentions behind the patriots' first attempt at forming a national government. Scholars have pointed to the victory of those congressmen who kept the word "white" out of a key section of the articles, the "privileges and immunities" clause, as clear evidence that at America's birth the ideals of universal citizenship were championed. But this myopic focus on one fleeting scuffle over the word "white" has misdirected attention from the overarching structure of citizenship and national belonging that the founders didn't debate because its elements were assumed by all. This larger structure was anchored in the shared belief that states had the right to include or exclude anyone they wished from the polity of citizenship. Founders did not grant any powers to define citizenship to the confederal government because any such power could ultimately limit the ability of states to discriminate in their choice of who was to enjoy the blessings of American liberty.

Clearly, preserving state autonomy over citizenship was vitally important to the founders as the articles did not grant Congress the power to set standards for naturalization. Nor did the articles specify

195

any qualifications for members of their own body, for judges, or even for the leader of the federal government, the president.

In crafting this blueprint of federal power, founders were careful not to use the word "citizen" which does not appear in the articles' original draft. Rather, the term "inhabitant" is employed six times while the term "natives," which was not then used in the sense of Native American ("Indians" being instead widely used), was used once. By the time the final amended version of the articles was approved, the word citizen was smuggled in once, the term "native" was dropped, and the word "inhabitant" was used four times. "Inhabitant" was clearly preferred because it did not imply any particular citizenship status, thus preserving states the power to define who was or wasn't a citizen. By employing these two different terms, one that invokes a state-defined status and one that is intentionally ambiguous, the drafters were able to preserve the widest possible degree of state autonomy.[38]

The racial meaning inherent in the founders' clever manipulation of the terms "inhabitant" and "citizen" is most evident in their phrasing of the responsibility each state has to treat those from another state in the same manner as they treat people of their own state. Such reciprocal responsibility extending the "privileges and immunities" of a state's own citizens to citizens of another state was not included in the original articles but was introduced along with six other amendments a year later.

The original competing drafts of the privileges and immunities clause, written by Connecticut jurist Richard Law and Virginia's Richard Henry Lee, varied slightly in who was entitled to equal treatment in other states. Lee said the "Citizens of every State" are entitled to the rights of "natural born free Citizens" of their host state, while Law said the "free Inhabitants" of each state "Paupers, Vagabonds and fugitives excepted" were entitled to the rights of "free Citizens" of the state they visited. Law's wording would have allowed for the non-citizen inhabitants of one state, such as black folks, to be treated as the "free Citizens" of the state they entered. In other words, the Yankee's legal wording allowed for northern states to discriminate against their black communities by not recognizing them as citizens, but protect them from abuse when they travelled south. Notably, both men's full amendments also provided a guarantee that enslavers could travel to states that did not recognize slavery without putting their human property in jeopardy.[39]

South Carolina's representatives moved to alter Law's draft by inserting the word "white" between Law's wording of "free" and "inhabitants." They did so because they recognized that free black people were legally the *inhabitants* of many states, not their citizens. Thus, this move was in part a recognition that citizenship was, actually, naturally white, and the "paupers, vagabonds and fugitives" exception provided plenty of opportunity for any state to deny a transient black person its protection of the law.[40]

Another controversy over the status of black Americans arose when New Jersey complained that the Ninth Article of the Confederation allocated each state's quota for contributing to the army based on whites alone. In arguing against the word white, New Jersey's representatives walked a tightrope over the abyss of racial equality, declaring that all people whatever the "colour of their complexion" were bound to support their country but at the same time they recognized that it was sometimes "improper, for special local reasons, to admit them in arms for the defence of the nation." Determined not to stand for racial equality, but to make their argument on the grounds of expediency, these northerners instead accepted the "necessity or expediency to justify the refusal of liberty in certain circumstances to persons of a particular colour, we think it unequal to reckon nothing upon such in this case." New Jersey's proposed changes failed miserably, six to three, with one state split. When Pennsylvania moved simply to strike the word "white" the vote shifted to seven to three.[41]

New Jersey's congressmen apparently were untroubled by the contradiction at the heart of their implied theory of government. The argument that all "inhabitants" of a state had a duty to defend it was a vestige of the ancient contract of subjecthood in which there was reciprocity between duties and rights. But one curious consequence of Americans discarding the aristocratic idea of subjecthood and replacing it with a new concept of racialized citizenship was severing rights from duties. Ancient subjecthood was consistent by universally including all those born of national soil and pairing obligations with protection, or duties and rights. Americans jettisoned the idea of universality for a citizenship that was bestowed or withheld by the state, thus demanding duties but denying their associated rights for those excluded.

While the purging of the word "white" from the articles seemed to be a step away from a racially based nationhood, it was actually a careful reservation of the power to define citizenship to states alone. Representatives from states most dependent on enslaved labor and with the highest black populations through this long period of debate and revision had come to realize that their prerogatives were best protected by simply preserving their own sovereign power to define the boundaries and qualifications of citizenship. Their elegant solution was to leave all power to define who enjoyed the protection of the state in the hands of the states.

Perhaps more revealing than the wording of the Articles of Confederation was the discourse involved in its creation that drew stark distinctions between whites who were eligible to be full-fledged members of the republic and people of color who were not. According to Jefferson's notes of the meeting, Maryland's Samuel Chase, who would go on to serve on the first Supreme Court, objected to federal taxes being levied in proportion to the population in each state. Chase "observed that negroes are property, and as such cannot be distinguished from the lands or personalities held in those states where there are few slaves." Chase's observation about the nature of slavery is notable, not only because of its casual definition of slaves as chattels, but for its equation of "negroes" and slaves. As his argument unfolded, Chase's general understanding that "negroes" had no place in an independent America became even more clear. "Negroes in fact should not be considered as members of the state more than cattle & that they have no more interest in it."[42]

As notable as was Chase's blunt assertion that black people had no place in a free America, the lack of objection to it by the other patriot legislators is just as telling. John Adams spoke next and did not rise to argue that "negroes" were in fact members of the body politic, but only that whether a man was called free or slave, they produced just as much wealth and therefore should be counted whatever term was used to describe them. Adams changed the terminology of the debate from "whites" and "negroes" to "slaves" and "freemen," a shift that drew an equivalency between whiteness and freedom, and blackness and slavery, an equivalency that implied a similar relationship between whiteness and citizenship, just as Chase had done more explicitly.

Virginia's Benjamin Harrison followed this logic by suggesting a compromise of counting slaves as one-half a freeman because "slaves did not do so much work."

Pennsylvania's James Wilson urged counting slaves because not doing so would give southern states all the benefits of slavery while shifting all the costs to the North. Wilson's prime reason was that slaves "increase the burthen of defence, which would of course fall so much the heavier on the Northern." Here Wilson was echoing the long-repeated assertion that slaves raised defense costs because they were prone not only to rebellion, but to treason by being easily seduced to the service of invading foreign armies. Wilson, generally viewed by historians of the Revolution as a foe of slavery, nevertheless offered an additional reason that even more clearly drew the boundaries of American belonging so as to exclude people of color, according to Jefferson's notes as saying, "slaves occupy the places of freemen and eat their food" (or according to John Adams' notes, arguing that "Slaves prevent freemen cultivating a Country"). Either way, people of color were assumed to be obstacles in the way of the development of a white man's country.[43]

South Carolinian Thomas Lynch interjected a warning, "If it is debated, whether their Slaves are their Property, there is an End of the Confederation."

Ben Franklin, as conflicted about the future of black people in America as any patriot, said sagely, "Slaves rather weaken than strengthen the State, and there is therefore some difference between them and Sheep. Sheep will never make any Insurrections." While cleverer than most, Franklin's quip still equated people of color with sheep and agreed that they "weaken" the government. In the end, at this time, the Congress voted to include "negroes and slaves" in the census used to allocate taxes and the balloting broke neatly along lines of North and South.

But this issue continued to flare up repeatedly over the life of the Continental Congress. In February of 1783, the Congress was still debating how to levy taxes and treat slaves and James Madison's notes of this recurrence of the debate repeats the revealing terminology of racial exclusion undergirding patriots' conception of American citizenship. Madison scrawled on his papers, "Mr. Wolcot ... declares his opinion that the confederation ought to be amended by substituting numbers of inhabitants as the rule; admits the difference between freemen & blacks; and suggests a compromise by including in the numeration such blacks only as were within 16 & 60 years of age."[44] Here again, "freemen" are white and "blacks" are objects to be negotiated and compromised for their good.

South Carolina went in the other direction, moving that the word "white" be squeezed before "free inhabitants" in Article Four's guarantee of state reciprocity: "the free inhabitants of each of these States ... shall be entitled to all privileges and immunities of free citizens in the several States." And appending to the tail end of this phrase: "according to the law of such states respectively for the government of their own free white inhabitants." Both proposals lost eight to two.[45]

BLACK SOLDIERS VS. CITIZENSHIP

Soon after the fighting began in the spring of 1775, the Massachusetts Committee of Safety considered the question of recruiting slaves into the army and resolved against it. On July 8, 1775, the Committee of Safety and Committee of Supplies of the Massachusetts Provincial Congress instructed the officers of all Massachusetts' regiments to exclude black recruits. "You are not to enlist any deserter from the ministerial army, nor any stroller, negro, or vagabond, or person suspected of being an enemy to the liberty of America, nor any under eighteen years of age" because, as they wrote, "the cause is the best that can engage men of courage and principle to take up arms, so it is expected that none but such will be accepted by the recruiting officer." These orders were sent to the Council of War for their approval.[46] Revealingly, the patriot leaders explained the source of their prejudice:

> Resolved, That it is the opinion of this committee, as the contest now between Great Britain and the colonies respects the liberties and privileges of the latter, which the colonies are determined to maintain, that the admission of any persons, as soldiers, into the army now raising, but only such as are freemen, will be inconsistent with the principles that are to be supported, and reflect dishonor on this colony, and that no slaves be admitted into this army upon any consideration whatever.[47]

Yankee patriots could have justified excluding enslaved people from their militia on many grounds. They could have, as others did at the time, noted that slaves were naturally unreliable as they would always be alert to an opportunity to escape. Or they could have fallen back on widely circulated racist tropes of black cowardice and criminality. Instead, they argued that fighting alongside men who were their property jeopardized their own "liberties and privileges," their "principles," and their honor. This was an admission that slavery was contradictory to the liberty that they fought for but at that same time it was a proclamation that their intention was to fight the war in a manner that did not alter the status of slaves. Rather, slaves, and by extension people of color in general, were exterior to the issue at stake, outside the realm of liberty and also the community of citizens.

Despite the famed actions of Peter Salem, the black hero of the Battle of Bunker Hill, the Massachusetts' Assembly, when it legislated to raise additional regiments to fight the British regulars in the summer of 1776, stipulated that "... no Negroes are to be admitted into said Regiments."[48]

Such sentiments were a reversal of long-standing practices in New England. Massachusetts had a long history of recruiting blacks and slaves into the army prior to the Revolution. Reverend Belknap, one of the early chroniclers of the colonies' history, reported, "I am inclined to think that slaves were more numerous before 1763, than at that time, because, in the two preceeding wars, many of them enlisted either into the army or on board vessels of war, with a view to procure their freedom."[49]

American patriots' refusal to recruit black troops was a departure from both English practices throughout the empire and their own colonial precedents. Afro-British soldiers fought in often all-black regiments regularly during the wars with Spain and France. Soldiers of color were numerous in the invasions of Cartagena in 1741, Martinique in 1759, and Havana in 1762.[50]

The widespread inclusion of black soldiers into English regiments was well known to American patriots. Patriot pamphleteer James Otis in his stirring 1764 attack on Parliament, *The Rights of the British Colonies Asserted and Proved*, contrasted the recruitment of soldiers in his own Massachusetts with the planters of the sugar islands in the wars with France and Spain:

> In the late war, the northern colonies not only rais'd their full quota of men, but they went even beyond their ability ... in the common, national, cause ... while the sugar colonies, have born little or no share in it: They indeed sent a company or two of Negroes and Molattoes, if this be worth mentioning, to the sieges of Gaudaloupe, Martineco and the Havanna.

Otis then goes into some detail, contrasting the character of the American people to the "mongrel mixture" found in the French islands:

> The climate and business of these islands is by nature much better adapted to Frenchmen and to Negroes, than to Britons. The labour of slaves, black or white, will be ever cheaper than that of freemen, because that of the individuals among the former, will never be worth so much as with the latter ...[51]

A generation earlier South Carolinians, feeling threatened from the Spanish in Florida, the indigenous peoples to the west, and the French from the sea, enacted a law requiring that all male slaves between sixteen and sixty be reported to local militia commanders and to be mustered into colonial regiments when an alarm was declared. The preamble to this law justified its scope by the common practices of the day:

> Whereas it hath been found by Experience, that several Negroes and other Slaves, have in Times of War behaved themselves with great Faithfulness and Courage, in repelling the Attacks of his Majesty's Enemies in their Descents on the Province, and have thereby demonstrated, that Trust and Confidence may in some Instances be reposed in them ...[52]

South Carolina military captains were permitted to fill out their companies to a total of one-third enslaved soldiers. The owners of enslaved soldiers were required to provide them with a gun, twenty rounds of shot, a hatchet, six flints and a full powder horn. In compensation for their service, enslaved soldiers' owners were paid 7s 6d per day of their enlistment and a compensation of their full market value upon their death.

Well before Virginia's governor, Lord Dunmore, issued his proclamation offering to provide sanctuary and freedom to any enslaved people who joined his army, patriots recognized the importance of black soldiers in the English army. In July 1775, James Warren wrote to John Adams with an estimate of the relative numbers of forces in the field:

> The General Estimation of our Army is about 16 or 17000, Ten of which are at Cambridge &c. the remainder at Roxbury. We cant with any Certainty determine the Numbers of the Enemy, we suppose from the Best Grounds we have that when the York Troops Arrive which are daily Expected they will amount to 9,000 at least, perhaps more Including the Black and White Negroes Engaged in their Service in Boston.[53]

Washington's Council of War made a similar assessment, highlighting the role of black redcoats:

1. A Question was proposed & considered viz. What is the Numbr of the Enemy in & near Boston, including the Troops formerly & lately arrived, & there expected, the Tories who may take Arms, such Sailors as may be spared from the Fleet & the Negroes— Upon which it was agreed, that from the best Intelligence the Force on the Side of the Enemy now amounts to about Eleven thousand, five hundred Men.[54]

Washington described the "embarrassed" State of the Army in his report to the Congress that Adams would have heard or read in July of 1775. Washington's worries over his inability to secure recruits in Massachusetts and "the Number of Men to fall short ... & below all Expectation" were compounded by his fear that more soldiers may be hard to find. "I entertain some Doubts whether the Number required can be raised," Washington confided, an opinion based on "the Number of Boys, Deserters, & Negroes which have been listed in the Troops of this Province ..."[55]

While serving the Continental Congress in Philadelphia in the fall of 1775, John Adams expressed concern that "there are great Numbers of Boys, Old Men, and Negroes" in the Massachusetts' regiments. Such troops, Adams wrote, "are unsuitable for the service, and therefore that the Continent is paying for a much greater Number of Men, than are fit for Action or any Service." He demanded that Major-General Heath inform him if there are more "Negroes in the [Massachusetts] service" than in "those of Connecticutt, Rhode Island and New Hampshire, or even among the Rifle Men.[56]

General Heath provided Adams with his estimate of the numbers of black soldiers in the army:

There are in the Massachusetts Regiments Some few Lads and Old men, and in Several Regiments, Some Negroes. Such is also the Case with the Regiments from the Other Colonies, Rhode Island has a Number of Negroes and Indians, Connecticut has fewer Negroes but a number of Indians. The New Hampshire Regiments have less of Both.[57]

Adams' racial prejudices were common in patriot ranks. Alexander Greydon, a Pennsylvanian who led a unit of the Continentals in 1776, had little good to say about the quality of the men being sent to him from the North, those "miserably constituted bands from New England." The best among them, a regiment from Marblehead, was spoiled by the presence of black men. "Even in this regiment, there were a number of negroes, which, to persons unaccustomed to such associations, had a disagreeable, degrading effect." Likewise, another Pennsylvanian, Captain Persifor Frazer, thought New England troops "the strangest mixture of Negroes, Indians and whites." Pennsylvania did not allow free black men to enlist in its militias and had very few black men in the units it sent to serve in the national army.[58]

Knowing the importance of black fighters and workers to the enemy's power, there was some urgency for the patriotic forces to respond in kind. But on October 8, 1775, at the Council of War, a group of three congressional delegates, Benjamin Franklin, Thomas Lynch, and Benjamin Harrison, with Washington presiding over the meeting, discussed the question of whether "it will be adviseable to re-inlist any Negroes in the new Army—or whether there be a Distinction between such as are Slaves & those who are free?" The Congressmen's minutes read: "7. Ought not Negroes to be excluded from the new Inlistment especially such as are Slaves? All were thought improper by the Council of Officers?" Washington and his council unanimously agreed to "reject all Slaves, & by a great Majority to reject Negroes altogether."

Washington formalized the ban on all black recruits in his General Orders issued October 31, 1775.[59]

New Jersey's delegate to the Continental Congress kept a diary of these heady days of 1775 and recounted how the subject of expelling all soldiers of African descent from the army divided the body in its first week of business. Edward Rutledge moved that the Congress order General Washington to "discharge all the Negroes as well Slaves as Freemen in his Army." Rutledge was "strongly supported by many of the Southern Delegates but so powerfully opposed that he lost the point."[60]

On November 12, 1775, Washington issued more general orders regarding enlistments and made clear again, "Neither Negroes, Boys unable to bare Arms, nor old men unfit to endure the fatigues of the campaign, are to be inlisted ..."[61] While Washington did not record his reasons for barring "Negroes" from his army, his thinking likely reflected that of his fellow general Philip Schuyler who did expose his rationale. General Schuyler wrote to Major General William Heath about the declining state of the Continental Army in the summer of 1777 from his fortifications at Saratoga saying that he doubted he could hold as his militia had dwindled away. General Schuyler was particularly bitter about having had to retreat from Ticonderoga for lack of provisions and support from the states and complained that "applications made for troops to the States" were met with a "shameful tardiness." Schuyler described many of the reinforcements he received as "boys, aged men, and negroes, who disgrace our arms." The general asked, "Is it consistent with the Sons of Freedom to trust their all to be defended by slaves?"[62]

Samuel Adams also complained to General Heath that he had heard from Schuyler of the sorry state of the army with its "negroes, and aged men not fit for the field or indeed any other service."[63] Heath wrote back agreeing, but noting that the "negroes" he had seen "were generally able bodied, but for my own part I must confess I am never pleased to see them mixed with white men."[64]

Years later, the war all but over, Heath was still complaining to General Washington that states were sending him soldiers of color. "Dear General ... the day before yesterday about eighty recruits arrived from Massachusetts, in general very indifferent; a number of them negroes, some old men & boys." A week later he wrote again, praising the recruits from Rhode Island, "as fine fellows as ever I saw, neither old countrymen, negroes, old men or boys among them."[65]

General Schuyler's rhetorical question, "Is it consistent with the Sons of Freedom to trust their all to be defended by slaves?" exposes a deeper connection between the reluctance of patriots to recruit people of color and their new ideas of citizenship. Schuyler here was not saying that black men were unfit to fight, as were boys and aged men, but they alone were beneath the *trust* of "Sons of Freedom." As he explained, "Every effort of the enemy would be in vain if our exertions equaled our abilities; if our virtue was not sinking under that infamous venality which pervades throughout and threatens us with ruin. America cannot be subdued by a foreign force: but her own corruption may bring on a fatal catastrophe."[66] Slaves, or perhaps slavery itself, were the agents of "venality" and "corruption." Either way, the slave was the embodiment of slavery and therefore by nature or condition untrustworthy, debasing, and unsuited to a free republic.

The heart of the issue of black soldiers was not simply the complicating one of recruiting men who were the property of other men. All those involved in discussions around the question of the recruitment of black soldiers employed a deliberate slipperiness of terminology, sliding freely between "negro," "slave," and "black." Rather, the main problem was derivative of the way patriots had constructed citizenship as a status that needed to be earned and proven, a quotient of virtue that had to be demonstrated in some tangible fashion. There was no clearer way of proving one's republican devotion and civic virtue than service in the nation's cause. Commission to carry arms in the nation's army was therefore not just a matter of defending against America's enemies, it was an act that defined the nation by marking one doorway of citizenship. The logic of republican citizenship demanded the formation of a white army.

Washington and Congress only lowered its color bar to recruitment under extreme pressure from the British army that was avidly recruiting men and women who fled their patriot masters. On December 2, 1775, John Hancock informed Washington that Virginia's Governor Dunmore had proclaimed freedom to slaves who fled their patriot masters and served his royal army.

This Day we Receiv'd Advice from Northampton in Virginia, that Lord Dunmore has Erected his Standard at Norfolk, proclaim'd Martial Law, invited the Negroes to Join him, and offer'd them Freedom, for which purpose he has issued a proclamation from on board the Ship where he Resides; and that Two Counties have been Obliged to Submitt to him—However I hope such measures are taking as will speedily and effectually Repel His Violences and secure the peace & safety of that Colony."[67]

General Washington recognized immediately the dire threat posed by Dunmore's Proclamation and wrote to his aide-de-camp, Joseph Reed (who had taken leave to serve in the Continental Congress), that Dunmore had to be immediately conquered.

If the Virginians are wise, that Arch Traitor to the Rights of Humanity, Lord Dunmore, should be instantly crushd, if it takes the force of the whole Colony to do it. otherwise, like a snow Ball in rolling, his army will get size—some through Fear—some through promises—and some from Inclination joining his Standard—But that which renders the measure indispensably necessary, is, the Negros; for if he gets formidable, numbers of [them] will be tempted to join who will be affraid to do it without.[68]

Washington repeated these sentiments to Richard Henry Lee a fortnight later, though with the greater urgency of demanding Dunmore dead or alive.

Lord Dunmores Letters to General Howe &ca wch very fortunately fell into my hands, & Inclosed by me to Congress, will let you pretty fully into his diabolical Schemes—If my Dear Sir that Man is not crushed before Spring, he will become the most formidable Enemy America has—his strength will Increase as a Snow ball by Rolling; and faster, if some expedient cannot be hit upon to convince the Slaves and Servants of the Impotency of His designs … nothing less than depriving him of life or liberty will secure peace to Virginia; as motives of Resentment actuates his conduct to a degree equal to the total destruction of the Colony.[69]

When Washington finally reversed himself on December 30, 1775, he did so out of necessity, not out of a change of heart. Washington wrote: "As the General is informed, that Numbers of Free Negroes are desirous of inlisting, he gives leave to the recruiting Officers, to entertain them, and promises to lay the matter before the Congress, who he doubts not will approve of it."[70] A day later he wrote to Hancock explaining why he did so—to prevent the black soldiers from switching sides:

> it has been represented to me that the free negroes who have Served in this Army, are very much disatisfied at being discarded—as it is to be apprehended, that they may Seek employ in the ministerial Army—I have presumed to depart from the Resolution respecting them, & have given Licence for their being enlisted, if this is disapproved of by Congress, I will put a Stop to it.[71]

It was just two weeks later, January 16, 1776, that Congress included in its funding bill for the army, a provision allowing Washington to reenlist free black soldiers, though the congressmen were careful not to open this door any further, resolving "that the free negroes who have served faithfully in the army at Cambridge, may be re-inlisted therein, but no others." Virginia's legislature made it a crime for any army recruiting officer to enroll a black soldier without him producing a valid certificate of freedom.[72]

The reluctant acceptance of free black men into the Continental Army highlighted the general understanding that they were not considered present or even future citizens of the republic they fought for. In late 1777, Brigadier General Thomas Nelson expressed to his commander, General Washington, his regret that black men were being kept in the army because they could not earn the rewards of citizenship.

> … the last plan adopted by the [Virginia] Assembly, of drafting in the manner there proposd, has been productive of much evil and little good, many of those drafted being unfit for service, or free Mulattoes and Negroes, as it was generally thought they could best be spar'd. This I think exceedingly unjust, because these poor Wretches, after they have risk'd their lives, & perhaps may have contributed to save America, will not be entitled to the priviledges of Freemen.[73]

General Nelson was not unsympathetic to the plight of the black recruits. He bemoaned that Virginia was unable to reward these "poor Wretches" for their service, for unlike slaves who were recruited with the faint promise of manumission, free black soldiers had little to fight for because, as Nelson phrased it, they "will not be entitled to the priviledges of Freemen." Nelson was not arguing that citizenship and the protection of the laws should be extended to black veterans, only that they should not have been drafted in the first place. Like most all other patriots, Nelson seemed to see the exclusion of African Americans from citizenship as a given, as something approaching common sense.[74]

Later in the war, Washington again moved to restrict at least the appearance that black men were a fighting force in the rebel army. Rhode Island's recruitment of an all-black regiment troubled the Continental Army's commanders, even though their greatest need was for more soldiers. Washington wrote to Major General William Heath on June 29, 1780, with instructions to dismantle the regiment officered by Colonel Greene that was composed mostly of black recruits once it arrived at their camp at Ramapough, New Jersey. Washington explained to Heath that he needed to "level the Regiments ... by dividing the Blacks in such a manner between the two [regiments], as to abolish the name and appearance of a Black Corps."[75]

There was no consistency among the states in their attitude toward black recruitment. Some states where antislavery sentiment seemed to be most apparent were least eager to court black recruits. New Hampshire and Massachusetts specifically barred African Americans from serving in their militias in 1776. New Hampshire rethought its color bar and allowed black enlistments the following year, but Massachusetts did not relent until the spring of 1778. New York barred black recruits from its military companies until pressured by the success of Iroquois fighters in 1779 and later offered land bounties to slave-owners who enlisted their slaves. New Jersey followed suit and allowed enslaved substitutes in 1777. Strikingly, Pennsylvania, that seeming hotbed of abolition, never permitted African Americans into its military companies.[76]

Whatever little tolerance had existed among American commanders for black troops evaporated quickly after the war. Secretary of War Henry Knox issued orders in April 1788 that "Neither Negroes Molatoes or Indians are to be recruited" by states to satisfy their quotas of soldiers.[77] Many states followed suit and barred people of color from their militias. Massachusetts' first general militia act of 1785 barred "negroes, Indians, and mulattoes" from even support duties and when the following year Governor Bowdoin was hard pressed to assembly enough eastern militias to confront the Shay's rebels marching from the west, he turned down an offer from Boston's black community to shoulder arms.[78]

Compared with the numbers of soldiers of color who fought in British or French regiments, relatively few African Americans served in patriot armies. Approximately 500 black men applied for military pensions under the federal pension acts of 1818 or 1832. Many enslaved black Americans enlisted against their will, forced to serve in the place of their white masters. Virginia allowed one enslaved recruit to count for two white draftees. Others were enticed to join by the prospect of earning the money needed to purchase family members out of slavery. For example, Jacob Francis agreed to serve a Continental enlistment for $75 and used the money to purchase his wife's liberty.[79]

Tellingly, when Samuel Bell filled out his application for a war pension in 1832, he made a point to note that the war he fought in was not for his own benefit. Bell said he enlisted because "he believed it his duty to assist his countrymen in arms in achievement of their independence." In that word "their" is a heaviness of meaning; a recognition that what independence had won was a country that did not choose to represent people of color.[80]

ANGLO-SAXON ELEMENTS OF CITIZENSHIP

Patriot leaders at first barred and then resisted black recruitment not only out of a desire to preserve the connection between citizenship and service, but also because buried within the patriot conception of citizenship was a belief that rights descended organically from ancestors to descendants. This belief was founded on several premises, some of them formal ideas forged in the fires of protest and others that were bits of folk wisdom and Anglo-chauvinism that pervaded British culture. For all their worship at the temple of Enlightenment reason and science, even the most rigorous patriot thinkers were not immune from the ethnocentric frameworks that informed their identity first as "British Subjects" and then as "American Citizens."

These structures of belief need to be pieced together into an incomplete mosaic from bits and shards of anecdote and comment, because eighteenth-century English writers thought them so obvious that they needed no commentary or explication. Start, for example, with this scene: At the end of the first week of business of the inaugural Continental Congress many of the delegates adjourned to the City Tavern at three in the afternoon. Later the ceremonial rounds of toasts were raised, thirty-two in all, among which were "May every American hand down to posterity pure and untainted the liberty he has derived from his ancestors." To which another delegate immediately offered, "May no man enjoy freedom who has not spirit to defend it."[81]

These tankards of ale were lifted in agreement with a raft of unstated but common understandings. These men believed that their English heritage bequeathed to them a unique entitlement to liberty and representation because their forefathers had fought and won them, just as they were prepared to expand this horizon of freedom and pass it down to their posterity. This is, in fact, a complicated mishmash of beliefs, some derived from English history, some related to a folk understanding of blood inheritance, even an ancient notion of right of conquest. None of these beliefs and common-sense understandings were ever teased apart from the others in this tangle but were expressed in concert when they bubbled to the surface.

Historians have portrayed the Americans' incessant complaints of their "slavery" at the hands of the Crown as being driven by the revolution in political thought sweeping Europe in the eighteenth century. While it is certainly true that the rhetoric of the time was fully saturated in ideas of natural rights and equality, the rise of liberal ideology does fully explain why white colonists freely saw themselves as suffering the bonds of slavery but not the men and women who they fastened in actual chains.

To a surprising degree patriot political and legal thought rested on a premise that rights were conferred by ethnic birth and lineage. White American colonists felt a deep connection to the mythical sources of their liberties, which was not simply that they were born as men, but that they were born as Englishmen. English people saw themselves as being distinct for the liberties they enjoyed, and these freedoms had passed into a legacy that raised Britons above the other nations of the world. James Otis, in making his case for American rights in the empire, claimed its whiteness lent support to its claims: "Divers of these colonies ... are well settled, not as the common people of England foolishly imagine, with a compound mongrel mixture of English, Indian and Negro, but with freeborn British white subjects, whose loyalty has never yet been suspected."[82]

Another poignant example is to be found in the wording in the petition of the First Continental Congress to Parliament in 1774 asking for relief from the "Intolerable Acts" that had closed Boston harbor and expanded powers of royal officials. These patriots praised God for having been "born the heirs of freedom, and ever enjoyed our right under the auspices of your Royal ancestors ..."

Similarly, there is this clause from Congress' 1776 Declaration of Rights: "Be not surprised, therefore, that we, who are descended from the same common ancestors; that we, whose forefathers participated in all the rights, the liberties, and the constitution you so justly boast of, and who have carefully conveyed the same fair inheritance to us ..."[83]

Such rights of Englishmen were birthrights not simply derived from nationhood, but from the struggles, sacrifices, and victories of their ancestors. For them the past was not simply a story of origins, but an accumulation of rights that were fought for and won. Patriot pamphleteer Levi Hart expressed the idea well when he wrote:

To assert and maintain the cause of Liberty, is far from being peculiar to the British colonies in North-America, at the present day; our venerable Ancestors fought and found it in this western world, and at no small expense of their treasure and blood, purchased it for, and conveyed it down to us.[84]

Hart's understanding of rights was that they were a sort of ethnic property, purchased and then inherited by each succeeding generation.

When Georgians drew up their resolutions against the stamp taxes in 1769, they prefaced their petition with claims of ethnic rights.

We, the inhabitants of Georgia, finding ourselves reduced to greatest distress and the most abject condition by the operation of several acts by the British Legislature, by means whereof, our property is arbitrarily wrested from us contrary to the true spirit of our constitution, and the repeatedly confirmed birthright of every Briton ...[85]

Protesting the closure of the Port of Boston, a crowd gathered at a liberty pole erected outside of Tondee's Tavern, in July of 1774 and agreed to a list of resolutions including one condemning "the act for the abolishing the charter of Massachusetts Bay [because it] tends to the subversion of the American rights; for besides those general liberties, the original settlers brought over with them as their birthright, particular immunities were granted by such charter ..."[86]

South Carolina patriot William Drayton regularly issued protests against the British Crown from his judicial bench. One of Drayton's protests against Parliament revealed the degree to which patriot leaders rooted their ideas of liberty in the soil of ethnic belonging and organic ancestry rather than in the air of Enlightenment philosophy. The first of Drayton's declarations reads: "That the Americans being descended from the same ancestors with the people of England, and owing fealty to the same Crown, are therefore equally with them, entitled to the common law of England, formed by their common ancestors ..."[87]

Drayton underscored the ethnic foundations of his conception of rights when he turned to consideration of the Quebec Act and its preservation of French law in the newly acquired territory that was "a despotism over English people." Drayton complained that Parliament acted "to deprive subjects of English blood of the right of representation in the colony of Quebec."[88] While the Crown may treat the conquered Papists however it wished, English settlers there cannot be stripped of those ancient rights they inherited from their forebears. Drayton then expressed this idea with a more direct natural metaphor—a literal family tree. Drayton denounced the tyranny of Parliament first with the analogy of blood, "... I cannot be of opinion that ... the crown can legally acquire a power over subjects of English blood, destructive of those rights which are peculiar to the blood—rights evidenced by Magna Charta, and defended by the fundamental laws of England," but then, carried off with thoughts of English blood, Drayton waxed poetically about tree sap:

[Parliament] cannot legally form any laws heterogeneous to the purposes of their own creation and existence. As the sap peculiar to a tree must necessarily and invariably produce similar effect in a plant of the same species, as far as the infancy of the latter will admit, being at the same time incapable of producing in it any appearance heterogeneous to the parent tree; so the American plant, being animated with the same species of sap with the English tree, the plant, however connected with the parent tree, cannot naturally produce any heterogeneous appearance.[89]

Many white Americans saw themselves as a particular people, sharing a lineage as being "born the heirs of freedom." This identity was not shared with that portion of benighted humanity who sprung from "a land of slavery." Such a division of mankind between the heirs of freedom and the heirs of slavery served to make sense of their world in which free whites could protest the slavery of being restricted from the fullest profitable uses of their own slaves. When white Americans employed rhetoric of natural rights, they often tied it to a concept of birthright, by which they may have meant that certain rights descended through national bloodlines, through the heroic achievements of past generations, and were inherited by them, not by every human being.[90]

Virginia patriot John Randolph's vision of the American future described in his 1774 pamphlet, *Considerations on the Present State of Virginia*, was all-white. It was one that replaced the "Savages, the original rude, though warlike Possessors, of the western Part of our Globe" with white settlers.

> Population is the principal Thing required to give Prosperity to America. It is a great Country, and wants nothing to bring it to Perfection but Numbers. Will the inhabitants of *England, Ireland,* or *Scotland,* leave their native Country, and migrate into one which, on their Entrance, instead of a friendly and quiet Welcome, will present to them a Scene of Confusion and Disorder?

Americans, Randolph wrote, had a unique racial heritage to preserve.

> The *Americans* are descended from the Loins of *Britons*, and therefore may, with Propriety, be called the Children, and *England* the Mother of them. We are not only allied by Blood, but are still farther united, by the extensive Trade and Commerce carried on between us. Our Manners are similar; our Religion, and Language, the same.[91]

The same year another anonymous patriot writing under the pseudonym "Backsettler" sounded the same idea:

> The Colonies were peopled and planted by British Subjects; at their Departure for America, they brought with them their Allegiance, an indelible Mark of their Subjection to a British Parliament; a Token of Obedience derived from their Ancestors, who were coeval with the Origin of the State, which no Change of Climate, no after-Act of theirs, could erase from their Persons.[92]

Legal scholar Jeremy Bierbach detected passages in the Declaration of Independence that expressed a narrow ethnocentric identity in stark contrast with the universalism of Thomas Jefferson's preamble to that document. Deeper in the Declaration the American patriots appealed to "our Brittish brethren" and pointed to "their native justice and magnanimity." American revolutionaries expressed their own identity as having "ties of our common kindred" and "consanguinity," the later term literally referencing their common blood.[93]

Such ethnocentric language of blood ties and ancient rights appears repeatedly in Jefferson's rhetoric. Jefferson drafted instructions for Virginia's delegates to the first Continental Congress. Jefferson detailed what he saw as the main issues facing Americans and shocked many with what was essentially a bold assertion that America was already by rights independent of England. Just as "their Saxon ancestors" had left the "woods in the north of Europe" and conquered England, Americans had emigrated from England and conquered America. Saxons would never have thought themselves subject to their old country, they would never have thought "to bow down the sovereignty of their state before such visionary pretensions." Ensuring that the purpose of this analogy was not lost, Jefferson added, "no circumstance has occurred to distinguish materially the British from the Saxon emigration." America, Jefferson argued, was already independent and whatever military aid and protection the empire had lent to the colonies did not convey obligation or ownership to England.[94]

New York's John Jay, in arguing for adoption of the Constitution in *Federalist* #2, described America as a nation united by common ancestry.

> With equal pleasure I have as often taken notice that Providence has been pleased to give this one connected country to one united people—a people descended from the same ancestors, speaking the same language, professing the same religion, attached to the same principles of government, very similar in their manners and customs, and who, by their joint counsels, arms, and efforts, fighting side by side throughout a long and bloody war, have nobly established general Liberty and Independence.

Jay's conception of shared heritage must have been one rooted in a concept of racial grouping rather than national differences as his progenitors were all French and Dutch. When Jay and his fellow founders spoke of common ancestors and being one people, they meant that America was one unified nation of white people.[95]

The deeply racialized nature of the American concept of citizenship was revealed in the patriots' treatment of the feared and reviled Crown mercenaries, the legendary Hessian soldiers. Tens of thousands of soldiers from the German principality of Hesse-Cassel were rented to the English and fought to suppress the American rebellion. Jefferson and the Continental Congress dipped their quill into a particularly venomous ink of their Declaration of Independence to denounce King George for "transporting large Armies of foreign Mercenaries to compleat the works of death, desolation and tyranny, already begun with circumstances of Cruelty & perfidy scarcely paralleled in the most barbarous ages, and totally unworthy of the Head of a civilized nation." Lurid stories of Hessian cruelty filled patriotic newspapers that called these mercenaries a "barbarous savage race" and "man monsters." Hessians were considered especially vicious because they supposedly had no loyalty to anything other than booty and plunder.[96]

But captured Hessians were quickly embraced as American citizens. Early in the war, the Congress charged a committee "to devise a plan for encouraging the Hessians, and other foreigners, employed by the King of Great Britain ... to quit that iniquitous service." A week later the committee recommended that any Hessians who defected should be "invested with the rights, privileges and immunities of natives" and given 50 acres of western lands.[97]

Even groups of Hessians who never voluntarily left the King's service, who were captured in battle, were welcomed into the American fold. The musical band of a Hessian unit captured at the Battle of Trenton was invited to attend a dinner in honor of the first anniversary of the declaration of American independence in Philadelphia and "heightened the festivity with some performances suited to the joyous occasion." After each toast artillery was discharged and the Hessian musicians played.[98] In 1779, the *Hartford Courant* reported the glad news that the former commander of the Hessian troops in America, General Reideful, had purchased a Virginia plantation and "has taken the oath of allegiance to the United States."[99]

Citizenship was the most important innovation of American political theory because it resolved the contradiction between the ideals of natural rights and equality and the fear of people of color. Citizenship, by providing a logic for excluding people from rights and equality, squared the circle of patriots' conflicting desires for both an end to slavery and a white republic.

Edmund Jenings, one of John Adams' longest and most prolific correspondents of his lifetime, offered his definition of republicanism to Adams soon after Yorktown. It captured much of the essence of the patriots' dilemma and their evolving solution to it. Jennings wrote "all Citizens in Republicks are Equal, altho one may have more Negroes than Another ... "[100]

The limits of racial citizenship were drawn by the views of revolutionary America's most active critics of slavery. Even white abolitionists recognized that there was no such thing as a national citizenship for people of color. The Philadelphia Society for the Abolition of Slavery understood that the new Constitution did not extend citizenship to any people of color:

When you reflect that the laws of some of the States acknowlege all the Blacks as free Citizens & that the population of some others is in the proportion of only eight white inhabitants to nine blacks, you will see the extreme difficulty of making a general arrangement at this moment, that should carry the American principles on this subject to their full lengths.[101]

When on rare occasions some white person suggested citizenship, or even openly wondered if such rights might extend to others regardless of their ancestry or complexion, their concerns were ignored or overruled. Once or twice, the protests of these dissenters prompted political leaders to soften their exclusionary language, but they never succeeded in extracting the guarantee of colorblind citizenship they sought.

One of these rare occasions happened when the state of Massachusetts crafted its first constitution in 1779. The Massachusetts' General Assembly debated excluding people of color from voting during a single session of their six months of work on the document. On that day, February 12, 1778, a tiny but vocal group attempted to strike the words "Indians, Negroes and Molattoes" from the list of those excluded from voting. They were outvoted eighty-three to eighteen.

When the draft constitution was then sent out to the towns for ratification, only a small minority listed among their objections the disenfranchisement of people of color. Out of the hundreds of towns that reported their votes, the great majority did not list their reasons for voting either for or against. Only twenty-seven towns detailed their reasons for rejecting the proposed state constitution. Nine of these listed prejudice against color or nation (among other reasons) and two others objected to Article V's voting restrictions without mentioning race. This means that at least a clear majority of towns, and possibly twice as many, didn't think the exclusion of African Americans and Indians was objectionable compared with those who did.[102]

Several of the town meetings that criticized the exclusion of black men from voting were motivated by concern for the well-being of the white community. Several towns feared that oppressing black neighbors would incur God's wrath—the same white frame through which much of the early white abolitionist movement viewed slavery. The town of Hardwick resolved that holding people in slavery "is very Contrary to the Law of god and Liberty that we Profess, and as we view this among many other, to be a Crying Sin which has Brought Gods Judgments upon the Land"[103] Likewise, voters in the town of Sutton thought that excluding "negroes … even tho they are free and men of property" would be "manifestly ading to the already acumulated Load of guilt lying upon the Land" and this would result in the *bringing or incurring more Wrath upon us*.[104] Boothbay also feared that their collective sin for slavery "reflects dishonour and Endangers the curse of heaven on our public Struggles for our own rights."[105]

That first draft constitution was overwhelmingly rejected by the people of Massachusetts, mostly because it unfairly favored the wealthier eastern districts over the poor western ones in allocating seats in the legislature. Bruised by this clamorous failure, Bay State leaders turned the drafting of a revised charter to an all-star patriot drafting committee consisting of John Adams and his cousin

Samuel, along with James Bowdoin, president of the state's Executive Council and chair of the Constitutional Convention. John Adams was reported to have had the primary role and the draft was viewed by others as his handiwork. John Adams' version was accepted by the other two men "with one or two trifling erasures."

Adams' revised constitution sidestepped the issue of black citizenship and rights by defining the right to vote vaguely: "All elections ought to be free; and all the [male] inhabitants of this commonwealth, having sufficient qualifications, have an equal right to elect officers, and to be elected, for public employments." Exactly who had "sufficient qualifications" was left to the legislature to decide.[106]

While free black men in Massachusetts were not specifically excluded from participating in elections, the general assumption on the part of leading patriots was that it was not proper for them to vote. After an election in that state in 1794, James Madison complained to Thomas Jefferson about the methods of his political opponents: "Ames is said to owe his success to the votes of negroes and British sailors smuggled under a very lax mode of conducting the election there." Madison's lumping of British sailors, a group clearly outside the boundaries of American citizenship, with "negroes" speaks volumes about how American citizenship was grounded in whiteness.[107]

Neither Massachusetts, New Hampshire, Pennsylvania, nor Vermont ever specifically introduced color bars to their voting statutes, but few, if any, free black men were allowed to enter the polls in the early republic. This was revealed when a group of black Bostonians, including the prominent spokesperson for the African American community, Paul Cuffe, protested their exclusion from citizenship in 1780:

Having no vote or Influence in the Election of those that Tax us yet many of our Colour (as is well known) have Cherfully Entered the field of Battle in the defense of the Common Cause and that (as we conceive) against a similar Exertion of Power (in Regard to taxation) too well known to need a Recital in this place ..."[108]

A similar petition on the part of black residents of Dartmouth, New Hampshire, echoed the old cries of white patriots. They wrote that they were "deprived of Injoying the Profits of our Labour or the advantage of Inheriting Estates from our Parents as our Neighbors the white people" and "are Taxed both in our Polls and that small Pittance of Estate which through much hard Labour & Industry we have got together" but "we are not allowed the Privilege of freemen of the State having no vote or Influence in the Election of those that tax us."[109] Decades later, Chief Justice Roger Taney gleefully noted in his Dred Scott decision that while New England laws did not specify race as a condition of voting, none of these states allowed black people to vote except, perhaps, in Maine.

Pennsylvania's disenfranchisement of African Americans was spotty and uneven across the state. Records indicate that at one time or another black voters were able to cast ballots in at least seven counties. In some of those places where they were firmly excluded, as in the city of Philadelphia itself, it was accomplished by not assessing them on the tax rolls which constituted being registered to vote. Benjamin Rush took an equivocal position on such exclusion of blacks from voting, commenting on Pennsylvania's law for gradual emancipation, "It does not admit free Negroes, it is true, to the privilege of voting, but then it exempts them from taxes."[110]

Rush was not alone among white abolitionists in advocating an end to slavery but unable to imagine freed people of color being equal citizens of the republic. Philadelphia's Thomas Branagan, a crusading abolitionist and member of the PAS, observed that

The policy of admitting Africans (who are, and indeed must be in their hearts enemies to the government that authorises their subjugation) to the rights and privileges of citizens, is not only obnoxious to the judgment and principles of all the advocates of slavery, but also a very large majority of the advocates for the emancipation of slaves ..."[111]

The first convention of antislavery societies met in Philadelphia in 1794 and quickly drafted a proclamation of their shared ideals and goals. Even for these leading abolitionists, envisioning the equal rights of freed people was difficult. Their discussion of the subject was bracketed with conditions: "to grant to such of them as have been, or may be emancipated, such a participation in civil privileges, as, by the diffusion of knowledge among them, they may, from time to time, be qualified to enjoy."[112] Who was to determine who or at what point a black person had obtained the requisite knowledge and character remained unexplained.

RACE AND CITIZENSHIP IN THE U.S. CONSTITUTION

Patriot leaders kept the issue of citizenship out of both the Articles of Confederation and the Constitution of 1787. This is a classic example of the key to a mystery being the lack of an expected clue rather than the presence of one, or what Sherlock Holmes discovered as "the dog that didn't bark in the night."[113] Having broken with monarchy and its comprehensive system of subjecthood, being anxiously aware both from a century of theorizing on the part of English dissenters and from an acute knowledge of the fates of classical republics, why did the patriots not address the question of legal membership in the nation directly?

The U.S. Constitution uses the word citizen ten times in specifying the terms of legislators, establishing the qualifications for president, drawing the jurisdiction of federal courts, and mandating state comity in the treatment of citizens of other states. It even counterposes the terms "citizen" and "subject" (Article 3, Section 2 gave federal courts the power to decide cases "between a State, or the Citizens thereof, and foreign States, Citizens or Subjects") reflecting the founders' awareness of the momentous difference they had cleaved between these concepts. But nowhere does it define who counts as a citizen. Rather, it consistently uses language that vests responsibility for defining citizenship in the states.

For example, Article 1, Section 8, gives Congress the power "To establish an uniform Rule of Naturalization." Note that the use of the adjective "uniform" which on its face appears to be redundant. Aren't all rules "uniform"? Isn't that the nature of being a rule? Here the word uniform is inserted to reflect the founders' assumption that citizenship primarily belonged to the states and that the federal government's role was merely to ensure that potential immigrants couldn't shop among various states for the easiest path to becoming an American.

Throughout the convention delegates assumed, without discussing it, that there would not be a singular national citizenship. They assumed that whatever criteria of citizenship was already established by their states would continue unimpaired by whatever arrangement the federal government adopted to choose who would be its citizens. Citizenship was conceived of as inclusion and exclusion—all assumed that if one was a citizen of their own state they would also be a citizen of the United States. James Wilson observed that a "citizen of America may be considered in two points of view—as a citizen of the general government, and as a citizen of the state, in which he may reside ... I am both a citizen of Pennsylvania and of the United States." But, at the same time, there was no federal citizenship that operated independently of the states. The federal government could not make a person a citizen of a state that did not want them.[114]

Most confusingly, Article 1, Section 1, defining the qualifications to become president, states that one must be a "natural born Citizen" or a "Citizen of the United States, at the time of the adoption of this Constitution." This phrase, "natural born Citizen" promises to be the start of a definition, but it immediately negates itself by opening the possibility that someone could be a citizen and not be natural born.

Such maddening hollowness of language could only be tolerated by a convention of men, most of whom were trained in law, if they shared a set of assumptions that backfilled this gap in their own thinking. One of these assumptions was that black people were not eligible to become citizens. Charles Pinckney may have been the only member to speak to these assumptions when years later he addressed Congress and detailed his thinking. He wrote, "at the time I drew that constitution, I perfectly knew that there did not then exist such a thing in the Union as a black or colored citizen, nor could I then have conceived it possible such a thing could have ever existed in it; nor, notwithstanding all that has been said on the subject, do I now believe one does exist in it.[115]

James Madison, like most of his colleagues, assumed that black people would never possess the right to vote. Unlike them, he outright said so as the convention dragged into its second month during a debate about whether to select the president through direct election or by some indirect arrangement like an electoral college:

The people at large was in his opinion the fittest in itself. It would be as likely as any that could be devised to produce an Executive Magistrate of distinguished Character ... There was one difficulty however of a serious nature attending an immediate choice by the people. The right of suffrage was much more diffusive in the Northern than the Southern States; and the latter could have no influence in the election on the score of the Negroes.[116]

Only once during the many months of the convention did any delegate voice the idea that black people might be citizens, and if they were then they should vote. Rising to debate proposals to allow states to count enslaved people for the purposes of allocating taxes and representatives in Congress, New Jersey's Gouverneur Morris asked rhetorically, "Upon what principle is it that the slaves shall be computed in the representation? Are they men? Then make them Citizens & let them vote?" Morris was not proposing that the constitution allow slaves to vote, but to exclude them by inserting the word "free" in front of the word "inhabitants" in the clause governing counting the population for these purposes. In this context his outburst was in the form of *reductio ad absurdum*.

James Madison fought not to burden the Constitution with restrictions on naturalization in order to best encourage the immigration of Europeans, who he referred to as "meritorious strangers" and the "most desirable class of people." Madison hoped that by placing few barriers to full citizenship, "great numbers of respectable Europeans; men who love liberty and wish to partake its blessings, will be ready to transfer their fortunes hither."[117]

Later when debating the naturalization bill of 1790 that barred all but "free white persons" from becoming citizens, Madison argued in favor of the bill saying that their rules should aim to not exclude "a single person of good fame that really meant to incorporate himself into our society" and that it should attract only those men that "would be a real addition to the wealth and strength of the United States."[118]

Alexander Hamilton suggested specifying as few qualifications for becoming a member of Congress as possible, as "the advantage of encouraging foreigners was obvious & admitted. Persons in Europe of moderate fortunes will be fond of coming here where they will be on a level with the first Citizens." James Madison seconded Hamilton's thinking, saying he "wished to invite foreigners of merit & republican principles among us" as that "part of America which had encouraged them most had advanced most rapidly in population, agriculture & the arts."

Roger Sherman spoke for the majority who were in favor of adding restrictions to foreigners becoming leaders of the nation and stated the general principle of citizenship upon which the nation was built. "The U. States have not invited foreigners nor pledged their faith that they should enjoy equal privileges with native Citizens. The Individual States alone have done this. The former therefore are at liberty to make any discriminations they may judge requisite." Citizenship was a sovereign power of states, and its purpose was to make discriminations between those who are to be called citizens and those who are not.[119]

NATURALIZATION AND WHITE CITIZENSHIP

Congress established whiteness as the standard for American citizenship in the Naturalization Act of 1790, allowing only "free white persons" the ability to become naturalized. Senator Maclay complained that the debate over the naturalization bill was "exceedingly lengthy" as debates raged in both chambers of Congress over the proposed two-year residency period, and especially the question of whether aliens could own land.[120] However, it appears no objections were raised to restricting naturalization to white people. Just as telling, no lawmaker suggested stating that those born on American soil were citizens as well.[121]

Senator Maclay, a Pennsylvanian, was proud of his state's record of welcoming European settlers from many countries and faiths and boasted that in "Pennsylvania, used as we are to the reception and adoption of strangers, we receive no class of men with such diffidence as the Eastern People." But Maclay had nothing good to say about his colleagues from New England who opposed the bill because it wasn't restrictive enough, "the Eastern people seem to think that he [God] made none but New England folks" and they "affect the greatest fear of being contaminated with foreign manners, customs, or vices."[122]

The only time the restriction of naturalization to whites was discussed was during discussion of an unrelated issue as members of the House of Representatives debated the extent of the limitations imposed on their lawmaking by the constitutional protection of the slave trade until the year 1808. In making the argument that Congress could regulate the slave trade if it wished, Thomas Scott of Pennsylvania noted that the Constitution granted to Congress the right to establish the rules for naturalization: "Congress ... may, whenever they please, declare, (by law) that every person, whether black, white, blue, or red, who from foreign parts can only get his or her foot on the American shore ... be not only free persons, but free citizens." Scott praised Congress' wisdom in limiting naturalization to whites, for "if this provision had not been made, the black man slave, as well as the white man free, could have availed himself of that law ..."[123]

IMPRESSMENT, SEAMEN, AND FEDERAL CITIZENSHIP

In early 1803, a petition from a group of people in Norfolk, Virginia, complaining of the free black migrants from Guadalupe who were arriving at their port from French colonies, was read on the House floor. The memorial charged that it was the "policy of the Government established by the French over several of their islands in the West Indies to expel therefrom all Negroes and Mulattoes to whom emancipation shall be accorded" and "by force or by fraud to have those people introduced into the United States."[124]

Apparently, many congressmen shared the Norfolk residents' alarm and within a week the House began discussing the matter and worked to craft a law that would "guard, by the imposition of heavy penalties, &c., against the introduction into the United States of brigands from the French West India islands." Forty-eight hours later, the House had written a bill intended to bar all people of color from the nation's shores. Titled "A Bill to Prevent the Importation of Certain Persons, Whose Admission is Prohibited by Certain Laws of the State Governments," it was the first proposed federal restriction of immigration in the nation's history.

The 1803 bill's title was reflective not of its purpose but of its method. Its point was to close America's ports to all people of color but it focused all of its sanctions on the owners and captains of the ships that could potentially transport those who America's central government wished to exclude. Penalties for violators were designed to be so costly as to render evasion of the law a risk no calculating person would take. For starters, each person landed in violation of the law, the "master or captain of any ship or vessel, or any other person" responsible was subject to a fine. But any fine paled to the ultimate maritime penalty that could be levied for the landing of a single person of the wrong complexion: forfeiture of the ship, "together with her tackle, apparel and furniture."[125]

While the Adams' administration during its saber-rattling with France signed the suite of laws collectively known as the Alien and Sedition Acts in 1798, even these repressive acts that extended the residency required for naturalization by five years and authorized the president to deport any alien kept America's borders open. Comparing the 1803 act that was prompted by vague fears of Afro-French immigrants with the Alien and Sedition Acts of five years earlier that were the result of fears of war with the French empire, the later law goes further than the earlier by excluding all people of color and establishing unusually steep penalties for violators. Apparently, free black people were seen as more dangerous than French spies.

When formally presented, the bill was met with some unspecified opposition and William H. Hill of North Carolina offered what he thought was a friendly amendment to delay the implementation of the law until after May Day. South Carolina's Thomas Lowndes rose to argue against the delay and Representative Hill withdrew his motion, but Peleg Wadsworth of Massachusetts employed a parliamentary maneuver to reinstate it and forced a discussion of its merits.

While the content of these debates was not recorded, the alignment of legislators on each side did not follow party lines, though those pushing for immediate implementation were all from the South. Those in favor of a few months' delay followed no similar sectional pattern as three of these delay-seekers were from the North, three were from the South, and one was from New York. In the end, the motion to delay closely failed, thirty six to forty, and the body narrowly agreed to a compromise that the law would go into effect on April 1st. Then, in the first full vote on the measure itself, the bill sailed through with sixty-two yeas and only twenty nays. But not one of these twenty negative votes were cast by a member from a southern state.[126]

An amended version of the bill was quickly agreed to by the House on February 4 that now specified only the amount of the fine, $1000 "for each and every negro, mulatto, or other person of color aforesaid, imported or brought into the United States." It also expanded the scope of the law by adding "the coasts of any state" to the previous language that had only mentioned "ports."[127] But when presented with these modifications, one representative from rural Massachusetts, Judge John Bacon of Stockbridge, took the floor to say he was "still dissatisfied with the principles of this bill" and proclaimed that he would not be "intimidated" by any "affected sneers" or "inhuman threats that can be uttered to supply the place of rational and manly discussion." Bacon then detailed the principles that he took exception to:

It makes a distinction between the citizens of the United States, which is not only unknown, but repugnant to the radical principles and general tenor of the Constitution, which secures an equality of rights to our citizens at large. A number of the persons described in the bill are citizens of the United States; they were such previous to the time of forming the Constitution, and actually had a voice in the adoption of the solemn compact. These persons, by the provisions of the bill, are to be deprived of the common rights of citizens; they may not, in a peaceable manner, either for the purpose of commerce, or in case of distress, enter the ports, or sail along the coast of particular States, without subjecting themselves to severe penalties.[128]

From a portion of his biography, it should not be surprising that John Bacon made this stand for black citizenship. Bacon was once a Presbyterian minister who had served Boston's Old South Church but was pushed out for reasons unrecorded and took up farming in the town of Stockbridge. He once voiced his opposition to the clause in the proposed 1778 state constitution that would have restricted "Negroes, Indians, and Mulattoes" from voting in the state.[129]

But Judge Bacon too was not eager to have black neighbors. Bacon had written to Samuel Phillips, president of the Massachusetts' Senate in the 1780s, complaining that northerners had to pay two-fifths more extra taxes in support of the federal government because southerners only paid three-fifths for their slaves. Adding insult to this injury, Bacon thought, was the continuing black presence in the Bay State: "I have not mentioned the large number of negroes in this State which are a nuisance to us ..."[130]

When pushed by his fellow representatives, Bacon admitted his objection was mostly theoretical as "few, if any, of this description of citizens will ever [be] the actual owners of vessels," nevertheless, he thought it an infringement of their "Constitutional rights" and, the Privileges and Immunities clause, which he quoted.

Perhaps knowing that an appeal to the equal citizenship rights of persons of color was an uphill argument, Bacon cleverly invoked the shining ideal of liberty of property. By practically prohibiting the employment of colored sailors, the bill conflicted with the right of ship masters of "employing in their service such other persons ... as they may see fit, whether mechanics, seamen, or common laborers." Granting Congress such a right, Bacon pointed out, would extend its powers to prohibit anyone from "employing a citizen of this descrip- tion to shoe my horse, or to labor on my farm." In his peroration, Bacon warned his colleagues that passage of such a bill that made a "sacrifice" of the "Constitutional rights of the citizens, of a certain description ... to gratify the wishes of the citizens of some other States" and would be viewed by many as "ample proof of the sovereign and despotic sway of the 'Ancient Dominion' over most of the other States in the Union." After alluding to the unfair reach of Virginia's slave power, Bacon added darkly, that such ideas, which he disingenuously claimed not to share, once made popular would sunder the nation: "nothing can have a more direct and powerful tendency to a dissolution of the Union, than the prevalence of a sentiment like this among our citizens."[131]

New Jersey's James Mott added that he too thought the bill unconstitutional. Samuel Mitchill of New York moved that the bill be recommitted and reconsidered for amendment. Mitchill said he "did not wish to vote against this or any other bill, providing for the security of the Union" and he was "very desirous of guarding the States of the nation from the introduction of the negroes, mulattoes, and persons of color, comprised in the bill" and "all other mischievous and evil-disposed people." He conceded that if the bill had specifically applied to the slave trade, he would have enthusiastically endorsed it.

Mitchill's concern with the bill was not its impact upon free black travelers or sailors, but upon ship-owners. He related the recent cases of American vessels sailing from Boston and from New York that made ports of call in the French West Indies and were forced to take on board "the banditti or brigands of the islands" who were "the most flagitious of mortal creatures." Captains faced the awful choice of sailing to their destination and being ruined by the confiscation of their ship or murdering his passengers and facing admiralty charges. (Mitchill seemed to lean toward murder in this scenario: "It would be easy for him to suffocate or strangle them in pesilential air. There would be no difficulty in throwing them overboard. There are many other methods of getting rid of them.")[132] Mitchill's bottom line was protecting white ship-owners and captains from such a Hobson's choice, and he declared that he would be satisfied if language were added indemnifying owners and captains if their colored cargo were forced upon them.

Mitchill moved to refer the bill to a select committee for amend-ment, prompting another round of debate that was only sketchily summarized in the record. Though "some" opposed the bill on the ground that as Bacon argued it was "unconstitutional in destroying and abridging the rights of free negroes and persons of color, who were citizens of one State," more of the opposition seemed to follow Mitchill in seeing the bill as being too severe on ship-owners and captains. Curiously, the clerk summarizing these proceedings noted: "All allowed the propriety of the General Government exerting every legitimate authority it possessed to enforce the State laws, and to avert the evil apprehended from the introduction of brigands from the West India Islands."

Supporters of the bill as it stood argued its harsh penalties were proportionate to the "imminent danger of the Southern States" and argued that the law was clearly constitutional because "it only pre-vented the importation of negroes and persons of color into those States which had already prohibited their admission." By a vote of forty-seven to forty-two, the bill was sent to a select committee for modification.[133]

The select committee was composed entirely of southern repre-sentatives, in fact representing all the prominent southern states. There was one representative from each of both Carolinas, Virginia, Georgia, and Maryland.[134] It was this committee that on February 10, amended the bill to permit ships to bring persons of color who were "a native citizen, or registered seaman of the United States." The new version also added the caveat: "nothing contained in this act shall be construed to prohibit the admission of Indians."[135]

The bill passed on February 17.[136] Just a few days earlier, Con-gress considered a militia act for the new District of Columbia that limited recruitment to "every able bodied white male, between the ages of eighteen and forty-five years" resident within the district.[137] One week later Supreme Court Chief Justice John Marshall made history by formally declaring an act of Congress to be "unconstitu-tional" in the case of *Marbury* v. *Madison*.

Passage of the amended "Bill to prevent the importation of certain persons" did not quiet the issue. The potential that blacks might be included in some sense of federally recognized citizenship pro-voked years of controversy. In 1796 Congress was driven to consider ways of protecting America's mariners by Britain's flagrant seizures of American sailors on the high seas, a form of kidnapping known as impressment. At the time, roughly one in five of America's sailors were men of color. A bill that some representatives thought would pass unanimously provoked controversy and debate by creating a federal system of registration that would protect sailors by issuing them a certificate of U.S. citizenship. Connecticut's Joshua Coit thought that the "proposed plan," by which any sailor for a fee of 25 cents could obtain a certificate on the sworn word of a single witness that he was born in America or had resided in America in 1783, "too loose" and urged that the law be changed so that "the proof of citizenship should be rendered so strict as to make it hard to obtain ..." Coit also worried that "this bill would supersede all other regulations with respect to naturalization."[138]

Coit's and other congressmen's objections caused the bill to run into opposition, but it passed in May and the certificates it provided for became tremendously popular among seamen, especially seamen of color. In Philadelphia alone, 26,000 certificates were issued in the law's first two decades of operation.[139]

Yet, almost as soon as this bill that recognized a sliver of black citizenship under the federal government became law, opponents in Congress pushed to restrict the ability of black seamen to make use of it. In January of 1804, Congress considered a bill restricting how certificates of citizenship were to be issued to people of color. Under this proposal, to obtain a citizenship certificate, black seamen would have to "produce to the collector, a certificate authenticated by the seal of some court of record in the United States, that such a person of color is a free man, either by birth or manumission ..."[140] Given the poor record keeping of many county courts, the difficulty of obtaining them, especially if they were kept in clerk's offices in southern states, and given the hostility of magistrates and courts to assist people of color, such a rule would have placed a serious obstacle in the way of many seamen. Accordingly, a month later, the Senate voted down this bill without comment or recorded debate.[141]

Southern states refused to recognize such certificates of citizenship or to extend to black sailors possessing them the "privileges and immunities" of their own citizens as required by the Constitution. South Carolina passed a "Negro Seaman's Act" that required all mariners of color entering the state, including those holding citizenship certificates, to be jailed while in port. In the face of this intransigence and what was a clear violation of the Constitution, Supreme Court Chief Justice John Marshall chose not to affirm national authority in this area. When he faced the prospect of ruling on the constitutionality of a Virginia law that barred black men from obtaining licenses to pilot ships in the state, Marshall recoiled from the depth of reaction a lower court justice provoked when he pointed out that South Carolina's law violated the Constitution. Marshall confided:

> The subject is one of much feeling in the South. Of this I was apprised, but did not think it would have shown itself in such strength as it has. The decision has been considered as another act of judicial usurpation; but the sentiment has been avowed that, if this be the Constitution, it is better to break that instrument than submit to the principle ... in Virginia; a case has been brought before me in which I might have considered its constitutionality, had I chosen to do so; but it was not absolutely necessary, and as I am not fond of butting against a wall in sport, I escaped on the construction of the act.[142]

PRESERVING WHITE CITIZENSHIP IN THE TERRITORIES

When James Monroe was sent to Paris to join America's ambassador Robert Livingston to finalize the purchase of the city of New Orleans, they were given a set of instructions, formulated by President Jefferson and Secretary of State Madison, that barred the diplomats from agreeing to grant citizenship to the polyglot people of the region.

As the final details of the purchase were being hammered out, Napoleon surprised the Americans by offering to sell the entirety of French Louisiana in addition to the port of New Orleans. Eager to secure this offer before Napoleon changed his mind, the Americans accepted a treaty whose language contradicted their instructions. Napoleon himself had insisted that the agreement specified that any French citizens handed over to the new sovereignty of the United States would be treated equally with American citizens. From a French legal perspective, this included the large community of free blacks who were a vital part of the city of New Orleans. Jefferson, however, had no intention of widening the concept of American citizenship to include people of color.[143]

Worried that the Constitution did not specifically permit the federal government to purchase whole territory from foreign powers, Jefferson drafted a constitutional amendment that would make his secret acquisition legal. After all, Jefferson was the leader of the political faction that took a dim view of the doctrine of implied powers and had insisted on the tenth amendment limiting federal actions to only those powers "delegated" in the Constitution. Jefferson crafted his amendment to both legalize his territorial acquisition and to overturn the provision in the treaty he had just signed promising to treat French subjects as American citizens.

The amendment Jefferson proposed began "Louisiana, as ceded by France to the U.S., is made part of the U.S. Its white inhabitants shall be citizens, and stand, as to their rights and obligations on the same footing with other citizens of the U.S ..." It provided the same racial definition of citizenship for a future Florida territory as well, "Florida, also, whensoever it may be rightfully obtained, shall become part of the U.S. Its white inhabitants shall thereupon be citizens ..."[144]

Jefferson shared his draft amendment with his secretary of state, James Madison, and his attorney general, Levi Lincoln, who was one of the few Yankees he relied on for political advice and counsel. Madison, though he made detailed suggestions for changes in other parts of the amendment, had no comment on the restriction of citizenship to "whites." This was consistent with American leaders casually excluding blacks from citizenship in their regular correspondence. Louisiana governor, William C.C. Clairborne, writing to James Madison, reported that "The late slight appearance of discontent among the people of Colour, of which in my last letter I advised you, excited some alarm among the white Citizens ..." thereby counterposing "people of Colour" with "white Citizens," even though everyone he was referring to had a few years before been French citizens.[145]

Levi Lincoln, who had earned a reputation as an opponent of slavery by representing Quack Walker in the series of cases that led to the Massachusetts' Supreme Court quietly declaring slavery unenforceable in the state, raised no objections to Jefferson's definition of citizenship as embracing only whites. Lincoln told Jefferson that he thought it was politically stronger to declare that there was no constitutional difficulty at all and undercut the opposition's only argument against the purchase, but at the same time, he told the president that he thought his amendment was well conceived. "Your proposed mode of amending the constitution appears to me the safest, & the freest from difficulty & exception of any I had contemplated."[146]

Jefferson's governor of the Mississippi territory pursued a policy of encouraging white settlement and discouraging the extension of plantation agriculture. In 1802, William C.C. Clairborne advocated legalizing the lands of the 2000 or so white settlers who had squatted on native lands with flimsy Spanish titles, rather than allowing these lands to be speculated on in the usual manner:

> The consequence would be that this most distant and infant settlement of the United States, at present insulated and defenceless, would be rendered more weak and defenceless, by the banishment of the poorer Class of White Citizens, and the introduction of a few wealthy characters, with a large increase of negroes, a description of inhabitants, already formidable to our present population.[147]

The newly elected senator from Massachusetts, John Quincy Adams, was furious at the news of Jefferson's grand purchase and called the president a hypocrite for taking office "blowing a trumpet against implied power" and then making the broadest possible constitutional interpretation of the treaty-power when opportunity presented. Adams also denounced the treaty's racial implications for the future of the union, writing, "It made a Union totally different

from that for which the Constitution had been formed ... It naturalizes foreign nations in a mass."[148]

The general question of whether free black Americans were citizens
never arose in national legislative debates until Missouri submitted
its constitution barring free blacks from entering the state to Congress in December of 1820. Many of the surviving founders in 1821
were less discomforted with Missouri becoming a slave state as they
were with what they saw as the more vexing issue of free blacks, an
issue that unlike slavery provoked legislative actions that threatened
to pose a direct challenge to the federal system. While no part of the
Constitution limited a state's ability to hold people in perpetual and
grinding bondage, one clause did restrict state powers to exclude free
black migrants and settlers.

Because states could theoretically choose to recognize free black
persons as citizens of their state, such citizens of color must be treated
by each state equally with their own citizens. This is the meaning of
Article 4, Section 2 of the U.S. Constitution that states that "The citizens of each state shall be entitled to all privileges and immunities
of citizens in the several states." Such constitutional provision would
not apply to free black people who were not recognized as citizens by
their home states, only those clothed with at least the barest raiment
of citizenship.

Article 3, Section 26 of the Missouri Constitution provided that it
would be the duty of the legislature "as soon as may be, to pass such
laws as may be necessary, First, to prevent free negroes and mulattoes from coming to, and settling in this state, under any pretext
whatsoever."

While other states, such as Indiana, had passed laws barring free
blacks from entering the state, none had as yet put such a provision in
their founding charter.[149]

When Missouri's draft constitution was submitted for congressional approval, several members of both the House and Senate rose
to point out that free black men were citizens and therefore Missouri's charter conflicted with the privileges and immunities clause
of the U.S. Constitution. A total of three New England Senators,
Burrill (R.I.), Morrill (New Hampshire), and Otis (Massachusetts)

argued that free black men were citizens. They were met by a pair of their colleagues representing both North and South, William Smith of South Carolina and Holmes of Maine, who argued that no black person in America was properly a citizen of either their own state or of the federal government.[150]

South Carolina's William Smith was the most systematic and thorough of those stating what seemed to them to be an extraordinarily obvious point, that the United States of America was a white man's nation that excluded all people of color from the fruits of citizenship. Smith correctly noted that this was the very first time in congressional history that the rights of citizenship of free "negroes" had ever been discussed and seemed surprised this was even a point worth debating. Smith saw no contradiction between a republican form of government, a government of the people, and one that excluded blacks: "we have always understood that sort of government which is administered by the people to be a republican form of government and does not obtain or lose this form when the free negroes and mulattoes are excluded from a participation. This is a case of *sui generis*."[151]

Beyond noting that no states treated African Americans as citizens when the nation was founded, Smith constructed a legal argument that no state treated their free black residents as citizens. Smith pointed out that no states allowed black men into their state militias, just as they were barred by federal law from serving in a national militia. The Naturalization Act of 1790 limited citizenship to only "whites." Moreover, some states specifically denied them the rudiments of citizenship; Kentucky, Ohio, and Louisiana all outlawed black voting and in Indiana they could not be witnesses in court.[152]

Smith's arguments were echoed in the other chamber. Virginia's Philip P. Barbour held that the fact that all free blacks were subject to discrimination, both civil and political, marked them as outside the realm of citizenship. No person could be called a citizen who lacked equal civil and political rights. Virginia's Smyth supported his colleague by pointing out that no state in the union allowed any of its black inhabitants all the rights allowed to naturalized aliens: namely, the right to hold and convey property, the right to vote, and the right to hold elected office. Therefore, no state treated them as citizens, but as mere "denizens." Storrs (New York), Barbour and Smyth (Virginia), and McLane (Delaware) rested on an even more fundamental argument. They charged that Congress had no constitutional power to define, expand, or restrict citizenship except as it relates to naturalization. This right, the Constitution reserved to the states exclusively.[153]

Advocates of recognizing black citizenship made their case most forcefully in the House of Representatives, but theirs was an uphill struggle. Congressmen Strong (Vermont), Hemphill (Pennsylvania), and Mallory (Vermont) could not deny Senator Smith's examples of state denial of citizen rights to their black residents and so made the weaker argument that state discrimination against black people did not cancel their status as citizens.[154]

In the end, those who wished to force Missouri to drop this provision failed to win a majority of their colleagues to their position and instead were forced to the face-saving compromise of admitting Missouri to statehood with the understanding that it not bar the entry of any migrant who was formally recognized as a citizen of another state. No state in the nation had yet rendered such a declaration. New Hampshire would thirty-seven years later.[155]

Even liberal Massachusetts never passed a law declaring African Americans to be citizens of the Bay State. Instead, what tenuous rights black people enjoyed rested on the high court ruling of *Commonwealth* v. *Jennison* (1783) that ended slavery in the Bay State by interpreting the state constitution's promise of liberty to extend to enslaved people of color. But such legal precedents were inferior to statutory affirmation of black citizenship as they could be overturned and reinterpreted at any time. Connecticut's highest judge, Chief Justice David Daggett upheld a state law outlawing Prudence Crandall's school for black children in 1834, declaring, "To my mind, it would be a perversion of terms, and the well known rules of construction, to say, that slaves, free blacks, and Indians, were citizens, within the meaning of that term, as used in the constitution."[156] That Daggett's decision (though not his argument about black citizenship) was subsequently overturned on appeal, only further illustrates the flimsiness of judicially mandated citizenship.

Pennsylvania's high courts also swung back and forth on the issue and never declared clearly on African Americans' citizenship rights. Tennessee's high court appeared to endorse black citizenship in 1827 and again in 1834. North Carolina followed suit in 1838, Judge William Gaston recalling that Great Britain drew no color bars on the citizenship of its subjects born within the realm. However, such liberal precedents were steadily overturned over the next decade.[157]

In November 1820, James Monroe wrote to his old friend James Madison, bemoaning the fact that Missouri's constitutional prohibition on the entry of free blacks threatened to derail the precarious agreements that had been reached to admit Missouri as a slave state, "The clause in the constitution of that State, authorising an inhibition of free negroes from emigrating into it, is understood to be that which will more particularly be laid hold of." Monroe then offered a legal formulation that he hoped would overcome the opposition and hasten Missouri's admittance. Monroe proposed that Missouri be admitted with the objectionable clause and the Congress could then simply issue a resolution "disapproving that clause & protesting against it." Such a resolution, Monroe thought, "would deprive it of such sanction & leave it subject to the decision of the court ..."[158] Monroe was confident that the Supreme Court would simply rule it a dead letter, as all provisions in any state laws contrary to the national constitution are null and void.

Madison agreed that the "obnoxious clause" was "to be regretted" as it might delay Missouri's statehood. Worse, Madison feared admitting Missouri with such a clause, not because of the effect this would have on the freedom of black citizens to move west, but because "it must, to say the least, be an awkward precedent, to sanction the Constitution of the new State containing a clause at variance with that of the U.S." The old lawyer then formulated another way that Missouri's exclusion clause could be worked around:

> ... may it not deserve consideration, whether the terms of the clause, would not be satisfied by referring the authority it gives, to the case of free people of colour, not citizens of other States. Not having the Constitution of Missouri at hand, I can form no opinion

on this point. But a right in the States to inhibit the entrance of that description of coloured people, it may be presumed, would be as little disrelished by the States having no slaves, as by the States retaining them. There is room also for a more critical examination of the Constitutional meaning of the term "Citizens" than has yet taken place; and of the effect of the various civil disqualifications applied by the laws of the States, to free people of Colour.[159]

In other words, either Missouri could clarify that its provision only applied to those people of color from states that did not recognize them as citizens, or, perhaps, the Supreme Court could simply declare that only white people could be citizens, as it would thirty-seven years later in the case of *Dred Scott* v. *Sandford*.

Those who wished to once and for all establish that free African Americans were disqualified from American citizenship only had to wait a few months for their arguments to receive a more official stamp. U.S. Attorney General William Wirt was asked by the collector of the port of Norfolk whether he had to allow "negro" pilots to command vessels, which was really a question of "Whether free persons of color are … citizens of the United States." Wirt began by echoing the premise of those in Congress who had opposed black citizenship: "that no person is included in the description of citizen of the United States who has not the full rights of a citizen in the State of his residence." This was due to the paradox of a free black man in Virginia, who shared none of the rights of whites in that state, who then moved to another, suddenly gained equal rights with all the whites of his new state by the Constitution's privileges and immunities clause. An even more absurd consequence of this doctrine, Wirt chortled, was that:

the only qualification required by the constitution to render a person eligible as President, senator, or representative of the United States, is, that he shall be a "citizen of the United States" of a given age and residence. Free, negroes and mulattoes can satisfy the requisitions of age and residence as well as the white man; and if nativity, residence, and allegiance combined, (without the rights and privileges of a white man) are sufficient to make him a "citizen of the United States" in the sense of the constitution, then free negroes and mulattoes are eligible to those high offices, and may command the purse and sword of the nation.

Like the pro-Missouri congressmen whose arguments he echoed, Wirt concluded that "For these and other reasons, which might easily be multiplied, I am of the opinion that the constitution, by the description of 'citizens of the United States,' intended those only who enjoyed the full and equal privileges of white citizens in the State of their residence." Because black men in Virginia cannot vote, cannot hold any public office, cannot testify against any white person in court, cannot serve in the state militia, may not own firearms, are subject to a different schedule of punishments for the same crime, and may not marry a white, then "free people of color in Virginia are not citizens of the United States in the sense of our shipping laws, or any other laws."[160]

In the end, while some states extended some of the privileges of citizenship to some free people of color, the republic had codified a federal system that defined citizenship as white while tolerating such local deviations in the interest of "states' rights." The white republic that the founders envisioned from the beginning of their struggles with the British empire remained unachieved due to the tenacity and collective strength of communities of color. But rather than abandon their dreams of a white nation, white patriots moved step by step to create a white republic within a multiracial one by exploiting all the exclusionary potential in the modern idea of citizenship they had invented in their revolutionary moment.

6

Gradual Emancipation as Racial Cleansing

The patriot's desire to eliminate from the republic the corrupting influences of slavery, because these corrupting influences included slaves themselves, could not be accomplished by simply setting enslaved people free. In demanding liberty for themselves but not for African Americans, patriot leaders did not see themselves as holding clashing principles. In their view their cherished values of liberty, equality, and republican democracy could temporarily coexist with slavery, if they believed themselves having no other reasonable path to emancipation than a slow and deliberate one. Proposals to simply free slaves were seen by most whites as irresponsible and self-defeating. Noah Webster, the great lexicographer, defended the Constitution in 1787 from criticisms that it protected slavery by observing that "An immediate abolition of slavery would bring ruin upon the whites, and misery upon the blacks, in the southern states. The constitution has therefore wisely left each state to pursue its own measures ..." Even America's foremost abolitionist in the years after America's victory in its war for independence, Warner Mifflin, confessed to a friend,

> if congress had unquestionably the power to emancipate all the slaves in America, I should be sorry to see them pass an act for their immediate liberation: although I firmly believe the Almighty will, in his own way and time, bring their deliverance about, I also believe if it be done in favour to us and them, it will be by gradation ... [then] the work may be brought about in safety.[1]

Just as slavery was widely viewed by American founders as an institution incompatible with republican principles, so were black people themselves. Part of the reason that slavery was seen as corrosive to the nation's foundations was because slavery encouraged and facili-

243

tated the growth of the black population and people of color were universally viewed as dangerous, disloyal, and feckless—the opposite of republican virtue and citizenship. Patriots could not solve one problem without addressing the other, so patriot schemes to abolish slavery gradually freed people from slavery while simultaneously ushering them out of their states.

While attempts to expel free blacks from southern states were clumsy and open for all to see, in the North systematic efforts to lower the black population were concealed beneath a thick rhetoric of benevolence. Given the relatively small African American populations in northern states and the existence of a vast slave market to the South eager to receive their cast-off populations, northern leaders did not need to actively expel people of color, they only needed to turn a blind eye to the logic of the marketplace and ensure that replacement black immigrants could not enter their states. When Quaker John Parrish complained to some men in "eminent stations" about the frequency of "man-stealing" they responded, "the country must be thinned of these people, they must be got rid of at any rate."[2]

Southerners were quite open about the benefit they received from the gradual emancipation laws crafted in the North containing loopholes that allowed slaves to be sold to them. South Carolina's William Smith stung his northern colleagues in the Senate in 1820 when he observed that at the time of the Revolution, "It was not then slaveholding States and non-slaveholding States, but all were slaveholding States. It is true since that time the Northern States, finding it their interest to do so, have sold the greater part of them to the Southern people, and have freed the rest."[3] Congressman David Ramsay, in urging his fellow South Carolinians to support the proposed federal constitution, pointed out that the distant threat of prohibiting "the importation of negroes after 21 years" was of slight importance as they would have two decades of importation "added to the natural increase of those we already have" plus "the influx from our northern neighbours, who are desirous of getting rid of their slaves."[4]

The hidden cornerstone of northern racial cleansing was laid at the Constitutional Convention. It occurred so quickly, in the dog days of a Philadelphia summer, ten weeks into the meeting, and with such scant discussion, that it is easy to overlook its significance. On August 28, South Carolina's C.C. Pinckney expressed his dissatisfaction with the privileges and immunities clause then on the floor, saying it did not provide enough protection for slavery and wishing "provision should be included in favor of property in slaves." No other delegates supported him, and South Carolina was the only state to vote against the clause. Without any further debate the delegates moved on to the next item, a clause that would require states to extradite fugitives to states requesting their return. C.C.'s cousin, Charles Pinckney and the other delegate from the Palmetto state, Pierce Butler, moved to change the wording to "require slaves and servants to be delivered up like criminals." Pennsylvania's James Wilson opposed this change, not because he was against returning runaway slaves, but because he did not think it was right for "the Executive of the State to do it, at public expense." Connecticut's Roger Sherman agreed that it was no more a public responsibility than capturing and returning "a horse."

Realizing he was not making any headway, Butler withdrew his motion but declared his intention to turn it into a separate measure. Butler offered his new fugitive slave clause the next morning. Cleverly, Butler modeled his article on the secret draft of the Northwest Ordinance that many members of the convention were simultaneously working on as members of the Confederation Congress, including himself.[5]

Revealingly, it was northerners who wrote the model for Butler's fugitive slave provision of the Constitution. Massachusetts' congressional delegate Rufus King chaired the committee that originally drafted the ordinance governing western territories in April of 1785. Among its various measures was one guaranteeing that the western territories, or the states carved from it, would not provide sanctuary to runaways.[6]

Like Jefferson a year earlier, whose first proposed law organizing the frontier territories included a provision ending slavery after 1800 (a period of delay that would allow slave-owners to sell their human property out of the country), King envisioned the western territories becoming free states, better able to attract white immigrants from Europe. Unlike King's proposed law restraining states from sheltering escapees, Jefferson's proposed territorial ordinance did not include a fugitive slave clause.

When during the Constitutional Convention, the Confederation Congress finally agreed on language governing at least the northern half of the western territories, the ordinances included both ambiguous language prohibiting slavery and clear language barring jurisdictions in the territories from harboring escaped slaves modeled on King's earlier language. The specific wording of these clauses was the product of a committee chaired by another Yankee, Massachusetts' Nathan Dane. Dane's committee included the fugitive slave clause as Article VI of the Northwest Ordinance, prominently the very last provision of that document: "That any person escaping into the same, from whom labor or service is lawfully claimed in any one of the original States, such fugitive may be lawfully reclaimed and conveyed to the person claiming his or her labor or service as aforesaid."

Such language requiring territories or states to return escaped slaves was novel and unique at the time. No such provision was included in the Articles of Confederation.[7] Under existing federal law, no state had any obligation to return fugitive slaves to another, a lacuna that had caused considerable friction between Massachusetts and South Carolina when sailors from the Bay State seized a privateer bearing thirty-four people claimed as their property by Charleston masters.

It is worth digressing for a moment to survey the meandering course of this incident as it vividly illustrates the problems, possibilities, and stakes involved in reconciling the different legal contexts of slavery in the North and the South.

In the summer of 1779, the *Victoria*, a pirate ship outfitted in Charleston and armed with a Spanish letter of marque sailed forth to prey on British shipping. It quickly overtook a British privateer and seized its cargo of slaves, tobacco, indigo, and wine. In the coming days, the *Victoria* herself was captured by British pirates but before they could make harbor in New York, the pirates were forced to surrender to a pair of prize-hunting American brigs, one bearing the rebellious name the *Tyrannicide*, who hauled *Victoria* to Boston. At the end of this torturous journey, the new-found state of Massachusetts was in possession of nineteen men, ten women, and five children that citizens of the new-found state of South Carolina claimed as their property.[8]

All thirty-four individuals were refused permission to land in Boston and held on board their ship for a week while the patriot Board of War determined what to do with them. The Board turned matters over to the Massachusetts' legislature that then ordered them to be imprisoned in a barracks on wind-swept Castle Island and for South Carolina's congressional representatives to be notified of their seizure "so proper measures may be taken for the return of the said Negroes, agreeable to their desire." The legislature also ordered that the commander of the fort, Lieutenant Paul Revere, put the men to labor shoring up the island's fortifications and the women to "Cooking, Washing, etc." A week or so later, a number of politically connected men were allowed to pick among the boys and take them home to be their servants. These included Henry Gardner, the state treasurer, and Joshua Brackett who was a friend of Paul Revere and owner of Cromwell's Head Tavern (where a young Colonel Washington boarded during part of the French and Indian War). Another child was sent to be the servant of Nathaniel Appleton who had earlier written against the institution of slavery in his 1767 pamphlet *Considerations on Slavery*.[9]

After being confined to Castle Island, going on four months, John Hancock informed the legislature that the "situation of these Negroes is pitiable with respect to clothing." A month later, agents for the South Carolinians claiming these people as their property arrived and with their local lawyer, John Winthrop, petitioned the legislature for permission to take them. A legislative committee then approved the request and ordered the Board of War to "deliver so many of the negroes therein mentioned, as are now alive."

To legally surrender the surviving prisoners to the South Carolinians the Massachusetts' government had to violate its own standing legal precedents. Earlier, in another case involving an American privateer seizing British slaves on the seas, the Massachusetts' legislature resolved that all such slaves captured in wartime should be freed and treated as prisoners of war. The resolution read in part: "the selling and enslaving the human species is a direct violation of the natural rights alike vested in all men by their Creator." In a lawyerly maneuver, legislators claimed that the men and women of Castle Island had asked to be returned to their owners and shipped off to South Carolina. Under cover of this legal fiction, the legislature posed as generally opposed to slavery, saying "Negroes should by no means be considered by this court as transferrable property," though transfer them as property they did. At least twenty men, women, and children were shipped back to slavery in South Carolina.[10]

However, one enslaving family, the Pawleys, failed to contract with the same slave catchers as the other owners, and the men and women claimed by them were taken to Boston as the personal charges and servants of John Hancock.

These ten quickly integrated into the vibrant black community in Boston and lived precariously between freedom and slavery. Four years passed until an agent sent by the Pawleys with power of attorney was refused assistance by a Boston magistrate. Together with the enslavers' attorney, John Winthrop, the agent drafted a petition to the state's governor, John Hancock, seeking his intervention in the case. Governor Hancock referred the case to the state supreme court for immediate adjudication. Meanwhile, at the request of a South Carolina lawyer, a Boston judge ordered the men and women seized from their homes and imprisoned while they waited for the arrival of a ship that would carry them into bondage. Nine of the ten were located and jailed. In the meantime, the supreme court issued an order to bring the enslaved to court where they were subsequently released on the grounds that their arrest warrants were improper. The slave catcher returned to South Carolina where he shared his experiences with northern justice to whoever would listen.

The Pawleys' lawyer, John Winthrop, wrote directly to his South Carolina employers with advice and support as to how to sidestep the Massachusetts' legal system entirely and expressed his strong advocacy of the cause of returning fugitive slaves because if southerners could not reclaim their chattel "all the Negroes from the Southern States will pour in upon us like a Torrent."[11] Following Winthrop's advice, the Pawleys wrote to Governor Guerard who drafted a letter of protest to Massachusetts' Governor Hancock, characterizing the high court's ruling as a "gross Attack on the Dignity, Independence & Sovereignty of this State."

Hancock and his highest justice, Samuel Cushing, the same jurist who had that very year issued rulings making slavery unenforceable, then backtracked and assured Governor Guerard that the decision did not vacate the South Carolinians' right to recover their slaves, it only released them from jail. Cushing clarified that his ruling in no way altered these men and women's obligation to "service." In the South Carolinians' view this was pure sophistry as the court had simply refused to aid them in reclaiming what they saw as their legal property.

All of the Yankees involved in this drama vacillated and prevaricated because they wished to diminish the power of slavery but not at the cost of encouraging a "torrent" of black escapees to enter their state. South Carolina's leaders certainly learned the lesson that their fellow northern states were not reliable partners in recovering runaways. In this context, it is not surprising that South Carolina's delegates to the Constitutional Convention pushed for a guarantee for the return of fugitive slaves. What they probably didn't expect was how easy obtaining one would be.

Well before the ratification of the Constitution, other northern state governors seemed little troubled in assisting the recapture of runaway persons claimed as property in other states. Pennsylvania's Vice-President Muhlenberg wrote to Governor Randolph of Virginia about a thirty-six-year-old black man claimed by a citizen of that state: "If, from an investigation of the matter, it should appear that the Negro is the property of a Citizen of Virginia, Council will (on receiving such information from your Excellency) with pleasure restore him to his owner." Pennsylvania officials lodged the black man in the Philadelphia jail while waiting for documentation from Virginia. Governor Randolph, however, merely provided his endorsement of the putative owner's good character: "he is satisfied of his title. My acquaintance with him enables me to say that he is an honest man, and that great reliance may be put in his assertions."[12]

Pennsylvania's act for gradual emancipation contained its own fugitive slave clause: "this act … shall not give any relief or shelter to any absconding or runaway negro." White persons claiming black men or women as their property were granted the "like right and aid to claim, seize, and take away his slave" and slave catchers were given the right to seize black people they claimed had run away in the past and have them legally registered as slaves for life "on due proof made before one Justice of the Peace." In one form or another, by the time of the Constitutional Convention, five other northern states, Connecticut, Rhode Island, Massachusetts, New York, and New Jersey also had statutes requiring the return of escapees from slavery.[13]

At the Constitutional Convention, Pierce Butler proposed that in addition to the clause requiring ordinary criminals be delivered up to states requesting their extradition, the Constitution should stipulate that

> If any person bound to service or labor in any of the U-States shall escape into another State, he or she shall not be discharged from such service or labor in consequence of any regulations subsisting in the state to which they escape, but shall be delivered up to the person justly claiming their service or labor.

This phrase then passed unanimously in the affirmative. In other words, perhaps the least debated, least controversial item considered by the founders gathered to draft a new Constitution was the requirement that states surrender their power to interfere with the seizure of African Americans by those claiming them as their property.[14]

Only one seemingly trivial change was made to the fugitive slave clause as reported by the drafting committee. The word "legally" was dropped from the phrase "legally held to service or labor." Lawyers (of which half the drafters were) knew that this was not simply streamlining the passage, but altering its fundamental nature by eliminating a vast array of legal impediments that astute administrators and jurists could have thrown in the way of slave-hunters. With the word "legally," courts or governments might have required a higher standard of proof that any individual was the property of another. They might create classes of claims that failed to meet their threshold for being "legal." At bottom, inserting the word "legally" provided purchase for courts and governments in one state to examine and judge the procedures for proving enslavement in another.

By this means the Constitution's fugitive slave clause was far stricter than the model it adopted its language from, the Northwest Ordinance, passed just six weeks earlier by Congress. Additionally, several instances of weaker language in the Ordinance "… may" were changed to the unambiguous "… shall."

The only sectional pressure that left its mark on the fugitive slave clause was the absence of the word "slave" and its replacement by the euphemistic "person bound to service or labor." It was northern delegates that pushed to keep the word "slave" out of the document but didn't similarly push against the more substantial consequence of tightening the procedures for returning them to bondage.

The importance of the fugitive slave clause's wording has been frequently misconstrued to mean that it simply required states to return escaped slaves to another claiming them. It stipulated more than an obligation. This clause rested on a restriction of state sovereignty by invalidating any state laws or regulations (and presumably also state court rulings) that infringed on the property rights of slave-owners from other states. Legal observers at the time would have immediately recognized that this clause overturned the shattering precedent set in the 1772 English King's Court ruling in *Somerset* v. *Stewart* that declared slavery unenforceable in England and effectively made that island free to all setting foot upon it. With this provision, no American state could follow the example of Lord Mansfield and declare that slave catchers could no longer pursue their victims within their borders. Had this clause been in effect four years earlier, it probably would not have been possible for Justice Cushing to have freed on a technicality the ten men and women praying not to be turned over to South Carolina manhunters.

The Fugitive Slave Clause was not only approved unanimously by all the states represented at the convention, but it was also rarely commented upon when the Constitution was taken up by state ratifying conventions. Only Moses Brown, a Rhode Island Quaker, recognized that the new Constitution gave a great boost to slavery, not only by protecting the international trade in slaves, but even more importantly, destroying the power of states to fully abolish slavery by requiring them to return runaways. Brown noted that this violated the English legal precedent that Massachusetts' high court ruling abolishing slavery was based upon:

> ... their doings on this subject aspecialy the 3d paragraph of the 2d sectn. of the 4th Article appears Calculated on purpose 'tho, Plauseably Coverd, to distroy the present Effect of the 1st Article of the Massachusetts Bill of Rights by which all Negroes when in that Jurisdiction are Declared free, as well and on the same ground as in England ...

Brown understood that while the Constitution scrupulously avoided violating any of the laws governing slavery in southern states, at a stroke it overturned the fundamental law of Massachusetts: "indeed I thought it an Indignity, or a violation of Right, accompanyd with Insult on the great Principle of that first Article of the Massachusets [constitution] ... "[15]

Moses Brown stands out alone in his dissent over the fugitive slave clause. A more typical white abolitionist view of this measure was highlighted by Benjamin Rush who remarked to his Boston friend Jeremy Belknap that the Quakers in Pennsylvania were well represented at that states' ratification convention and "with an exception of three or four persons only" they all voted in favor of approval. Though they were solidly against slavery, they thought the future restriction of the slave trade "was a great point obtained from the Southern States." To these white abolitionists, punting emancipation to some distant time was a prudent course. "They consider very wisely that the Abolition of slavery in our country must be gradual in order to be effectual ... "[16]

To follow Occam's Razor, the simplest explanation of how the fugitive slave clause sailed through the convention riding a wave of intersectional consensus is, as George Van Cleve concluded, it served every stakeholder's interest (except, of course, people of color themselves). Southerners received a double benefit: the status of fugitives would be determined by their own state laws and foreclosed the slight possibility that America could follow the example of the English empire and allow some privileged areas to be "free soil" where slaves would be at liberty. Northerners understood that the fugitive slave clause acted as a great wall that would keep black people out. By designing their lengthy programs of emancipation in ways that turned a blind eye to the taking and selling of slaves out of their states, such a law would facilitate a gradual program of black banishment.[17]

Northerners, for their part, felt they needed to protect slavery in the South to abolish slavery in their own states: the existence of a ready market to dispose of enslaved people made emancipation laws politically feasible and reduced the future population of liberated African Americans. Agreeing to a blueprint of government that gave the North control of international commerce in exchange for protecting slavery in the South and overturning the Somerset precedent by promising to return fugitives from slave states was hardly a devil's bargain for white northerners as southern slavery and a fugitive slave clause assisted them in banishing blacks from their community. At the end of the day, the form in which antislavery took hold (a movement for the safety and purification of the white community by the removal of people of color), combined with African Americans' refusal to accept a choice between enslavement and banishment, determined the basic outline and spirit of the American nation.

Congress was moved to further define and strengthen the Constitution's provisions for returning fugitive slaves in the new federal government's second year of operation. Ironically, the impetus for tightening procedures for returning fugitive slaves was a case involving white kidnappers of people of color whose extradition was sought by Governor Mifflin of Pennsylvania. In the end, rather than obtaining the return of men charged under his state's kidnapping statutes, the action Mifflin initiated led to President Washington asking Congress to create more specific standards for the capture and rendition between states of both fugitives and escapees from slavery.

The law Congress fashioned in 1793 allowed anyone claiming another person as their slave to seize them, hold them by force and then simply provide "proof to the satisfaction of the judge or magistrate," which could be simply "oral testimony" and receive a license to carry their prisoner back to slavery in their home state.

As this bill was redrafted in committee (a committee that included Roger Sherman of Connecticut) the legal threshold of proof for a master to obtain a warrant was lowered from requiring a deposition under oath to the court, to simply submitting an affidavit endorsed in the master's home state. States were removed from responsibility for hunting escapees and instead private enslavers were allowed to seize people on their own and merely had to obtain a "removal certificate" from a local court to leave with their captives. After deliberation in the House chamber, some of the only remaining protections for black residents accused of being fugitives were removed from the bill and the law passed forty-eight to seven in the House with two of the most vocal critics of slavery, New Jersey's Elias Boudinot and Jonathan Dayton, approving of it. The law was signed by George Washington just fifty-four days after it was first introduced.[18]

While the Pennsylvania Abolition Society routinely sent petitions to Congress in this era, there are no records of any being sent opposing the Fugitive Slave Act. At best, the PAS records contain but one mention of the pending law, a warning issued to its own members that the new law would be "productive of mischievous consequences to the poor Negro Slaves appearing to be calculated with very unfavorable intentions towards them."[19] The first convention of abolitionist societies that took place a few months after passage of the Fugitive Slave law did not mention it. Not until its eighth annual meeting in 1803 did the national convention of abolitionist societies have anything to say about "persons who have taken advantage of the provisions of the fugitive act to found improper claims on the blacks, and thus drag them from their homes to distant parts." But then it only mildly urged that "this subject may very properly be also recommended to the careful attention of the societies."

White abolitionists seem to have drawn a bright line between the *legal* reclaiming of *actual* fugitives from slavery, who they saw as outlaws and outside the scope of their concern, and freed men and women who were *unlawfully* abducted into slavery. Abolition societies devoted much of their time and resources to protecting free black communities from such predation and even appealing to states to tighten penalties for outright kidnapping. But they chose not to challenge the principle that the entire edifice of the republic was founded upon, namely, that slave-owners had the right to reclaim their wayward property in any corner of the nation. No state or citizen had the right to interfere in this natural operation of private property. White abolitionist inaction in the case of the federal Fugitive Slave Act is highly significant in plumbing the distance between the views and goals of black abolitionists and white ones as the first two petitions ever sent to Congress by groups of African Americans prayed for repeal of this hated law.[20]

Congress briefly toyed with the idea of employing federal power to prevent abductions of free people of color by requiring all ship captains to maintain certificates of the "number and situation of negroes or mulattoes he may have on board." When South Carolina's William Smith opposed the measure as an infringement of state's rights, the law's main promoter, John Swanwick of Pennsylvania, pointed out that it was the federal government's responsibility to police the interstate waterways. Few congressmen seemed to care much that kidnappers operated freely along the eastern coast and after sending the bill back to committee, and allowing it to languish for nine months, voted it down on the grounds that it was not "expedient" to "interfere" with state laws. When Congress did contemplate revising the Fugitive Slave Act of 1793 during its session in 1818, the bill it produced made it easier for enslavers to recover their claimed human property. Congress would not actually pass anti-kidnapping legislation until after the Civil War.[21]

There is evidence buried deep in the voluminous records of the House of Representatives that some members of Congress were well aware of the problem of the abduction of free people of color but intentionally ignored the problem. In 1800 a petition from a group of African Americans from Philadelphia pleading for more protections from kidnappers was referred to a special committee on the slave trade. Members of this committee produced an extensive report that concluded that "many Blacks & People of Colour entitled to their Freedom ... are under color of the Fugitive Law entrapped, kidnapped & carried off" to the lower South and to the West Indies where "their color is sufficient Evidence to hold them in a State of Slavery." The authors of the report noted that state laws contained a "Defect of Power" to intercept this trafficking in kidnapped people, especially when the kidnappers stole people away by ship. This report was never read out or released by the committee, and its existence was only discovered much later when a handwritten copy was found in the National Archives.[22]

GRADUAL EMANCIPATION AS RACIAL CLEANSING

When the Pennsylvania legislature began debating some form of gradual emancipation of slavery in 1778 the state's patriot leaders emphasized that the time was ripe for action because the war had reduced the region's black population. Pennsylvania's Executive Council proclaimed, "no period seems more happy for the attempt than the present, as the number of such unhappy characters, ever few in Pennsylvania, has been much reduced by the practices & plunder of our late invaders." It then referred to the effect of the bill freeing only the children of parents then enslaved as "divesting the State of Slaves," which by focusing on the slave as a person, rather than slavery as a legal system, implied that such a law would have the effect of further reducing the black population or at least preventing its growth. Partly this was to be accomplished by prohibiting all slave importations, but the "divesting" of slaves was widely understood at the time to also mean pushing them beyond the state's borders.[23]

Pennsylvania declared that no person born in the state after March 1780 would be a slave for life, but instead would be emancipated when they reach the age of twenty-eight. Enslavers were given until November of that same year to register those people they claimed as their property or they would be declared free as well. Pennsylvania attempted to block the further importation of enslaved people by declaring any slaves brought into the state to be free. However, Philadelphia being the nation's capital at the time, an exception was made for members of Congress and foreign ambassadors who were allowed to keep their slaves with them for up to six months, which was a term long enough to cover one session of Congress.

In contrast to other northern states that had passed weak and probably unenforceable laws to restrict masters from evading emancipation by selling their slaves out of the state, Pennsylvania granted no loophole for moving to reside in a different state or set a legal standard of knowingly or having "designs" to evade the law. The penalty for violation was higher than neighboring states at £75 but was still well below the average sale price of human beings in southern states.[24]

At the same time, Pennsylvania's patriot policymakers made it clear that their vision of ending slavery over a succession of generations was not a plan for including freed men and women into the republic. "It is not proposed that the present Slaves, most of whom are scarcely competent of freedom should be meddled with ..." Pennsylvania's gradual emancipation law contained a provision reinforcing the connection between whiteness and citizenship. "That no man or woman of any nation or color, coming or brought into ... this commonwealth ... shall be entitled unto all the privileges of a freeman, who is not a citizen of this state, allowed to free negroes by this act ..."[25] Also buried in Pennsylvania's proposed gradual emancipation law was a clause that allowed for the auctioning of former slaves for one year if found loitering or "mispending his time" in the view of two justices of the peace.[26]

M. Brissot de Warville observed in 1788 in his book *Travels in North America* that when Pennsylvania enacted its emancipation law, many former slaves were sold south:

this act ... was eluded in many points. A foreign commerce of slaves was carried on by speculators; and some barbarous masters sold their blacks, to be carried into foreign countries; others sent the negro children into neighboring states, that they might there be sold, and deprived of the benefit of the law of Pennsylvania, when they should come of age: others sent their black pregnant women into another state, that the offspring might be slaves; and others stole free negroes, and carried them to the islands for sale.

257

It took a second act of the legislature to establish penalties for these actions.[27]

New York loosened its manumission laws and tightened its slave importation statute in February 1788. After that date, not only was the trade in slaves brought into the state from abroad prohibited, but so was the bringing of slaves into the state from other states. (In 1801, New York narrowed this limitation by allowing enslavers to bring slaves into the state if they planned to become permanent residents.) Up until 1799, it was legal for New York masters to sell the men and women they held in bondage out of state.[28] After 1801, the state opened a legal escape hatch for masters to evade this sale restriction by simply moving out of the state with their human property.[29] According to some estimates, these laws operated to ship a large proportion of the black population of New York to the South. One economist calculated that 24,000 enslaved New Yorkers were sold to slave states, twice as many as were freed by legislation.[30]

In November of 1788, New Jersey's law emancipating the children of slaves upon their twenty-fifth or twenty-first birthdays, placed weak restrictions on masters who preferred to turn a profit by selling their slaves out of state rather than enslaving for a term of years. Rather than prohibiting out-of-state sales entirely, New Jersey's legislature in 1788, in expectation of some form of gradual emancipation being passed in a future session, required a slave-owner to obtain an enslaved person's assent to such a sale (this law was reenacted in 1812). Even sales outside of this broad loophole were difficult to prosecute as New Jersey followed Connecticut's lead and established a high bar of proof for prosecutions: prosecutors had to prove that there was a "design" to remove them for sale rather than simply moving with their slaves to "reside" in another state. Additionally, the fine for violators was far smaller than the potential profit from such sales, in this case just £20.[31]

In 1818, an enterprising Louisiana plantation owner and state legislator named Charles Morgan teamed up with his New Jersey brother-in-law, Jacob Van Wickle, who was a judge in Middlesex County, to turn the sale of New Jersey slaves into a regular and large-scale business. As many of New Jersey's enslaved men and women were to be freed upon reaching adulthood, and the demand for agricultural laborers was not nearly as acute in New Jersey as in the Delta region, their market price was a fraction of similar human commodities in the New Orleans slave markets. Morgan provided the capital, $45,000 to start, and Judge Van Wickle had the power to certify that enslaved men and women had "consented" to being sold "down the river." After setting up a private jail on Van Wickle's estate, the judge's son acted as shipping agent and arranged shipping from Perth Amboy. In the first six months of operation, Morgan and Van Wickle shipped seventy-three enslaved people out of the state, thirteen of whom were infants and children.

Though legal questions about the accuracy of the ship's manifest in recording the names and ages of its human cargo were raised when the first of the Morgan syndicate ships reached New Orleans, an attempted prosecution of the ship captain failed to persuade a local jury. Later, a New Jersey grand jury indicted Charles Morgan but not Judge Van Wickle on charges of violating the law on consent for selling children incompetent to make such an agreement.

New Jersey's legislature lightly revised the consent law in November of 1818, prohibiting sales of slaves to non-residents and barring anyone who had not been five years resident from transporting a slave out of the state. The new law would have prohibited Charles Morgan from purchasing and transporting enslaved people, but not Jacob Van Wickle.

As the law was being debated, some New Jersey masters seized the opportunity and bought up slaves before the law became effective for the purpose of selling them South. John Marsh purchased several men and organized a forced march in chains overland to Louisiana. Though his coffle was detained, and Marsh arrested in Pennsylvania, Marsh returned to New Jersey, successfully sued to reclaim his slaves, and sailed them to Louisiana. William Raburgh bought up eleven slaves from eight separate owners and, like Marsh, was arrested upon crossing the border into Pennsylvania but prevailed in the New Jersey courts who obliged him by imprisoning his chattel in the New Brunswick jail while he arranged their transportation. Raburgh's plans derailed when he attempted to embark his human cargo through

New York and the New York Manumission Society successfully sued in state court on their behalf.

Computing the number of people of color who were dragged or sold out of the state by their masters to avoid their eventual emancipation is highly speculative given the lack of records and the easy evasions of state's mild legal restrictions by slave entrepreneurs. But the most informed estimates are in the hundreds of people who joined the great exodus to the cotton and sugar delta.[32]

Connecticut's gradual emancipation law passed in 1784 encouraged the out-of-state shipment and sale of slaves by setting a date for freedom well in the future and specifically allowing slaveholders to move their human property out of the state. "... nothing in this act shall operate to prevent persons removing out of this state, for the purpose of residence, from carrying or transporting with them such negroes or molattoes as belong to them ..." This clause trumped the weak prohibition on out-of-state sales by requiring that authorities prove an intent to transport for the purpose of sale in order to obtain a conviction. Even in the unlikely event such intent (as opposed to movement for purpose of residency followed by a separate sale) was punishable by a fine that was one-tenth of the profit to be made by selling a human being at then-typical prices. William Fowler, one of the first scholars to write about Connecticut's gradual emancipation law, noted that "slaves were transported out of the State to other States" and recalled that "when I was in Georgia, I heard of a family of Connecticut slaves there."[33]

In 1794, a group of Delaware Quakers petitioned their legislature for more effective prohibition of sales of free black people out of state and into slavery:

> a practice has hitherto prevailed, of assigning the indentures of black servants, to people who at the time reside in this state, but who are immediately going out of it for elsewhere; and who, by means of such assignment, carry such indented black servants out of this state, and afterwards sell them as slaves for life ...[34]

They were ignored.

Connecticut's legislature revised its scattered statutes regulating slavery in 1784 by collecting them together in one section and adding provisions that would prohibit bringing any enslaved people into the state and free the children of enslaved mothers in their twenty-fifth year. As there were no prohibitions placed on the sale of enslaved people out of the state, the force of the law was obviously to encourage the removal of as many black people as possible. When such sales were prohibited in 1788, the penalties for selling enslaved people out of the state were so minimal that the law was rewritten in 1792, but even then it tightened only restrictions on the sale of youth subject to the twenty-five year sunset law leaving those enslaved for life at risk of being sold out of the state. The logic of the marketplace put downward pressure on Connecticut's black population. In 1782 the black population of the state stood at 6273. By 1790 this number had been pushed down to 5572, of whom 2764 were enslaved. Even twenty years later, this number remained largely unchanged as the census counted 310 enslaved people and 6453 "Free Non-White."[35]

Rhode Island passed a gradual emancipation act in 1784 that was designed not to free anyone before 1802. Only those born after the law's passage would become free, girls upon reaching the age of eighteen and boys twenty-one. Like its neighbors, Rhode Island's scheme for eliminating slavery had the effect of accelerating sales and kidnapping of black people out of the state. Judging by the numbers that exist, very few enslaved people had changed status over the course of the first decade of the emancipation law's operation. Then, in the decade leading up to the sunsetting of legalized slavery in 1802, the numbers of enslaved people rapidly dropped by two-thirds, from 948 to 380. However, during this same period, the total black population in the state fell from 4355 to 3684, or 671 souls. As the free population also declined by 103, all this decrease must be accounted for by either the death or out-migration of enslaved people from the state. Clearly, the law worked as intended in driving down the black population. Rhode Island's black community would not grow back to its numbers before the law's implementation for another seventy years, or until 1870, after slavery had been abolished throughout the nation.

Even war heroes were not safe. John Burroughs fought in Rhode Island's famed black regiment until the end of the war. In 1791 he was freed but Burroughs was soon seized and re-enslaved while working on a ship bound for New Orleans. Likewise, a fellow black private from his regiment, Jack Champlin, was somehow also re-enslaved, though the details of his travails have been lost. Burroughs' white commander appealed to the legislature for help in securing both men's freedom but the state government made no efforts to reclaim them.[36]

In Massachusetts a ruling of the state's highest court effectively abolished slavery in the state in 1783. However, it was not until 1788 that a court ruled that the sale or abduction of black people from the state was illegal. Even then, state court rulings and later even specific laws banning the sale of people out-of-state did little to reduce the frequency that freed black people were sold or stolen.[37]

The failure of white officials to enforce even the weak protections against selling enslaved people southward left black communities to struggle to protect themselves. Because such efforts were clandestine (as any efforts to organize independently of white control attracted immediate retaliation and suppression) few are documented and the occasions where actions for black community self-protection surface in the early republic are rare. One collective effort that was recorded happened in 1801 in New York City, when it was learned that a wealthy woman, Jeanne Mathusine Droibillan Volunbrun, who had arrived four years earlier fleeing the revolution in Haiti, was preparing to depart for the South with twenty enslaved people whose status as slaves was cast in doubt by the gradual emancipation law passed two years earlier. Taking matters into their own hands, a crowd of hundreds of people of color surrounded Volunbrun's house threatening to set it afire unless she freed the people she kept in bondage.

In response to this angry protest of African Americans, the city rallied all its force, fifty members of the watch, to disburse it. In the ensuing melee twenty-three black New Yorkers were arrested and later sentenced to two months in the local jail. In the wake of the riot the New York Manumission Society abandoned its quiet legal actions aimed at preventing Madam Volunbrun from absconding from the city, with one of its members declaring that he did not wish to free slaves and thereby contribute to such disorder. Volunbrun then decamped for Baltimore with the people she enslaved where she started a tobacco factory. Later Volunbrun sold an unknown number of the people she had taken from New York further "down the river" to New Orleans.[38]

SOUTHERN BANS ON BLACK TRAVELERS AND MIGRANTS

American leaders had long understood that the most direct way of limiting the growth of the free black population was to prohibit any free people of color from immigrating into their states. Throughout the era of American state formation in the last quarter of the 1700s, states both northern and southern moved to bar the entrance of all people of color, slave or free, whether from abroad or from neighboring states. Southern states were the innovators of these laws prohibiting black migrants and travelers, but northern states adopted them quickly also.

Virginia barred the entrance of free blacks several years before banning foreign slave importations. Following the logic of a general policy of whitening the state population, Virginia legislators permitted an exception to this ban on international importation of slaves when it allowed a West Indian trader to import enslaved people to the state from abroad on one condition, that he "at the same time, import the like number of white laborers or mechanics."[39]

In late 1793, Virginia's legislature approved "An Act to Prevent the Migration of Free Negroes and Mulattoes into this Commonwealth" that prohibited any free black persons from entering the state. Free people of color resident in the state were required to register with their local county officials and to re-register whenever they relocated. Unlike South Carolina's prohibition of free blacks, Virginia, already having a surplus of enslaved people, did not require that violators be sold into slavery but instead required justices of the peace to "send and remove every such negro or mulatto out of this commonwealth, into that state or island from whence it shall appear he or she last

263

came ..." Exceptions for black sailors and the personal servants of travelers were allowed.[40]

Eventually, in 1806, twenty years after expanding the ability of whites to free their slaves, the Virginia Assembly ordered that all slaves freed by their will or by deed leave the state entirely within one calendar year. Other states followed suit and soon five states (Alabama, Kentucky, North Carolina, Virginia, and Tennessee) passed laws requiring all slaves voluntarily freed by their masters to promptly leave the state.[41]

The racial exclusionary character of state laws banning slave importation is highlighted by the fact that many of these laws also barred the entry of free people of color. South Carolina's two-year slave import ban of 1792 began with a preamble that baldly proclaimed its purpose as limiting the black population, "WHEREAS it is deemed inexpedient to increase the number of slaves within this state, in our present circumstances and situation ..." It then added alongside its suspension of the importation of enslaved people, any "negro Indian, Moor, mulatto or mutizo, bound to service for a term of years." At the time, the vast majority of free people of color, especially those arriving from foreign ports, would have struck some sort of labor contract that fell under this clause. An exception was made for any white settlers migrating to South Carolina, or those who obtained slaves from other lands by marriage, all such were allowed to import their own human property.[42] Reviving the ban of 1792 in its 1794 session, South Carolina's legislature firmed up its limitations on black migration to the state, prohibiting all free people of color, not just those arriving on labor contracts.[43]

When South Carolina again temporarily prohibited the importation of slaves in 1800, it significantly tightened its language and its mechanisms of enforcement. The 1800 statute followed the 1794 statute banning any person of color from entering the state: "... nor shall it be lawful for any free negro, mulatto or mestizo, any time after the passing of this act, to enter into this state ..." But added to this law were detailed and specific procedures for how it should be enforced. Any free person could inform a magistrate and force a warrant to jail suspected prohibited immigrants to be issued. Warrants were then handed over to militia captains who were empowered to dragoon white citizens into their posse and were explicitly given the power to use deadly force ("if need be, to attack, wound and kill any person who shall resist"), in apprehending fugitives and anyone, white or black, who assisted them. After being seized, jailed, and convicted, the person who had illegally entered the state was sold at auction, half the proceeds going to the informant who began the whole process, the other half being divided among the posse members who rode to the capture.[44]

Slave-owners passing through the state or residing for up to two years were exempted from these provisions, though they were prohibited from bringing more than ten enslaved persons temporarily into South Carolina. Likewise, exceptions were made for black sailors working ships that docked in the state, if bonds were posted to ensure their timely departure.

South Carolina's legislature added to this black exclusion law a full measure of all the methods a state that had few actual law enforcement officials employed in this era to compel officials and citizens to comply with its rules. To ensure enforcement, the state allowed local justices only twelve hours to issue an arrest warrant upon being informed of the presence of a prohibited black person by any white citizen. Failure to do so was punished by a fine of $200, half payable to the informant, along with disqualification from the bench for a period of five years. Militia captains were threatened with court martial if they failed to execute the warrants they were given. Tax collectors who learned that any person had entered the state illegally were required to inform the nearest court or be sacked and fined $200. Even ferry boat captains and bridge tenders who knowingly conveyed prohibited passengers were subject to a $5 fine per colored person.

Slave-owning South Carolinians found these restrictions "too rigorous and inconvenient" and later loosened the requirements for masters traveling through the state with their slaves, though the general ban on the admission of free people of color remained in force.[45]

Kentucky in 1808 closed its borders to free people of color.

Whereas it is represented to the present general assembly that a very serious evil is likely to be produced by the emigration of emancipated slaves from different parts of the union to this state, and that many of the states have passed laws compelling slaves when emancipated by citizens of their respective states to remove out of such state within a given time: for remedy whereof ... it shall not be lawful for any free negro or mulatto to migrate or be brought into this state from any territory or state within the United States, or elsewhere ...

Penalties for violation of Kentucky's exclusion law were all aimed at achieving the removal of the person of color from the state. Upon being found to be in the state in violation of the law, the accused was required to post a $500 bond that would be forfeited if they did not leave the state within twenty days. Failure to post such bond resulted in the sale of the person at auction for a term of service of one year, the proceeds of which constituted their departure bond. Failure to leave at the end of that term of service resulted in another cycle of sale and bonding that could repeat in perpetuity.[46]

On September 21, 1776, Delaware finalized its constitution that prohibited both the slave trade and the importation of any slaves into the state for the purposes of sale.[47] A decade later, Delaware prohibited the importation of all enslaved people. Legislators apparently had a greater interest in limiting the growth of the enslaved black population than in accommodating the needs of slave-owners and denied the petition of Charles Thomas who in 1793 moved into the state from Maryland and asked to bring "one negro Man, named Sam, Two negro women, named Fanny & Hannah, Three negro boys, named Jack, Reuben & Perry, and one negro girl named Nanee" with him. Likewise, Samuel Dredden inherited a "negro boy named Levin" from the estate of a Maryland relative but was denied legislative permission to bring the child across state lines.[48]

White Delawareans grew increasingly perturbed by the presence of African Americans in their communities. Thirty-nine individuals signed their name to a petition asking that the state government pass additional restrictions on the movements of black people. They complained that it was too difficult to distinguish free and black and that "many idle and evil-disposed Slaves througout this County stroll thro' the same, some with, and some without passes or certificates." Not only were they concerned with the easy counterfeiting of slave passes, but they worried that black "stragglers and vagabonds," freed from surrounding states, found their way into their county and became "chargeable."[49]

Delaware later expanded this policy to prohibit all free people of color from entering the state in 1807 and innovated a novel legal provision that had the potential of gradually diminishing the black population. Any free black resident of Delaware, except "any sea-faring person or persons of colour, who may be following his or their occupation," who left the state for a period of two years was deemed ineligible to return. The same statute also prohibited racial inter-marriage and established harsher penalties for theft and other petty crimes committed by free people of color. Unsatisfied with the effec-tiveness of this law, the state government passed a stronger one in 1811 that sold violators into slavery and fined anyone who gave them shelter or employment.[50]

Delaware also was a pioneer in state-sanctioned sale of freemen out of the state on the pretense that they were "leased convicts." Black men convicted of crimes were routinely "leased" as indentured serv-ants to out-of-state masters. In 1839 the state's governor reported that in all the years in which this practice had been routine, not a single convict was ever returned at the expiration of their term, rather they were all sold as slaves.[51]

Neighboring Maryland first banned the importation of slaves "by land or water" in 1783 and then as its free black population contin-ued to climb strengthened the letter of this law to include them in 1796. It too required that free black men, women, and children regis-ter their manumission or certify their birthright freedom at the local courthouse or risk being fined, jailed, or deported. It was these laws that Frederick Douglass recalled in his *Autobiography*: "Any white man is authorized to stop a man of color, on any road, and examine him, and arrest him, if he so desires ... freemen have been called upon to show their papers ... and on the presentation of the papers, the ruffians have torn them up, and seized their victim, and sold him to a life of endless bondage."[52]

Georgia included in its 1793 "Act to Prevent the Importation of Negroes into This State, from the Places herein Mentioned" both a ban on the importation of slaves from the West Indies and Florida, and on the admission of any free people of color who could not obtain a certificate of "honesty and industry" from two different county magistrates.[53] Further restrictions were enacted in 1810 when a prohibitive tax of $20 was required of each free person of color entering the state and the registration provisions were made even more stringent. Georgia followed Delaware's precedent and stipulated that any free person of color leaving the state for more than six months was from that time forward no longer considered a resident.[54]

North Carolina strengthened its laws excluding free black people from the colony in 1723. By that time the law required that any slave set free by their owners was required to leave the colony within six months or be sold at public auction. However, to prevent those freed and banished from returning, the North Carolina Assembly created a bounty system where

if any Slave or Slaves being so freed and set at Liberty, having departed as before directed, shall presume to return back into this Province, it shall and may be lawful for any Person or Persons whatsoever to apprehend and take up such Slave or Slaves so offending, and carry him or them before some Magistrate ...

Upon the judge's order the accused was then to be sold for a term of seven years, half of the proceeds given to "the Apprehender." At the expiration of the seven-year term, the formerly enslaved person was still required to leave North Carolina or the process would begin again.[55] Such laws were not repealed when the patriots took over but tightened.

North Carolina's legal code established after the Revolution included a mechanism for easily expelling free African Americans from any town in the state. Under the pretense of preventing free black people from trading with slaves (who it was presumed would only traffic stolen goods) and to prevent them from aiding runaways, the penalties for selling or buying goods from slaves, or harboring an escapee, were increased to include banishment for seven years. As a further incentive to local officials to expel free black people, expulsion was accompanied by a hefty fine of £10 that "commissioners, trustees, or directors as the case may be" may take "payable to themselves." And further, to make free black people "more easily be convicted" the standard of proof of illegal buying or selling was for any slave, not licensed to trade on behalf of their master, to carry into the house or store of a free black person any article that "may be supposed for sale."[56]

Louisiana's territorial legislature barred the entry of free people of color from the island of Hispaniola or any French islands. In 1807 it broadened this restriction and declared the Territory of Orleans closed to all free people of color.[57]

When Congress passed legislation authorizing the incorporation of the City of Washington, they included a provision that allowed the city to exclude people of color. The city was given authority to "prescribe the terms and conditions upon which free negroes and mulattoes may reside in the city." As Congressman Smith noted a couple years later, "Giving power to prescribe the terms, is, in effect, giving power to expel."[58]

NORTHERN BLACK EXCLUSION

The deep desire of Americans in northern states to limit the growth of African Americans is well illustrated by a law passed by Rhode Island in 1770. Titled "An Act Prohibiting the Importation of Negroes into this Colony," the law began with a ringing preamble: "Whereas, the inhabitants of America are generally engaged in the preservation of their own rights and liberties, among which, that of personal freedom must be considered as the greatest; as those who are desirous of enjoying all the advantages of liberty themselves, should be willing to extend personal liberty to others ..." So as to ease this contradiction, the Rhode Island Assembly declared it was banning the further importation of slaves and established a self-enforcing mechanism whereby the courts would not recognize claims of ownership over people brought into the colony in violation of the law.

While on its face a large step in the direction of containing the further growth of slavery, the act was at the same time a declaration that people of color were not legitimate members of society. The legislation continued: "in case any slave shall hereafter be brought in, he or she shall be, and are hereby, rendered immediately free, so far as respects personal freedom, and the enjoyment of private property, in the same manner as the native Indians." As in all parts of New England, "native Indians" were defined as existing outside society, as neither subject to colonial rule nor protected by its laws. Those Indians who were not properly registered and living within the jurisdictions of "praying towns" were outlaws who could be hunted and murdered in exchange for bounty payments.

Underneath this law's rhetoric was a rather toothless mechanism that allowed most everyday operations of slavery to continue unhindered. Travelers to the state were allowed to enter and leave with their slaves; immigrants who arrived with human property were allowed to retain ownership (but if they subsequently emigrated, they were obligated to take their slaves with them out of Rhode Island). Slaves leased out to ship masters and returned after their voyages were not freed, and, most egregiously, slaves seized out of Africa for sale in the West Indies but could not be sold at a desirable price could be imported, and held in the colony for up to a year while waiting for a more favorable market.[59]

New Jersey's colonial slave code of 1713 specified that "no negro, indian, or molatto, who shall thereafter be made free" could legally own or "possess" any "houses, lands, tenements or hereditaments" and this apparently remained in force in 1786 when the state also loosened manumissions so as to "exempt the master's estate from maintaining the slave so freed if he or she, at a future time becomes chargable ..."[60] While giving masters more power to free their own slaves, New Jersey's law was focused on limiting the growth of the number of black people in the state and restricting the movements of those already there. It banned the importation of African slaves, prohibited any freed people from "travelling in this state," and established penalties for anyone employing or housing such a person. All free people of color in New Jersey were prohibited from traveling outside the township or county where they lived as a slave, unless they first secured a certificate from two justices and the clerk of their county court.[61]

Other northern states provided for the exclusion of racially unwelcome visitors and migrants without having to refer to their race. Vermont on November 6, 1801, passed a law giving selectmen "power to remove from the State any persons who come there to reside. And any person removed, and returning without permission of the selectmen, shall be whipped ..."[62] One politician wryly noted: "there would be but few, either black or white, who would become citizens, until there should be some other mode of naturalizing than at the whipping post." Other New England states, such as Connecticut, had extensive and clearly defined "warning out" procedures whereby town authorities, without any sort of judicial procedure, could order the expulsion of any unwanted arrivals on pain of being jailed and whipped and then conducted to town limits.

Warning out proved effective in driving many people of color from the smaller towns to New England's urban centers. Massachusetts' Jeremy Belknap observed of free black people that "They have generally, though not wholly left the country, and resorted to the maritime towns ... the number of blacks in Boston probably exceeds one thousand."[63]

Apparently even this broad authority was not sufficient to police their racial boundaries and in 1796 Connecticut required free people of color to obtain travel passes from local authorities. "Whatsoever negro, mulatto, or Indian servant, shall be found wandering out of the bounds of the town or place to which they belong, without a ticket, or pass, in writing, to be taken up ... No free negro is to travel without a pass from the selectmen or justices." Whites in Connecticut were subject to fines for "buying or receiving any thing from a free negro, mulatto, or Indian servant ..."[64] When Connecticut abolished slave importations into the state it also required all "free negroes" to obtain certificates of their freedom from a local magistrate and always carry them.

Careful studies of town records conducted by Ruth Herndon found the warning out process was disproportionately used to expel people of color throughout the eighteenth century. Tellingly, the already high figures for black and native people forced to leave towns began to rise with the formation of the new independent American state. Herndon finds that "white officials began to target people of color for removal in the 1780s and 1790s" and that many towns began specifically rounding up their communities of color. East Greenwich, Connecticut, in a fit of ethnic cleansing, ordered "all the Indians, mulattoes & Negros" to leave in 1786. While some towns made exceptions for black individuals born in the area, Providence compiled a list of "blacks of all descriptions whatever dwelling in this Town" and warned them all out.[65]

Massachusetts passed its first racial exclusion law in 1788. This law seems to have been prompted by a state supreme court ruling in the case of *Exeter* v. *Hanchett* (1783) that allowed slave-owners to bring enslaved people into the state without fear the state would free them.[66] When the court ruled that it was unconstitutional to negate the human property of citizens from another state, it potentially opened the door for an influx of enslaved people of color from neighboring states. While the state was restricted by its judiciary from altering the status of enslaved people once they arrived in the state, it was not restrained from simply barring all people of color from entering.

Like most other states, Massachusetts' legislature moved vigorously to bar people of color from the state, passing three separate exclusion laws between 1788 and 1802. These laws drew no differences between free and enslaved people of color, though it did provide an exemption for those who could prove their citizenship by a certificate, which at the time were generally only provided to sailors or, in New York, those who otherwise qualified to vote. Penalties for violators included deportation out of the state, imprisonment, and whipping. At least 158 African Americans and seventy-six Indians were thrown out of the state through the operation of these laws.[67]

Just to be certain that their constabulary had all the discretion they needed to expel people they thought troublesome, in 1800 Massachusetts passed a "loiterers law" that allowed officials the power to declare any newcomer a "loiterer" and require them to leave the state within sixty days.[68]

White abolitionists in the Bay State did not campaign against such laws. Reverend Jeremy Belknap, generally considered an opponent of slavery at the time, described this law as preventing "deserting negroes from resorting hither, in hopes to obtain freedom, and then being thrown as a dead weight on this community."[69]

Black sailmaker James Forten successfully fought against a similar proposed law in Pennsylvania and vividly described what its effects would be, perhaps drawing on what he knew of its operation on the other side of the Delaware River. Not only did such laws render every black person easy prey for kidnappers and at risk for being sold back into slavery in their own state, but it also forced them to be informers and enforcers of the hated law as well. "The man of colour receiving as a visiter any other person of colour, is bound to turn informer, and rudely report to the Register, that a friend or brother has come to visit him for a few days ..." Forten gave the example of a brother of his who lived in a "distant part of the Union" and "after a separation of years" drawn by "fraternal affection" comes and visits. "Unless that brother be registered in twenty four hours after, and be able to produce a certificate to that effect, he is liable ... to arrest, imprisonment, and sale."

Forten goes behind the letter of the law to illustrate how it would give force to the prejudices of the public and encourage and empower every white person to lord over every black person.

The Constable, whose antipathy generally against the black is very great, will take every opportunity of hurting his feelings!—Perhaps, he sees him at a distance, and having a mind to raise the boys in hue and cry against him, exclaims, "Halloa! Stop the Negro!" The boys, delighting in sport, immediately begin to hunt him, and immediately from a hundred tongues, is heard the cry—"*Hoa, Negro, where is your Certificate!*"

Such laws that seemed minor and administrative to most whites, merely requiring "registration" after all, Forten showed undermined all other rights. Registration laws not only undermined a black person's liberty but even their ability to hold property. Forten wrote, "our property is jeopardized, since the same power which can expose to sale an unfortunate fellow creature, can wrest from him those estates, which years of honest industry have accumulated."[70]

White abolitionist ranks dwindled in the last decade of the eighteenth century because most white opponents of slavery felt that by then everything that needed to be done to end it had been accomplished. In 1791, Zephaniah Swift, a member of the Connecticut House of Representatives, addressed the Connecticut Society for the Promotion of Freedom, and the Relief of Persons Unlawfully Holden in Bondage. Swift, then working on compiling the first legal treatise to be published by an American, asked his audience, "what measures can be suggested, adopted, and executed to accomplish the important purpose of abolition"? Swift's answer was surprisingly self-congratulatory. "In our own State a punctual observance of the laws in being will eventually answer the design." As for the less enlightened parts of their young nation, the "principles that constitute the basis of the government of the United States will infallibly produce an extinction of slavery throughout the empire, as soon as will be compatible with the safety of the public and the welfare of the slaves themselves." For Swift, and presumably for his audience, nothing further had to be done to accomplish their mission as a slow gradual process of liberation best served white interests.[71]

While white abolitionists fought against kidnappings of freed men, women, and children, they were curiously inactive in pushing for stronger laws prohibiting the sale of enslaved people out of the state much farther away from the slim prospect of ever one day being free. Why this was is not well documented, mostly because white antislavery organizations and activists rarely discussed it. However, glimpses of the deeper motivations behind this inactivity can be found scattered through the detritus of history. For example, one famed Connecticut abolitionist, Theodore Dwight, when speaking before the Society for the Promotion of Freedom in 1794, let slip his pleasure at the effect of the gradual emancipation laws in reducing the black population. While urging "the total abolition of slavery" and even defending the rights of enslaved people to violently resist their oppressors as the people of Santo Domingo had done, Dwight asked, "Can it be urged as a reason for its continuance, that the slaves, not being numerous enough to become troublesome, are unworthy of the public attention?" Like an unbuttoned garment, Dwight's rhetorical question revealed more than he intended; abolition, even one that was immediate, could be accomplished in the Nutmeg State because the number of slaves had safely dwindled (according to plan) to an unthreatening number.[72]

Northern states had the luxury of passing emancipation laws that everyone expected would gradually reduce both the number of slaves and the number of black people. Southern states attempted to craft similar programs, but these failed because of powerful and self-interested factions of planters but also because the size of their populations of enslaved people was too large to simply push freed men, women, and children out of their states. For them, slavery was a solution to both problems as slaves could be sold west, thereby building the empire and reducing the black proportion of their home populaces. Whatever residue of free black people that remained could be ethnically cleansed through banishment to Liberia, or Haiti, or South America.

Almost to a man, patriot founding fathers hated slavery in principle. They also knew that slavery was not just a system of labor, but a system of social control and their vision of America had no place for citizens who were not white. From their perspective, emancipation solved no problems because changing a black slave into a black freed person still left the black. Emancipation simply multiplied a free black population that no whites, not even abolitionists, wanted in their towns or counties.

While drafting their fundamental charters of law to make it easier to rid their communities of black people, they also knew they would probably not be successful in pushing beyond the nation's borders every single one. The other solution to their racial dilemma was to punch a series of loopholes through their belief in equality before the law that rendered all black people subject to the authority and control of whites.

275

7

The Patriots' Solution—Civil Slavery

The current fashion among historians of eighteenth-century abolitionism is to depict it as an interracial movement in which white
and black activists struggled together to achieve the same goals of
freedom. This revisionism is only possible by overlooking the vast
differences of social, economic, and political power between the two
communities. Even the most established and respected leaders of the
black community wielded less influence than the least accomplished
members of any white antislavery organization. Black leaders navi-
gated an unequal relationship where whites held the keys to access
to education, to employment, to property, and to law, both its formulation and its protection. Both black leaders and regular members
of the black community sought white patronage as it was necessary
for social and economic advancement and the security of anything
anyone had already acquired.[1]

Moreover, while both black and white antislavery activists loudly
denounced slavery and organized to end it, their motivations and
underlying interests never aligned. As has been shown, white activists
were fundamentally concerned with the self-interest of their white
nation, a community threatened by God's worldly punishments for
violating his laws, by otherworldly damnation for sin, by the corruption of their republic, by the discouragement of white immigration,
by the retardation of economic growth, by foreign invasion, and by
servile insurrection. Black activists' goals were simpler: they demanded
their immediate liberation and their equal rights as citizens. In order
to maintain their theory that eighteenth-century abolitionism was
"interracial," revisionist historians have to ignore the stark and irrefu-
table fact that no record exists of any white abolitionist calling for the
immediate liberation of enslaved people until 1816, thirty years after
the drafting of the U.S. Constitution and after most of the white anti-

slavery organizations founded in the eighteenth century had folded up their tents and retired. When George Bourne became the first white American to demand the "total and immediate" abolition of slavery he broke with the century-long precedent of white antislavery crusaders crafting their programs of reform by prioritizing what was most beneficial to the white community.[2]

At the first convention of abolitionist societies held in Philadelphia in 1794, the organization's leadership and its broader representation of delegates had diverging views on the scope and purpose of combating slavery. Organizers of the conference, led by Benjamin Rush, opened their meeting by proposing that the body prepare a series of five resolutions and memorials. None of these proposals passed through the remainder of the week's proceedings without being significantly toned down. Rather, their appeals shifted from benevolent concern for the well-being of those in bondage to the best interests of whites.

As had all their antislavery precursors, this convention's organizers prioritized ending the slave trade, making this their first resolution. After three days' debate, the resolution that was finally approved urged ending the slave trade on the grounds that it was responsible for increasing the black population. Only by ending the trade was it possible to "diminish the number of Slaves in the United States," to "prohibit an accumulation of the evil, by further importation." All could agree, these memorialists believed, that this "evil" was of such "great magnitude" they had "to prevent its growth, and gradually to destroy it."

Throughout this resolution slavery was never named. Rather, it is referred to as "an evil, entailed upon us by our ancestors," a construction that allowed for various impressions as to what constituted such "evil." Was it evil because of the cruelty and abuse of fellow human beings? Or was it evil because it propagated a debased race of savages in a white nation? Nothing in the resolution itself precluded the later reading. Indeed, a racist interpretation is encouraged in such phrases as describing the "evil" as "a dishonorable stain upon a country, the basis of whose political happiness is man's equal rights." (The usage of the word "man" here need not include those of African ancestry whose status as men was an open question at the time.) The abolitionists' resolution closes by equating what ending the slave trade would mean to enslaved people and what it meant to the interests of white Americans by calling on the states to "abolish a practice, no less destructive to the interests of the United States, than to the general cause of humanity."

This convention also demonstrated that even the more empathetic leaders of America's abolitionists expressed some hesitation about the extension of equal rights to those they had successfully freed, hoping that freed men be granted "such participation in civil privileges, as, by the diffusion of knowledge among them, they may, from time to time, be qualified to enjoy." These reformers saw their role as tutoring and supervising those emancipated from slavery toward the light of citizenship and to this end, they urged the founding of schools and for opponents of slavery "to use their utmost endeavours to have the children of the free and other Africans, instructed in common literature in the principles of virtue and religion, and afterwards in useful mechanical arts; thereby to prepare them for becoming good citizens of the United States." It wasn't clear from the skeletal minutes of their early conventions how long a period of tutelage would be required to qualify formerly enslaved people to enjoy rights and duties as American citizens, or who would confirm their readiness, though, presumably, these activists believed they would have some role in it.

On a superficial level, the rhetoric of these abolitionists can be seen to support the assumption that they supported the idea that freed men should be granted citizenship and equal rights. But a deeper reading of their idea of rights shows that these were not the same as whites enjoyed. Their view of black citizenship was contingent on a judgment of good behavior and character whites were not subjected to. Black rights were different from white ones as they were based on white generosity, rather than a claim of equality. Rather, these white abolitionists acknowledged that emancipated African Americans had to demonstrate their fitness before their white patrons could, or should, bestow upon them additional "protections." They did not dispute that at the present black people had an unacceptably and even dangerous character. "We are all too much accustomed to the reproaches of the enemies of our cause, on the subject of the ignorance and crimes of the Blacks, not to wish that they were ill-founded." Rather, they pinned their hopes on some distant future day when black character could be elevated and then, and only then, could they be entrusted with something approaching "certain rights" that "legislative justice might safely admit him." Such progress was premised on proper white supervision; "we have witnessed an increase of the useful qualities in the African citizen, keeping pace with the kindness and protection of which he partakes." These concerns were embodied in the name Delaware's abolitionists gave the organization they founded in 1788: the "Delaware Society for Promoting the Abolition of Slavery, for Superintending the Cultivation of Young Free Negroes, and for the Relief of Those Who May Be Unlawfully Held in Bondage."[3]

Kris Manjapra is one recent scholar who has broken from the herd of historians who have recuperated eighteenth-century white antislavery activists and see only their altruism. Manjapra objects to such uncritical celebrations of abolition that don't take account of the content of the freedom they implemented through law. Not only did their approach to abolition prolong the captivity of those they claimed to champion, but these forms of emancipation "established a historical manual for how to breach human rights" and for distinguishing "who counts as human." Schemes of "gradual emancipation" were neither gradual nor emancipatory as much as mechanisms for giving "reparations" to enslavers that were paid for with the continuing labor of those scheduled at some future time to be gradually freed. Moreover, they institutionalized in law a chasm between those who could enjoy the blessings of republican government and law and those who were subject to its surveillance and repression. Worst, these were not failures or defeats of better-intentioned plans but the consequences of their fundamental design.[4]

What Manjapra traced through the course of projects of emancipation throughout the Atlantic world was the predictable result of an antislavery movement motivated and structured primarily by white activists whose overriding priority was advancing the interests and safety of the white community. Such white priorities have been obscured by historians who have selectively highlighted white abolitionists' benevolent rhetoric and suppressed their equally insistent appeals to white interests. Whether reading through histories of abolitionism published a century ago or this week, one will find only infrequent, scattered, and deemphasized references to abolitionists' fear and disgust of the black people they claimed to represent.

The fact that even the most celebratory accounts of white abolitionism occasionally mention a dissonant note, such as that some of those calling for the end of the slave trade did so because the trade increased the black population, raises a methodological question that is never pursued. When confronted with evidence of both altruistic and selfish motivations for wishing slavery to end, how does one decide which was sincere, which was foremost, and which was mere rhetoric? Manjapra's approach provides one clear answer: the contours of abolitionists' actual attempts to legislate an end to slavery expose their true concerns. In the case of the so-called "gradual emancipation laws" that were passed by northern states, New Jersey being last in 1804, such laws not only made the enslaved compensate their owners through continued years of exploitation, they forced those technically freed into subservient relationships to whites whose patronage they needed to protect their liberty and their property. The simple fact that white abolitionists were the architects of these oppressive plans and cheered their passage as the fulfillment of their crusade should cast a harsh light upon their original motivations.

A new wave of historians, motivated by previous generations' dismissal of early abolitionists as meek, elitist, or worse, crypto-capitalists, have worked to burnish their halos. Rightly suspicious of interpretations of antislavery activists as psychologically irrational, fanatical, or wracked with status anxiety, these academics have recovered the record of their astute campaigns built upon persuasive oratory and effective political strategies. This upcoming generation of historians of pre-Garrisonian abolitionism thought earlier scholars had ignored the voices of black activists and consequently overlooked the powerful way that African Americans themselves had influenced even the white antislavery activists of the eighteenth century. Manisha Sinha, a leader of this revisionist school, slammed the famed historians of the 1960s such as David Brion Davis and Winthrop Jordan for their

blindness to the interracial character of the early abolitionist movement. "The interracialism of this first wave of abolition lay forgotten
as many subsequent historians dismissed this revolutionary phase of
abolition as gradualist, conservative, and predominantly white-dom-
inated," Sinha opined in the flagship journal of American history.[5]

The problem with this, as Kris Manjapra abundantly documents,
is that black abolitionists had a completely different vision of emancipation than their white counterparts. Their petitions to state
governments and to Congress contained appeals not only for an immediate end to slavery, but their recognition of their rights as citizens,
and for "land, education, and for social protection." White antislavery
campaigners pushed for no specific provisions in their emancipation
laws respecting or restoring freed people's property, protecting their
basic human rights such as maintaining the integrity of families, educating children, or shielding them from discrimination. States only
begrudgingly extended limited rights and protections, such as the
right to vote, largely because of their impact on whites, such as issuing
certificates of citizenship to black sailors as part of a larger program
of protecting white sailors from English impressment.[6]

It should not be surprising that instances of cooperation and coor-
dination can be found between black leaders and white activists.
Given the pervasive climate of racism and discrimination, the disregard of black rights by legal authorities, and their tenuous ability
to even lodge complaints, it should be expected that black communities welcomed any allyship from powerful whites, even when such
alliances were unequal and patronizing. What is a mistake is to read
these moments of interracial organization as black leaders' valida-
tion of white activist goals or rhetoric. It is hard to imagine how it
would have been possible for black leaders to both court the protec-
tive patronage of politically connected whites and to publicly criticize
them. Rather, such interactions should be read within the framework
of disproportionate white power and presumed to involve the compro-
mising of black hopes for the attainment of limited goals. Moreover,
it can be presumed that when black and white activists came together,
the true black interests and viewpoints rarely passed into a historical record that was written and preserved by whites. Rather, what

survives in these journals and papers is a record of strategic black engagement with a white movement that did not represent their true aspirations but could offer halting and temporary gains that had to be seized or lost.[7]

For example, Black Philadelphian James Forten anonymously published *Letters from a Man of Colour* in 1813 and besides defending the rights of African Americans and arguing for their full citizenship in the republic, Forten's book reveals the unequal relationship of black leaders like Forten with their supposed white abolitionist allies. On its first page, Forten appeals to "the white men, whom we should look upon as our protectors." In his second letter after lamenting the death of the "zealous friend" and "sincere advisor" Benjamin Rush, Forten appealed again to "Ye, who should be our protectors." In his last letter, Forten refers to various "societies" formed to "ameliorate the condition of our unfortunate brethren," undoubtedly alluding to the Pennsylvania Abolition Society. Such societies, Forten explains, uplift his "brethren" in their attempts "to correct their morals and to render them not only honest but useful members to society."

All of Forten's references to whites, including or, perhaps especially, those who proclaimed themselves opposed to slavery, implied more than just an unequal relationship. Throughout his letters Forten's voice is deferential rather than confrontational, reflecting the grossly disproportionate power in Forten's relationship with even his supposed allies.[8]

The combining of the old laws of slavery with the sunsetting of slavery far into the future after the death of the last living enslaved person effectively transformed slavery from a system of private ownership to one where African Americans became what Joanne Pope Melish called "slaves of the community." Under these laws, no black person, free or enslaved, could move about without passes and the scrutiny and permission of whites, had to abide by curfews, and any deemed "vagrant" could be jailed. The enslaved remained prohibited from buying and selling goods or "entertaining" other black folks. Melish peels back the rhetoric of these laws to uncover their grounding in the "rights, safety, and welfare" of a "presumptively white" public

282

and their expression as "republican entitlements within the domain of citizenship from which slaves were and would remain excluded."⁹

"Liberty" and "freedom" meant different things in eighteenth-century America depending on whether one was deemed black or white. When white abolitionists campaigned to free some enslaved people from their bondage, they also understood that this freedom was not, and could not be, the same liberty that they themselves enjoyed. Emancipation to these white abolitionists meant release from private ownership and control but not the absence of control, for free black persons were subject to harsh supervisory regimes that effectively made all whites their collective masters.

White abolitionists were responsible for first formulating arguments that tied black liberation to white supervision and control. Even the renowned abolitionist Anthony Benezet, who was unusual in imagining emancipated black people as enjoying a more equal share of liberty with whites than most patriots were willing to concede, consigned free black families to the close supervision of whites.¹⁰

Benezet's specific proposal for emancipation required that enslaved people continue to serve their present owners until they could be justly compensated for the loss of their property, or as Benezet phrased it, "after serving so long as may appear to be equitable." Those freed would then be required to register with their county court and not be allowed to move or travel about freely, or "be obliged to be a resident during a certain number of years." For this period of years, (Benezet did not specify the term) free black people were to be "under the care of the overseers of the poor." At the time he wrote, to be under such public care meant being subject to being bound out and indentured to labor and being under the discipline of some white private citizen. Benezet was in favor of returning black families to the authority of whites because he believed "they would be obliged to act the more circumspectly, and make proper use of their liberty." Children would all be bound out to other white families which Benezet thought would given them "an opportunity of obtaining such instructions as are necessary to the common occasions of life." Such a system, Benezet exclaimed, was one where "both parents and children might gradually become useful members of the community." Benezet did not venture to suggest how long this state of white community control, this system of parole and probation, should last, other than suggesting that it should be "years."[11]

John Pleasants, a leader of his Upper Quarterly Meeting in Virginia and father of the famed antislavery activist Robert Pleasants, made provision in his 1771 will for the manumission of his slaves, but this freedom was provisional and remained tied to Pleasants' heirs' judgment of their behavior.

> But if either of the above eight slaves should make so bad a use of this liberty given them as not to labor for their support according to their capacity, or disobey the laws and will (in the judgment of a majority of my trustees) be better for them or any of them so deficient to return to their former servitude it may be in the power of my trustees to divide them among my children, or my poor friends that will use them well as much to the comfort and satisfaction of the poor unhappy creatures as they possibly can.[12]

Likewise, Robert Pleasants drafted manumission papers for a fourteen-year-old boy named Jamey in 1772 that conditioned his freedom on his behavior. Pleasants provided that Jamey would serve his cousin in Philadelphia until he reached the age of twenty-one, except that "in case of misbehaviour" his cousin should "have the liberty of returning him," or, in other words, sending him back to Virginian slavery.[13]

To North Carolina Quaker Thomas Nicholson and many other early white abolitionists, even the offer of manumission was made with strings attached. Nicholson wrote that he was willing to give up his own slaves "on reasonable and lawful Terms." Until such "reasonable" terms could be obtained, Nicholson thought it best "to keep them and use them well, and after a reasonable number of Years of Servitude to defray the Cost ... to make them free." Even those freed after working years to further compensate their owners were never truly free in this slave society, for Nicholson advocated a continuing regime of control and discipline enforced by the threat of being resold back into slavery. After their release, freed men and women should be put "under proper Guardians and Restrictions to keep them from becoming a public Charge or Offense to Government, and such as behave badly ... to be sold to other masters ..."[14]

When a group of antislavery Methodists from Frederick County, Virginia, petitioned for a law that would gradually emancipate slaves in the state, they conceded their opponents' arguments that freeing the enslaved would lead to violence and crime, but reassured the legislators that the police powers of the state were adequate to meet this challenge.

> That the fear of the Enormities which the Negroes may commit, will be groundless, at least if the Emancipation be gradual, as the Activity of the Majestrates and the provision of Houses of Correction where Occasion may require, will easily Suppress the gross, flagrant, Idleness either of Whites or Blacks.

In other words, private slavery may be safely exchanged for a public regime of social surveillance and discipline.[15]

Likewise, when a group of Virginia Quakers attempted to justify their releasing their slaves in 1780 against the laws of the state, they stressed their "care and caution" to "give no just occasion for their good design therein to be evil spoken of." Not wanting to be seen as disregarding the safety and peace of their white neighbors and the white community at large, they detailed how they took "care and caution" to only release those they deemed as capable of their own support. Minors remained under the discipline and supervision of masters who simply treated them as bound apprentices. The elderly and infirm continued to be held in slavery. Those men and women who were set at liberty remained under the thumb of their former masters who set up a system for policing their behavior. Quakers were eager to portray themselves as responsible citizens and so they stressed that "... after manumitting those of a suitable Age and Capacity for Freedom, they have engaged still to act as Guardians over them, and have their names annually entered upon the publick List, that the Community might suffer no Damage thereby."[16]

The Virginia Society for Promoting the Abolition of Slavery sent a petition proposing a gradual abolition law to the Virginia Assembly in October of 1791. Its preamble mingled religious and what they conceived as practical reasons for adopting a plan to gradually end legal human bondage, or what they stated was that "slavery is not only a moral but political Evil" that was "an outrageous violation, and an odious degradation of human nature", but also a practice "tending to weaken the bands of society, discourage trades & manufacturers, endanger the peace, and obstruct the prosperity of the country." By 1791 the arguments as to how slavery weakened the "bands of society," endangered peace, and retarded trade, manufacturing and prosperity were so commonly aired that the drafters of the petition didn't think it necessary to rehearse them.

Anticipating their opponents' arguments, the Virginia Society thought to head off criticism by conceding a key point; "Your petitioners are aware of the objection that probably would arise to a general and immediate Emancipation," namely, the "unfitness of individuals for freedom."

> They are not insensible that a people long destitute of the means of mental improvement may in some instances, be such below the common standard of human nature; accustomed to move at the will of a master or overseer, reflection, may in some degree be suspended, and reason & conviction have but little influence on their conduct …

For that reason, the petitioners were not pleading for such "general and immediate emancipation" but a law that would allow for eventual freedom while keeping black people under the close supervision and discipline of whites.

> They humbly propose and pray, that a law may pass, declaring the Children of Slaves now born, or to be born after the passing of such Act to be Free, as they come to proper ages: to enjoin their instruction to Read &c, and to invest with suitable privilidges, as an excitement to become useful citizens …[17]

Benjamin Rush, who penned his first antislavery tract in 1773, recoiled when faced with the reformer's enduring question, "What is to be done?" Rush could not bring himself to imagine a world in which those in bondage were immediately freed:

> As for the Negroes among us, who, from having acquired all the low vices of slavery, or who, from age or infirmities are unfit to be set at liberty, I would propose, for the good of society, that they should continue the property of those with whom they grew old, or from whom they contracted those vices and infirmities. But let the young Negroes be educated in the principles of virtue and religion—let them be taught to read, and write—and afterwards instructed in some business, whereby they may be able to maintain themselves.[18]

Rush's logic here flowed naturally from the assumption, common among learned liberal thinkers like himself, that while all men were truly created equally, they quickly developed strikingly different characters depending on the conditions of their upbringing and environment. Such "environmental" thinking was popular among patriots who were influenced by the main currents of the European Enlightenment. While environmentalist thinking held out the hope that one day all races of men could bask in equality, in the short term it made little difference whether one considered people of color savage and depraved by birth or by environment. A belief in either cause led to a conviction that African Americans required repressive supervision in order to exist in white society.

Like practically all other white abolitionists, Quaker John Parrish viewed people of color, especially those who had suffered enslavement, as permanently rendered inferior to whites by their experiences.

> It is necessary to make great allowances for the poor blacks, considering their education and condition. It may, therefore, well be accounted for, why the Indians' mental capacities appear stronger than theirs. The Indians have never had their spirits broken down by hard labour and oppression as the injured Africans, under severe task-masters ...[19]

287

Another white abolitionist, Moses Fisk, based his rejection of slavery on the Bible and the certitude of God's wrath and punishment for sin. But more openly than most of his like-minded reformers, Fisk admitted that there was some usefulness in maintaining slavery, if just as an intermediate step to freedom: "they are and ought to be considered as slaves, till government shall take effectual measures, as their guardians, to see, that they are in fact free."

Fisk satired the attitudes of his fellow Americans who he found regretted the Africans' "misfortune in being brought into a situation, which renders it *necessary*, that they should be continued in bondage." Most Americans advocated a version of emancipation that stretched into a biblical span of time:

> There shall be an abolition; but it shall begin moderately, and proceed leisurely, and be completed sometime or never. Thus the poor slave may comfort himself, that at some distant period, when GOD only know, he, or his children, or his children's children, may hope for deliverance.

While not quite an advocate of immediate abolition, Fisk wished for a speedier delivery from the evil of slavery than that. However, he agreed that there were practical considerations to be heeded, such as that "if so many myriads of wretches were turned out of doors, destitute ... uncultivated as they now are, they would be a nuisance in society." Such "nuisances" Fisk anticipated were "idleness and beggary, we should see uncomfortable disorders, perhaps outrages, perhaps fatal crimes; some through ignorance, some through wantonness, some from impelling hunger, and some from revenge."

As freed African Americans were dangerous to the white community and to themselves, or as Fisk phrased it, "They are not fit to be their own guides," they needed to be "considered, for a time, as in a state of minority. It must be a state of dependence and discipline, not servitude." Fisk spoke for many white abolitionists in this era when he detailed what had to be done to "fit" freed men and women to live in white society:

They must therefore be taken away from their masters, and, by direction of the magistrate, put under temporary guardians, governours, and instructors, to be educated, to be made acquainted with their rights and duties, and some honest method of acquiring a livelihood; to be prepared for citizenship.[20]

Fisk was critical of Massachusetts, a state that seemed to have simply torn down the edifice of slavery with no thought to the moral improvement of the newly freed. "Massachusetts ... had they fallen upon the plan of carrying their negroes through such a preparation state before manumission, they would, I firmly believe, have found it a salutary measure ..."

Philadelphia's Thomas Branagan, like these other white abolitionists, did not wish slaves to simply be freed, but for a "gradual emancipation" that began with the "instruction of slaves" at public expense, and then continued "in the employ of their masters" but "holding a rank as men in society, and receiving an equivalent reward for their services."[21]

Branagan exemplifies the predominant views of both abolitionists and patriots who condemned slavery and favored the forced removal of all people of color from the United States. In Branagan's first antislavery tract, he argued at length for the physical, mental, and moral equality of blacks and whites, observing that the great distance between the "savage tribes of Africa and the uncivilized nations of Europe is adventitious ... fortuitous and accidental." While Branagan holds that in principle Africans were by nature equal to other races, he also accepts that the "inhumanizing" nature of slavery had rendered them "brutes" by "sinking them to a level with the brutal creatures."

Branagan repeated all the usual arguments against slavery, both those rooted in the betterment of enslaved people and the well-being of the white community, in his long pamphlet. Slavery is cruel and unjust. Slavery is antithetical to a republic because it corrupts white citizens. Slavery is dangerous because it leads to servile insurrections with "thousands of mortal enemies scattered through other states." Slavery is "ungenerous as it respects the poor white people, who have

to labour for their own support." Slavery angers a just God who punishes sin both in this world and the next. But in contemplating what
to do about enslaved people's bondage, Branagan falls entirely on the
side of white interest as he concedes that it is "impolitic to attempt
this at once" as "prudential considerations ... plead for a postpone-
ment of the final abolition of slavery, and the universal emancipation
of the slaves." Rather than immediately release their fetters, "let their
slavery be mitigated ... rendering their servile condition tolerable"
by bringing them Christianity, providing better provisions, allowing families to stay together, and protecting enslaved women from
becoming "prostitutes to their brutal masters." Such reforms would
only "enhance, instead of injure, the interest of their masters" as they
will then be more productive laborers.[22]

When Connecticut was debating the terms of its emancipation law
in 1783, Noah Webster, a well-known opponent of slavery, warned
that "the restoration to freedom" does not "correct the depravity of
their hearts." Webster detailed how the enslaved were "born and bred
beneath the frowns of power, neglected and despised in youth," and
abandoned "to ill company, and low, vicious pleasures, till their habits
are formed ..." The problem, as Webster saw it, was that "manumission, instead of destroying their habits, and repressing their corrupt
inclinations, serves to afford them more numerous opportunities of
indulging both." Webster worried that "strict justice to the slave, very
often renders him a worse member of society."[23]

For many white abolitionists their fear and distrust of black people
as a group, their hatred of slavery, and their priority of ensuring the
safety and betterment of the white community when mixed produced
an odd comfort with holding people of color in a status that was
neither freedom nor chattel slavery but leaned closer to the latter.
A clear example of this is the lengths to which leading members of
the Philadelphia Abolition Society went to recapture a group of men
who fled rather than submit to the terms of their "rescue."

Sometime in 1802, as he had done numerous times over the previous years, Thomas Harrison organized a group of other white
abolitionists to pool their money and purchase a group of enslaved
men. Harrison was a Quaker tailor who served a five-year term on the

Committee of Guardians and another long stint on the Committee of Inspection. Harrison often took the lead in organizing the rescue of illegally enslaved men and women.[24] Their method was not to free them outright but to keep them as bound laborers and use their labor to pay off their own freedom expenses.

Not all members of their Abolition Society thought this scheme was appropriate. This arrangement didn't sit well with Harrison's fellow abolitionist, William Newbold, who wrote to his friend saying he "cannot approve either in a religious or political point of view especially in cases where it can be reasonably dispensed with or superceded by an other perhaps more consistent with mutual justice …" Nevertheless, Harrison and a few others went ahead but their plan went awry when the men who he thought had agreed to exchange permanent enslavement for a temporary version ran away. This act of rebellion against the Abolition Society prompted another member to write Harrison his condolences and to complain of the runaways' "ingratitude" and offering to help him bring the "ungrateful blacks" to "justice."

To hunt down the escapees, Harrison enlisted the aid of several members of New York's Manumission Society, including Thomas Eddy who was a well-known financier and philanthropist. Eddy and another member of the society formulated a plan of pressing the one black man of the group who was in their possession to divulge the whereabouts of his fellows. They enlisted a pair of New York constables to go to Eddy's farm where the man, Pete, worked, and haul him into New York City for interrogation. As Eddy told Harrison, "we supposed would frighten him and induce him to tell the truth sooner than if I had undertaken to question him." Pete was threatened with being sent to the notorious Bridewell jail "unless he would tell the truth & give every requisite satisfaction."

Pete insisted that he knew nothing about where the other men had gone and Eddy was satisfied because he had been spying on Pete for some time and "since he lived with me and when he did not expect to be detected I never heard him speak about his Brother(s)." Pete then bargained with his captors saying that he did not know thee had paid any Money for him or he would never have come away—he said he was very willing to stay with me and leave his Wages in my hands, (10 Dollars p month) except what he should want for cloathing (sic) till thy debt or his proportion of it was paid.

Eddy agreed because he found him a "good Servant" and "believed he will be faithfull" but he also warned Pete that "in case he should attempt to leave me and run off that he might depend on it I would have him advertised and offer a reward for taking him."

Eddy and the other Manumission officer continued to question and threaten Pete but Pete either refused to give up the others or genuinely didn't know where they were. In the meantime, a member of the New York Manumission Society offered to sell Pete to Eddy on an indenture contract, but Eddy refused on principle to do such a thing. Instead, Pete was sold to a man from Philadelphia for $35 and the money was sent to Harrison to repay part of what he had given to Pete's original captors.[25]

THE SOCIALIZATION OF SLAVERY

Slavery was a system of both economic exploitation and social control. Each of these two factors were at odds, as the cost of policing, punishing, and terrorizing the enslaved population lowered its profitability. In states with large numbers of enslaved people, the costs of repressing and keeping people in bondage were a large proportion of its returns and slave-owners successfully shifted much of their policing costs onto the public in the form of expanded slave patrols, courts, jails, and public compensation for the criminal execution of slaves. In New England and Pennsylvania, where enslaved people were a small proportion of the population, the public had little role in upholding the institution and practically all the costs of repression fell to enslavers themselves.

Keeping this dynamic relationship between the profits of slavery and the costs of repression in mind, the era of gradual emancipation in the North, which was also the era of manumission in the South, can be seen in its true light. Emancipation laws were passed first in those areas where the private costs of enslavement threatened to exceed its productivity and profits and enslavers acquiesced in a grand bargain. They agreed to convert their intergenerational claims of ownership in other humans into a fixed term of service in exchange for shifting all the costs of repressing and enslaving onto the public. To fulfill this bargain, northern states invested in expanding their militias and their constabulary, they built jails and workhouses and passed rafts of new criminal laws that rendered all people of color subject to a regime of surveillance and policing that treated them all as a criminal element.

In effect, those states north of Maryland slowly converted their regimes of slavery into regimes of black social control, or what can be termed systems of civil slavery. As people of color were not citizens of the republic, they could be subjected to an entirely different set of laws and enforcement procedures and were effectively transformed from private property into public property overseen by the state.

Such socialization of slavery also advanced in the South, but it took a different form. In those areas where the profitability of slavery lagged behind the costs of repression, slave-owners used their power in state legislatures to relax prohibitions on manumissions. Such prohibitions had been put in place long before to prevent slave-owners from shifting their costs onto landless and slaveless colonists. Masters in Virginia, Maryland, and Delaware reaped great benefits from manumission laws that gave them leverage to coerce more labor from the enslaved, to lower their costs of repression, and to shed unproductive workers entirely. As the freed population in those states multiplied as a result, the state assumed much of the costs of policing and repression of those who had once been privately controlled by their owner's lash.

At the beginning of the 1700s, slavery was a private institution supported by the state and over time it evolved into a state institution upheld by private interests. As the numbers of slaves grew and the institution of slavery became ever more central to the colonial economy, white communities expected that individual slave-owners would protect them from the fears they had of blacks—that African Americans were disorderly, prone to crime, vices, and possibly even capable of undertaking bloody rebellions or acting as a fifth column for foreign invaders. Colonial governments passed laws empowering masters with nearly unrestrained power to beat, flog, torture, or kill their own slaves in the interest of preserving public safety. Under this regime of privatized slave policing, barring slave-owners from freeing their own slaves was necessary; allowing slave masters to free their slaves was tantamount to allowing them to abdicate their legal responsibility for preserving the peace and safety of their communities.

For example, when Georgia passed its first slave code, it specified that policing slaves was a private responsibility, but one so vital that the state established detailed specifications about it. For every twenty people enslaved on a plantation, the law required the master to provide at least one "white Servant … Capable of bearing arms." Masters who wantonly killed their own slave were subject not to criminal penalties, but at worst a fine limited to £50. Any white person could kill someone else's slave without fear of punishment beyond paying restitution to the owner. Masters were required to control their own slaves upon threat of fines: a master who neglected his duties and allowed slaves to "beat Drums blow Horns or other Loud Instruments" were fined not only for disturbing the peace but for possibly endangering the community by allowing secret signals to be communicated.[26]

Over time, colonial governments began to shoulder more of the burden of slave repression and policing from slave-owners. In a real sense, as the slave-owning class rose in power, wealth, and influence, they pushed off more of their private responsibilities (meaning risks and expenses) onto the public. Socialized slavery meant public slave patrols, public jails, public slave markets, and more courts, judges, clerks, and constables to organize, surveil, record, regiment, categorize, and manage a burgeoning system of growing complexity.

Colonial governments first passed laws organizing slave patrols, a public service that obligated all white landowners in the community, slave-owners or not, to serve when called. Over time, the powers of slave patrols were codified and defined and expanded, especially during the war for independence when many slaves sought their chance to flee to enemy lines, or assisted the British regulars who represented an army of liberation.

Laws governing the conduct and policing of slaves increasingly and intentionally blurred the lines between slavery and freedom for black colonists. The terms "slave" and "negro" were used interchangeably establishing codes that granted slave police the same rights to search, seize, and punish without civil process, any black person they wished.

In a longer historical perspective, the liberalization of manumission laws must be viewed as part of the wider trajectory of governmental modernization. From the eighteenth century onward, states were gradually discovering means of operating more efficiently by first delegating deliberative responsibilities onto boards and committees, and then separating these entities into specialized executive bodies.

Governments in their primitive states operated with few administrative units. Government administration began as a system of proclamation of policy whose inevitable problems and inconsistencies returned through the direct petition of the affected subject to the sovereign whose word was law. As the number of proclamations, laws, precedents, and exceptions multiplied, some functions were distributed to local entities; in England and its colonies these were the county, shire, or parish. To maintain consistency and linkages to the central head of state, a handful of higher officials, crown tax collectors, appellate judges, and military officials moved among their circuits or "ridings."

Over time, when legislative bodies became inundated with rising numbers of petitions for permissions or exceptions, they found ways of shifting this burden to lower courts or to new, expanding, or specialized administrative bureaus.

Slavery laws that required legislative approval for citizens to divest themselves of their human property were doomed by this dynamic. As petitions for manumission, especially those involving bequests and their gaggles of heirs and creditors, became more frequent, legislators were motivated to establish uniform standards for manumission and push their review to lower courts. This is exactly how the revised manumission laws of Virginia operated: they sloughed the adjudication of manumission claims to county courts and widened qualifications to limit the number of exceptions that would rise to their attention.

Manumission laws were relaxed at the same time systems of discipline and surveillance of the free black community were tightened. In this sense, the southern states' movement to ease the terms of manumission was the direct counterpart of northern states' adoption of gradual emancipation laws. Both were steps away from private systems of control and toward the socialization of the policing of black people.

PRE-REVOLUTIONARY REGIMES
OF RACIAL SURVEILLANCE

After the 1739 Stono uprising, a mass insurrection of the enslaved in South Carolina, that colony went furthest in its attempt to legally define all people of color as slaves and all whites as freemen. In 1740, "An Act for the better Ordering and Governing Negroes and other Slaves" declared that all "Negroes, Indians ... Mulatos or Mestizos, who now or shall hereafter be in this Province, and all their Issue and Off-spring born or to be born, shall be and they are hereby declared to be and remain for ever hereafter absolute Slaves, and shall follow the Condition of the Mother ..." Exemptions were made for "free Indians in Amity with this Government" and people of color who were at the time of the law's passage deemed free.

However, freedom for people of color was narrowly circumscribed and legally contingent upon the ongoing surveillance and approval of some white person. All people of color claiming their freedom had to arrange for a white "Guardian" who would be the only legal representative of that person in a court of law. It was up to the white Guardian to petition the court to initially recognize and certify a black person's free status. Such a status of legal dependency was effectively permanent as any white person could seize and claim a black person at large and claim them as their property and only their white Guardian could represent their defense in court. As the law placed the burden of proof in determining free status upon the person of color, or more accurately, their white Guardian, the system of guardianship placed all free black people in the colony under the thumb of a white person. The law specifically defined every free black person as a "Ward" of a white person.

Free people of color accused of crimes were tried according to the rules established for the prosecution of slaves. Such courts consisted of any handy justice of the peace and any two other white persons who together all served as both judges and jurors (capital cases required two justices and three to five white freemen). Conviction required the agreement of the judge and one of the two other whites. Trials were speedy, the law required that the proceedings be held no more than three days after the apprehension of the accused.

Any white person was legally permitted to seize any black person out in public "not being on lawful Business ... or not having a white person with them" on Saturday nights, Sundays, and holidays and administer then and there "a moderate Whipping." Persons of color could also be apprehended for beating drums or blowing horns or "use of any loud Instruments" and fined £10. Any person of color who could not pay a fine was to be auctioned back into slavery.[27]

As Charles Town rapidly grew into a major port, the colonial assembly innovated regulations for the surveillance of its tiny free black community.

> ... whereas it may prove of dangerous Consequence to the Peace and Security of the said Town, to suffer Negroes and other Slaves to be lurking and caballing about the Streets of the said Town after Night ... and that all Negroes and other Slaves who go abroad about the Streets may be seen, known and discovered ... all Negroes and other slaves ... shall be obliged to have and carry with them during all such time as they are abroad ... a Lantorn with a Candle lighted therein ...

The penalty was to be whipped in public the next morning. It was also illegal to sell "rum and other strong Liquors" to "Negroes and Slaves" on Sunday or any day after dark.[28]

South Carolina tightened its regulations on slave patrols in 1740, empowering patrol captains to levy fines on their deputies for dereliction of their duty including drunkenness, gave them permission to enter any house they suspected of harboring fugitives, and the authority to issue summary justice in the form of "Whipping with a Switch or Cow-skin not exceeding Twenty Lashes."[29]

From the 1730s to the 1750s, South Carolina's grand juries complained most about the disorderly behaviors of enslaved people and usually placed their appeals for stronger laws to curb what they saw as these public nuisances and dangers at the top of their list of complaints. One presentment from 1744 complained that tippling houses were serving slaves alcohol, blacks wore clothes that were of finer quality than their rank in society, and they went about seeking their own work. As a category of actions, what was common about all these doings was that they were expressions of a degree of personal freedom.[30]

Such complaints about enslaved people claiming too much public liberty continued on a regular basis down to the American Revolution. These complaints were expressions of a white society that universally agreed that people of color needed to be repressed, contained, and kept on the lowest rung of society's ladder.

In 1785, North Carolina tightened its regulation of free African Americans with a law that required all free black inhabitants (and newcomers to the state) to register with their county commissioners and pay a special tax of 8s and a fee of 2s to the clerk. Upon registration they were to be given "a badge of cloth, of such colour or colours as they shall respectively direct, to be fixed on the left shoulder, and to have thereon wrought in legible capital letters the word FREE." Failure to register resulted in being hired out as a slave of the county.[31] North Carolina's legislature resumed its efforts to restrict the activities of free African Americans the following year and made it illegal for any person of color to board a ship after dark or to entertain any enslaved person in their home on the Sabbath day or any nighttime. Penalties were again set as high at £10 with failure to pay them resulting in the violator being sold at auction with bidders offering different lengths of service for their £10 payment.[32]

By the time the constitutional ban on slave trade restrictions had expired in 1807, Virginia had successfully constructed a comprehensive system of social controls on its free black population. African Americans in that state who were not the property of another were barred from owning firearms, they could not travel about without identity papers, they were required to register with the local court wherever they resided. They could not testify against whites in court which rendered it nearly impossible for them to protect their property or conduct business. They were subject to special taxes that white citizens were not. Black men could not vote, and many professions were closed to them by laws which restricted the allocation of licenses to citizens, such as piloting or captaining any ship in the merchant marine.[33]

Northern states followed suit and established numerous laws disciplining and controlling their free black communities. Soon after the war for independence was over, the New York council moved to tighten restrictions on the 2000 people enslaved in the city. Upon pain of public whipping, enslaved people were required to carry lanterns at night and were prohibited from gambling. Flogging was no idle threat, as a Mr. Joseph Shelvy, the "public Whipper" was paid £8 15s each quarter to perform this service.[34]

More threatening, the council ordered its constables to go door to door and compile a report on the

Names Ages & Places of Abode of every Negro & Molatto in his Ward; Distinguishing, if they are Slaves, the Names of their respective Masters & Mistresses And if they are or claim to be free the Place & Manner in which they were made free & the time of their Residence in this City ...

Aldermen were to report regularly on the "Cases of such Negro's or Molatto's as shall claim to be free." All this was an attempt on the part of the city's elites to force black people into the designated categories of free and slave after the upheaval of war and British occupation had thrown these distinctions into doubt.[35]

Just as threatening to the black community as such repressive and demeaning regulations was the systematic closure of the legal system to African Americans, who even in states where they enjoyed theoretical citizenship, this status was rarely observed or fulfilled.

The experiences of Jeffrey Brace illustrate the hollow nature of even supposed citizenship for people of color. Brace was a former slave whose patriot army service and residency in New England states that purported to recognize black citizenship amounted to precious little protection for him and his family.

Boyrereau Brinch, aka Jeffrey Brace, was born in Africa and suffered the Middle Passage. He served numerous masters until he was mustered into a patriot regiment (it is not clear from Brace's memoir if he served as his master's replacement or was mustered as his servant). Brace did not view the patriot's fight for liberty as his own, writing that he was sent "to liberate freemen, my tyrants." Secretly he dreamed of escaping to Barbados and returning to fight against the Americans who he called "the Philistines."

Being three inches above six feet in height and strongly built, Brace was placed in the infantry and saw action at Salem, Mud-Fort, North Castle, Hackensack, Cambridge, White plains, Monmouth, Princeton, Newark, Froggs-point, Horseneck and while foraging around West Point he lost his middle finger in combat with a British officer. Brace killed that man and took his horse and a cutlass that had taken off his finger as prizes, which he sold to a white colonel who never paid him.

After five years of wartime service, Brace was discharged as a free man and headed to Vermont where he worked for various employers who one after another cheated him of his wages. Unable to save any money as the men who hired him never paid fully what they had agreed to, Brace turned to farming and made an agreement to purchase twenty-five acres of wooded land in exchange for six months service. He married and built a "snug log house" and made money by chopping firewood and hauling iron, by the hundred weights, over his shoulder from a furnace in the mountains to Manchester and exchanging it for grain which he carried back to his growing family.

While farming a plot near Manchester and raising "good crops of Corn and other Grain, and life glided along greatly to my satisfaction," the "Selectmen" of the town demanded that Brace surrender his children and allow them to be indentured to white farmers until they reached maturity. Brace describes this experience with bitterness:

> I was a black man. The corruption and superstition, mingled with the old Connecticut bigatry and puritanism, made certain people

think a Negro had no right to raise their own Children. Therefore I was complained of, that the selectmen might be enabled to bind out the children, which my wife had by her first husband. Dixon wanted the boy; that was the moving spring to the complaint.

As he was about twelve years of age, and began to be useful, and could earn more than his living, it was sufficient to induce almost any honest selectman to induce a complaint to be entered, that he might have the profits of his labors. They took away the boy and bound him out. One further reason I gave them, which was that I came to Manchester to stay for a season, and that I had Land in Poultney, which was paid for, and that I intended to move there immediately, and very much wanted the boys assistance in clearing the same ... this had no effect.

Another child, a girl named Bersheba, Brace and his wife agreed to bind out to a Mrs. Powell who promised to teach the girl to read and to give her "a good feather bed, when she should arrive at the age of eighteen." Powell never did either and Brace had no recourse, for as he said, "what Lawyer would undertake the cause of an old African Negro, against a respectable Widow in Manchester"?[36]

Even without the aid of his son, Brace managed to clear about a third of his land and plant a field of wheat fenced in with an "excellent pole and log fence." But when Brace refused to sell his land to a white neighbor, the man "pulled down my fence and let in cattle." Cheated repeatedly by his neighbor, who also attempted to have his remaining children bound out, Brace was forced to sell at a loss and move to a different town and make a new start. Brace's troubles continued as he was again cheated by white "benefactors" who offered to give him land if he cleared it and once the work was completed reneged. In the end, Brace lost his sight and died in poverty except for the Revolutionary war pension he successfully fought for at the end of his life.

THE ERA OF PHILANTHROPIC POLICING

Fully professional governmental systems of policing would not coalesce until the antebellum era and so early republican governments depended upon organizations of private citizens to perform much of the labor of repression. In Pennsylvania and New York, antislavery societies acted as surrogate overseers for the free black community. In effect, these associations constituted public-private partnerships whose function was to keep black communities under surveillance and to wield their monopoly of access to courts, schools, and jobs to compel adherence to their own standards of behavior.

Abolition societies boasted that they were the self-deputized police-men of the black community. A few months before the Pennsylvania Society for Promoting the Abolition of Slavery sent its petition to Congress that provoked one of the most extensive debates about slavery at any level of government in the history of the young repub-lic, the society published an "Address to the Public" in the Federalist *Gazette of the United States*. The *Address* was written by Benjamin Franklin, the society's president, and noted as being "signed by order of the society."

It began by repeating the usual white abolitionist bromides about black people requiring white tutelage and discipline due to being degraded by slavery into a people unsuited to citizenship. "Slavery is such an attrocious debasement of human nature, that its very extir-pation, if not performed with solicitous care, may sometimes open a source of serous evils." Franklin and his fellow reformers developed a detailed theory about how this "debasement" operated:

> The unhappy man who has long been treated as a brute animal, too frequently sinks beneath the common standard of the human species. The galling chains that bind his body, do also fetter his intellectual faculties, and impair the social affectations of the heart. Accustomed to move like a mere machine, by the will of a master, reflection is suspended; he has not the power of choice; and reason and conscience have but little influence over his conduct; because he is chiefly governed by the passion of fear. He is poor and friend-less—perhaps worn out by extreme labor, age and disease.

So far had African Americans sunk "beneath the common standard" of humanity that these self-proclaimed abolitionists harbored doubts about their own mission and wondered if "Under such circumstances, freedom may often prove a misfortune to himself, and prejudicial to society." Ideally, Franklin and his fellow crusaders thought, the federal government should supervise, control, and discipline black people. "Attention to emancipated black people, it is therefore to be hoped, will become a branch of our national police." But until such a special federal race police service could be established, organizations like Pennsylvania's Society for Promoting the Abolition of Slavery would have to step into the breach and do this work themselves: "that attention is evidently a serious duty, incumbent on us, and which we mean to discharge to the best of our judgment and abilities."

In the view of Franklin and the Philadelphia abolitionists, such duty required them not only to "instruct" and "to advise" but to serve as the gatekeepers to any opportunities and privileges black people might seek. As Franklin phrased this ostiary function, white society members were "to qualify those who have been restored to freedom, for the exercise and enjoyment of civil liberty." Their duty was not just to "promote in them habits of industry" but "to furnish them with employments suited to their age, sex, talents, and other circumstances," implying that Abolition Society members would decide for their black wards what was suitable and what was not. Likewise, their mission was not just to "procure their children an education" but to provide an education "calculated for their future situation in life," a calculation, undoubtedly, to be made without reference to what black families themselves may dream of what the future could hold for their children.[37]

To accomplish this daunting task of supervising the black population with "expedition, regularity, and energy," the Pennsylvania Society for the Abolition of Slavery hammered out a detailed plan that divided their organization into four committees. (Copies of this plan were sent to each member of each house of Congress and "also to the members of a Convention lately assembled in this city for forming a new Constitution for the State of Pennyslvania ..."[38])

The first of these, a "Committee of Inspection" whose duty was to "superintend the morals, general conduct, and ordinary situation of the Free Negroes," indicated that the peace and safety of the white community was a top priority.

As Pennsylvania had passed a gradual emancipation law that converted the lifetime servitude of enslaved people in the state to a lengthy servitude, the Philadelphia abolitionists conceived that all free black children should be similarly bound. These white abolitionists saw the reluctance of black families to part with their children as an obstacle to their plans and gave their Committee of Guardians the power to coerce them either on their own or by enlisting the force of the state. "The committee may effect this partly by persuasive influence on parents ... and partly by co-operating with the laws ..."

A Committee of Education was formed and charged with superintending the instruction of the "youth of the Free blacks" in what they saw as "necessary for their future situation in life" according to "moral and religious principles." This committee was also tasked with keeping track of the entire black community by developing a "regular record of the marriages, births and manumissions of all Free Blacks."

Rounding out the fourth leg of their plan of control was a "Committee of Employ" which was to "procure constant employment for those Free Negroes, who are able to work" because a lack of employment "occasion poverty, idleness, and many vicious habits."[39]

The Committee of Guardians proved the most active agency of the Pennsylvania Abolition Society in its early years. The demand for bound children outstripped the ability of the society to supply them. In describing their activities, the Guardians let slip the reason for this discrepancy: black families were not so eager to hand their children over to these moral crusaders. At its meeting of September 25, 1790, the Guardians reported twelve people applied for apprentices

whom we cannot at present supply, but hope, when the plan has been established for a greater length of Time, & its value is more amply known, so that the black people can have full confidence in our exertions to serve them, that we shall be able to give the Business that importance which it evidently merits ...

Following this the Guardians held meetings to convince skeptical black Philadelphians of their good intentions.

> We had an early Meeting with some of the Black People, and soon after a general one with the people of that color at which we endeavored to explain to them the Society's plan and views for their benefit, on which occasion the Blacks behaved with great decorum and appeared well Satisfied.[40]

By the beginning of 1791, the Committee of Guardians was growing frustrated in its lack of progress in removing children from their homes and binding them out with strangers. Though the Guardians did not admit in their minutes that they were facing stiff resistance from black families who understandably did not wish to be separated, what they did record underscores this possibility. At their January 25th meeting, the Committee of Guardians proposed drafting an address for the next general meeting of the society requesting that the organization put its muscle behind "procuring an Act vesting in the Committee of Guardians, in such way as may be thought most proper, full power to bind out all those colored Minors who may come under their notice ..." Those in attendance were "expressing generally their approbation thereof" but had to defer approving the motion for lack of a quorum.

Later that spring, the Committee of Guardians' members were still "wanting of more power ... when they have a Child to be bound, to make that service more easy and expeditious, which cannot be remedied without the Legislature of the State's interference."[41] Philadelphia's Guardians were much perturbed that the city's African Americans were not relying on them exclusively as their employment agents. "That we have reason to believe some others have found places by Virtue of our Recommendations altho they have not informed us thereof; which duty is too much neglected by those negroes, to whom our Care has been extended." Black families had good reason to bypass the intervention of the white abolitionists as they routinely brokered longer terms for those indentured than black families were able to negotiate on their own.[42]

Though claiming that their interest in binding out children was to place them in situations where they would be educated and taught a trade, most of the children bound out in 1792, for which fairly complete records exist, were sent to work on farms, not placed with artisans and tradesmen. Others were bound out as household servants. A few years later the Committee of Guardians reported they had successfully bound out "four servants," but only two of them were contracted to have "schooling." So many free people of color were bound out to farms that the population surrounding Philadelphia tripled in the last fifth of the eighteenth century as did the proportion of African Americans living in white households.[43]

To better carry out its charge, the Committee of Inspection divided its members into teams of two, each team charged with inspecting African American homes in one particular district "at least once in every Two Months every family in their inspection department." The city was divided up into "the Northern Liberties," "the District of Southwark," and the city proper.

These white inspectors "with great pains" compiled "a very Accurate" list containing names of heads of black families, the number, sex, and age of their children "& Inmates, together with the Names of the Streets or alleys in which they liv'd." However, once this list was completed, the committee decided that it was "still inadequate to the important purpose which they had in view" and they began expanding it to include the ages of the parents, their occupations, "Religious Professions, Competency, or poverty," "neat or sordid manners of living," "whether they possess Credentials of Their freedom," whether the family was "in Health or Sickness," "which of their Children it is proper to Send to School," which children "are already Bound or Hired Servants," and "whether they are satisfied with the treatment of such as are thus already Bound or Hired." The committee tried to document "whether any Individuals suffer a particular grievance" and "if any of their Parents, Husbands, Wives, or Children are Slaves," and, if so, to determine the name and address of their master and "whether there is any uncommon Hardship in Such Slavery."[44]

White inspectors did more than just inspect, they directed free black families in ways that should change their behavior. In April 1791, in its report, the Committee of Inspection noted that "it has given the Committee great satisfaction to find that in General, their advice has been followed with alacrity, their dicisions submitted to with Cheerfullness & their interposition considered as a favour & acknowledged with Gratitude." It also reported helping 250 families for a total of nearly 1000 people, 400 of whom were minors. Such a large number to inspect is "arduous; but it would be much too Laborious, for the small number that Compose it, where it not for the docile, tractable disposition of the free Blacks & the great deference with which they receive the advice & admonitions of the Committee."[45]

Soon, the Committee of Inspection used its detailed knowledge of black neighborhoods to attempt to suppress activities it disapproved of. In 1797, it held a special meeting at the house of Thomas Harrison to temporarily combine all the various committees into one grand committee "to discourage the practice which sometimes prevails amongst the black People of assembling in large numbers to dance and frolic & the irregularities and disorders arising therefrom." Inspectors were dispatched and reported on these gatherings and what they viewed as the "indecent and licentious manners and appearance of divers, both men and women." Representatives of the organization then showed up to discourage a "large company assembled on a like occasion" using "much expostulation" and "discouragement given to such practices." This combined committee quickly moved from ad hoc to regular status and took the name "Committees ... for suppressing of irregularities amongst the Black People" which eventually was reworked to become the "Committees to attend to the conduct of the Black people."[46]

New York's Manumission Society similarly prioritized supervising the conduct of the black community. One of its first tasks was to "Keep a watchful eye over the conduct of such Negroes as have been or may be liberated; and ... to prevent them from running into immorality or sinking into idleness." This society also organized the door-to-door inspection of black homes and the recording of their whereabouts, relationships, and other vital information.

Eventually, the New York Manumission Society institutionalized this activity by creating a "Committee for Preventing Irregular

Conduct in Free Negroes." Members of this conduct committee were directed to warn free people of color "against admitting slaves or servants into their homes, receiving or purchasing anything from them, against fiddling, dancing or any other noisy entertainment in their houses, whereby the tranquility of the neighborhood be disturbed."[47]

All the white abolition and manumission societies proclaimed as part of their mission the "education" of freed people of color. The Philadelphia society established a committee on education that sponsored several "schools for colored children" in various parts of the city. New York's Manumission Society formed the "African Free School" in 1787.

When white abolitionists spoke of "educating negroes" they meant far more than what education usually means today. "Education," in the sense they used the term, meant both being instructed in reading, writing, and the Gospel, but also a general disciplining and overseeing. When Anthony Benezet wrote to Robert Pleasants about the importance of setting up a school for blacks in Philadelphia, he made it clear that he thought "education" should not lead to skilled employments that would compete with white workers:

I am very avere [averse] to placing young Negros Lads in this City except it be to some of the Low trades Shoemaking to place them for menial service in the kitchin or stable. I refuse to be concerned as from the leisure they have & conversation of servants & they are mostly corrupted; to be brought up in religious Familis to husbandry or trade in the country is I am persuaded best for them.[48]

New York's Manumission Society used their "African Free School" as an instrument of control and discipline of the black community. From the school's inception, black parents wishing their children to be admitted to the school were required to allow a committee of white inspectors to visit their home and to allow their continuous surveillance. The society's committee charged with preventing "the irregular behavior of free negroes" recommended:

That negroes when registered be informed of the benefits derived from this society [and] are not to be extended to any except such as maintain good characters for sobriety and peaceable and orderly living.[49]

New York Manumission Society leader and slave-owner John Jay revealed the underlying and primary purpose of what white abolitionists called "negro education" in a letter to a fellow NYMS member:

Be pleased to inform me whether any particular attention is paid by the superintendents to the children after they have left it, and whether it is part of the plan to endeavour to have them bound out to trades or to service in decent families. To me it appears important that they be not left entirely either to their parents or to themselves, it being difficult to give them good morals, manners, or habits in any other way than by placing them under the care and direction of persons better qualified for those purposes than their parents generally are.[50]

Jay was merely expressing the common view of white abolitionists that while slavery must be abolished, white society's control of the black population must continue on. This was the natural outcome of the ideas implanted at the birth of white abolitionism, a movement that learned to oppose slavery because slavery was incompatible with the broadest white interests. Such concerns did not end just because slavery did, but they found new outlets in drawing clear distinctions between the nature of white citizenship and a black presence that was, after all, the purpose of the invention of citizenship in the first place.

The cumulative effects of state efforts to found a regime of civil slavery over the people of color combined with the philanthropic activities of white abolitionists that extended that power through their close supervision of black neighborhoods created an environment that left African Americans few choices. African Americans who enjoyed some degree of self-ownership or those who had successfully fled the more comprehensive regimes of slavery in the South depended upon the patronage of powerful whites to maintain their freedom. In some states, those of New England and New York for a few decades, where the dependency of black communities on white patrons was firmly established, even the elective franchise was extended to a select few black citizens who could be depended upon to support the party of their patrons. But even in those most liberal corners of the nation, black liberty remained tenuous and contingent on white control.[51]

One of the most celebrated white abolitionists of the last years of the eighteenth century was a Methodist minister, the Reverend Francis Asbury. Asbury bravely urged the Virginia legislature to abolish slavery and to this end circulated several petitions, including one he personally carried to George Washington but which the great general refused to sign. Legislators quickly voted to table them in 1785. Asbury's attempts to argue for black equality were overwhelmed by his framing of the question as a choice between perpetuating slavery (and living with a dangerous people who are not "Interested in the support of its Government"), freeing slaves gradually under white supervision, or releasing them and unleashing anarchy. Asbury's rhetoric of slavery and freedom stubbornly aligned with popular understandings of the black presence as alien and dangerous. "That the fear of the Enormities which the Negroes may commit, will be groundless, at least if the Emancipation be gradual, as the Activity of the Magistrates and the provision of Houses of Correction where Occasion may require will easily Suppress the gross, flagrant, Idleness either of Whites or Blacks." Asbury's gratuitous attempt to temper what is a litany of slurs against people of color by capping it with a reference to both "Whites or Blacks" didn't reverse the valence of the passage, as it hued closely to popular prejudice and ideologies of exclusion to begin with.[52]

Typical of Virginian attitudes that Asbury encountered at that time was his visit at the home of I. Wilson, an "old gentleman" who Asbury noted was "kind beyond measure." As the evening wore on, "the subject of slavery being introduced, he acknowledged the wrong done the blacks by taking them from their own country, but defended the right of holding them …" Later, Asbury wrote how he had dinner with "Dr. Samuel Smith" and a "Mr. M'K" at the home of General Roberdeau, and how their conversation "turned upon slavery; the difficulties attending emancipation, and the resentment some of the members of the Virginia legislature expressed against those who favored a general abolition."[53]

Reading more deeply into Reverend Asbury's journal, while glorying in the sight of "sable faces" bathed in tears at the joy of the news of the Lord he brought to them, he was also deeply uncomfortable with their company. Asbury rarely missed an occasion to note how the black people he encountered danced and drank and cursed. He recorded how he scolded an old black ferry hand on the banks of the Susquehanna River that if he didn't repent he would drown and be damned and the poor fellow did just that on his next trip across the river. Asbury consoled himself by noting that "the negroes were intoxicated." When Asbury returned to Massachusetts, he felt at home, not just for the familiar countryside, but because of its whiteness: "I was refreshed in soul and body … The simplicity and frugality of New-England is desirable … here are no noisy negroes running and lounging."[54] It only took another decade for Reverend Asbury to dampen his enthusiasm for abolition and wonder in his diary, "Would not an *amelioration* in the condition and treatment of slaves have produced more practical good to the poor Africans, than any attempt at their *emancipation?*"[55]

Asbury's questioning of the benefits of abolitionism brings the arc of white abolitionism full circle from its origins in fears of a growing black presence and God's worldly retribution for sin. White abolitionism, in honing its own self-interested rejection of slavery, had constructed a religious language of emancipation that was soon to prove readily adaptable to secular purposes as well. The propertied slave masters who rose to leadership in the course of the American colonies' rebellion against British imperial policies merged the ideals of evangelical abolitionism with secular theories of republicanism. Their achievement was launching a new nation that rejected both slavery and the slave.

All of the proposed policies and programs of abolition up to the year 1816 were ultimately crafted to advance white interests, hopes, and dreams. Whatever benefits these plans conferred on the black community were incidental, a secondary effect and not their primary purpose. Viewing white abolitionism in this way parallels the insights of legal scholar Derrick Bell who, after analyzing the failures of Reconstruction in the last quarter of the nineteenth century or of the movement for school desegregation in the mid-twentieth century, theorized that in America the advancement of black rights was a byproduct of white interests. Only when black interests momentarily converged with white agendas did civil rights take a step forward, and then this progress was shallow and fragile because it was never the point in the first place. Or as Bell put it, "policymakers recognize and act to remedy racial injustices when, and only when, they perceive that such action will benefit the nation's interests without significantly diminishing whites' sense of entitlement." Bell's theory of "interest convergence" helps peel back the layers of mystification that have obscured the self-interested nature of white actions to curtail slavery in the early republic.[56]

That patriots both hated slavery and wished it to be abolished and yet organized their war of independence to defend it, and their federal system to protect it seems on its face to be a contradiction of the highest order. Pushed by this jarring inconsistency, many have charged the founders with hypocrisy and questioned the sincerity of their principles. But these views grow out of misunderstandings of the patriot opposition to slavery and their vision for their future nation; the remedy lies in appreciating the extent to which both anti-slavery and independence were tied to cleansing America of a black presence. In this solution the patriot's duplicity dissolves away.

While slavery accustomed all white people to be suspicious and vigilant against all people of color, so did the rhetoric of white abolitionism. White patriots' benevolence toward people of color was a byproduct rather than a purpose of their abolitionism. Slavery as the sinful or corrupting enemy was an abstraction, an idea removed from the actual forcing of fellow humans to bend to a will, and it was hoped it could be expunged without much altering the essential relationship between master and servant. Patriots imagined they could remake the world, and their vision of their own nation was either purged of both slavery and black people or somehow the black presence was to be contained and repressed into invisibility.

Even while living in a country in which more than one in five people were not white, white patriots stubbornly thought of their nation as a white one and erected its legal and constitutional foundations on this fantasy. Americans lived in one of the most multiracial societies in the world but imagined themselves as if they were Englishmen and women in a homogeneous one. In the end, their dilemma was irresolvable. In the end, they could not both abolish slavery and remove all black people to some distant foreign land, so they did the next best thing and banished people of color from their newly invented ideal of citizenship. Thus, the seeds of Dred Scott and Jim Crow and all their more hidden modern versions were planted the day Jefferson dipped his quill and wrote: "We Hold These Truths to Be Self-Evident …"[57]

Notes

INTRODUCTION

1. Mark Binelli, "'Hamilton' Creator Lin-Manuel Miranda: The Rolling Stone Interview," *Rolling Stone*, June 1, 2016; Maya Phillips, "'Hamilton,' 'The Simpsons' and the Problem with Colorblind Casting," *New York Times*, July 8, 2020.

2. "'The Past Isn't Done with Us,' Says 'Hamilton' Creator Lin-Manuel Miranda," NPR.org, June 29, 2020.

3. Ron Chernow, *Alexander Hamilton* (New York: Penguin Books, 2004), pp. 210–11; Arthur Scherr, "Alexander Hamilton and Slavery: A Closer Look at the Founder," *The Historian* (Kingston), 83:2 (April 2021), pp. 130–70; Gregory D. Massey, *John Laurens and the American Revolution* (Columbia: University of South Carolina Press, 2000), passim; Hercules Mulligan was a New York tailor who famously passed the information he overheard as he fitted British officers in his shop to General Washington. Mulligan, like many skilled artisans at the time, owned a man named Cato, even while he enrolled his name on the membership lists of the New York Manumission Society. Recently, a plan by the Northern Ireland town where Mulligan was born, Coleraine, to honor its famous American spy, was scrapped when a local historian revealed that Mulligan didn't emancipate his slaves as long believed, but was recorded as owning another human being as late as 1791, five years after he joined the antislavery society. Nathan Schachner, "Alexander Hamilton Viewed by His Friends: The Narratives of Robert Troup and Hercules Mulligan," *The William and Mary Quarterly*, 4:2 (April 1947), pp. 203–25; Michael J. O'Brien, *Hercules Mulligan: Confidential Correspondent of General Washington* (New York: P.J. Kennedy & Sons, 1937), pp. 100, 123; Rory Carroll, "Northern Ireland Council Withdraws Plan to Honour Hercules Mulligan," *Guardian* (London), March 3, 2021, p. 24.

4. "From George Washington to John Francis Mercer, 9 September 1786," *The Papers of George Washington, Confederation Series, vol. 4, 2 April 1786–31 January 1787*, W.W. Abbot, ed. (Charlottesville, VA: University of Virginia Press, 1995), pp. 243–4.

5. Benjamin Franklin, "An Address to the Public from the Pennsylvania Society for Promoting the Abolition of Slavery, and the Relief of Free Negroes Unlawfully Held in Bondage," November 9, 1789, in *The Works of Benjamin Franklin*, vol. 12, John Bigelow, ed. (New York: G.P. Putnam's Sons, 1904), pp. 157–8.

6. Martin Bernal notes that this quote from the 1794 edition of the *Encyclopedia Britannica* follows pages of racist descriptions of African savage characters and concludes that this era mixed racism and antiracism in ways that appear strange to our own. Martin Bernal, *Black Athena Writes Back: Martin Bernal Responds to His Critics* (Durham, NC: Duke University Press, 2001), pp. 180–1.

7. Winthrop Jordan was one of the first scholars to recognize how abolition and colonization were tied together in the eighteenth century: "...wholesale emanci-

pation looked as if it would result in wholesale intermixture. The most common antislavery solution at least had the virtue of simplicity: remove emancipated Negroes from America" (p. 546). Winthrop D. Jordan, *White over Black: American Attitudes toward the Negro, 1550–1812* (Chapel Hill, NC: University of North Carolina Press, 1968).

8. According to the scholar who most thoroughly documented proslavery thinking in the eighteenth century, Larry Tise, there were a total of just five pamphlets defending slavery published in the last quarter of the eighteenth century. Larry E. Tise, *Proslavery: A History of the Defense of Slavery in America, 1701–1840* (Athens, GA: University of Georgia Press, 1988), pp. 24–30.

9. The first generation of academic historians to study abolitionism as a political movement recognized that their motivations were not entirely altruistic. Albert Bushnell Hart noted that most of the nations' founders took antislavery positions "not so much out of sympathy with the oppressed negro, as from the belief that slavery was an injury to their own neighbors and constituents, and that the influence of the slave power in national affairs was harmful." Albert Bushnell Hart, *Slavery and Abolition, 1831–1841* (New York: Harper & Brothers, 1906), pp. 172–3.

10. Many scholars of abolitionism have confused these debaters. Examples include Tise, *Proslavery*, p. 30; Paul J. Polgar, *Standard-Bearers of Equality: America's First Abolition Movement* (Chapel Hill, NC: University of North Carolina Press, 2019), p. 39; and Maurice Jackson, *Let This Voice Be Heard: Anthony Benezet, Father of Atlantic Abolitionism* (Philadelphia, PA: University of Pennsylvania Press, 2010), p. 132. It was Harvard's Peter Galison who discovered the true identities of the debaters. Peter Galison, "21 July 1773: Disputation, Poetry, Slavery," *Critical Inquiry*, 45 (Winter 2019), pp. 351–79.

11. *A Forensic Dispute on the Legality of Enslaving the Africans, Held At The Public Commencement In Cambridge, New-England, July 21st, 1773* (Boston: Printed by John Boyle, for Thomas Leverett, near the post-office in Cornhill, 1773).

12. J.R. Oldfield describes this pamphlet by Rush as "a devastating critique of slavery and slaveholders, as well as white racist attitudes." J.R. Oldfield, *Transatlantic Abolitionism in the Age of Revolution: An International History of Anti-Slavery, c.1787–1820* (Cambridge: Cambridge University Press, 2013), p. 13. Paul Polgar notes the "limits of … antislavery environmentalism" in supporting black equal rights but generally describes the debate over slavery in the Revolutionary era as one that pitted those arguing for "natural rights of man to liberty" and "black inequality [as] … a transitory state capable of being overcome" against those holding blacks' "inherent incapacity for freedom" and "enslaved Africans' natural suitability for slavery." Polgar, *Standard-Bearers of Equality*, pp. 38, 40.

13. Stephen Fried, *Rush: Revolution, Madness, and the Visionary Doctor Who Became a Founding Father* (New York: Crown, 2018), pp. 289–91; Gideon Mailer, "Between Enlightenment and Evangelicalism: Presbyterian Diversity and American Slavery, 1700–1800," in *Faith and Slavery in the Presbyterian Diaspora*, William Harrison Taylor & Peter C. Messer, eds. (New York: Rowman & Littlefield, 2016), p. 60.

14. Robert C. Smith, "Liberty Displaying the Arts and Sciences: A Philadelphia Allegory by Samuel Jennings," *Winterthur Portfolio*, 2 (1965), pp. 85–105.

15. Gaillard Hunt, "William Thornton and Negro Colonization," *American Antiquarian Society* (April 1920), pp. 32–61.

16. Barbara E. Lacey, "Visual Images of Blacks in Early American Imprints," *The William and Mary Quarterly*, 53:1 (January 1996), pp. 137–80.

17. None of these arguments will be new to specialists in a field in which there is a long and detailed literature documenting the racism of early abolitionists, the self-interested nature of much of white antislavery activism, the clash between democratic ideals and the practical concerns of controlling black populations, or white schemes of black removal. Among the historians who have highlighted how racism undergirded the worldview, political strategies, and actions of early opponents of slavery are the following: David Brion Davis, *The Problem of Slavery in the Age of Revolution, 1770–1823* (Ithaca, NY: Cornell University Press, 1975); Donald L. Robinson, *Slavery in the Structure of American Politics* (New York: Harcourt Brace Jovanovich, 1971); Duncan J. MacLeod, *Slavery, Race and the American Revolution* (New York: Cambridge University Press, 1974); Winthrop Jordan, *White over Black: American Attitudes toward the Negro, 1550–1812* (Chapel Hill, NC: University of North Carolina Press, 1968); Gary B. Nash & Jean R. Soderlund, *Freedom by Degrees: Emancipation in Pennsylvania and Its Aftermath* (New York: Oxford University Press, 1991); Joanne P. Melish, *Disowning Slavery: Gradual Emancipation and "Race" in New England, 1780–1860* (Ithaca, NY: Cornell University Press, 1998); Matthew Spooner, "'I Know This Scheme Is from God:'Toward a Reconsideration of the Origins of the American Colonization Society," *Slavery & Abolition*, 35:4 (December 2014), pp. 559–75; Matthew Spooner, "Freedom, Reenslavement, and Movement in the Revolutionary South," in *Race and Nation in the Age of Emancipations*, Whitney Nell Stewart & John Garrison Marks, eds. (Athens, GA: University of Georgia Press, 2018), pp. 13–34; Shane White, *Somewhat More Independent: The End of Slavery in New York City, 1770–1810* (Athens, GA: University of Georgia Press, 1991); Nicholas Guyatt, *Bind Us Apart: How Enlightened Americans Invented Racial Segregation* (New York: Basic Books, 2016); Beverly Tomek, *Colonization and Its Discontents: Emancipation, Emigration, and Antislavery in Antebellum Pennsylvania.* (New York: New York University Press, 2011); Martha S. Jones, *Birthright Citizens: A History of Race and Rights in Antebellum America* (New York: Cambridge University Press, 2018); David N. Gellman, *Emancipating New York: The Politics of Slavery and Freedom, 1777–1827* (Baton Rouge, LA: Louisiana State University Press, 2006); Christopher Leslie Brown, *Moral Capital: Foundations of British Abolitionism* (Chapel Hill, NC: University of North Carolina Press, 2006); and Robert G. Parkinson, *The Common Cause: Creating Race and Nation in the American Revolution* (Chapel Hill, NC: University of North Carolina Press, 2016).

18. George Bourne, *The Book and Slavery Irreconcilable* (Philadelphia: J.M. Sanderson & Co., 1816); Ryan McIlhenny, *To Preach Deliverance to the Captives: Antislavery and Anti-Catholicism in the Religious Writings of George Bourne (1780–1845)* (Ph.D. Diss., University of California, Irvine, 2008); John Christie & Dwight Dumond, *George Bourne and the Book and Slavery Irreconcilable* (Wilmington, DE: Historical Society of Delaware, 1969); Theodore Bourne, "Rev. George Bourne: The Pioneer of American Antislavery," *Methodist Quarterly Review*, 42 (January 1882), pp. 68–90.

CHAPTER 1

1. Charles F. Irons, *The Origins of Proslavery Christianity* (Chapel Hill, NC: University of North Carolina Press, 2008); Patricia Bonomi, *Under the Cope of Heaven: Religion, Society, and Politics in Colonial America* (New York: Oxford University Press, 1986); James Essig, *The Bonds of Wickedness: American Evangelicals against Slavery, 1770–1808* (Philadelphia, PA: Temple University Press, 1982).

2. Elliot to Belknap, 1795, *Collections of the Massachusetts Historical Society*, ser. 5, vol. 3 (Cambridge, 1877), p. 383.

3. Winthrop Jordan, *White over Black: American Attitudes toward the Negro, 1550–1812* (Baltimore, MD: Pelican Books, 1969, orig. 1968), pp. 4–11.

4. Brycchan Carey, *From Peace to Freedom: Quaker Rhetoric and the Birth of American Antislavery, 1657–1761* (New Haven, CT: Yale University Press, 2012), pp. 51–2; George Fox, *Gospel Family-order Being a Short Discourse Concerning the Ordering of Families, Both of Whites, Blacks, and Indians* (London, 1676), pp. 17, 20.

5. Joseph Besse, "A Collection of the Sufferings of the People Called Quakers," Quaker Collection BX7650.B5 C6 vol. 2, Haverford College Special Collections, Haverford College; Carey, *From Peace to Freedom*, p. 45.

6. A. Loomba & J. Burton (2007) "Morgan Godwyn (1640–ca. 1686)," in *Race in Early Modern England: A Documentary Companion*, Ania Loomba & Jonathan Burton, eds. (New York: Palgrave Macmillan, 2007), pp. 269–72.

7. Morgan Godwyn, *The Negro's & Indians Advocate* (London, 1680), pp. 7–10.

8. George H. Moore, *Notes on the History of Slavery in Massachusetts* (New York: D. Appleton & Co., 1866), p. 94.

9. Samuel Sewall, *The Selling of Joseph: A Memorial* (Boston: Bartholomew Green and John Allen, 1700), Massachusetts Historical Society. Winthrop Jordan naturalizes the process of identity formation, saying white Americans had "a well-defined sense of Englishness, a sense which came automatically to bear when they were confronted with peoples who for whatever reason seemed appreciably dissimilar." On the same page Jordan also attributes a quote to Sewell's *Selling of Joseph*, that blacks "cannot mix with us and become members of society" that does not exist in the original. Jordan, *White over Black*, p. 142. See also Albert J. Von Frank, "John Saffin: Slavery and Racism in Colonial Massachusetts," *Early American Literature*, 29:3 (1994), pp. 254–72.

10. John Saffin, "A Brief and Candid Answer to a Late Printed Sheet, Entitled, The Selling of Joseph," in Moore, *Notes on the History of Slavery in Massachusetts*, pp. 252–3.

11. C.E. Pierre, "The Work of the Society for the Propagation of the Gospel in Foreign Parts among the Negroes in the Colonies," *The Journal of Negro History*, 1:4 (October 1916), pp. 349–60.

12. *A Narrative of Some of the Proceedings of North Carolina Yearly Meeting on the Subject of Slavery …* (Greensboro, NC: North Carolina Yearly Meeting, Printed by Swaim & Sherwood, 1848), p. 5, Bd.Pam.326.4 F912 vol. 2, no. 9, Rare Book, Manuscript and Special Collections Library, Duke University Libraries.

13. As most English colonies had clarified their laws by the late 1600s so that Christian baptism did not automatically grant emancipation from slavery, such

missionary efforts were not a direct threat to slaveholders. Virginia passed a law in 1667 declaring that "Baptisme doth not alter the condition of the person as to his bondage or freedom ..." and Locke's constitution for Carolina proclaimed both that slaves could become members of the church and that doing so does not alter "the state or condition he was in before." Maryland followed suit in 1671. *The Negro Church*, W.E.B. Du Bois, ed. (New York: Rowman & Littlefield, 2003, reprint of 1903 ed.), pp. 8–9.

14. Considering the French Revolution, Lynn Hunt theorizes that modern racism arose to prominence during the revolutionary eighteenth century because "in contrast to simple prejudice, the systematic denigration of what you are not requires a doctrine, and such doctrines only appeared once inequality had to be justified." But such doctrine does not need only justification, it can also be critique. Ethno-abolitionists constructed a doctrine of what slavery and inequality was a century before the American and French Revolutions. Lynn Hunt, "The World We Have Gained: The Future of the French Revolution," *American Historical Review*, 108:1 (February 2003), p. 19.

15. Beverly C. Tomek, *Colonization and Its Discontents: Emancipation, Emigration, and Antislavery in Antebellum Pennsylvania* (New York: New York University Press, 2010), pp. 20–1.

16. "Quaker Protest against Slavery in the New World, Germantown (Pa.) 1688," Manuscript Collection 990 B-R, Haverford College Special Collections, Haverford College.

17. J. William Frost, "The Origins of the Quaker Crusade against Slavery: A Review of Recent Literature," *Quaker History* 67:1 (1978), pp. 42–58; Gary B. Nash, "Slaves and Slaveowners in Colonial Philadelphia," *William and Mary Quarterly*, 30:2 (April 1973), p. 223.

18. Some historians of early abolitionism have overly emphasized the altruism and benevolence of white critics of slavery. Manisha Sinha quotes only the 1688 Germantown Quakers' declarations of racial equality ("We shall doe to all men like as we will be done ourselves; making no difference of what ... colour they are") and describes their protest as being against other "Quaker slaveholders for treating human beings like cattle," omitting their stated reasons for standing against slavery, namely, that there were too many blacks and they were a dangerous presence in their colony. Manisha Sinha, *The Slave's Cause: A History of Abolition* (New Haven, CT: Yale University Press, 2016), p. 12. Paul Goodman described the early abolitionists as a "a feeble band, made up of a handful of benevolently minded men." Goodman recognized that "[s]upport for abolition did not imply belief in racial equality" but then distanced racist policies from abolitionist intentions, writing that the backlash that ensued after the passage of limited emancipation laws – state laws banning black migration and calls for black colonization – were the result of these "benevolently minded men" having "not thought through the implications, civic or spiritual, of emancipation." Paul Goodman, *Of One Blood: Abolitionism and the Origins of Racial Equality* (Berkeley, CA: University of California Press, 1998), pp. 6–7. Joanne Pope Melish was one of the first historians to see through the thick fog of romanticism about the abolitionists and point out how their crusade was grounded in racist self-interest. Melish observed that even such vociferous crusaders as Anthony Benezet focused most of their energies on ending the slave trade and not slavery directly, revealing

their interest in eradicating slavery was to expunge the enslaved. Melish observed that "pre-Revolutionary antislavery protest structured the problem as one of the presence or absence of enslaved Africans ... ending slavery was understood to mean eliminating the presence of slaves." Joanne Pope Melish, *Disowning Slavery: Gradual Emancipation and "Race" in New England, 1780–1860* (Ithaca, NY: Cornell University Press, 1998), p. 53. Stanley Harrold finds even the much-lauded early Quakers as having a self-interest in abolishing slavery as they feared "God's wrath in the form of slave revolt awaited those who forced servitude on others." Harrold also observed that "Economic considerations, fear of slave revolt, and desire to limit black population, rather than moral antipathy, often inspired early abolitionist effort." Stanley Harrold, *American Abolitionism: Its Direct Political Impact from Colonial Times into Reconstruction* (Charlottesville, VA: University of Virginia Press, 2019), pp. 16, 18. Gary B. Nash and Jean R. Soderlund describe the Germantown Quakers' motives as being partly "practical because they saw the spread of slavery as threatening the stability and welfare of Pennsylvania society." Gary B. Nash & Jean R. Soderlund, *Freedom by Degrees: Emancipation in Pennsylvania and Its Aftermath* (New York: Oxford University Press, 1991), p. 47. See also Jean Soderlund, *Quakers and Slavery: A Divided Spirit* (Princeton, NJ: Princeton University Press, 1985). J.R. Oldfield found a similar dynamic among English abolitionists and wrote that "After 1807 ... British activists set out to make abolition 'universal', partly out of self-interest and partly out of humanitarian zeal." J.R. Oldfield, *Transatlantic Abolitionism in the Age of Revolution: An International History of Anti-Slavery, c.1787–1820* (Cambridge: Cambridge University Press, 2013), p. 5.

19. Kay Wright Lewis, notes that stories of the cruelty of African warfare circulated widely in the American colonies in the eighteenth century, adding a particular terror to the prospect of slave rebellions. Kay Wright Lewis, *A Curse upon the Nation: Race, Freedom, and Extermination in America and the Atlantic World* (Athens, GA: University of Georgia Press, 2017), esp. pp. 50–8.

20. Katherine Gerbner notes that the Germantown Protest expressed concern that the holding of slaves in Pennsylvania made it harder to attract Europeans to the colony, but concludes "their primary concern, and the core of their argument, remained humanitarian." Katherine Gerbner, *Christian Slavery: Conversion and Race in the Protestant Atlantic World* (Philadelphia, PA: University of Pennsylvania Press, 2018), p. 70; Gary B. Nash and Jean R. Soderlund describe the Germantown Quakers' motives as being partly "practical because they saw the spread of slavery as threatening the stability and welfare of Pennsylvania society" but they stress that their position was "morally based" and "deeply moral and religious." Nash & Soderlund, *Freedom by Degrees*, p. 47; Soderlund, *Quakers and Slavery*.

21. Beverly C. Tomek points out that the Quaker "focus on importation reveals an element of self-interest. Even the most benevolent whites feared the growing black population and the threat of insurrection. Stopping the trade as soon as possible limited the threat of insurrection." Tomek also notes how early Quakers feared that slavery discouraged white immigration, debouched the white master class, and invited divine retribution. Tomek, *Colonization and Its Discontents*, p. 23. Margaret Abruzzo notes the self-interest of Quaker abolitionism: "By 1737, individual Friends viewed slaveholding violence as incompatible with

319

Quaker values, but their concern centered on the moral taint on slaveholders and the Society, not the suffering of the enslaved." Margaret Abruzzo, *Polemical Pain: Slavery, Cruelty, and the Rise of Humanitarianism* (Baltimore, MD: Johns Hopkins University Press, 2011), p. 25.

22. Abruzzo, *Polemical Pain*, p. 21.

23. Anthony Benezet, *Observations on the Inslaving, Importing and Purchasing of Negroes* ... (Germantown, PA: Christopher Sower, 1759).

24. Anthony Benezet, "A Short Account of That Part of Africa Inhabited by the Negroes," in *Am I Not a Man and Brother: The Antislavery Crusade of Revolutionary America, 1688–1788*, Roger Bruns, ed. (New York: Chelsea House Publishers, 1977), pp. 80–1.

25. Anthony Benezet, "A Caution and Warning," 1767, in Bruns, *Am I Not a Man and Brother*, p. 112. See also Benezet to Grenville Sharp, May 14, 1772, in Bruns, *Am I Not a Man and Brother*, p. 194.

26. Benezet to John Smith, February 20, 1759, Manuscript Collection 852, Haverford Special Collections, Haverford College.

27. Benezet to Samuel Fothergill, October 24, 1771, Manuscript Collection 852, Haverford Special Collections, Haverford College.

28. John Woolman, *The Journal with Other Writings of John Woolman* (New York: E.P. Dutton & Co., 1922), p. 33.

29. John Woolman, *Some Considerations on the Keeping of Negroes*, in Bruns, *Am I Not a Man and Brother*, p. 78.

30. Abner Woolman's Journal, Manuscript collection 1250 B5.1 1772 15a, p. 33, Haverford College Quaker and Special Collections, Haverford College.

31. Bruns, *Am I Not a Man and Brother*, p. 141.

32. Many scholars have recognized that much opposition to slavery was both rooted in Christian moralism and self-interest. Winthrop Jordan boiled the sermons of generations of divines into the observation that by the time of the Revolution, slavery was widely understood to be a sin. Jordan, *White over Black*. Gary Nash observed that Calvinists in New England warned that "holding slaves was to deprive themselves of divine protection." Gary B. Nash, *Race and Revolution* (Madison, WI: Madison House Press, 1990), p. 10.

33. Bernard Bailyn was one of the first historians to identify the use of the jeremiad in antislavery appeals. Bernard Bailyn, *Ideological Origins of the American Revolution* (Cambridge, MA: Harvard University Press, 1967), pp. 242–3. Likewise, Winthrop Jordan notes that New England antislavery ministers used language "virtually the same as that used by their grandfathers in warning of God's dealings with a faithless people ..." Jordan, *White over Black*, p. 298. Perry Miller traced the importance of the jeremiad generally in Protestant America in "From Covenant to the Revival," in *Religion in American Life: The Shaping of American Religion*, vol 1, James W. Smith, A.L. Jamison, & Nelson R. Burr, eds. (Princeton, NJ: Princeton University Press, 1961), pp. 322–68; William Gribbin extends Miller's arguments through the early national period in "The Covenant Transformed: The Jeremiad Tradition and the War of 1812," *Church History*, 40:3 (1971), pp. 297–305. See also Tomek, *Colonization and Its Discontents*, p. 23.

34. *A Collection of Many Select and Christian Epistles, Letters and Testimonies ... by George Fox* (Philadelphia: Marcus T.C. Gould, 1831), pp. 43–4.

35. Cadwalader Morgan (Merion, PA) to friends at Philadelphia Yearly Meeting, July 5, 1696, Manuscript Collection 990 B-R, Haverford College Quaker and Special Collections, Haverford College.

36. *The Complete Antislavery Writings of Anthony Benezet, 1754–1783*, David L. Crosby, ed. (Baton Rouge, LA: Louisiana State University Press, 2013), p. 67. Arguably no individual was more central to the early antislavery movement than Anthony Benezet. Roger Bruns, "A Quaker's Antislavery Crusade: Anthony Benezet," *Quaker History*, 65:2 (Autumn 1976), pp. 81–92; "Anthony Benezet's Assertion of Negro Equality," *Journal of Negro History*, LVI (July 1971), p. 23.

37. Beverly Tomak observes, "Benezet saw the slave trade as both morally wrong and dangerous to white interests." Tomek, *Colonization and Its Discontents*, p. 24.

38. Anthony Benezet to Joseph Phipps, May 28, 1763, in Bruns, *Am I Not a Man and Brother*, pp. 97–9.

39. Bruns, *Am I Not a Man and Brother*, p. 71.

40. Sewall, *The Selling of Joseph*. www.masshist.org/database/53 (accessed December 12, 2023).

41. Kenneth P. Minkema & Harry S. Stout, "The Edwardsean Tradition and the Antislavery Debate, 1740–1865," *The Journal of American History*, 92:1 (June 2005), pp. 47–74.

42. Bruns, *Am I Not a Man and Brother*, p. 321.

43. John Wesley, *Thoughts on Slavery*, 5th ed. (London, 1792), p. 22.

44. John Allen, *An Oration on the Beauties of Liberty, or The Essential Rights of the Americans. Delivered at the Second Baptist-Church in Boston ... Dec. 3d, 1772*, 4th ed. (Boston, 1773), pp. 74–5; Bruns, *Am I Not a Man and Brother*, pp. 335–6.

45. Richard Wells, *A Few Political Reflections Submitted to the Consideration of the British Colonies...* (Philadelphia: John Dunlap, 1774), pp. 80, 82.

46. Ibid., pp. 83, 85.

47. *American Museum* (Philadelphia), August 1790, p. 61.

48. Quoted in Gary Nash, *Warner Mifflin: Unflinching Quaker Abolitionist* (Philadelphia, PA: University of Pennsylvania Press, 2017), p. 51.

49. *American Museum* (Philadelphia), August 1790, p. 62.

50. David Ferris, *Memoirs of the Life of David Ferris* (Philadelphia: Merrihew & Thompson's Steam Power Press, 1855), pp. 87–90.

51. Martha P. Grundy, "David Ferris: Arguments against Quaker Slaveholding," *Quaker History*, 103:2 (Fall 2014), pp. 18–29.

52. Ferris, *Memoirs of the Life of David Ferris*, p. 91.

53. Grundy, "David Ferris," p. 25.

54. James Otis, *The Rights of the British Colonists, Asserted and Proven* (Boston, 1764), in Bruns, *Am I Not a Man and Brother*, p. 104. Douglas Egerton also perceived the antiblack thrust of Otis' argument, writing: "Otis did not merely assail the presence of racial slavery in New England but came perilously close to attacking the very presence of slaves *themselves*." Douglas R. Egerton, *Death or Liberty: African Americans and Revolutionary America* (New York: Oxford University Press, 2009), p. 45.

55. "Journal of Josiah Quincy, Junior," *Proceedings of the Massachusetts Historical Society* (June 1916), p. 463.

56. Quoted in *Documents Relating to the Revolutionary History of the State of New Jersey*, vol. 4, William Nelson, ed. (Trenton, NJ: John L. Murphy Publishing Co., 1914), p. 367.

57. Arthur Lee, "Address on Slavery," March 19, 1767, in Bruns, *Am I Not a Man and Brother*, pp. 107–11.
58. "Notices of David Cooper #17," Friend's Review (Philadelphia), 15:45 (July 12, 1862), p. 722.
59. Ibid., p. 723. Quote from David Cooper, A *Serious Address to the Rulers of America on the Inconsistency of Their Conduct Respecting Slavery* (Trenton: Isaac Collins, 1783), p. 14.
60. Bruns, *Am I Not a Man and Brother*, p. 399; *The Works of Samuel Hopkins*, vol. 2, Sewal Harding, ed. (Boston: Doctrinal Tract and Book Society, 1852), p. 584.
61. Bruns, *Am I Not a Man and Brother*, p. 424.
62. *Pennsylvania Archives*, Samuel Hazard, ed. (Philadelphia: Joseph Severns & Co., 1853), ser. 1, vol. 7, p. 79.
63. William B. Reed, *Life and Correspondence of Joseph Reed*, vol. 2 (Philadelphia: Lindsay and Blackiston, 1847), p. 174.
64. *The Pennsylvania Packet* (Philadelphia), March 4, 1779, p. 1.
65. *American Convention for Promoting the Abolition of Slavery and Improving the Condition of the African Race: Minutes, Constitution, Addresses, Memorials ...*, vol. 1 (New York: Bergman Publishers, 1969), pp. 23–4.
66. *Virginia Gazette*, October 21, 1775, p. 1.
67. *The Public Records of the Colony of Connecticut*, vol. 4, Charles J. Hoadly, ed. (August 1689–May 1706) (Hartford: Case, Lockwood & Brainard, 1868), pp. 375–6. Connecticut did not move to ease its restrictions on manumissions until October of 1777. Amending its "Act Concerning Indian, Molatto and Negro Servants and Slaves," the state assembly allowed any master to petition their local town selectmen to free a person they held in bondage. Town select-men had then to certify whether or not it was "consistent with the real advantage of such servant or slave" to be free, whether it was "probable that the servant or slave will be able to support his or her own person," and certify that the person in question was "of good and peaceable life and conversation." If they affirmed all these conditions, they would issue a certificate to the master that they were at "liberty to emancipate and set at liberty such servant or slave" that indemnified them from any future liability for the freed person's upkeep or misbehavior (*The Public Records of the State of Connecticut*, vol. 1, Charles J. Hoadly, ed. (Hartford: Lockwood Brainard Co., 1894), p. 415).
68. *The Charters and General Laws of the Colony and Province of Massachusetts Bay* (Boston: T.B. Wait & Co., 1814), p. 746.
69. *Records of the Colony of Rhode Island and Providence Plantations*, vol. 4, John Russell Bartlett, ed. (Providence: Knowles, Anthony & Co., State Printers, 1859), pp. 415–16.
70. Emily Blanck, *Revolutionizing Slavery: The Legal Culture of Slavery in Revolutionary Massachusetts and South Carolina* (Ph.D. Diss., Emory University, 2003), p. 209.
71. *The Acts of Assembly of the Province of Pennsylvania* (Philadelphia: Hall and Sellers, 1775), p. 144.
72. Marcus Rediker, *The Fearless Benjamin Lay: The Quaker Dwarf Who Became the First Revolutionary Abolitionist* (Boston, MA: Beacon Press, 2017), p. 66.
73. Arthur Zilversmit, *The First Emancipation: The Abolition of Slavery in the North* (Chicago, IL: University of Chicago Press, 1967), pp. 16–18.

74. Peter Force, *American Archives*, ser. 4, vol. 3 (Washington, 1840), pp. 1854–5.

75. William Waller Hening, *The Statutes at Large: Being a collection of all the laws of Virginia, from the first session of the legislature, in the year 1619*, vol. 3 (Richmond: Printed by and for Samuel Pleasants, junior, printer to the commonwealth, 1809–23), pp. 87–8.

76. John H. Russell, *The Free Negro in Virginia, 1619–1865* (Baltimore, MD: Johns Hopkins Press, 1913), p. 53.

77. Jon Cox, Jr. *Quakerism in the City of New York, 1657–1930* (New York, 1930), pp. 58–9.

78. Among the few recorded manumissions executed in compliance with the law, and therefore conferring a freedom defensible in court, was the 1757 will of Eve Scurlock, a tavern-keeper in New York City. Scurlock released Ann and four other people she owned and the heavy bond of £200 was paid by her relatives who were also working people in the city, a nephew shoemaker and a brother cooper. "Witnessing 200 pound bond for manumission of slave by Philip Livingston, New York, New York, May 4, 1757," GLC03943, The Gilder Lehrman Collection, Gilder Lehrman Institute of American History. Susana Bond who lived in the Hudson Valley, freed her slave Christian Bran after posting the necessary security with the Ulster County court. "Manumission of slave, Christian Bran," Records of the Court of General Sessions of the Peace, November 4, 1740, Ulster County Clerk's Office, New Paltz, NY.

79. David Brion Davis, *The Problem of Slavery in the Age of Revolution, 1770–1823* (Ithaca, NY: Cornell University Press, 1975), pp. 197–8.

80. Jean R. Sonderland, *Quakers & Slavery: A Divided Spirit* (Princeton, NJ: Princeton University Press, 1985), pp. 88, 98.

81. Ibid., pp. 102–3.

82. Ferris, *Memoirs of the Life of David Ferris*, p. 90.

83. Ibid., pp. 93–4.

84. Ibid., p. 9.

85. Michael J. Crawford, *The Having of Negroes Is Become a Burden: The Quaker Struggle to Free Slaves in Revolutionary North Carolina* (Gainesville, FL: University Press of Florida, 2010), p. 88.

86. Ibid., pp. 89–90.

87. Records of the County Court, Slave Records 1759–1864 Repository: North Carolina Department of Archives and History, Raleigh, North Carolina, Accession #21279603, Race and Slavery Petitions Project Series 2, County Court Petitions University of North Carolina at Greensboro.

88. *A Narrative of Some of the Proceedings North Carolina Yearly Meeting on the Subject of Slavery within Its Limits* (Greensboro, NC: Swaim & Sherwood, 1848), p. 10.

89. Ibid., pp. 11–13.

90. Ibid, p. 13.

91. Records of the County Court, Slave Records 1759–1864, North Carolina Department of Archives and History, Raleigh, North Carolina, Accession: #21278201, Race and Slavery Petitions Project Series 2, County Court Petitions University of North Carolina at Greensboro.

92. Ibid.

93. "To the Editor of the American Universal Magazine: SIR, The Petition…" *The American Universal Magazine* (Philadelphia), February 6, 1797, pp. 1, 5; see also

Jupiter Nicholson case petition to Congress 1797—Congress allowed Nicholson and three others to be returned to NC for slavery, Petition of Manumited Slaves to the U.S. Congress, *Annals of Congress*, 4th Cong., 2nd sess., 1796–97 (January 1797), House of Rep. 2015-2024.

94. "Deed of Manumission," October 1, 1772, in Betsy August, *Robert Pleasants Letterbook, 1771–1773* (M.A. Thesis, College of William and Mary, Virginia), p. 103.

95. *The Edward Pleasants Valentine Papers*, vol. 2 (Richmond, VA: The Valentine Museum, 1927), p. 1247.

96. Glen Crothers, *Quakers Living in the Lion's Mouth: The Society of Friends in Northern Virginia, 1730–1865* (Gainesville, FL: University Press of Florida, 2012), pp. 42, 45.

97. Thomas Jefferson to Edward Bancroft, January 26, 1789, *The Papers of Thomas Jefferson, vol. 14, 8 October 1788–26 March 1789,* Julian P. Boyd, ed. (Princeton, NJ: Princeton University Press, 1958), pp. 492–4.

98. Report of the Committee of Propositions and Grievances, November 17, 1790, General Assembly, Session Records, Joint Standing Committee of Propositions and Grievances, November–December 1790, North Carolina Department of Archives and History, Raleigh, North Carolina, Race and Slavery Petitions Project Series 1, Legislative Petitions, The University of North Carolina Greensboro; Matthew Spooner, "Freedom, Reenslavement, and Movement in the Revolutionary South," in *Race and Nation in the Age of Emancipations*, Whitney Nell Stewart & John Garrison Marks, eds. (Athens, GA: University of Georgia Press, 2018), p. 26.

99. Thomas Jordan, Perquimans County, September 1795, General Assembly, Session Records, Emancipation Petitions, November–December 1795, North Carolina Department of Archives and History, Raleigh, North Carolina, Race and Slavery Petitions Project Series 1, PAR #11279507, Legislative Petitions, The University of North Carolina Greensboro.

100. Petition of November 29, 1780, Legislative Petitions of the General Assembly, 1776–1865, Accession Number 36121, Box 289, Folder 107, Library of Virginia, Richmond.

101. Crothers, *Quakers Living in the Lion's Mouth*, p. 60.

102. Petition of November 29, 1780, Legislative Petitions of the General Assembly, 1776–1865, Accession Number 36121, Box 289, Folder 107, Library of Virginia, Richmond.

103. Petition of November 29, 1780, Accession Number 36121, Box 289, Folder 107; May 29, 1782, ibid.

104. Cox, Jr., *Quakerism in the City of New York, 1657–1930*, p. 61; see also *Judicial Cases Concerning American Slavery and the Negro*, vol. 4, Helen Tunnicliff Catterall, ed. (Washington, DC: Carnegie Institution, 1936), p. 363.

105. Sheppard to Ellicott, July 17, 1845, RG5/137, Friends Historical Library, Swarthmore College.

106. Katherine Gerbner notes that the Germantown Protest expressed concern that the holding of slaves in Pennsylvania made it harder to attract Europeans to the colony, but concludes "their primary concern, and the core of their argument, remained humanitarian." Gerbner, *Christian Slavery*, p. 70; John Wood Sweet transposes the old idea of benevolence to a theory of "sentimentality" but

it remains the same old altruism obscuring white self-interest: "In the era of the American Revolution, public support for slavery was challenged less by concepts of liberty or equality than by humanitarian sensibility." John Wood Sweet, *Bodies Politic: Negotiating Race in the American North, 1730–1830* (Baltimore, MD: Johns Hopkins University Press, 2003), p. 240.

107. Sean Wilentz, *No Property in Man: Slavery and Antislavery at the Nation's Founding* (Cambridge, MA: Harvard University Press, 2018), p. 28; Richard D. Brown, *Self-Evident Truths: Contesting Equal Rights from the Revolution to the Civil War* (New Haven, CT: Yale University Press, 2016), p. 9; George H. Moore, *Notes on the History of Slavery in Massachusetts* (New York: D. Appleton & Co., 1866), pp. 124–5; *Free Negroes and Mulattoes: House of Representatives, Jan. 16, 1822, Report,* Theodore Lyman, ed. (Boston: True & Green, 1822); *A Report of the Record Commissioners of the City of Boston Containing the Boston Town Records, 1758–1769* (Boston: Rockwell and Churchill, 1886), p. 183. In the end the assembly amended the proposed bill by simply imposing a tax on the importation of enslaved people and then failed to pass it and no further calls for "total abolition" were aired by Boston's leaders. For a very complete discussion of Lyman's Report, see Margot Minardi, *Making Slavery History: Abolitionism and the Politics of Memory in Massachusetts* (New York: Oxford University Press, 2010), pp. 31–3.

CHAPTER 2

1. Alexis De Tocqueville, *Democracy in America*, vol. 1, Henry Reeve, trans. 3rd. ed. (Cambridge: Sever and Francis, 1863), p. 462.

2. Many historians have noted this relationship, including William Freehling. Freehling wrote in 1994, "Jefferson and fellow racists hated the African slave trade partly because it brought more blacks to America." Freeling also noted that the "first step in removing blacks from the United States was to stop Africans from coming, and the last step was to deport those already in the nation." William Freehling, *The Reintegration of American History: Slavery and the Civil War* (Oxford: Oxford University Press, 1994), pp. 16, 23. The first scholar to uncover the white self-interest underlying opposition to the slave trade was W.E.B. Du Bois in his early work, *The Suppression of the African Slave-Trade.* Surveying all the attempts to restrict the trade up to the time of the Revolution, Du Bois concluded that a fear of "insurrections and acts of violence" and a "condition of vague dread and unrest ... was the prime motive back of all the earlier efforts to check the further importation of slaves." W.E.B. Du Bois, *The Suppression of the African Slave-Trade* (New York, 1896), pp. 42–3. Du Bois' contentions received more attention in the early 1970s as Donald L. Robinson, Duncan J. MacLeod and others reexamined the politics underlying opposition to the slave trade. MacLeod found this opposition to be "frequently crass rather than humanitarian in its motivation." Duncan J. MacLeod, *Slavery, Race and the American Revolution* (New York: Cambridge University Press, 1974), p. 31. Donald L. Robinson also thought slave trade restrictions were "produced more by fear of slave insurrections and by the desire not to discourage white immigration than by genuine antipathy toward slavery." Donald L. Robinson, *Slavery in the Structure of American Politics* (New York: Harcourt Brace Jovanovich, 1971), pp. 78–9.

Others have continued to misrepresent the movement for restriction of the slave trade as being primarily rooted in egalitarianism. Bernard Bailyn depicted these measures as unambiguous achievements "to extend the reign of liberty to the enslaved Negroes." He noted that the Continental Congress pledged to discontinue the slave trade in 1776 and sums up this moment as one in which slavery "had been subjected to severe pressure as a result of the extension of Revolutionary ideas, and it bore the marks ever after." Bernard Bailyn, *Ideological Origins of the American Revolution* (Cambridge, MA: Harvard University Press, 1967), pp. 245–6. Richard D. Brown described proposals to restrict the slave trade not only as a desire for abolition but as evidence of a broader antiracism: "The plantation gentry's votes against the slave trade suggest that natural rights idealism sustained the language of equal rights." Richard D. Brown, *Self-Evident Truths: Contesting Equal Rights from the Revolution to the Civil War* (New Haven, CT: Yale University Press, 2017), p. 7.

3. Philadelphia Yearly Meeting of the Religious Society of Friends, July 23, 1696, Manuscript Collection 1250, A1.2, Haverford College Quaker and Special Collections, Haverford College.
4. Philadelphia Yearly Meeting Minutes, Meeting of July 23, 1696, Manuscript Collection 1250, A1.2, Haverford College Quaker and Special Collections, Haverford College.
5. Quoted in Brycchan Carey, *From Peace to Freedom: Quaker Rhetoric and the Birth of American Antislavery, 1657–1761* (New Haven, CT: Yale University Press, 2012), p. 99.
6. Philadelphia Yearly Meeting of the Religious Society of Friends, September 20, 1729, Manuscript Collection 1250, A1.2, Haverford College Quaker and Special Collections, Haverford College.
7. Philadelphia Yearly Meeting of the Religious Society of Friends, September 19, 1730, Manuscript Collection 1250, A1.2, Haverford College Quaker and Special Collections, Haverford College.
8. Philadelphia Yearly Meeting, *Epistle of Caution and Advice*, 1754, Manuscript collection 1250, A1.3, Haverford College Quaker and Special Collections, Haverford College.
9. *Journal of the Commissioners for Trade and Plantations 1728–1734*, vol. 6 (London: Her Britannic Majesty's Stationery Office, 1928), pp. 64–8.
10. *Documents Illustrative of the History of the Slave Trade to America*, vol. 4, Elizabeth Donnan, ed. (New York: Octagon Books, 1969), p. 66, 86.
11. Ibid., pp. 91, 93.
12. Ibid., pp. 94, 115–17.
13. Ibid., pp. 122–3, 127.
14. Ibid., p. 107.
15. Ibid., pp. 131–2.
16. Ibid., p. 145.
17. Ibid., pp. 151–2.
18. Ibid., p. 458.
19. George H. Moore, *Notes on the History of Slavery in Massachusetts* (New York: D. Appleton & Co., 1866), p. 52.
20. Ralph Sandiford, "A Brief Examination of the Practice of the Times" (1729), in *Am I Not A Man and a Brother: The Antislavery Crusade of Revolutionary America,*

1688–1788, Roger Burns, ed. (New York: Chelsea House Publishers, 1977), p. 37.

21. John Hepburn, "Arguments against Making Slaves of Men" (1715), in Bruns, *Am I Not A Man and a Brother*, pp. 29–30.

22. "Darien Protest, January 3, 1739," in Bruns, *Am I Not A Man and a Brother*, p. 65.

23. Twentieth Assembly, Sixth Session, April 25, 1734, in *Journal of the Legislative Council of the Colony of New York*, vol. 1 (Albany: Weed, Parsons & Co., 1861), p. 630.

24. Anthony Benezet, *A Short Account of the Part of Africa Inhabited by the Negroes*, 3rd ed. (London: W. Baker & J.W. Galabin, 1768, orig. 1762), p. 79. See also Anthony Benezet, "A Caution and Warning" (1767), in Bruns, *Am I Not a Man and Brother*, p. 112.

25. Bernard Bailyn wildly exaggerated the extent of Reverend Samuel Cooke's criticism of slavery. Bailyn wrote that Reverend Cooke "devoted most of text to 'the cause of our African slaves.'" In fact, in only one of the forty-seven pages of his homily, did Cooke "plead the cause of our African slaves." Bernard Bailyn, *The Ideological Origins of the American Revolution* (Cambridge, MA: The Belknap Press of Harvard University Press, 2017, orig. 1967), p. 239; Samuel Cooke, *A Sermon Preached at Cambridge, in the Audience of His Honor Thomas Hutchinson, Esq ... May 30th, 1770* (Boston: Edes and Gill, printers to the Honorable House of Representatives, 1770).

26. Benjamin Lay, "All Slave-keepers ... Apostates" (1737), in Bruns, *Am I Not A Man and a Brother*, pp. 57, 61.

27. Peter Wood, "The Changing Population of the Colonial South: An Overview by Race and Region, 1685–1790," in *Powhatan's Mantle: Indians in the Colonial Southeast*, Gregory A. Waselkov, Peter H. Wood, & Tom Hatley, eds. (Lincoln, NE: University of Nebraska Press, rev. ed., 2006, orig. 1989), pp. 57–132; *The Virginia Gazette* (Williamsburg), March 20, 1752, p. 1.

28. "Observations Concerning the Increase of Mankind, 1751," *The Papers of Benjamin Franklin, vol. 4, July 1, 1750, through June 30, 1753*, Leonard W. Labaree, ed. (New Haven, CT: Yale University Press, 1961), pp. 225–34. See also Eva S. Wolf, "Early Free-Labor Thought and the Contest over Slavery in the Early Republic," in *Contesting Slavery*, John Craig Hammond & Matthew Mason, eds. (Charlottesville, VA: University of Virginia Press, 2011), pp. 32–48. Christa Dierksheide observes that "[thinkers of] the period of the later eighteenth century believed that slavery was incompatible with human progress. To them, the slave trade and the plantation slavery it spawned constituted an archaic system that retarded moral, economic, and political development in the Atlantic world. They imagined a world without slaves, a world in which legitimate commerce and free labor encouraged the perfection of mankind." Christa Dierksheide, *Amelioration and Empire: Progress and Slavery in the Plantation Americas* (Charlottesville, VA: University of Virginia Press, 2014), p. 2.

29. "From Benjamin Franklin to Richard Jackson, 11 February 1764," *The Papers of Benjamin Franklin, vol. 11, January 1, through December 31, 1764*, Leonard W. Labaree, ed. (New Haven, CT and London: Yale University Press, 1967), pp. 76–8.

30. J.A. Leo Lemay, *The Life of Benjamin Franklin, Volume 3: Soldier, Scientist, and Politician, 1748–1757* (Philadelphia, PA: University of Pennsylvania Press, 2009), pp. 605–12.

31. George Mason to George William Fairfax and George Washington, December 23, 1765, Washington Papers, Library of Congress, Washington, DC, Printed in Robert A. Rutland, *The Papers of George Mason, 1725–1792*, vol. 1 (Chapel Hill, 1970), pp. 61–2.

32. Philip D. Morgan, "'To Get Quit of Negroes': George Washington and Slavery," *Journal of American Studies*, 39:3 (December, 2005), pp. 403–29.

33. *Pennsylvania Gazette* (Philadelphia), February 18, 1756, p. 2.

34. Bruns, *Am I Not a Man and Brother*, pp. 210–11.

35. Ibid,, p. 213.

36. Nathaniel Appleton, *Considerations on Slavery, In a Letter to a Friend* (Boston: Printed by Edes and Gill in Queen-Street, 1767), p. 20; Bruns, *Am I Not a Man and Brother*, pp. 128–37.

37. David Eastburn et al., 1801, General Assembly, Legislative Papers, Delaware State Archives, Dover, Delaware, Race and Slavery Petitions Project Series 1, PAR #10380101, Legislative Petitions, The University of North Carolina Greensboro.

38. To Thomas Jefferson from Thomas Paine, January 25, 1805, *The Papers of Thomas Jefferson, vol. 45, 11 November 1804 to 8 March 1805*, James P. McClure et al., eds. (Princeton, NJ: Princeton University Press, 2021), pp. 378–89.

39. Douglas Egerton concluded from his study of early antislavery pamphlets, speeches, and sermons that "the proposition that slavery was wrong primarily because it was harmful to *white* society was a prominent feature of these essays and letters." Douglas R. Egerton, *Death or Liberty: African Americans and Revolutionary America* (New York: Oxford University Press, 2009), p. 49. Beverly Tomek argued that American antislavery "proceeded from several motives, one of which was an effort to limit the black population from the beginning." Beverly C. Tomek, *Colonization and Its Discontents: Emancipation, Emigration, and Antislavery in Antebellum Pennsylvania* (New York: New York University Press, 2010), p. 14.

40. *Documents Illustrative of the History of the Slave Trade*, pp. 257–8, 276.

41. Ibid., pp. 315, 415.

42. Ibid., pp. 151–2, 484, 493.

43. Ibid., pp. 142–3.

44. An ACT for laying a Duty upon Negroes and Mulatto Slaves, imported into this Province. 1762, 4, in Bernard Bush, *Laws of the Royal Colony of New Jersey* (New Jersey Archives, Third Series, vols. 2–5, published 1977–86), pp. 171–5.

45. An ACT for laying a Duty on the Purchasers of Slaves imported into this Colony. June 24, 1767, in Bush, *Laws of the Royal Colony of New Jersey*, vol. 4 (New Jersey Archives, Third Series, vols. 2–5, published 1977–86), pp. 435–6.

46. Robert W. Gibbes, *Documentary History of the American Revolution*, vol. 1, "The First Remonstrance from South Carolina against the Stamp Act, Sept. 4, 1764," pp. 5–6.

47. *Documents Illustrative of the History of the Slave Trade*, pp. 422–3.

48. Ibid., pp. 433, 450.

49. Ibid., pp. 153–4.

50. Ibid., pp. 154–6.

51. *A Narrative of Some of the Proceedings of North Carolina Yearly Meeting on the Subject of Slavery* ... (Greensboro, NC: North Carolina Yearly Meeting, Printed by Swaim & Sherwood, 1848), pp. 7–8, Manuscript and Special Collections Library, Duke University Libraries.

52. Salem Monthly Meeting, "The Petition of Sundry Inhabitants of the County of Salem" (1774), RG2/Ph/S26, Friends Historical Library, Swarthmore College.

53. Culpepper County Resolutions, July 7, 1774, Force, ser. 4, vol. 1, p. 523.

54. *Documents Illustrative of the History of the Slave Trade*, pp. 162, 237; Prince George's County Resolutions, Force, ser. 4, vol. 1, p. 493–4. Joanne Melish describes early Revolutionary-era antislavery protest as involving black exclusion, finding such "antislavery protest structured the problem as one of the presence or absence of enslaved Americans, of introducing closure to the process of open-ended increase in their numbers and in fact reducing their physical presence by attrition of one kind or another." Joanne P. Melish, *Disowning Slavery: Gradual Emancipation and "Race" in New England, 1780–1860* (Ithaca, NY: Cornell University Press, 998), p. 53. Matthew Spooner refers to historians overlooking this white Americans' long and widespread desire to exclude and banish black people from their communities as "neglect." Matthew Spooner, "'I Know This Scheme Is from God:' Toward a Reconsideration of the Origins of the American Colonization Society," *Slavery & Abolition*, 35:4 (December 2014), pp. 559–75.

55. "Letters from Sir James Wright," in *Collections of the Georgia Historical Society*, vol. 3 (Savannah: Morning News, 1873), pp. 210, 215.

56. *The Statutes at Large, Being a Collection of all the Laws of Virginia*, vol. 9 (Richmond, 1821), October 5, 1778, p. 471.

57. *Documents Illustrative of the History of the Slave Trade*, p. 164.

58. *Pennsylvania Archives*, Samuel Hazard, ed. (Philadelphia: Joseph Severns & Co., 1853), ser. 1, vol. 6, p. 685.

59. Ibid., p. 518.

60. *Gazette of the United States*, March 24, 1790, p. 3; *American Museum* (Philadelphia), August 1790, p. 63.

61. *American Museum* (Philadelphia), 1792, Appendix II, p. 22.

62. *Journals of the House of Representatives, 1792–1794*, Michael E. Stevens, ed. (Columbia, SC: University of South Carolina Press, 1988), p. xxiii.

CHAPTER 3

1. Woody Holton, *Forced Founders: Indians, Debtors, Slaves, and the Making of the American Revolution in Virginia* (Chapel Hill, NC: University of North Carolina Press, 1999), pp. 67–8.

2. "To John Adams from Unknown, 9 June 1775," *The Adams Papers, Papers of John Adams, vol. 3, May 1775–January 1776*, Robert J. Taylor, ed. (Cambridge, MA: Harvard University Press, 1979), pp. 18–20.

3. Robert G. Parkinson also discusses this anonymous letter but infers from it, without any evidence, that Adams was not fearful of black freedom but rather that such a policy "might alienate southern colonies from the cause." In this way, Adams' abolitionist credentials are preserved and patriot anxieties are deflected from fears of free blacks to worries about colonial unity. Robert G. Parkin-

son, *The Common Cause: Creating Race and Nation in the American Revolution* (Chapel Hill, NC: University of North Carolina Press, 2016), pp. 99–101.

4. "September 1775," *The Adams Papers, Diary and Autobiography of John Adams, vol. 2, 1771–1781*, L.H. Butterfield, ed. (Cambridge, MA: Harvard University Press, 1961), pp. 172–88.

5. "William Lee to Robert Carter Nicholas," March 6, 1775, in *Letters of William Lee*, vol. 1, Worthington Chauncey Ford, ed. (Brooklyn, NY: Historical Printing Club, 1891), pp. 143, 144.

6. "William Lee to Richard Henry Lee," February 25, 1775, in *Letters of William Lee*, p. 130.

7. Christopher Leslie Brown, *Moral Capital: Foundations of British Abolitionism* (Chapel Hill, NC: University of North Carolina Press, 2006), pp. 146–8; James E. Bradley, *Religion, Revolution and English Radicalism: Non-Conformity in Eighteenth-Century Politics and Society* (New York: Cambridge University Press, 2002), pp. 292–3; see also B. Zorina Khan, *Inventing Ideas: Patents, Prizes, and the Knowledge Economy* (New York: Oxford University Press, 2020), p. 352.

8. *The Public Advertiser* (London), December 8, 1775, p. 2.

9. *The Pennsylvania Gazette*, February 28, 1776, p. 2. See, for example, *The Public Advertiser* (London), December 8, 1775, p. 2.

10. *The Pennsylvania Packet*, March 4, 1776, p. 4; *Maryland Gazette* (Annapolis), March 7, 1776, p. 2.

11. *The Public Advertiser* (London), December 21, 1775, p. 1.

12. *The Maryland Gazette* (Annapolis), June 13, 1776, p. 1.

13. *The Pennsylvania Gazette*, April 17, 1776, p. 2. Two years later, and far too late, the English government proposed something close to that suggestion. A secret diplomatic mission to the war-torn American colonies offered to allow Americans to prohibit the importation of slaves to America. As he sailed across the North Atlantic on his way to bargain for peace with a secret rebel delegation in May of 1778, Lord Carlisle spent his time making notes on how the Americans might be induced to rejoin the empire. On board the *Trident* he hammered out a draft list of concessions, beginning with allowing newly formed state governments and the Continental Congress to remain in their powers, though governors and the president would be appointed by the King. These royal governors would be largely ceremonial, their powers shriveled to merely overseeing that no acts of assembly conflicted with the international commerce regulations of the empire (the same power conceded to the federal government in the American Constitution of 1787). Carlisle and his collaborator, Governor Johnstone, thought it important to clarify that this commerce power would not extend to the slave trade: "But no negative as to acts for the prohibition of Negroes ..." Lord Carlisle was not offering the empire's support for ending the transatlantic slave trade to America out of sympathy with enslaved people. While anchored in Delaware, he wrote to his wife that he had "been looking out for a little black slave" but worried that his son George "should choose to make a plaything of him when I come home." *The Manuscripts of the Earl of Carlisle* (London: Eyre and Spottiswoode, 1897), pp. 346, 387–8.

14. *The Diplomatic Correspondence of the American Revolution*, vol. 1., Jared Sparks, ed. (Boston: N. Hale & Gray & Bowen, 1829), pp. 48–9, 92.

15. "To John Jay from Silas Deane," 3 December 1776," *The Selected Papers of John Jay, vol. 1, 1760–1779*, Elizabeth M. Nuxoll, ed. (Charlottesville, VA: University of Virginia Press, 2010), pp. 313–18.

16. "Seasonable Thoughts," in the *Pennsylvania Journal*, January 3, 1776, in *Diary of the American Revolution: From Newspapers and Original Documents*, vol. 1, Frank Moore, ed. (New York: C. Scribner, 1860), pp. 188–9.

17. *Diary of the American Revolution: From Newspapers and Original Documents*, pp. 24–5.

18. Bessie Lewis Whitaker, *The Provincial Council and Committees of Safety in North Carolina* ... (Chapel Hill, NC: The University Press, 1908), pp. 33, 40.

19. Newburgh (New-York) Committee, May 15, 1775, Peter Force, *American Archives*, ser. 4, vol. 2 (Washington, 1837–53), p. 607.

20. July 6, 1776, *Journals of the Provincial Congress ... of the State of New York*, vol. 1 (Albany: Thurlow Weed, 1842), p. 480.

21. Militia Bill August 22, 1775, *Journals of the Provincial Congress*, p. 114.

22. *Journals of the Provincial Congress*, p. 215.

23. Force, *American Archives*, ser. 4, vol. 6 (Washington, 1846), p. 549.

24. G.A. Gilbert, "The Connecticut Loyalists," *American Historical Review*, 4:2 (January 1899), p. 284.

25. *Pennsylvania Archives*, Samuel Hazard, ed. (Philadelphia: Joseph Severns & Co., 1853), ser. 1, vol. 4, p. 792.

26. Force, *American Archives*, ser. 4, vol. 6, pp. 1262–3.

27. Minutes of the Provincial Congress of New Jersey, p. 492.

28. Samuel Tucker to John Hancock, July 5, 1776, Force, *American Archives*, ser. 5, vol. 1 (Washington, 1848–53, p. 16.

29. *Journals of the Provincial Congress*, p. 567.

30. Ibid., p. 606.

31. Ibid., p. 1091.

32. *Journal of the House of Delegates of the Commonwealth of Virginia*, June 4, 1777 (Richmond, 1827), p. 59.

33. Force, *American Archives*, vol. 1, p. 490.

34. *The Revolutionary Records of the State of Georgia*, vol. 1, Allen D. Candler, ed. (Atlanta, GA: Franklin-Turner Co., 1908), pp. 300–3.

35. Robert W. Gibbes, *Documentary History of the American Revolution*, "The First Remonstrance from South Carolina against the Stamp Act, Sept. 4, 1764," vol. 1, p. 205.

36. Jeffrey R. Young, *Domesticating Slavery: The Master Class in Georgia and South Carolina, 1670–1837* (Chapel Hill, NC: University of North Carolina Press, 1999), p. 74.

37. "To George Washington from Brigadier General Henry Knox, 29 March 1780," *The Papers of George Washington, Revolutionary War Series, vol. 25, 10 March–12 May 1780*, William M. Ferraro, ed. (Charlottesville, VA: University of Virginia Press, 2017), pp. 222–5.

38. Georgia Council of Safety, August 19, 1776, Force, *American Archives*, vol. 1, p. 1052; Extract of a letter to a Gentleman in London, dated St. Augustine, August 20, 1776, Force, *American Archives*, vol. 1, p. 1076.

39. Gen. Lee to Board of War and Ordinance, August 24, 1776, Force, *American Archives*, vol. 1, p. 1132.

40. "To George Washington from Major General Benjamin Lincoln, 7 November 1779," *The Papers of George Washington, Revolutionary War Series, vol. 23, 22 October–31 December 1779*, William M. Ferraro, ed. (Charlottesville, VA: University of Virginia Press, 2015), pp. 192–5.

41. "To Alexander Hamilton from Lieutenant Colonel John Laurens, 14 July 1779," *The Papers of Alexander Hamilton, vol. 2, 1779–1781*, Harold C. Syrett, ed. (New York: Columbia University Press, 1961), pp. 102–4.

42. "To George Washington from Henry Laurens, 24 October 1779," *The Papers of George Washington, Revolutionary War Series, vol. 23, 22 October–31 December 1779*, pp. 24–8.

43. Philip M. Hamer et al., eds., *The Papers of Henry Laurens*, vol. 12 (Columbia, SC: University of South Carolina Press, 2003), p. 392.

44. "From George Washington to a Continental Congress Camp Committee, 29 January 1778," *The Papers of George Washington, Revolutionary War Series, vol. 13, 26 December 1777–28 February 1778*, Edward G. Lengel, ed. (Charlottesville, VA: University of Virginia Press, 2003), pp. 376–409.

45. Major General Pigot wrote to General Howe, "Several of the Inhabitants from the Narraganzet Shore are come over to us, and enlisted with Col°- Wightman and Days are fixed for bringing off more of them. Negroes likewise come to us for protection, their Masters wanting them to enlist in a Regiment raising at Boston upon Terms of granting them their Freedom after three Years Service." Pigot to Howe, April 10, 1778, *Report on American Manuscripts in the Royal Institution of Great Britain*, vol. 1 (London: 1904), p. 229.

46. "To George Washington from Henry Laurens, 16 March 1779," *The Papers of George Washington, Revolutionary War Series, vol. 19, 15 January–7 April 1779*, Philander D. Chase and William M. Ferraro, eds. (Charlottesville, VA: University of Virginia Press, 2009), pp. 503–5.

47. *The Manuscripts of the Earl of Carlisle*, p. 429.

48. "From Alexander Hamilton to John Jay, March 14, 1779," *The Papers of Alexander Hamilton, vol. 2, 1779–1781*, pp. 17–19.

49. "From Alexander Hamilton to Lieutenant Colonel John Laurens, 11 September 11, 1779," *The Papers of Alexander Hamilton, vol. 2, 1779–1781*, pp. 165–9.

50. "From George Washington to Henry Laurens, March 20, 1779," *The Papers of George Washington*, vol. 19, pp. 542–3.

51. "To Alexander Hamilton from Lieutenant Colonel John Laurens, July 14, 1779," *The Papers of Alexander Hamilton, vol. 2, 1779–1781*, pp. 102–4.

52. Ryan A. Quintana, *Making a Slave State : Political Development in Early South Carolina* (Chapel Hill, NC: University of North Carolina Press, 2018), p. 56; *The Royal Gazette* (New York) July, 21, 1779, p. 1; *Report on American Manuscripts in the Royal Institution of Great Britain*, p. 463.

53. "To James Madison from Joseph Jones, November 18, 1780," *The Papers of James Madison, vol. 2, 20 March 1780–23 February 1781*, William T. Hutchinson and William M.E. Rachal, eds. (Chicago, IL: University of Chicago Press, 1962), pp. 182–5.

54. "From James Madison to Joseph Jones, November 28, 1780," *The Papers of James Madison*, vol. 2, pp. 209–11.

55. Jones to Madison, December 8, 1780, in *Letters of Joseph Jones of Virginia, 1777–1787*, Worthington C. Ford, ed. (Washington: Department of State, 1889),

pp. 63–4. Note how Jones casually assumes that emancipation would require that those freed would "go off" and be replaced by "labourers," by which he clearly meant whites.

CHAPTER 4

1. Arthur Lee, *An Essay in Vindication of the Continental Colonies of America* (London, 1764), pp. 9–10; Richard K. MacMaster, "Arthur Lee's 'Address on Slavery': An Aspect of Virginia's Struggle to End the Slave Trade, 1765–1774," *The Virginia Magazine of History and Biography*, 80:2 (April 1972), pp. 141–57.
2. Lee, *An Essay in Vindication of the Continental Colonies of America*, p. 30.
3. Ibid., p. 25.
4. Ibid., p. 43.
5. Ibid., p. 45.
6. *Penn. Chronicle and Universal Advertiser*, August 31–September 7, 1767, quoted in Edmund S. Morgan, "The Puritan Ethic and the American Revolution," *The William and Mary Quarterly*, 24:1 (January 1967), pp. 3, 23. See also Arthur Lee, "Monitor II," *The Virginia Gazette* (Williamsburg), March 3, 1768, p. 1.
7. Some historians have questioned the sincerity of elite southern antislavery sentiment. Robert McColley notes that "Virginia's leaders ... denounce[d] slavery as an evil institution" but then finds that this was mostly window-dressing for "outsiders," like Yankees and the French. McColley overlooks Lee and others when he writes: "But among the class of wealthy planters whom they chiefly represented not one Virginia statesman of the Jeffersonian era ever advanced a practical proposal for the elimination of slavery ... with the single exception of St. George Tucker ..." Robert McColley, *Slavery and Jeffersonian Virginia* (Urbana, IL: University of Illinois Press, 1964), p. 115.
8. See, for example, Douglas Egerton, "'It's Origin Is Not a Little Curious': A New Look at the American Colonization Society," *Journal of the Early Republic*, 5:4 (1985), pp. 463–80; Nicholas Guyatt in his brilliant *Bind Us Apart: How Enlightened Americans Invented Racial Segregation* recounts that "In the decades between the Revolution and the Civil War, the idea that the races might be separated became a mainstay of the movement against slavery in North and South alike ... In fact, racial separation served as a rallying point for slavery's opponents for more than seventy years, from the publication of Jefferson's Notes on the State of Virginia in 1785 to the first years of the Civil War ..." Nicholas Guyatt, *Bind Us Apart: How Enlightened Americans Invented Racial Segregation* (New York: Basic Books, 2016), pp. 4, 5.
9. "[thinkers of] the period of the later eighteenth century believed that slavery was incompatible with human progress. To them, the slave trade and the plantation slavery it spawned constituted an archaic system that retarded moral, economic, and political development in the Atlantic world. They imagined a world without slaves, a world in which legitimate commerce and free labor encouraged the perfection of mankind." Christa Dierksheide, *Amelioration and Empire: Progress and Slavery in the Plantation Americas* (Charlottesville, VA: University of Virginia Press, 2014), p. 2.
10. Charles W. Mills, *The Racial Contract* (Ithaca, NY: Cornell University Press, 1997). See also Charles W. Mills, *Black Rights/White Wrongs: The Critique of*

Racial Liberalism (New York: Oxford University Press, 2017). Considering the French Revolution, Lynn Hunt theorizes that modern racism arose to prominence during the revolutionary eighteenth century because "in contrast to simple prejudice, the systematic denigration of what you are not requires a doctrine, and such doctrines only appeared once inequality had to be justified." But such doctrine does not need only justification, it can also be critique. Ethno-abolitionists constructed a doctrine of what slavery and inequality was a century before the American and French Revolutions. Lynn Hunt, "The World We Have Gained: The Future of the French Revolution," *American Historical Review*, 108:1 (February 2003), p. 19. For a dissenting view from Mills, see Jimmy C. Klausen, *Fugitive Rousseau: Slavery, Primitivism, and Political Freedom* (New York: Fordham University Press, 2014). See also Emmanuel Chukwudi Eze, "Hume, Race, and Human Nature," *Journal of the History of Ideas*, 81:4 (October 2000), pp. 691–8; Emmanuel Chukwudi Eze, "The Color of Reason: The Idea of 'Race' in Kant's Anthropology," in *Postcolonial African Philosophy: A Critical Reader*, Emmanuel Chukwudi Eze, ed. (Cambridge, MA: Blackwell Publishers, 1997), pp. 103–40; Robert Bernasconi & Anika Maaza Mann, "The Contradictions of Racism: Locke, Slavery, and the Two Treatises" and Anthony Bogues, "John Stuart Mill and 'The Negro Question': Race, Colonialism, and the Ladder of Civilization," in *Race and Racism in Modern Philosophy*, Andrew Valls, ed. (Ithaca, NY: Cornell University Press, 2005), pp. 89–107, 217–34; Holly Brewer, "Slavery, Sovereignty, and 'Inheritable Blood': Reconsidering John Locke and the Origins of American Slavery," *American Historical Review* 122:4 (October 2017), pp. 1038–78.

11. John Christman, "Rousseau's Silence on trans-Atlantic Slavery: Philosophical Implications," *European Journal of Philosophy*, 30:4 (December 2022), pp. 1458–72.

12. Montesquieu, *The Spirit of the Laws*, Anne M. Cohler, Basia Carolyn Miller, & Harold Samuel Stone, trans. and eds. (New York: Cambridge University Press, 1989). These sections of Montesquieu are often mistaken for simply denying that there is such a thing as a "natural" slave. Arthur Scherr, "Intellectual Roots of Thomas Jefferson's Opinions on Slavery: Montesquieu's Impact," *Journal of Transatlantic Studies*, 19:2 (2021), pp. 189–214.

13. Debate over whether Montesquieu wrote about slavery ironically, as in the mode of Jonathan Swift, or implicitly condoned it, has taken passionate forms in France with Odile Tobner in *French Racism: Four Centuries of Negrophobia* (Paris: Les Arènes, 2007) arguing that the philosopher was a racist and colonizer and René Pommier in *Defense of Montesquieu: On an Absurd Reading of the Chapter "On Negro Slavery"* (Paris: Eurédit, 2014) calling such a reading "absurd." While it is undoubtedly true that Montesquieu engages in an ironic defense of slavery in Book XV, ch. 5 that is clearly parody, the same cannot be said for those passages detailing the ancient precedents in law cited above. Ashleen Menchaca-Bagnulo, "Madison as Reformer: The Montesquieuan Roots of Madison on Slavery," *Perspectives on Political Science*, 51:2 (2022), pp. 67–80. Montesquieu's importance to the abolition movement in England was traced nearly a century ago by F.T.H. Fletcher, "Montesquieu's Influence on Anti-Slavery Opinion in England," *The Journal of Negro History*, 18:1 (1933), p. 414.

14. Diana J. Schaub, "Montesquieu on Slavery," *Perspectives on Political Science*, 34:2 (March 2005), pp. 70–8.

15. Colonization schemes are discussed widely in the literature on abolitionism, though their true pervasiveness has not been fully appreciated . See Winthrop Jordan, *White over Black: American Attitudes Toward the Negro 1550–1812* (Chapel Hill, NC: North Carolina University Press, 1968), pp. 542–69; David Kazanjian, *The Colonizing Trick: National Culture and Imperial Citizenship in Early America* (Minneapolis, MN: University of Minnesota Press, 2003), pp. 89–138; Samantha Seeley, *Race, Removal, and the Right to Remain: Migration and the Making of the United States* (Chapel Hill, NC: University of North Carolina Press, 2021); Peter S. Onuf, "Every Generation Is an 'Independent Nation': Colonization, Miscegenation, and the Fate of Jefferson's Children," *William and Mary Quarterly*, 57:1 (January 2000), pp. 153–70; Matthew Spooner, "'I Know this Scheme is from God:' Toward a Reconsideration of the Origins of the American Colonization Society," *Slavery & Abolition*, 35:4 (December 2014), pp. 559–75; Guyatt, *Bind Us Apart* (2016); Beverly C.Tomek, *Colonization and Uts Discontents: Emancipation, Emigration, and Antislavery in Antebellum Pennsylvania* (New York: New York University Press, 2011); Martha S. Jones, *Birthright Citizens: A History of Race and Rights in Antebellum America* (New York: Cambridge University Press, 2018).

16. John Hepburn, "Arguments against Making Slaves of Men" (1715), in *Am I Not A Man and a Brother: The Antislavery Crusade of Revolutionary America, 1688–1788*, Roger Burns, ed. (New York: Chelsea House Publishers, 1977), pp. 29–30.

17. Benjamin Rush, *Essays, Literary, Moral & Philosophical* (Philadelphia: Thomas & Samuel F. Bradford, 1798), pp. 315–20; Nina Reid-Maroney, "Benezet's Ghost: Revisiting the Antislavery Culture of Benjamin Rush's Philadelphia," in *The Atlantic World of Anthony Benezet (1713–1784): From French Reformation to North American Quaker Antislavery Activism*, Marie-Jeanne Rossignol & Bertrand Van Ruymbeke, eds. (Brill, 2016), pp. 199–220.

18. John Stauffer, "In the Shadow of a Dream: White Abolitionists and Race," *Proceedings of the Fifth Annual Gilder Lehrman Center International Conference* (New Haven, CT: Yale University Press, 2003), pp. 1–44.

19. *The Universal Asylum and Columbian Magazine*, November 1792, p. 311.

20. "Peter Bestes and Other Slaves Petition for Freedom (April 20, 1773)," in Aptheker, ed, *A Documentary History of the Negro People in the United States*, vol. I, pp. 7–8.

21. Guyatt, *Bind Us Apart* (2016).

22. Frank Moore, *Diary of the American Revolution from Newspapers and Original Documents*, vol. 2 (New York: Charles T. Evans, 1863), pp. 365–6.

23. *Christian World* (Boston), October 14, 1843, p. 1.

24. Samuel Hopkins, "A Dialogue on Slavery," in *Am I Not a Man and Brother*, p. 423. Hopkins eventually learned from a veteran who had marched through North Carolina that Chloe was alive and missed Newport where she could hear the Bible read. She thought her master and mistress "kind," though "I have lost many comforts by coming here." She had several children and the oldest was already separated from here "gone away to Georgia to live with my master's brother, and I shall never see him again ..." *Christian World* (Boston), October 28, 1843, p. 1.

25. Hopkins to Brown, April 29, 1784, in *The Works of Samuel Hopkins*, vol. 1 (Boston: Doctrinal Tract and Book Society, 1852), p. 139.
26. Hopkins to Sharpe, January 15, 1789, in *The Works of Samuel Hopkins*, pp. 140–1.
27. *The Works of Samuel Hopkins*, p. 144.
28. Ibid., pp. 145–6.
29. Jonathan Edwards, *The Injustice and Impolicy of the Slave Trade, and of the Slavery of the Africans* (New Haven: Thomas and Samuel Green, 1791), pp. 5, 10–12, 37–8. Jordan, *White over Black*, pp. 543–4.
30. Jacques-Pierre Brissot de Warville, *A Critical Examination of the Marquis de Chatellux's Travels in North America ...* (Philadelphia: Joseph James, 1788).
31. *The Golden Age; or, Future Glory of North-America Discovered by an Angel to Celadon* (United States: s.n. 1785). For meaning of Celadon, see E. Cobham Brewer, *The Reader's Handbook: Famous Names in Fiction, Allusions, References, Proverbs, Plots, Stories, and Poems* (Philadelphia, PA: J.B. Lippincott Company, 1904), p. 191; see also Werner Sollors, *Beyond Ethnicity: Consent and Descent in American Culture* (New York: Oxford University Press, 1986), pp. 174–5. Leo Marx describes Celadon's encounter with the American angel in *The Machine in the Garden* which he notes is a statement of the "pastoral ideal" of America. Marx, however, does not mention that this pastoral ideal rested on racial segregation. Leo Marx, *The Machine in the Garden: Technology and the Pastoral Ideal in America* (Oxford University Press, 1964), pp. 106–7.
32. *The American Museum, or Universal Magazine* (Philadelphia), 8:6 (December 1790), pp. 285–7. Fairfax's colonization ideas are discussed in Robert G. Parkinson, *The Common Cause: Creating Race and Nation in the American Revolution* (Chapel Hill, NC: University of North Carolina Press, 2016), p. 631; Manisha Sinha, *The Slave's Cause: A History of Abolition* (New Haven, CT: Yale University Press, 2016), p. 90.
33. Brandon Mills, *The World Colonization Made: The Racial Geography of Early American Empire* (Philadelphia, PA: University of Pennsylvania Press, 2020), p. 18.
34. George Tucker, *Letter to a Member of the General Assembly of Virginia on the Subject of the Late Conspiracy of the Slaves* (Baltimore: Bonsal & Niles, 1801).
35. Tucker is frequently misunderstood as experiencing a major conversion in his life from abolitionist to proslavery apologist. This confusion begins with seeing his earlier advocacy of emancipation as a position of moral benevolence rather than one firmly situated in the self-interest of whites. See Tucker's biographers, Robert Colin McLean, *George Tucker, Moral Philosopher and Man of Letters* (Chapel Hill, NC: University of North Carolina Press, 1961), and Tipton R. Snavely, *George Tucker as Political Economist* (Charlottesville, VA: University of Virginia Press, 1964). James Fieser grants some element of self-interest in Tucker's abolitionism, saying that Tucker "staunchly rejects slavery on moral grounds" though his "principal argument ... is practical" warning that slave rebellions "place the whole country at risk." *The Life of George Tucker*, James Fieser, ed. (Thoemmes Continuum, 2004), p. xi.
36. Mills, *The World Colonization Made*, p. 16; Nicholas Guyatt, "'An Impossible Idea?': The Curious Career of Internal Colonization," *The Journal of the Civil War Era*, 4:2 (May 2014), pp. 234–63; Moses Fisk, *Tyrannical Libertymen: A Discourse upon Negro-Slavery in the United States* (Hanover: Eagle Office, 1795); *The*

American Quarterly Register, B.B. Edwards & W. Cogswell, eds. (Boston: Perkins & Marvin, 1840), p. 382.

37. "Memorandum on an African Colony for Freed Slaves (ca. 20 October) 1789," *The Papers of James Madison*, vol. 12, Charles F. Hobson & Robert A. Rutland, eds. (Charlottesville, VA: University of Virginia Press, 1979), pp. 437–8; Gaillard Hunt, "William Thornton and Negro Colonization," *Proceedings of the American Antiquarian Society*, 30 (Worcester, MA, 1920), pp. 32–61.

38. Madison quote from "Memorandum on an African Colony for Freed Slaves (ca. 20 October) 1789," pp. 437–8; see also Hunt, "William Thornton and Negro Colonization," pp. 32–61. See also Mills, *The World Colonization Made*, p. 12.

39. David Lummis to Thomas Jefferson, February 15th. 1802, *The Papers of Thomas Jefferson, vol. 36, 1 December 1801 to 3 March 1802*, James P. McClure & J. Jefferson Looney, eds. (Charlottesville, VA: University of Virginia Press, 2008–19), p. 582; J. Thomas Scharf & Thompson Westcott, *History of Philadelphia*, vol. 1 (Philadelphia: L.H. Everts & Co., 1884), p. 483.

40. Lyon N. Richardson, *A History of Early American Magazines* (New York: Thomas Nelson & Sons, 1931), pp. 198–207.

41. Robert G. Parkinson notes Brackenridge, like Jefferson, "Neither advocate of abolition could envision an independent America that included free blacks as citizens." Parkinson, *The Common Cause*, p. 592.

42. *Gazette of the United States* (New York), March 10, 1790, p. 1. Evidence for Duer's authorship is traced in "Unmasking the Authors of the Great Rusticus and Africanus Debate of 1790," forthcoming.

43. Gary Nash, "Race and Citizenship in the Early Republic," in *Antislavery and Abolition in Philadelphia*, Richard Newman & James Mueller, eds. (Baton Rouge, LA: Louisiana State University Press, 2011), pp. 90–117.

44. Some scholars have had difficulty reconciling the seeming benevolence of Branagan's antislavery with the authoritarianism of his plans for forced expatriation of African Americans. Such positions only conflict within the false assumption that those who opposed slavery in these years did so primarily out of benevolent concern for the enslaved rather than for betterment of whites. For example, Gary Nash depicts Branagan's *Serious Remonstrances* as being a reversal from his earlier abolitionism and writes: "Branagan's turnabout was stunning" (ibid., p. 99). Manisha Sinha calls Branagan an "apostate to abolition" because he was a "staunch advocate of black removal." By implication, then, other abolitionists opposed black removal, which is totally wrong. In order to sustain this distorted picture of Branagan and of the early abolitionists generally, Sinha has to depict Branagan as moving from an antislavery position in his tract, *A Preliminary Essay on the Oppression of the Exiled Sons of Africa*, his epic poem "Avenia," and his children's verse, "The Penitential Tyrant" to advocating black removal in his work *Serious Remonstrances, Addressed to the Citizens of the Northern States*. In fact, there is a great consistency in his principles and policies throughout all these works typical of all the white abolitionists (Sinha, *The Slave's Cause*, pp. 112–13). Even Branagan's obsessive fears of race mixing were not unique—similar worries about black men taking white wives can be found in John Parrish's abolitionist tract but Sinha does not describe Parrish as an apostate. Sinha's charge is doubly absurd when it is considered that one of Branagan's most full-throated denunciations of slavery came *after* "Serious Remonstrances," in his *Political & Theological*

Disquisitions on the Signs of the Times which was published in 1807. As noted in Rachel Hope Cleves, *Mortal Eloquence: Violence, Slavery, and Anti-Jacobinism in the Early American Republic* (Ph.D. Diss., University of California, Berkeley, 2005), pp. 86–7. Branagan's first work, *Preliminary Essay*, actually concedes that rapid abolition of slavery was impractical and instead slaves' conditions should be improved and a very gradual transition to a system of servitude should replace it (see the discussion of Branagan in ch. 8). Moreover, later abolitionists did not view him as an "apostate." The *National Anti-Slavery Standard* published an obituary of Branagan in 1843 that called him "an old soldier" in the antislavery cause. *National Anti-Slavery Standard* (New York), June 29, 1843, p. 15.

45. Thomas Branagan, *Serious Remonstrances, Addressed to the Citizens of the Northern States* (Philadelphia: Thomas T. Stiles, 1805).

46. Vivien Sandlund, "To Arouse and Awaken the American People": The Ideas and Strategies of the Gradual Emancipationists, 1800–1850" (Ph.D. Diss., Emory University, 1995), pp. 108–75.

47. Branagan, *Serious Remonstrances*, pp. 36, 64.

48. John Parrish, *Remarks on the Slavery of the Black People: Addressed to the Citizens of the United States…* (Philadelphia: Kimber, Conrad & Co., 1805), p. 25.

49. Ibid., p. 42.

50. Thomas Jefferson, *Notes on the State of Virginia* (London: John Stockdale, 1787), p. 240.

51. Winthrop Jordan stressed the importance of Jefferson's *Notes on Virginia* which he saw as a turning point, saying there had been just "a scattering of such proposals prior even to the Notes on Virginia" and these were but "highly miscellaneous" compared with the rigor and clarity of Jefferson's vision of an American empire swept free of its black population. Jefferson's arguments "catalyzed sentiment for colonization of Negroes." Jordan, *White over Black*, p. 547.

52. John Adams to Timothy Pickering, August. 6, 1822, reprinted in *The Works of John Adams, Second President of the United States: with a Life of the Author*, vol. 2, Charles Francis Adams, ed. (Boston, 1850–1856), p. 512.

53. *The Papers of Thomas Jefferson, vol. 2, January 1777 to June 1779*, Julian P. Boyd, ed. (Princeton, NJ: Princeton University Press, 1951), p. 306.

54. Ibid., pp. 307–8.

55. Kevin J. Hayes "In addition to the bills regarding religious freedom and crime and punishment, Jefferson's bills concerning education are the most important ones he drafted as part of the revision of the laws of Virginia." Kevin J. Hayes, *The Road to Monticello: The Life and Mind of Thomas Jefferson* (New York: Oxford University Press, 2008), p. 213.

56. William Cohen was one of the few historians to note the racially exclusionary elements of Jefferson's plans for revision and wrote: "the bill was more than a digest of earlier codes and it contained some significant additions which were designed to prevent the increase of the state's free Negro population." However, Cohen thought Jefferson was mostly interested in protecting slavery out of fear that a growing population of free blacks would encourage insurrections. Cohen didn't connect the elements dealing with the slave trade and interracial procreation with those dealing with manumission and criminal penalties. Without these pieces, he was justified in surmising, "It has been argued that Jefferson may have included these provisions in the belief that slavery would gradually

die out because of an absence of new recruits to replenish the stock. This may have been his reason, but it seems unlikely … It must have been obvious to him that preventing further importations and limiting the growth of the free-Negro population would not stop the increase of the slave population due to natural causes." William Cohen, "Thomas Jefferson and the Problem of Slavery," *The Journal of American History*, 56:3 (December 1969), pp. 503–26. Paul Finkelman also recognized the connection between Jefferson's desire "to eliminate slavery … while at the same time preventing the growth of a free black population." Paul Finkelman, *Slavery and the Founders: Race and Liberty in the Age of Jefferson*, 2nd ed. (New York: M.E. Sharpe, 2001), p. 147. William Jeremiah Moses documents Jefferson's later interest and involvement in colonization schemes, calling these "ethnic cleansing." William Jeremiah Moses, *Thomas Jefferson: A Modern Prometheus* (New York: Cambridge University Press, 2019), pp. 291–8.

57. *Autobiography of Thomas Jefferson 1743–1790*, Paul Leicester Ford, ed. (New York: G.P. Putnam's Sons, 1914), p. 76.

58. William Waller Hening, *The Statutes at Large: Being a collection of all the laws of Virginia, from the first session of the legislature, in the year 1619*, vol. 8 (Richmond: Printed by and for Samuel Pleasants, junior, printer to the commonwealth, 1809–23), p. 134.

59. *Journals of the House of Burgesses of Virginia, 1766–1769*, John P. Kennedy, ed. (Richmond: The Colonial Press, 1906), pp. 198, 203.

60. Hening, *The Statutes at Large*, vol. 8, p. 393.

61. Hayes, *The Road to Monticello*, p. 111; Advertisement for a Runaway Slave, September 7, 1769, *The Papers of Thomas Jefferson, vol. 1, 1760 to 1776*, Julian P. Boyd, ed. (Princeton, NJ: Princeton University Press, 1950), p. 33.

62. *Journals of the House of Burgesses of Virginia*, p. 259; Hening, *The Statutes at Large*, vol. 3, vol. 6, p. 111.

63. Hening, *The Statutes at Large*, vol. 8, p. 358.

64. Ibid., pp. 522–3.

65. The names of the 117 members of the 1773 House of Burgesses were compiled from *The Colonial Virginia Register*, William G. & Mary Newton Stanard, eds. (Albany, NY: Joel Munsell's Sons, 1902), pp. 190–2. This was then cross-indexed with the members of the 1776 House of Delegates that is found at the *The Virginia Elections and State Elected Officials Database Project, 1776–2007*, Charles A. Kromkowski, ed., University of Virginia, http://vavh.electionstats.com/ (accessed June 1, 2020).

66. Hening, *The Statutes at Large*, vol. 3, p. 252.

67. *The Papers of Thomas Jefferson*, vol. 2, , p. 476; ibid., p. 252.

68. Hening, *The Statutes at Large*, vol. 6, p. 357.

69. Ibid., p. 112.

70. Ibid., pp. 87–8.

71. Ibid., pp. 361–2.

72. *The Papers of Thomas Jefferson*, vol. 2, pp. 470–1.

73. Ibid., p. 504.

74. Cohen, "Thomas Jefferson and the Problem of Slavery," pp. 503–26.

75. While the Virginia Assembly considered Jefferson's revisions of the state code during the legislative session of 1785, petitions were introduced on both sides of the issue of slavery. One petition appealed for a general and gradual eman-

cipation of all enslaved people, the other demanded repeal of the recently passed provisions allowing owners to liberate their own human property. James Madison observed the reaction of the legislators to these measures and said they revealed the "pulse of the H. of D ... with regard to a general manumission." The petition for general emancipation was received with a motion "to throw it under the table, which was treated with as much indignation on one side, as the petition itself was on the other." In spite of the "indignation" of a few, it was voted to table unanimously. "To George Washington from James Madison, 11 November 1785," *The Papers of George Washington, Confederation Series, vol. 3, 19 May 1785–31 March 1786*, W.W. Abbot, ed. (Charlottesville, VA: University of Virginia Press, 1994), pp. 355–8. No text of the bill or record of the debate exists for it appears to have been quickly dismissed. Its trace in history is slight; a passing mention by Jefferson in his *Notes on Virginia* and a letter from Virginia planter Peter Minor to his nephew, a Continental officer and one of the youngest members of the Virginia Assembly, John Minor, Jr. He wrote: "As to your first Bill for the Emancipating Slaves I think it met with a very good fate for we might as well let Loose a parcel of Indians or Lions as to Let our Slaves free without they could be sent from the Continent." *Fragments of Revolutionary History*, Gaillard Hunt, ed. (Brooklyn, NY: Historical Printing Club, 1892), p. 187; John B. Minor, *The Minor Family of Virginia* (Lynchburg, VA: J.P. Bell, Co., 1923).

76. *Autobiography of Thomas Jefferson 1743–1790*, p. 77.
77. Other of his notes indicate that one point of disagreement in the assembly may have been about Catholics and another was whether to include Jews: "Religion—is theirs less moral" and "all who have not full rights are secret enem[ies]" and "Jews advantageous." "Bill for the Naturalization of Foreigners (October 14, 1776)," *The Papers of Thomas Jefferson*, vol. 1, pp. 558–9.
78. *The Statutes at Large of Virginia, from October Session 1792 to December Session 1806*, vol. 3, Samuel Shepherd, ed. (Richmond: Samuel Shepherd, 1836), pp. 251–3.
79. *The Papers of Thomas Jefferson, vol. 6, May 1781 to March 1784*, Julian P. Boyd, ed. (Princeton, NJ: Princeton University Press, 1952), pp. 294–8.
80. Paul Finkelman makes this argument in Paul Finkelman, *Slavery and the Founders: Race and Liberty in the Age of Jefferson*, 2nd ed. (New York: M.E. Sharpe, 2001), pp. 147–8.
81. St. George Tucker, *A Dissertation on Slavery and a Proposal for the Gradual Abolition of It* (Philadelphia: Mathew Carey, 1796), p. 84.
82. Simon Newman, "The World Turned Upside down: Revolutionary Politics, Fries' and Gabriel's Rebellions, and the Fears of the Federalists," *Pennsylvania History: A Journal of Mid-Atlantic Studies*, 67:1 (Winter 2000), pp. 5–20.
83. Document no. 215, *American State Papers: Documents, Legislative and Executive, of the Congress of the United States*, Walter Lowrie & Walter S. Franklin, eds., vol 1, Miscellaneous (Washington: Gales and Seaton, 1834), p. 464.
84. Ibid.
85. Jefferson to Monroe, November 24, 1801, *American State Papers*, p. 465.
86. On Patrick Henry, see William W. Henry, *Patrick Henry: Life, Correspondence and Speeches*, vol. 1 (New York: Charles Scribner's Sons, 1891), p. 114. Jordan, *White over Black*, p. 544.

87. David Rice, *Slavery Inconsistent with Justice* ... (Philadelphia: M. Gurney, 1792); Guyatt, *Bind Us Apart*, pp. 35–36, 249.

88. All quotes of Smith are from his "On the Relation of Master and Servant," Lecture XXI, in *The Lectures, Corrected and Improved ... vol. 2* (New York: Whiting and Watson, 1812).

89. Manisha Sinha, in her eagerness to reclaim early abolitionists from the slanders of earlier historians who called them insincere, portrays abolitionists as anti-racists. She incorrectly observes, "Racism suited proslavery aims and crippled antislavery efforts." The example she employed to illustrate this overbroad and misleading characterization was Smith, saying he fought Jefferson on his "speculations on innate racial differences." While Sinha put Smith on the side of abolitionist antiracists, she separated Jedidiah Morse on the other, saying he was influenced by Jefferson's biologism to "deplore racial intermixture" and support colonization. The inconvenient facts that Sinha leaves out are that all these men, Jefferson, Smith, and Morse, all deplored race mixing, supported gradual emancipation, and planned schemes of colonization. Sinha, *The Slave's Cause*, p. 89. Likewise, Paul Polgar throws Smith off the abolitionist boat saying he was "no antislavery activist." In addition to suppressing Smith's public lecturing and pamphleting against slavery, Polgar chooses not to discuss his proposals for gradual emancipation or for black colonization. Paul J. Polgar, *Standard-Bearers of Equality: America's First Abolition Movement* (Chapel Hill, NC: University of North Carolina Press, 2019), pp. 128–9. One of the few scholars to devote a dissertation to Smith's preaching, teaching, and writing, Charles Bow, concluded Smith was "an ardent slavery abolitionist." Charles Bow, *End of the Scottish Enlightenment in Its Transatlantic Context: Moral Education in the Thought of Dugald Stewart and Samuel Stanhope Smith, 1790–1812* (Ph.D. Diss. University of Edinburgh, 2012), p. 157.

90. Nicholas Guyatt discusses Smith's colonization plan in *Bind Us Apart*, pp. 131–2.

91. Ibid., pp. 92–3. Eva Sheppard Wolf, *Race and Liberty in the New Nation: Emancipation in Virginia from the Revolution to Nat Turner's Rebellion* (Baton Rouge, LA: Louisiana State University Press, 2006), pp. 104–7.

92. Letterbook of Robert Pleasants, p. 189 (listed as p. 200 in archival index), Manuscript Collection 1116/168, Haverford Special Collections, Haverford College.

93. Citizen Free Born to Thomas Jefferson, October 30th. 1802, *The Papers of Thomas Jefferson, vol. 38, 1 July to 12 November 1802*, James P. McClure & J. Jefferson Looney, eds. (Charlottesville, VA: University of Virginia Press, 2008–19), p. 602.

94. "To Thomas Jefferson from Michael Walton, January 20, 1809," Founders Online, National Archives, https://founders.archives.gov/documents/Jefferson/99-01-02-9603 (accessed December 12, 2023).

95. To Thomas Jefferson from Thomas Paine, January 25, 1805, *The Papers of Thomas Jefferson, vol. 45, 11 November 1804 to 8 March 1805*, James P. McClure et al. eds. (Princeton, NJ: Princeton University Press, 2021), pp. 378–89.

96. Livingston to King, May 7, 1803, in Edward Alexander Parsons, *The Original Letters of Robert R. Livingston, 1801–1803* (New Orleans, LA: Louisiana Historical Society, 1953), pp. 59–60.

97. Jason E. Pierce, *Making the White Man's West: Whiteness and the Creation of the American West* (Boulder, CO: University of Colorado Press, 2016), p. 30.

98. Thomas Jefferson to James Monroe, November, 24, 1801, *The Papers of Thomas Jefferson, vol. 35, 1 August–30 November 1801*, Barbara B. Oberg, ed. (Princeton, NJ: Princeton University Press, 2008), pp. 718–22.

99. James Monroe to Thomas Jefferson, December 21, 1801, *The Papers of Thomas Jefferson, vol. 36, 1 December 1801–3 March 1802*, Barbara B. Oberg, ed. (Princeton, NJ: Princeton University Press, 2009), pp. 185–7.

100. Jefferson to King, July 13, 1802, *The Papers of Thomas Jefferson, vol. 28, 1 January 1794 to 29 February 1796*, James P. McClure & J. Jefferson Looney, eds. (Charlottesville, VA: University of Virginia Press, 200).

101. Arthur Scherr, "Light at the End of the Road: Thomas Jefferson's Endorsement of Free Haiti in His Final Years," *Journal of Haitian Studies*, 15:1/2 (Spring/Fall 2009), pp. 203–16.

102. "To John Adams from Robert J. Evans, June 3, 1819," Founders Online, National Archives, https://founders.archives.gov/documents/Adams/99-02-02-7147 (accessed September 29, 2019); "To James Madison from Robert J. Evans, June 3, 1819," *The Papers of James Madison, Retirement Series, vol. 1, 4 March 1817–31 January 1820*, David B. Mattern, J.C.A. Stagg, Mary Parke Johnson, & Anne Mandeville Colony, eds. (Charlottesville, VA: University of Virginia Press, 2009), pp. 464–5; "To Thomas Jefferson from Robert J. Evans, 3 June 1819," Founders Online, National Archives, https://founders.archives.gov/documents/Jefferson/98-01-02-0465 (accessed September 29, 2019). See Evans' articles (signed as "Benjamin Rush") in the *Daily National Intelligencer*, May 22, 29, 1819.

103. "From John Adams to Robert J. Evans, 8 June 1819," Founders Online, National Archives, https://founders.archives.gov/documents/Adams/99-02-02-7148 (accessed September 29, 2019).

104. "From James Madison to Robert J. Evans, 15 June 1819," *The Papers of James Madison*, vol. 1, , pp. 468–72.

105. Beverly Tomek, "Seeking 'an Immutable Pledge from the Slave Holding States': The Pennsylvania Abolition Society and Black Resettlement," *Pennsylvania History*, 75:1 (Winter 2008), pp. 26–53. See also Tomek, *Colonization and Its Discontents*, esp. chs. 3–4.

106. *Minutes of the Proceedings of the Fourteenth American Convention for Promoting the Abolition of Slavery* (1816), p. 32. The existence of this memorial contradicts Paul Polgar's thesis that the early abolition societies were antiracist allies of the black community. In order to mash it into this box, Polgar distorts this resolution, falsely claiming that "the petition proposed federally sanctioned colonization only for manumitted southern blacks, not for all persons of color in the United States." There is no such restriction in the wording of the petition. Rather, it applied equally to the more than 17,856 enslaved people in the mid-Atlantic region that Polgar counts on p. 281. Polgar then tries to insulate Yankee abolitionists from the obvious racism of the resolution by attributing the clause about limiting the mixture of blacks in "white people of our country" to southern members. Then, in the face of the obvious words he had just quoted, Polgar concludes, "the Convention was reacting, not to white prejudice ... but to specific instances in which the prospective freedom of bondspersons could not be obtained without their being removed from the state in which they were enslaved." Polgar implies colonization was chosen as the only option, but does

not mention that there was a simpler and more obvious solution that white abolitionists chose not to advocate and which Polgar does not mention in this context, namely, advocating for the revocation of laws barring the migration of freed people into northern states. Polgar, *Standard-Bearers of Equality*, pp. 285–6.

107. P.J. Staudenraus, *The African Colonization Movement, 1816–1865* (New York: Columbia University Press, 1961), p. 27.

108. *A View of Exertions Lately Made for the Purpose of Colonizing the Free People of Colour* (Washington: Jonathan Elliot, 1817).

109. *Minutes of the Proceedings of the Fifteenth American Convention for Promoting the Abolition of Slavery* (1817), pp. 30–1.

110. *Minutes of the Proceedings of a Special Meeting of the Fifteenth American Convention for Promoting the Abolition of Slavery* (Philadelphia: Hall & Atkinson, 1818), p. 3.

111. *Minutes of the Proceedings of the Sixteenth American Convention for Promoting the Abolition of Slavery* (Philadelphia: William Fry, 1819), pp. 50–5.

CHAPTER 5

1. Robert Parkinson noted the conceptual break that citizenship made with subjecthood in his *The Common Cause: Creating Race and Nation in the American Revolution* (Chapel Hill, NC: University of North Carolina Press, 2016). Parkinson astutely observes that the patriot's invention of citizenship allowed them "to choose whom they let in and whom they exclude" (p. 23) See also Nicholas Guyatt, *Bind Us Apart: How Enlightened Americans Invented Racial Segregation* (New York: Basic Books, 2016), p. 3; Douglas Bradburn, *The Citizenship Revolution: Politics and the Creation of the American Union, 1774–1804* (Charlottesville, VA: University of Virginia Press, 2009), p. 239; Joel Olson, *The Abolition of White Democracy* (Minneapolis, MN: University of Minnesota Press, 2004).

2. Jeremy B. Bierbach, *Frontiers of Equality in the Development of EU and US Citizenship* (The Hague, the Netherlands: T.M.C. Asser Press, 2017), pp. 18–29.

3. Polly J. Price, "Natural Law and Birthright Citizenship in Calvin's Case (1608)," 9 *Yale Journal of Law & the Humanities* (1997), pp. 81–5.

4. Ibid.

5. William Blackstone, *Commentaries on the Laws of England* (4th ed., Oxford: Printed at the Clarendon Press, 1770), Book 1, passim.

6. Ibid., pp. 366, 370.

7. Ibid., p. 371.

8. "Humprey's History of the Propagation Society," *The Church Review*, 5:3 (October 1852), p. 437.

9. Eliga H. Gould. *Among the Powers of the Earth* (Cambridge, MA: Harvard University Press, 2012), pp. 57–8.

10. Ibid., pp. 373–4. Christopher Brown highlights the "multiethnic" character of subjecthood in which all subjects were in compact with the sovereign, a compact in which the subjects owed loyalty in exchange for protection. Brown notes that while subjects may "hold different ranks" each was also entitled to "hold real property" and "the right to equal consideration under the law." Christopher Leslie Brown, *Moral Capital: Foundations of British Abolitionism* (Chapel Hill, NC: University of North Carolina Press, 2006), pp. 221–2.

11. Douglas R. Egerton, *Death or Liberty: African Americans and Revolutionary America* (New York: Oxford University Press, 2009), p. 44.

12. Robert Francis Seybolt, *The Colonial Citizen of New York City: A Comparative Study of Certain Aspects of Citizenship Practice in Fourteenth Century England and Colonial New York City* (Madison, WI: University of Wisconsin Press, 1918). See also Phil Withington, *The Politics of Commonwealth: Citizens and Freemen in Early Modern England* (Cambridge and New York: Cambridge University Press, 2005); Ben Herzog, *Revoking Citizenship: Expatriation in America from the Colonial Era to the War on Terror* (New York: New York University Press, 2015), ch. 2.

13. Treaty of Paris, September 3, 1783; Perfected Treaties, 1778–1945; General Records of the United States Government, Record Group 11, National Archives Building, Washington, DC.

14. Act VII, 1733 (reaffirmed in 1752), William Waller Hening, *The Statutes at Large: Being a collection of all the laws of Virginia, from the first session of the legislature, in the year 1619*, vol. 3 (Richmond: Printed by and for Samuel Pleasants, junior, printer to the commonwealth, 1809–23), vol. 2, p. 267.

15. "A great number of Servants and Poor and indigent Persons, voted promiscuously with their Masters and Creditors, as also several free Negroes were Receiv'd, and taken for as good Electors as the best Freeholders in the Province." "So that we leave it with your Lordships to Judge, whether admitting Aliens, Strangers, Servants, Negroes, etc., as good and qualify'd Voters, can be thought any ways agreeable to King Charles's Patent to your Lordship's, or the English Constitution or Government." Daniel Defoe, "Party-Tyranny" (1705) in *Narratives of Early Carolina, 1650–1708*, Alexander S. Salley, Jr., ed. (New York: Charles Scribner's Sons, 1911), p. 239. "in the beginning of the Year 1701 … Mr. Moore perceiving, That that Assembly could not be prevailed with to answer his Ends, he dissolved the Assembly, and about the latter End of that Year a new one was chosen, at the Election of which, tho' the Right of Electing be by the Charter in the Freeholders only, he so Influenc'd the Sheriff, that Strangers, Servants, Aliens, nay Malatoes and Negroes were Polled, and Returns made accordingly." John Ash, "The Present State of Affairs in Carolina," *Narratives of Early Carolina, 1650–1708*, Alexander S. Salley, Jr. (New York: Charles Scribner's Sons, 1911), pp. 265–76. Ibid., p. 271.

16. Hening, *The Statutes at Large*, vol. 1, p. 412, vol. 3, p. 172; John Henderson Russell, *The Free Negro in Virginia, 1619–1865* (Baltimore, MD: Johns Hopkins Press, 1913), pp. 118–19. Bradburn, *The Citizenship Revolution*, pp. 239–40.

17. Edward D. Neill, *Virginia Carolorum: The Colony under the Rule of Charles the First and Second, A. D. 1625–A.D. 1685* (Albany, NY, J. Munsell's Sons, 1886), p. 330; Russell, *The Free Negro in Virginia*, pp. 119–20.

18. The first generation of academic political scientists who began their studies in the early years of Jim Crow, were surprised to find that there were no racial restrictions on voting during most of the colonial era, except in the southernmost colonies. Stephen B. Weeks, "The History of Negro Suffrage in the South: I. Before the Revolution," *Political Science Quarterly*, 9:4, December 1894, p. 4; Cortland F. Bishop, *History of Elections in the American Colonies* (New York: Burt Franklin, orig. 1893), p. 52. Similarly, Christopher Brown documents that some advisors and strategists in the imperial administration considered "slaves as British subjects as well as the property of slaveholders." Christopher L. Brown,

"Empire without Slaves: British Concepts of Emancipation in the Age of the American Revolution," *The William and Mary Quarterly*, 56:2 (April 1999), pp. 273–306.

19. T.H. Breen calls the shift from "subjects" to "citizens" one of "far-reaching consequences" including allowing the state to formulate citizenship "in such a way that it deprived certain groups of individuals of the very 'rights' and 'equality' that they … had claimed as "subjects." Breen also correctly observes that in the decade preceding the American Revolution when firmly ensconced in an English legal framework, James Otis operated with the "assumption that New World Africans and Europeans alike were colonists, all equally subjects of the empire." Breen describes Otis' assumption as "striking," though it wasn't all that striking to other English lawyers. Nevertheless, Breen insightfully highlights the racially egalitarian nature of subjecthood: "It was their common 'subjecthood' that gave the colonists, blacks as well as whites, equal standing within an empire ruled by a constitutional monarch." And "The rhetoric of subjecthood, therefore, was categorically nonhierarchical and inclusive; it encouraged egalitarian thinking." Breen also connects the rising "proslavery" attitude of American patriots to Otis' lack of popularity after independence: "Otis's reputation as a radical liberal theorist languished largely because he championed universal human rights within a conceptual framework that every American writer rejected at the moment of the signing of the Declaration of Independence." T.H. Breen, "Subjecthood and Citizenship: The Context of James Otis's Radical Critique of John Locke," *The New England Quarterly*, 71:3 (September 1998), pp. 378–403.

20. Michael G. Hanchard, *The Spectre of Race: How Discrimination Haunts Western Democracy* (Princeton, NJ: Princeton University Press, 2018), p. 2; Rogers M. Smith, *Civic Ideals: Conflicting Visions of Citizenship in U.S. History* (New Haven, CT: Yale University Press, 1997), p. 14.

21. "Edmund Randolph's Essay on the Revolutionary History of Virginia 1774–1782 (Continued)," *The Virginia Magazine of History and Biography*, 44:1 (January 1936), p. 45. Many historians have assumed without evidence that Mason and the Virginia Assembly *meant* to express a non-racial basis of citizenship. Richard D. Brown incorrectly claims "Virginia's revolutionary convention—a body of privileged, slave holding aristocrats—endorsed such apparently egalitarian language" and though they "excluded slaves" their "expression of universal, natural rights idealism is best understood as an aspirational statement of principles." Richard D. Brown, *Self-Evident Truths: Contesting Equal Rights from the Revolution to the Civil War* (New Haven, CT: Yale University Press, 2017), p. 6.

22. Hening, *The Statutes at Large*; *The Papers of Thomas Jefferson, vol. 2, January 1777 to June 1779*, Julian P. Boyd, ed. (Princeton, NJ: Princeton University Press, 1951), pp. 476–8.

23. James H. Kettner, *The Development of American Citizenship, 1608–1870* (Chapel Hill, NC: University of North Carolina Press, 1978), pp. 215–16. Kettner calls the prototypical form of American citizenship "volitional allegiance" that sealed a contract between the citizen and his government. But Kettner overlooks how it is the state in the first instance that is choosing which inhabitants to qualify for this volitional allegiance (p. 185).

24. *The Law of Freedom and Bondage in the United States*, vol. 2, John C. Hurd, ed. (Boston: Little, Brown & Co., 1862), p. 72.

25. The apparent lack of direct exclusions of people of color from voting during the Revolutionary years (which is mistaken, as will be shown below) has allowed those historians eager to burnish their founding heroes into paragons of racial equality to claim, as Gordon Wood erroneously does, that patriots considered "all men ... to be equally free citizens." Gordon S. Wood, *The Radicalism of the American Revolution* (New York: Alfred A. Knopf, 1992), p. 187.

26. *The Statutes at Large of Pennsylvania from 1682*, vol. 9, James T. Mitchell & Henry Flanders, eds. (Pennsylvania: Wm. Stanley Ray, 1903), pp. 147, 303. *The Diplomatic Correspondence of the American Revolution*, vol. 4, Jared Sparks, ed. (Boston: Nathan Hale and Gray & Bowen, 1829), p. 38.

27. St. George Tucker, *A Dissertation on Slavery and a Proposal for the Gradual Abolition of It* (Philadelphia: Mathew Carey, 1796), p. 89.

28. *The Articles of Confederation; the Declaration of rights; the Constitution of the Commonwealth, and the articles of the definitive treaty between Great-Britain and the United States of America. Published by order of the General Assembly* (Richmond: Dixon & Holt, 1784 or 1795).

29. David Ramsay, *A Dissertation on the Manner of Acquiring the Character and Privileges of a Citizen of the United States* (Charleston: 1789). See also T.H. Breen, "Subjecthood and Citizenship," pp. 378–403.

30. Kettner, *The Development of American Citizenship*, p. 217.

31. *Documents and Records relating to the State of New Hampshire during the Period of the American Revolution*, vol. 8, Nathaniel Bouton, ed. (Concord, NH: Edward A. Jenks, State Printer, 1874), pp. 204–6; *Miscellaneous Documents and Records Relating to New Hampshire*, Nathaniel Bouton, ed., vol. 10 (Concord, NH: Edward A. Jenks, State Printer, 1877), pp. 637–9; *Journals of the Continental Congress, 1774–1789*, vol. 4, Worthington Chauncey Ford, ed. (Washington, DC: Government Printing Office, 1906), p. 205.

32. *Pennsylvania Archives*, Samuel Hazard, ed. (Philadelphia: Joseph Severns & Co., 1853), ser. 1, vol. 5, p. 418.

33. *The Statutes at Large of Pennsylvania from 1682*, vol. 9, pp 76–7.

34. Hazard, *Pennsylvania Archives*, vol. 5, p. 601.

35. Ibid., p. 509.

36. Ibid., pp. 574, 582, 586, 589, 604–5.

37. Edward Raymond Turner, *The Negro in Pennsylvania* (Washington, DC: The American Historical Association, 1911), pp. 179–80. Other ceremonies of white citizenship were enacted in South Carolina, even though that state's constitution made no references to "citizens" and instead used the word "freeman" that was presumed to combine white, free, and citizen into one synthesis. South Carolina required an "oath of allegiance and fidelity" of "every free male inhabitant of the State ... above a certain age." *The South Carolina Gazette; and Country Journal* (Charleston), October 21, 1778, p. 4.

38. *Journals of the Continental Congres*, vol. 5, pp. 546–54.

39. *Journals of the Continental Congress*, vol. 9, pp. 887–9, 899; *The Debates in the Several State Conventions on the Adoption of the Federal Constitution*, Jonathan Elliot, ed., vol 1. (Philadelphia: J.B. Lippincott, 1941, orig. 1836), pp. 79–84; see also George Van Cleve, *A Slaveholders' Union: Slavery, Politics, and the Constitution in the Early American Republic* (Chicago, IL: University of Chicago Press, 2010), pp. 51–5.

40. *Journals of the Continental Congress*, vol. 11, p. 652. Rogers Smith sees only the surface appearances of this episode rather than the more important structural implications when he writes: "Congress decisively defeated a South Carolina motion to limit the clause's guarantees to whites. In this era of the First Emancipation, many Northerners rejected official denials of citizenship to free blacks as inconsistent with the egalitarianism of the Declaration. The privileges and immunities clause thus represented a country-wide shield for the rights of free, propertied nonwhites, making it a tentative but recognizable expression of liberal and nationalistic precepts." In this case a northerner, Connecticut's Richard Law, employed the word "inhabitant" so as to preserve a state's ability to exclude blacks from citizenship but not have them seized and abused when they traveled to southern states, which many black mariners did. Smith, *Civic Ideals*, p. 97.

41. *Journals of the Continental Congress*, vol. 11, pp. 650–2; Elliot, *The Debates in the Several State Conventions*, p. 89.

42. Elliot, *The Debates in the Several State Conventions*, pp. 70–1.

43. "Notes of Proceedings in the Continental Congress, 7 June–1 August 1776," *The Papers of Thomas Jefferson, vol. 1, 1760–1776*, Julian P. Boyd, ed. (Princeton, NJ: Princeton University Press, 1950), pp. 299–329.; "July 1776," *The Adams Papers, vol. 2, 1771–1781*, L.H. Butterfield, ed. (Cambridge, MA: Harvard University Press, 1961), pp. 241–6.

44. "Notes on Debates, 11 February 1783," *The Papers of James Madison, vol. 6, 1 January 1783–30 April 1783*, William T. Hutchinson and William M.E. Rachal, eds. (Chicago, IL: University of Chicago Press, 1969), pp. 215–17.

45. Bradburn, *The Citizenship Revolution*, p. 246.

46. *Journals of Each Provincial Congress of Massachusetts in 1774 and 1775*, William Lincoln, ed. (Boston: Dutton & Wentworth, State Printers, 1838), p. 592.

47. Massachusetts Commitee of Safety, May 20, 1775, ibid., pp. 553, 302.

48. Massachusetts Assembly, June 10, 1776, Peter Force, *American Archives*, ser. 4, vol. 6 (Washington, 1846), p. 802.

49. "Queries Respecting the Slavery and Emancipation of Negroes in Massachusetts, Proposed by the Hon. Judge Tucker of Virginia, and Answered by the Rev. Dr. Belknap," *From the Collections of the Massachusetts Historical Society*, ser. 1, vol. 4 (Boston: 1835, reprint of 1795 publication), pp. 191–211.

50. Peter Voelz, *Slave and Soldier: The Military Impact of Blacks in the Colonial Americas* (New York, 1993), pp. 77–81.

51. James Otis, *The Rights of the British Colonies Asserted and Proved* (Boston, 1764), pp. 24, 57–58, 75.

52. *Acts Passed by the General Assembly of South Carolina, Nov. 15, 1733–May 29, 1736* (Charles Town: Lewis Timothy, 1736), pp. 105–6; Voelz, *Slave and Soldier*, pp. 77–81.

53. "To John Adams from James Warren, 7 July 1775," *The Adams Papers, Papers of John Adams, vol. 3, May 1775–January 1776*, Robert J. Taylor, ed. (Cambridge, MA: Harvard University Press, 1979), pp. 68–70.

54. "Council of War, July 9, 1775," *The Papers of George Washington, Revolutionary War Series, vol. 1, 16 June 1775–15 September 1775*, Philander D. Chase, ed. (Charlottesville, VA: University of Virginia Press, 1985), pp. 79–82.

55. "II. Letter Sent, 10–11 July 1775," *The Papers of George Washington*, vol. 1, pp. 85–97.

56. "From John Adams to William Heath, 5 October 1775," *The Adams Papers*, vol. 3, pp. 183–4.

57. "To John Adams from William Heath, 23 October 1775," *The Adams Papers*, vol. 3, pp. 230–1.

58. Judith L. Van Buskirk, *Standing in Their Own Light: African American Patriots in the American Revolution* (Norman OK: University of Oklahoma Press, 2017), p. 70.

59. "Council of War, 8 October 1775," *The Papers of George Washington, Revolutionary War Series, vol. 2, 16 September 1775–31 December 1775*, Philander D. Chase, ed. (Charlottesville, VA: University of Virginia Press, 1987), pp. 123–8; "Minutes of the Conference between a Committee of Congress, Washington, and Representatives of the New England Colonies, 18[–24] October 1775," *The Papers of Benjamin Franklin, vol. 22, March 23, 1775, through October 27, 1776*, William B. Willcox, ed. (New Haven, CT and London: Yale University Press, 1982), pp. 224–41. See also Philip D. Morgan, "'To Get Quit of Negroes': George Washington and Slavery," *Journal of American Studies*, 39:3 (December 2005), pp. 403–29.

60. "Diary of Richard Smith in the Continental Congress, 1775–1776," *The American Historical Review*, 1:2 (January 1896), p. 292.

61. "General Orders, 12 November 1775," *The Papers of George Washington*, vol. 2, pp. 353–5.

62. Schuyler to Heath, July 28, 1777, in *The Heath Papers*, vol. 2 (Boston, MA: Massachusetts Historical Society, 1904), p. 135.

63. Samuel Adams to Heath, August 13, 1777, in *The Heath Papers*, vol. 2, p. 140.

64. Heath to Samuel Adams, August 27, 1777, in *The Heath Papers*, vol. 2, p. 148.

65. Heath to Washington, May 7, 1782 and May 10, 1782, in *The Heath Papers*, vol. 3 (Boston: Massachusetts Historical Society, 1904), pp. 373, 377.

66. Schuyler to Heath, July 28, 1777, in *The Heath Papers*, vol. 2, p. 135.

67. "To George Washington from John Hancock, 2 December 1775," *The Papers of George Washington*, vol. 2, pp. 469–71.

68. George Washington to Joseph Reed, December 15, 1775, *The Papers of George Washington*, vol. 2, pp. 551–4.

69. George Washington to Richard Henry Lee, December 26, 1775, *The Papers of George Washington*, vol. 2, pp. 610–13.

70. "General Orders, 30 December 1775," *The Papers of George Washington*, vol. 2, p. 620.

71. See also "From George Washington to John Hancock, 31 December 1775," *The Papers of George Washington*, vol. 2, pp. 622–6.

72. *Journal of the House of Delegates of the Commonwealth of Virginia*, June 26, 1777 (Richmond, 1827), p. 102; *Letters of Members of the Continental Congress*, vol. 1, Edmund C. Burnett, ed. (Washington, DC: Carnegie Institute, 1921), p. 313.

73. "To George Washington from Brigadier General Thomas Nelson, Jr., 21–22 November 1777," *The Papers of George Washington, Revolutionary War Series, vol. 12, 26 October 1777–25 December 1777*, Frank E. Grizzard, Jr. & David R. Hoth, eds. (Charlottesville, VA: University of Virginia Pree, 2002), pp. 341–3; see also fn. 21, Morgan, "To Get Quit of Negroes'," pp. 403–29.

74. Washington's letters of December 19, 1777 is mentioned in Nelson's letter to him dated January 20, but has not been found. "To George Washington from Brigadier General Thomas Nelson, Jr., 20 January 1778," *The Papers of George Washington*, vol. 13, pp. 298–9. Washington's thoughts on Nelson's report are unfortunately lost to history along with a letter he wrote to Nelson in response to this one.

75. "From George Washington to Major General William Heath, 29 June 1780," *The Papers of George Washington, Revolutionary War Series, vol. 26, 13 May–4 July 1780*, William M. Ferraro, ed. (Charlottesville, VA: University of Virginia Press, 2018), pp. 593–4. Historians have long repeated the supposed fact that 5000 black men fought on the revolutionary side in the war with England. However, none have ever cited a source for this figure. Judith L. Van Buskirk, "Review of Death or Liberty: African Americans and Revolutionary America," *Journal of the Early Republic*, 31:2 (2011), pp. 324–7.

76. Van Buskirk, *Standing in Their Own Light*, pp. 61–7; David N. Gellman, *Emancipating New York: The Politics of Slavery and Freedom, 1777–1827* (Baton Rouge, LA: Louisiana State University Press, 2006), p. 37.

77. "Henry Knox Orders to Lieutenant John Pratt," The Henry Knox Papers GLC09055.01; also "Rules for Enlisting Men for Service," n.d., The Henry Knox Papers, GLC02437.08189, The Gilder Lehrman Institute of American History, New York.

78. George H. Moore, *Notes on the History of Slavery in Massachusetts* (New York: D. Appleton & Co., 1866), pp. 245–6.

79. Van Buskirk, *Standing in Their Own Light*, pp. 19, 63.

80. Ibid., p. 61.

81. Force, *American Archives*, ser. 4, vol. 1 (Washington, 1837–53), p. 900.

82. Otis, *The Rights of the British Colonies Asserted and Proved*, pp. 24, 57–8, 75.

83. *Weekly National Intelligencer*, September 4, 1847, p. 1. See also Congress' petition to the King of October 26, 1774, which was heavy with allusions to the virtuous character of Britons. *Journals of the Continental Congress*, vol. 1, pp. 115–22.

84. Levi Hart, *Liberty Described and Recommended in a Sermon Preached ... in Farmington, Sept. 20, 1774* (Eben Watson, Hartford: 1775), Antislavery Pamphlet Collection (RB 003). Special Collections and University Archives, University of Massachusetts Amherst Libraries.

85. Walter McElreath, *A Treatise on the Constitution of Georgia* (Atlanta, GA: The Harrison Co., 1912), p. 41.

86. Ibid., p. 47.

87. Ibid., p. 16.

88. Ibid., p. 16.

89. William Drayton, *A Charge on the Rise of the American Empire* (Charlestown: David Bruce, 1776), p. 23.

90. Some historians, reading these passages through the lens of an Enlightenment philosophy they presumed was universal, thought they were expressions that pertained to all people. However, they can just as consistently be read as making the narrower claim of certain rights by direct descent. Take, for example, this passage from the Chief Justice of the South Carolina Supreme Courts' celebration of American Independence in 1776: "Carolinians ! heretofore you were bound. By the American Revolution you are now free. The change is most important—

most honourable—most beneficial. It is your birthright by the law of nature—." Force, *American Archives*, ser. 4, vol. 2 (Washington, 1837–53)), p. 1047.

91. *Considerations on the Present State of Virginia Attributed to John Randolph*, Earl Gregg Swem, ed. (New York: Charles F. Heartman, 1919), p. 23; see also Gould, *Among the Powers of the Earth*, p. 51.

92. "Some Fugitive Thoughts on a Letter Signed Freeman, Addressed to the Deputies, Assembled at the High Court of Congress in Philadelphia. By a Back Settler" (South Carolina, 1774), p. 5.

93. Bierbach, *Frontiers of Equality*, pp. 62–4.

94. "Draft of Instructions to the Virginia Delegates in the Continental Congress," *The Papers of Thomas Jefferson*, vol. 1, pp. 121–37; Thomas Jefferson, *A Summary View of the Rights of British America* (1774). Though the Virginia Assembly tabled his draft and members were sworn to secrecy "under the strongest obligations of honor," in 1774 Jefferson's friends published his essay as a pamphlet entitled *A Summary View of the Rights of British America. A Summary View* was read as a declaration of independence by many in London. One Londoner wrote to a friend in New York that the "author of the 'Summary' seems to have laboured to convince the People of England, that nothing but Independence will satisfy America." This correspondent advised that such talk would ruin the patriot cause: "Your Patriots, by contending for too much, will probably lose all." He noted that others have been able to allude to these ideas without crossing over into outright treason: "your warm partisans have only a little too soon exposed those conclusions, which intelligent men long ago perceived to be concealed under their principles. The sum total of these claims is Independence …" Force, *American Archives*, vol. 2, pp. 1035–7.

95. *The Federalist*, Jacob E. Cooke, ed. (Middletown, CN, Wesleyan University Press, 1961), p. 9; Gordon S. Wood, *Empire of Liberty: A History of the Early Republic, 1789–1815* (New York: Oxford University Press, 2009), pp. 39–40.

96. Parkinson, *The Common Cause*, p. 629.

97. Kettner, *The Development of American Citizenship*, p. 220.

98. *The Pennsylvania Packet* (Philadelphia), July 8, 1777, p. 3.

99. *The Hartford Courant* (Hartford, Conn.), June 22, 1779, p. 3.

100. "To John Adams from Edmund Jenings, 3 June 1783," *The Adams Papers, Papers of John Adams, vol. 15, June 1783–January 1784*, Gregg L. Lint, C. James Taylor, Robert F. Karachuk, Hobson Woodward, Margaret A. Hogan, Sara B. Sikes, Mary T. Claffey, & Karen N. Barzilay, eds. (Cambridge, MA: Harvard University Press, 2010), pp. 10–15.

101. [Letter to Abolition Society in London, n.d., probably very end of 1789], PAS Papers Series II—Correspondence, Loose Correspondence, outgoing 1783–1914, The Pennsylvania Abolition Society at The Historical Society of Pennsylvania.

102. Robert G. Parkinson first pointed out that the support for removing the color bar from the Massachusetts constitution was much less than previous sources had claimed. Parkinson, *The Common Cause*, pp. 370–3. *The Popular Sources of Political Authority: Documents on the Massachusetts Constitution of 1780*, Oscar Handlin & Mary Flug Handlin, eds. (Cambridge, MA: Harvard University Belknap Press, 1966), p. 186. A. Leon Higginbotham strains his sources when he writes that the Massachusetts Constitutional Convention of 1778 "revolved

around the conflict between those for and those against black equality" (*In the Matter of Color: Race and the American Legal Process* (New York: Oxford University Press, 1978), p. 89).

103. Handlin & Handlin, *The Popular Sources of Political Authority*, p. 216.

104. Ibid., p. 231.

105. Ibid., pp. 248–9.

106. *The Works of John Adams*, vol. 4, Charles Francis Adams, ed. (Boston: Charles C. Little & James Brown, 1851), p. 225. John Adams was further delegated to formulate a declaration of rights which he did entirely on his own. Adams' first phrase has long been misquoted due to a mix-up in the state's official records. It is widely claimed that Adams wrote: "All men are born free and equal" when in fact his original read: "All men are born equally free and independent," a slight variation from George Mason's earlier wording in the Virginia Bill of Rights that read, "All men are created equally free and independent." (Mason's original was later amended to read: "All men are by nature equally free and independent.") Adams' and Mason's wording stresses the equality of birth, which was a secularized version of the Christian concept that all people are the children of God. At the time, this was usually understood as a statement of human oneness, not of any particular rights that people possessed in society or under a particular government. Following Rousseau, who is the innovator of this language, having been born in a state of nature that is equal, man then surrenders some of his freedom and independence in order to enjoy the security and blessings of society. What begins in swadling as a state of freedom and equality quickly grows up into the classes, orders, ranks, nationalities, and other distinctions of human society. These divisions of rights and privileges are not necessarily overturned by saying that "All men are born equally free and independent." The question is not how men are born but how they are to live together. See *Proceedings of the Massachusetts Historical Society*, vol. 5 (Boston: John Wilson & Son, 1862), p. 92.

107. Madison to Jefferson, December 21, 1794, *The Papers of Thomas Jefferson, vol. 28, 1 January 1794 to 29 February 1796*, John Catanzariti, ed. (Princeton, NJ: Princeton University Press, 2000), p. 221.

108. Henry Noble Sherwood, "Problems of Citizenship," *The Journal of Negro History*, 8:2 (April 1923), pp. 162–6.

109. Ibid., pp. 162–6; Massachusetts Anti-Slavery and Anti-Segregation Petitions; Massachusetts Archives Collection. V.186-Revolution Petitions, 1779–1780. SC1/series 45X. Massachusetts Archives. Boston, Mass. V.186: p.134-136a: Petition of John Cuffe, Page (seq. 4), Repository Collection Development Department. Widener Library. HCL Institution, Harvard University.

110. Edward Raymond Turner, *The Negro in Pennsylvania* (Washington, DC: The American Historical Association, 1911), pp. 180, 185.

111. Thomas Branagan, *Serious Remonstrances, Addressed to the Citizens of the Northern States* (Philadelphia: Thomas T. Stiles, 1805), p. 64. Manisha Sinha writes that "Abolitionists' plans for the protection and improvement of black included securing citizenship for them" but none of the sources she cites actually advocate equal citizenship as a policy. Manisha Sinha, *The Slave's Cause: A History of Abolition* (New Haven, CT: Yale University Press, 2016), p. 113.

112. *The American Convention for Promoting the Abolition of Slavery*, vol. 1 (New York: Bergman Printers, 1939), p. 3.

113. The dog that didn't bark was a plot element in "The Adventure of Silver Blaze," collected in Arthur Conan Doyle, *The Memoirs of Sherlock Holmes* (Oxford: Oxford University Press, 1993, orig. 1894).

114. *The Records of the Federal Convention of 1787*, vol. 1, p. 413.

115. Ferrand, *The Records of the Federal Convention*, vol. 3, p. 446.

116. Madison's notes, July 19, Ferrand, *The Records of the Federal Convention*, vol. 2, p. 57.

117. Bierbach, *Frontiers of Equality*, p. 91.

118. *Annals of Congress, House of Representatives, 1st Congress, 2nd Session*, p. 1150.

119. Ferrand, *Records of the Federal Convention*, vol. 2, pp. 269–70.

120. *Journal of William Maclay, United States Senator from Pennsylvania, 1789–1791*, Edgar S. Maclay, ed. (New York: D. Appleton and Company, 1890), p. 208.

121. Summaries of the debates can be found in the *Annals of Congress, House of Representatives, 1st Congress, 2nd Session*, pp. 1147–64. *The Gazette of the United States* (New York), February 6, 1790, p. 2. This account was reprinted in other papers, such as the *Connecticut Courant* (Hartford, Conn.), February 18, 1790, p. 1 and the *Pennsylvania Packet* (Philadelphia), February 12, 1790, p. 2; March 11, 1790, p. 2.

122. *Journal of William Maclay*, p. 210.

123. *The Pennsylvania Packet* (Philadelphia), April 1, 1790, p. 2.

124. Memorial of January 17, 1803, Record Group 59: General Records of the Department of State, 1763–2002, Office of the Secretary, Letters Received, January–December 1803, #55287285, National Archives.

125. Bill #20, January 26, 1803, Bills and Resolutions, House of Representatives, 7th Congress, 2nd Session (Washington: Duane & Son, Printers, 1803), Library of Congress.

126. *Annals of Congress*, House of Representatives, 7th Congress, 2nd Session, p. 461.

127. Bill #21, February 4, 1803, Bills and Resolutions, House of Representatives, 7th Congress, 2nd Session.

128. *Annals of Congress*, House of Representatives, 7th Congress, 2nd Session, p. 468.

129. Padraig Riley, *Slavery and the Democratic Conscience: Political Life in Jeffersonian America* (Philadelphia, PA: University of Pennsylvania Press, 2016), p. 26.

130. "Letter of Hon. John Bacon" (September 22, 1785), *Proceedings of the Massachusetts Historical Society*, vol. 5 (Boston: John Wilson & Son, 1862), pp. 477–85.

131. *Annals of Congress*, House of Representatives, 7th Congress, 2nd Session, pp. 468–9.

132. Ibid., pp. 469–70.

133. *Annals of Congress*, House of Representatives, 7th Congress, 2nd Session, pp. 471–2.

134. Ibid., p. 324. (Monday, February 7).

135. Bill #32, February 10, 1803, Bills and Resolutions, House of Representatives, 7th Congress, 2nd Session. While this copy of the bill is the last in the series in the Library of Congress Bills and Resolutions, it is different from the final published version of the bill in the *Statutes at Large* (vol. 2, pp. 205–6). It "being a native citizen, or registered seaman of the United States" but the version in the *Statutes at Large* reads "being a native, a citizen, or registered seamen of the United States."

136. *Journal of the House of Representatives of the United States, 1801–1804,* Thursday, February 17, 1803, pp. 347–8.

137. Bill #36, February 14, 1803, Bills and Resolutions, House of Representatives, 7th Congress, 2nd Session.

138. W. Jeffrey Bolster, "To Feel Like a Man": Black Seamen in the Northern States, 1800–1860," *The Journal of American History,* 76:4 (March, 1990), pp. 1173–99; *Annals of Congress,* House of Representatives, 4th Congress, 1st Session, p. 803. See also Michael A. Schoeppner, *Moral Contagion: Black Atlantic Sailors, Citizenship, and Diplomacy in Antebellum America* (Cambridge: Cambridge University Press, 2019).

139. Ira Dye, "The Philadelphia Seamen's Protection Certificate Applications," *Prologue: Sources at the National Archives for Genealogical and Local History Research,* 18 (1986); W. Jeffrey Bolster, *Black Jacks: African American Seamen in the Age of Sail* (Cambridge, MA: Harvard University Press, 1997), pp. 5, 115; Denver Brunsman, "Subjects vs. Citizens: Impressment and Identity in the Anglo-American Atlantic," *Journal of the Early Republic,* 30:4 (Winter 2010), pp. 557–86; Edlie L. Wong, *Neither Fugitive Nor Free: Atlantic Slavery, Freedom Suits, and the Legal Culture of Travel* (2009), pp. 189–90.

140. Bill 26, January 10, 1804, Bills and Resolutions, House of Representatives, 8th Congress, 1st Session.

141. February 8, 1804, *Journal of the House of Representatives of the United States,* 8th Congress, 1st Session.

142. Alan Frank, *The First Nullification: The Negro Seamen Acts Controversy in South Carolina, 1822–1860* (Ph.D. Diss., University of Iowa, 1976), pp. 178–9.

143. Christopher Green, *Equal Citizenship, Civil Rights, and the Constitution: The Original Sense of the Privileges or Immunities Clause* (New York: Routledge, 2015), pp. 24–5.

144. Jon Kukla, *A Wilderness so Immense, the Louisiana Purchase and the Destiny of America* (New York: A.A. Knopf, 2003), p. 570.

145. Claiborne to Madison, July 7, 1804, *The Papers of James Madison, Secretary of State Series,* vol. 7, David B. Mattern, J.C.A. Stagg, Ellen J. Barber, Anne Mandeville Colony, Angela Kreider, & Jeanne Kerr Cross, eds. (Charlottesville, VA: University of Virginia Press, 2005), pp. 428–9.

146. Lincoln to Jefferson, September 10, 1803, *The Papers of Thomas Jefferson, vol. 41, 11 July–15 November 1803,* Barbara B. Oberg, ed. (Princeton, NJ: Princeton University Press, 2015), pp. 359–61.

147. Claiborne to Madison, November 5, 1802, *The Papers of James Madison, Secretary of State Series,* vol. 4, Mary A. Hackett, J.C.A. Stagg, Jeanne Kerr Cross, Susan Holbrook Perdue, & Ellen J. Barber, eds. (Charlottesville, VA: University of Virginia Press, 1998), pp. 91–5.

148. *Memoirs of John Quincy Adams,* vol. 5, Charles Francis Adams, ed. (Philadelphia: J.B. Lippincott, 1875), p. 401.

149. Niles' Weekly Register 19 [23 September 1820], p. 52; Robert Pierce Forbes, *The Missouri Compromise and Its Aftermath: Slavery & the Meaning of America* (Chapel Hill, NC, 2007), pp. 108, 110.

150. Duane Smith, "The Evolution of the Legal Concept of Citizenship in the United States" (Ph.D. Diss., Ohio State University, 1936); *Annals,* 16 Cong. 2 Sess., pp. 42, 45, 102, 47–8, 93–4, 105, 112.

151. "Proceedings and Debates of the Senate of the United States, at the Second Session of the Sixteenth Congress, begun at the City of Washington, Monday, November 13, 1820," *Annals of the Congress of the United States*, vol. 37 (1820–21), p. 57.

152. *Annals*, 16 C-ong. 1 Sess., pp. 59–60, 86–7.

153. Ibid., pp. 536–7, 557, 615.

154. Ibid., pp. 570–1, 576, 599, 633.

155. Kettner, *The Development of American Citizenship*, p. 314.

156. Ibid., pp. 314–15.

157. Ibid., p. 317.

158. *The Papers of James Madison, Retirement Series*, vol. 2 (*1 February 1820–26 February 1823*), J.C.A. Stagg, ed. (Charlottesville, VA: University of Virginia Press, 2010), p. 149.

159. "From James Madison to James Monroe, 19 November 1820," *The Papers of James Madison*, vol. 2, pp. 151–153.

160. Kettner, *The Development of American Citizenship*, p. 321; *Opinions of Attorney Generals*, vol. 1 (Washington, DC: Government Printing Office, 1851), p. 336.

CHAPTER 6

1. Noah Webster, "An Examination into the Leading Principles of the Federal Constitution. By a Citizen of America" (Philadelphia, 1787), in *Pamphlets on the Constitution of the United States*, Paul Leicester Ford, ed. (Brooklyn, NY, 1888); *American Museum* (Philadelphia), August 1790, p. 63.

2. John Parrish, *Remarks on the Slavery of the Black People: Addressed to the Citizens of the United States…* (Philadelphia: Kimber, Conrad & Co., 1805), p. 21.

3. "Proceedings and Debates of the Senate of the United States, at the Second Session of the Sixteenth Congress, begun at the City of Washington, Monday, November 13, 1820," *Annals of the Congress of the United States*, vol. 37 (1820–21), p. 57.

4. David Ramsay, *An Address to the Freemen of South Carolina on the Subject of the Federal Constitution* (Charleston: Bowen & Co., 1787), p. 8.

5. *The Records of the Federal Convention of 1787*, vol. 1, Max Ferrand, ed. (New Haven, CT: Yale University Press, 1911),, pp. 594, 603–5; Ferrand, *The Records of the Federal Convention*, vol. 2, pp. 95, 443, 453.

6. Emily Blanck, *Tyrannicide: Forging an American Law of Slavery in Revolutionary South Carolina and Massachusetts* (Athens, GA: University of Georgia Press, 2014), pp. 151–2. See also Douglas Bradburn, *The Citizenship Revolution: Politics & the Creation of the American Union 1774–1804* (Charlottesville, VA: University of Virginia Press, 2009), p. 246.

7. George Van Cleve argued that though the articles did not have a separate fugitive slavery clause, the sweeping nature of its privileges and immunities clause achieved the same purpose. See George Van Cleve, *A Slaveholders' Union: Slavery, Politics, and the Constitution in the Early American Republic* (Chicago, IL: University of Chicago Press, 2010), pp. 52–6. Emily Blanck documents how the articles were judged in state courts to restrict states from harboring or freeing fugitives from slavery. Emily Blanck, *Tyrannicide*.

8. George H. Moore, *Notes on the History of Slavery in Massachusetts* (New York: D. Appleton & Co., 1866), p. 166–8.

9. Joseph Palmer, *Necrology of Alumni of Harvard College, 1851–52 to 1862–63* (Boston: J. Wilson & Son, 1864), p. 169; Samuel Adams Drake, *Old Boston Taverns* (Boston: W.A. Butterfield, 1917), pp. 43–4, 62; Blanck, *Tyrannicide*, p. 103.

10. Blanck, *Tyrannicide*, pp. 101–3.

11. Ibid., p. 132.

12. *Pennsylvania Archives*, Samuel Hazard, ed. (Philadelphia: Joseph Severns & Co., 1853), ser. 1, vol. 11, pp. 249, 256.

13. *Pennsylvania Packet* (Philadelphia), March 4, 1779, p. 1; Paul Finkelman, *Slavery and the Founders: Race and Liberty in the Age of Jefferson*, 2nd ed. (New York: M.E. Sharpe, 2001), p. 103.

14. *The Debates in the Several State Conventions on the Adoption of the Federal Constitution*, 2nd ed., vol. 1, Jonathan Elliot, ed. (Washington: Taylor & Maury, 1854), p. 273. Paul Finkelman, "Slavery and the Northwest Ordinance: A Study in Ambiguity," *Journal of the Early Republic*, 6:4 (Winter, 1986), pp. 343–70. Sean Wilentz incorrectly identifies the fugitive slave clause of the Northwest Territories Ordinance as "Article Five." It was Article VI. Sean Wilentz, *No Property in Man: Slavery and Antislavery at the Nation's Founding* (Cambridge, MA: Harvard University Press, 2018), p. 103.

15. Moses Brown to possibly Joseph Townsend, November 13, 1787, Manuscript Collection 954, Haverford College Quaker and Special Collections; Moses Brown to James Thornton, Sr., Providence, November 13, 1787, *The Documentary History of the Ratification of the Constitution*, Digital Edition, ed. John P. Kaminski, Gaspare J. Saladino, Richard Leffler, Charles H. Schoenleber, & Margaret A. Hogan (Charlottesville, VA: University of Virginia Press, 2009).

16. *A Necessary Evil?: Slavery and the Debate over the Constitution*, John P. Kaminski, ed. (Madison, WI: Madison House, 1995), p. 147.

17. Van Cleve offered a variant of these positions, arguing the clause was simply part of a national consensus surrounding fugitive slaves. Northerners were "unwilling to permit black 'freedom from slavery' to become black equality." Van Cleve even touches on the possibility that "'black removal' [was] … a part of slavery's abolition." Van Cleve, *A Slaveholders' Union*, pp. 167–72. Paul Finkelman speculates "The delegates to the Constitutional Convention may have been simply too exhausted for further strenuous debate. It is more likely, however, that the northern delegates failed to appreciate the legal problems and moral dilemmas that the rendition of fugitive slaves would pose." Paul Finkelman, "The Kidnapping of John Davis and the Adoption of the Fugitive Slave Law of 1793," *Journal of Southern History*, 56:3 (August 1990), p. 398. Mark Boonshoft observed how some historians "explain the lack of commentary on the fugitive slave clause as evidence that it was not actually proslavery. Rather, they suggest that by regulating fugitive issues at the federal level, northern opponents of slavery would have an easier time defending free blacks from the possibility of kidnapping. If left entirely to the states, southern lawmakers would be able to provide legal cover for slave catchers who illegally kidnapped free blacks in the North and transported them to the South as slaves. In reality, antislavery activists at the time understood that this clause meant that 'Massachusetts will no Longer be an

Asylum to the Negroes.'" Mark Boonshoft, "Doughfaces at the Founding: Federalists, Anti-Federalists, Slavery, and the Ratification of the Constitution in New York," *New York History*, 93:3 (2012), pp. 187–218.

18. Thomas Mifflin to George Washington, July 18, 1791, *The Papers of George Washington, Presidential Series*, vol. 8, Mark A. Mastromarino, ed. (Charlottesville, VA: University of Virginia Press, 1999), pp. 345–8; Finkelman, "The Kidnapping of John Davis," pp. 397–422; H. Robert Baker, "The Fugitive Slave Clause and the Antebellum Constitution," *Law and History Review* 30:4 (November 2012), pp. 1133–74; Stanley Harrold, *Border War: Fighting over Slavery before the Civil War* (Chapel Hill, NC: University of North Carolina Press, 2010), pp. 21–3; Matthew Mason, *Slavery and Politics in the Early American Republic* (Chapel Hill, NC: University of North Carolina Press, 2006), pp. 17–18.

19. Finkelman, "The Kidnapping of John Davis," pp. 397–422.

20. Thomas D. Morris, *Free Men All: The Personal Liberty Laws of the North, 1780–1861* (Union, NJ: The Lawbook Exchange, 2001), pp. 26–8. Nicolas P. Wood rifled through an impressive pile of records of Pennsylvania Quakers and the Pennsylvania Abolition Society to find evidence that some white abolitionists "assisted" with the drafting of one of these petitions. From this article, Wood conjures a full-blown interracial community: "previously unexamined manuscript evidence—including rough drafts of both petitions—reveals the interracial and interregional networks that helped the nation's first black petitioners achieve political voice." Nicholas P. Wood, "A 'class of Citizens': The Earliest Black Petitioners to Congress and Their Quaker Allies," *The William and Mary Quarterly*, 74:1 (January 2017), pp. 109–44; *Minutes of the Proceedings of the Eighth Convention of Delegates of the American Convention for Promoting the Abolition of Slavery and Improving the Condition of the African Race* (Philadelphia, 1803), p. 23. See also M. Scott Heerman, "Abolishing Slavery in Motion: Foreign Captivity and International Abolitionism in the Early United States," *The William and Mary Quarterly*, 77:2 (April 2020), pp. 245–72.

21. Morris, *Free Men All*, pp. 30, 35; Baker, "The Fugitive Slave Clause," pp. 1133–74.

22. Morris, *Free Men All*, p. 32.

23. Hazard, *Pennsylvania Archives*, vol. 7, p. 79.

24. *Minutes of the Proceedings of the Fourth Convention of Delegates from the Abolition Societies* ... (Philadelphia: Zachariah Poulson, Jr., 1797), pp. 51–2.

25. Hazard, *Pennsylvania Archives*, vol. 7, p. 79.

26. David Brion Davis, *The Problem of Slavery in the Age of Revolution, 1770–1823* (Ithaca, NY: Cornell University Press, 1975), p. 305. After compiling and analyzing all the slave registrations required by the manumission law, Cory James Young observed that the law actually reinforced the hold of masters on their human property. "The 1780 law was as much an act for the conditional preservation of slavery as it was an act for its gradual abolition." *For Life Or Otherwise: Abolition and Slavery in South Central Pennsylvania, 1780–1847* (Ph.D. Diss., Georgetown University, 2021), p. 48.

27. *The Universal Asylum and Columbian Magazine*, November 1792, p. 311.

28. *Minutes of the Proceedings of the Fourth Convention of Delegates from the Abolition Societies*, pp. 47–8.

29. Morris, *Free Men All*, p. 27.

30. Claudia Golden, "The Economics of Emancipation," *The Journal of Economic History*, 33:1 (March 1973), p. 70.

31. *Minutes of the Proceedings of the Fourth Convention of Delegates from the Abolition Societies*, pp. 50–1.

32. James J. Gigantino II, "Trading in Jersey Souls: New Jersey and the Inter-state Slave Trade," *Pennsylvania History: A Journal of Mid-Atlantic Studies*, 77:3 (Summer 2010), pp. 281–302.

33. William C. Fowler, *The Historical Status of the Negro in Connecticut* (Charleston, SC: Walker, Evans & Cogswell, 1901, orig. in *Historical Magazine and Notes and Queries*, vol. 23–24, 1874–75), p. 18.

34. Record Group: #1111, General Assembly, Legislative Papers, Delaware State Archives, Dover, Delaware, Race and Slavery Petitions Project Series 1, PAR #10379402, Legislative Petitions, The University of North Carolina Greensboro.

35. David, Menschel, "Abolition without Deliverance: The Law of Connecticut Slavery 1784–1848," *The Yale Law Journal*, 111:1 (October 2001), pp. 183–222; 1782 Census. "A return of the Number of inhabitants in the State of Connecti-cut, February 1, 1782; and also of the Indians and Negroes." Connecticut State Library; 1790 Census, "Heads of Families at the First Census of the United States Taken in the year 1790: Connecticut," Bureau of the Census (Washing-ton, DC: Government Printing Office, 1908), p. 9; Campbell Gibson and Kay Jung, "Historical Census Statistics on Population Totals by Race, 1790 to 1990," Population Division, Working Paper 56, U.S. Census Bureau (September 2002), pp. 39–40.

36. *Records of the State of Rhode Island ...* vol. IX, John Russell Bartlett, ed. (Prov-idence: Alfred Anthony, 1864), p. 169; *Records of the State of Rhode Island ...* vol. VII, John Russell Bartlett, ed. (Providence: Alfred Anthony, 1862), p. 253; Lorenzo Johnston Greene, *The Negro in Colonial New England* (New York: Atheneum, 1969), p. 96; John Wood Sweet believes that the records show the opposite effect. Sweet writes that emancipation ran ahead of the law and claims that two-thirds of that state's enslaved were freed by 1790. This is only pos-sible if the enslaved population before 1790 was three times larger than the 948 counted that year. The state census of 1778 counted 518 slaves. John Wood Sweet, *Bodies Politic: Negotiating Race in the American North, 1730–1830* (Balti-more, MD: Johns Hopkins University Press, 2003), p. 252; Sidney S. Rider, *An Historical Inquiry Concerning the Attempt to Raise a Regiment of Slaves by Rhode Island* (Providence: Sidney S. Rider, 1880), 57-58, 71. Judith L. Van Buskirk, *Standing in their Own Light: African American Patriots in the American Revolu-tion* (Norman: Univ. of Oklahoma Press, 2017), 188.

37. Margot Minardi, *Making Slavery History* (New York: Oxford University Press, 2012), pp. 17–20; Joanne P. Melish, *Disowning Slavery: Gradual Emancipation and "Race" in New England, 1780–1860* (Ithaca, NY: Cornell University Press, 1998), pp. 101–4.

38. Paul A. Gilje, *The Road to Mobocracy: Popular Disorder in New York City, 1763–1834* (Chapel Hill, NC: University of North Carolina Press, 1987), pp. 147–9; Shane White, *Somewhat More Independent: The End of Slavery in New York City, 1770–1810* (Athens, GA: University of Georgia Press, 1991), pp. 144–5; *Baptiste v. De Volunbrun*, 5 Har. and John, 86, June 1820.

39. *Journal of the House of Delegates of the Commonwealth of Virginia*, November 29, 1783 (Richmond, 1828), p. 39.

40. "An Act to prevent the Migration of Free Negroes and Mulattoes into this Commonwealth," Virginia–October Session, 1793, p. 28. Bradburn, *The Citizenship Revolution*, pp. 236–7.

41. Thomas D. Morris, *Southern Slavery and the Law, 1619–1860* (Chapel Hill, NC: University of North Carolina Press., 1996), p. 372; Ellen Eslinger, "Free Black Residency in Two Antebellum Virginia Counties: How the Laws Functioned," *The Journal of Southern History*, 79:2 (May 2013), pp. 261–98. *The Statutes at Large of Virginia*, vol. 1, Samuel Shepherd, ed. (Richmond: 1835–36), pp. 238–9; for the 1806 manumission law, vol. 3, pp. 251–3; for the 1782 manumission law, see William Waller Hening, *The Statutes at Large: Being a collection of all the laws of Virginia, from the first session of the legislature, in the year 1619*, vol. 11 (Richmond: Printed by and for Samuel Pleasants, junior, printer to the commonwealth, 1809–23), pp. 39–40.

42. *Acts of the General Assembly of the State of South Carolina, from February 1791, to December 1794*, vol. 1 (Columbia: J.J. Faust, State Printers, 1808), pp. 215–16.

43. Ibid., pp. 391–2.

44. *Acts of the General Assembly of the State of South Carolina, from December, 1795, to December 1804*, vol. 1 (Columbia: J.J. Faust, State Printers, 1808), pp. 344–5.

45. Ibid., pp. 449–50.

46. *The Statute Law of Kentucky*, vol. 3, William Littell, ed. (Frankfort: William Hunter, 1811), p. 449.

47. *The Federal and State Constitutions*, Francis Newton Thorpe, ed. (Washington, DC: Government Printing Office, 1909), p. 178.

48. *Judicial Cases Concerning American Slavery and the Negro*, vol. 4, Helen Tunnicliff Catterall, ed. (Washington, DC: Carnegie Institution, 1936), p. 213; Record Group: #1111, General Assembly, Legislative Papers, Delaware StateArchives, Dover, Delaware, Accession #10379602 and Accession #10379701, Race and Slavery Petitions Project Series 1, Legislative Petitions, The University of North Carolina Greensboro.

49. Ibid.

50. *The Law of Freedom and Bondage in the United States*, vol. 2, John C. Hurd, ed. (Boston: Little, Brown & Co., 1862), pp. 77–8.

51. Carol Wilson, *Freedom at Risk: The Kidnapping of Free Blacks in America, 1780–1865* (Lexington, KY: University Press of Kentucky, 1994), p. 67–71.

52. T. Stephen Whitman, *Slavery, Manumission, and Free Black Workers in Early National Baltimore* (Ph.D. Diss., Johns Hopkins University, 1993), p. 161.

53. *Digest of Laws of the State of Georgia*, Robert & George Watkins, eds. (Philadelphia: R. Aitken, 1800), p. 530. Frederick Douglass, *My Bondage and My Freedom* (1855), ch. 19. Jennifer Hull Dorsey studied applications for such certificates in Maryland and concluded that they were not nearly as important as Douglass claimed they were. Calculating the proportion of freed people who applied for such documents, she found that "only a fraction" did so and that "Free African Americans did not apply ... because they thought the certificates would protect their freedom. They filed for certificates because the papers facilitated migration and thereby created opportunities." Her evidence for this claim was her data showing that "only a fraction of manumitted or freeborn African Americans in

Maryland ever applied ..." She concludes that "as late as 1830, twenty-five years after the legislature standardized the certificates, only 10 percent of the free African Americans" applied. However, her data is miscalculated. Dorsey calculates the proportion of the free black population that applied for certificates in each of four periods. For example, she finds that Talbot County had 12 percent applications from 1805 to 1810, 30 percent from 1810–19, just 10 percent from 1820 to 1829. The error here is that each period's applications should have been subtracted from the next overall population total as these individuals *had their certificates* and did not need to apply again. When those who already had obtained certificates are subtracted from the population, Dorsey's sequence of 12, 30, and 10 percent can be recalculated to be 12, 38, and 18 percent. (Thus the correct number for 1830 should be 18, not 10 percent.) For some reason, Dorsey does not include the simple overall proportion of applications and population as of her final date, which calculates to the impressive number of 48.5 percent of all free black people in Talbot County having applied for their certificates in this period, a figure that seems in line with Douglass' description of a general fear of consequences. Jennifer Hull Dorsey, *Hirelings: African American Workers and Free Labor in Early Maryland* (Ithaca, NY: Cornell University Press, 2011), pp. 50–3.

54. *A Compilation of the Laws of the State of Georgia,* Augustin Smith Clayton, ed. (Augusta: Adams & Duyckinck, 1812), p. 655.

55. *Acts of the North Carolina General Assembly, 1723, North Carolina, General Assembly,* vol. 23 (November 23, 1723), p. 107.

56. "An Additional Act ... to Regulate and Restrain the Conduct of Slaves and Others," in *The State Records of North Carolina,* vol. 24, Walter Clark, ed. (Goldsboro, NC: Nash Brothers, 1905), pp. 727–8.

57. *An Exposition of the Criminal Laws of the State of Louisiana* (Plaquemine: J. Hawkins Peoples, 1840), p. 77.

58. "Proceedings and Debates of the Senate of the United States, at the Second Session of the Sixteenth Congress, begun at the City of Washington, Monday, November 13, 1820," *Annals of the Congress of the United States,* vol. 37 (1820–21), p. 61.

59. *Records of the Colony of Rhode Island and Providence Plantations,* vol. 7, John Russell Bartlett, ed. (Providence: A. Crawford Greene, State Printer, 1862), pp. 415–16, 251–3. See also Christy Clark-Pujara, *Dark Work: The Business of Slavery in Rhode Island* (New York: New York University Press, 2017).

60. *Minutes of the Proceedings of the Fourth Convention of Delegates from the Abolition Societies,* pp. 49–50.

61. Ibid., p. 50.

62. "Proceedings and Debates of the Senate of the United States, at the Second Session of the Sixteenth Congress, begun at the City of Washington, Monday, November 13, 1820," *Annals of the Congress of the United States,* vol. 37 (1820–21), p. 64.

63. "Queries Respecting the Slavery and Emancipation of Negroes in Massachusetts," *Collections of the Massachusetts Historical Society,* ser. 1, vol. 4 (Boston: 1835, reprint of 1795), pp. 191–211.

64. *Annals of the Congress,* vol. 37 (1820–21), p. 69.

65. Ruth Wallis Herndon, *Unwelcome Americans: Living on the Margin in Early New England* (Philadelphia, PA: University of Pennsylvania Press, 2001), pp. 19–20.

66. Emily Blanck, *Revolutionizing Slavery: The Legal Culture of Slavery in Revolutionary Massachusetts and South Carolina* (Ph.D. Diss., Emory University, 2003), pp. 250–1.

67. "Proceedings and Debates of the Senate of the United States," *Annals of the Congress*, vol. 37 (1820–21), p. 66. James O. Horton & Lois E. Horton, *In Hope of Liberty: Culture, Community and Protest among Northern Free Blacks, 1700–1860* (New York: Oxford University Press, 1997), p. 101.

68. *The Acts and Resolves of Massachusetts, 1786–1787* (1889), pp. 625, 635; *Massachusetts Mercury*, September 16, 1800.

69. "Queries Respecting the Slavery and Emancipation of Negroes in Massachusetts," pp. 191–211.

70. James Forten, "Letters from a Man of Colour, on a Late Bill before the Senate of Pennsylvania" (1813), Gilder Lehrman Collection # GLC06046, The Gilder Lehrman Institute of American History. See also Julie Winch, *A Gentleman of Color: The Life of James Forten* (New York: Oxford University Press, 2002).

71. Zephaniah Swift, *An Oration on Domestic Slavery. Delivered at the North Meeting-House in Hartford, on the 12th day of May, A.D. 1791* (Hartford: Hudson and Goodwin, 1791).

72. Theodore Dwight, *An Oration, Spoken Before "The Connecticut Society, for the Promotion of Freedom and the Relief of Persons Unlawfully Holden in Bondage," ... 8th day of May, A.D. 1794* (Hartford: Hudson and Goodwin, 1794).

CHAPTER 7

1. See Manisha Sinha, *The Slave's Cause: A History of Abolition* (New Haven, CT: Yale University Press, 2016); Paul J. Polgar, *Standard-Bearers of Equality: America's First Abolition Movement* (Chapel Hill, NC: University of North Carolina Press, 2019); and Sean Wilentz, "The Revolution within the Revolution," *New York Review of Books*, October 23, 2023.

2. George Bourne, *The Book and Slavery Irreconcilable* (Philadelphia: J.M. Sanderson & Co., 1816).

3. *The American Convention for Promoting the Abolition of Slavery and Improving the Condition of the African Race Minutes, Constitution, Addresses, Memorials, Resolutions, Reports, Committees and Anti-Slavery Tracts Complete and Unabridged in Three Volumes*, vol. 1 (New York: Bergman Publishers, 1969), pp. 8–11. Paul Polgar notes the "limits of ... antislavery environmentalism" in supporting black equal rights but generally describes the debate over slavery in the Revolutionary era as one that pitted those arguing for "natural rights of man to liberty" and "black inequality [as] ... a transitory state capable of being overcome" against those holding blacks' "inherent incapacity for freedom" and "enslaved Africans' natural suitability for slavery." Polgar, *Standard-Bearers of Equality*, pp. 38, 40.

4. Kris Manjapra, *Black Ghost of Empire: The Long Death of Slavery and the Failure of Emancipation* (New York: Scribner, 2022), p. 5.

5. Manisha Sinha, "The Problem of Abolition in the Age of Capitalism: The Problem of Slavery in the Age of Revolution, 1770–1823, by David Brion Davis," *The American Historical Review*, 124:1 (February 2019), pp. 144–63.

6. Manjapra, *Black Ghost of Empire*, p. 16.

NOTES

7. Paul Polgar writes as if white abolitionists had identical commitments to blacks themselves: *"first movement abolitionism* was composed of an ideological and strategic coalition of black and white activists with three shared goals for abolishing slavery ..." (p. 4). Polgar's credulousness toward white abolitionists seems to have no bounds. In explaining the seemingly contradictory fact that the New York Manumission Society did not expel slaveholders from its membership until it was over twenty years old, in 1809, Polgar insists "That the NYMS permitted slaveholding among their members should not detract from their activism or raise questions regarding the goals of the society" (p. 54) Polgar uses expressions like African Americans "teaming up with white activists," implying some sort of relationship of equals (p. 75). Polgar, *Standard-Bearers of Equality.*

8. James Forten, "Letters From a Man of Colour, on a Late Bill before the Senate of Pennsylvania" (1813), Gilder Lehrman Collection # GLC06046, The Gilder Lehrman Institute of American History.

9. Joanne Pope Melish, *Disowning Slavery: Gradual Emancipation and "Race" in New England, 1780–1860* (Ithaca, NY: Cornell University Press, 1998), p. 70.

10. Beverly Tomek writes: "Benezet's crusade to educate the freed was also an attempt to control them ..." Beverly C. Tomek, *Colonization and Its Discontents: Emancipation, Emigration, and Antislavery in Antebellum Pennsylvania* (New York: New York University Press, 2010), p. 29.

11. Anthony Benezet, *Some Historical Account of Guinea*, in *The Complete Antislavery Writings of Anthony Benezet, 1754–1783*, David L. Crosby, ed. (Baton Rouge, LA: Louisiana State University Press, 2013), p. 182.

12. *The Edward Pleasants Valentine Papers*, vol. 2 (Richmond, VA: The Valentine Museum, 1927), p. 1117.

13. "Robert Pleasants to Samuel Pleasants, Oct. 1, 1772," Betsy August, "Robert Pleasants Letterbook, 1771–1773," (M.A. Thesis, College of William and Mary, Virginia), pp. 99–100.

14. Michael J. Crawford, *The Having of Negroes Is Become a Burden: The Quaker Struggle to Free Slaves in Revolutionary North Carolina* (Gainesville, FL: University Press of Florida, 2010), pp. 73–5.

15. *Am I Not a Man and Brother: The Antislavery Crusade of Revolutionary America, 1688–1788*, Roger Bruns, ed. (New York: Chelsea House Publishers, 1977), p. 507.

16. Petition of November 29, 1780, Legislative Petitions of the General Assembly, 1776–1865, Accession Number 36121, Box 289, Folder 107, Library of Virginia, Richmond.

17. Letterbook of Robert Pleasants, pp. 198–9 (listed as pp. 209–210 in archival index), Manuscript Collection 1116/168, Haverford Special Collections, Haverford College.

18. Bruns, *Am I Not a Man and Brother*, p. 229.

19. John Parrish, *Remarks on the Slavery of the Black People: Addressed to the Citizens of the United States...* (Philadelphia: Kimber, Conrad & Co., 1805), p. 24.

20. Moses Fisk, *Tyrannical Libertymen: A Discourse upon Negro-Slavery in the United States* (Hanover: Eagle Office, 1795).

21. Thomas Branagan, *Preliminary Essay on the Oppression of the Exiled Sons of Africa* (Philadelphia: John W. Scott, 1804), pp. 232–3.

361

22. Ibid., pp. 117–19, 125, 127, 217, 221.

23. William C. Fowler, *The Historical Status of the Negro in Connecticut* (Charleston, SC: Walker, Evans & Cogswell, 1901, orig. in *Historical Magazine and Notes and Queries*, vol. 23–24, 1874–75), p. 34.

24. Special Meeting of Aug. 10, 1797, PAS Papers Series I—Minutes and Reports; Committee for Improving the Condition of Free Blacks, Minutes 1790–1803, The Historical Society of Pennsylvania, p. 154; Gary B. Nash & Jean R. Soderlund, *Freedom by Degrees: Emancipation in Pennsylvania and Its Aftermath* (New York: Oxford University Press, 1991), pp. 130–1.

25. The thread of this correspondence can be found in William Newbold to Thomas Harrison, June 1, 1802; Sam Browne to Thomas Harrison, June 7, 1802; George Newbold to Thomas Harrison, July 1, 1802; Thomas Eddy, New York, to Thomas Harrison, July 13, 1802; George Newbold to Thomas Harrison, July 14, 1802; Geo. Newbold to Thomas Harrison, October 16, 1802, PAS Papers Series II—Correspondence, Loose Correspondence, incoming 1796–1819, The Pennsylvania Abolition Society at The Historical Society of Pennsylvania.

26. Glenn McNair, *Criminal Injustice: Slaves and Free Blacks in Georgia's Criminal Justice System* (Charlottesville, VA: University of Virginia Press, 2009), pp. 38–40.

27. *Acts Passed by the General Assembly of South Carolina, November 15, 1733–May 29, 1736* (Charles Town: Lewis Timothy, 1736).

28. Ibid., p. 83.

29. *The South Carolina Gazette* (Charleston), June 24, 1740, p. 1.

30. Sally E. Hadden, "South Carolina's Grand Jury Presentments: The Eighteenth Century Experience," in *Signposts: New Directions in Southern Legal History* (Athens, GA: University of Georgia Press, 2013). pp. 89–109.

31. "An Additional Act … to Regulate and Restrain the Conduct of Slaves and Others," in *The State Records of North Carolina*, vol. 24, Walter Clark, ed. (Goldsboro, NC: Nash Brothers, 1905), pp. 727–8.

32. *The State Records of North Carolina*, vol. 24, pp. 890–1.

33. Douglas Bradburn, *The Citizenship Revolution: Politics and the Creation of the American Union, 1774–1804* (Charlottesville, VA: University of Virginia Press, 2009), pp. 236–7.

34. *Minutes of the Common Council of the City of New York, 1784–1831*, vol. 1, January 21, 1791 (New York, 1917), p. 693. David N. Gellman, *Emancipating New York: The Politics of Slavery and Freedom, 1777–1827* (Baton Rouge, LA: Louisiana State University Press, 2006), p. 45. David Brion Davis recognized this movement toward repression: "As private manumissions increased in the North, even antislavery spokesmen looked for substitute controls that could serve the functions of slavery, especially in keeping blacks at work and insulated from the corruptions of the lower white "counterculture." David Brion Davis, *The Problem of Slavery in the Age of Revolution, 1770–1823* (Ithaca, NY: Cornell University Press, 1975), p. 305; see also Ben Bascom, "Queer Anachronism: Jeffrey Brace and the Racialized Republic," *The Arizona Quarterly*, 75:1 (Spring 2019), pp. 23–47. See also Khalil Gibran Muhammad, *The Condemnation of Blackness: Race, Crime, and the Making of Modern Urban America* (Cambridge, MA: Harvard University Press, 2010); Simone Browne, *Dark Matters: On the Surveillance of Blackness* (Durham, NC: Duke University Press, 2015).

35. *Minutes of the Common Council of the City of New York, 1784–1831*, vol. 1, September 1, 1784 (New York, 1917). p. 68.

36. Benjamin F. Prentiss, *The Blind African Slave, Or Memoirs of Boyrereau Brinch, Nick-named Jeffrey Brace* (St. Albans, Vt.: Harry Whitney, 1810), pp. 175–8.

37. *Gazette of the United States* (New York), November 25, 1789, p. 2.

38. PAS Papers Series II—Correspondence, Loose Correspondence, outgoing 1783–1914, The Pennsylvania Abolition Society at The Historical Society of Pennsylvania.

39. *Gazette of the United States* (New York), November 28, 1789, p. 1.

40. PAS Papers Series I—Minutes and Reports; Committee for Improving the Condition of Free Blacks, Minutes 1790–1803, pp. 18–20.

41. Ibid., pp. 23–4, 31.

42. Ibid., p. 28. Gary B. Nash & Jean R. Soderlund, *Freedom by Degrees*, pp. 178–9.

43. Entry for March 22, 1792, PAS Papers Series I—Minutes and Reports; Committee for Improving the Condition of Free Blacksp, p. 43; Meeting of March 21, 1795, PAS Papers Series I—Minutes and Reports; Committee for Improving the Condition of Free Blacks, p. 95. Nash & Soderlund, *Freedom by Degrees*, p. 190.

44. PAS Papers Series I—Minutes and Reports; Committee for Improving the Condition of Free Blacks, pp. 17–18.

45. Ibid., pp. 29–30.

46. Meeting of August 26, 1797, ibid., pp. 155–6.

47. John L. Rury, Philanthropy, Self Help, and Social Control: The New York Manumission Society and Free Blacks, 1785–1810, *Phylon*, 46:3 (3rd Qtr., 1985), pp. 231–41.

48. Anthony Benezet to Robert Pleasants, March 17, 1781, Manuscript Collection 852, Haverford Special Collections, Haverford College.

49. Robert J. Swan, "John Teasman: African-American Educator and the Emergence of Community in Early Black New York City, 1787–1815," *Journal of the Early Republic*, 12:3 (Autumn, 1992), pp. 331–56. See also Gellman, *Emancipating New York*, pp. 72–4.

50. Jay to John Murray, Jr. October 18, 1805, in *The Correspondence and Public Papers of John Jay*, vol. 4, Henry P. Johnston, ed. (New York: G.P. Putnam's Sons, 1898), p. 304, cited in Swan, "John Teasman."

51. See Richard Newman, "The Pennsylvania Abolition Society and the Struggle for Racial Justice," in *Antislavery and Abolition in Philadelphia: Emancipation and the Long Struggle for Racial Justice in the City of Brotherly Love*, Richard Newman & James Mueller, eds. (Baton Rouge, LA: Louisiana State University Press, 2011), pp. 130–3.

52. Bruns, *Am I Not a Man and Brother*, p. 507.

53. *Journal of Rev. Francis Asbury*, vol. 1 (New York: Land & Scott, 1852), pp. 460, 502.

54. *Journal of Rev. Francis Asbury*, vol. 2 pp. 412, 458.

55. *Journal of Rev. Francis Asbury*, vol. 3, p. 298.

56. Derrick Bell, *Silent Covenants: Brown v. Board of Education and the Unfulfilled Hopes for Racial Reform* (New York: Oxford University Press, 2004), p. 9.

57. Christopher Tomlins observes that Taney's decision in Dred Scott was a continuation of the logic set in motion by the American Revolution and Jefferson's Declaration of Independence, not a repudiation of it. Tomlins is certainly correct in seeing Lincoln's Second Inaugural Address as declaring "an end to the particular conjunction of un/freedom that the law and work of colonizing had brought into being." Tomlins, *Freedom Bound: Law, Labor, and Civic Identity in Colonizing English America, 1580–1865* (New York: Cambridge University Press, 2010), p. 524.

Index

Laurens, Henry, 75, 86, 112
Laurens, John, 2–3, 111–16
Law, Richard, 196
Lay, Benjamin, 19, 27
Lee, Arthur, 43, 119–21
Lee, General Charles, 110
Lee, Richard Henry, 98, 196, 208
Lee, William, 97–8
Library Company of Philadelphia, 10–11
Lincoln, Gen. Benjamin, 110–12
Lincoln, Levi, 235, 236
Livingston, Robert, 170, 234
Livingston, William, 142
Lords of Trade and Plantations, see Commissioners of Trade and Plantations
Lowndes, Thomas 229
loyalty tests, see citizenship, ceremonies of
Lummis, David, 141
Lyman's Report of 1822, 64
Lynch, Thomas, 229

Maclay, Sen. William, 226–7
Madison, James, 12, 117, 139–40, 142, 158–9, 173, 221, 225–6, 234–5, 240–1
Mallory, Rollin, 239
Manjapra, Kris, 279–81
manumission laws, 3, 48–53, 61–3, 249–50, 256–7, 258–9, 295–6
Marion, Gen. Francis, 109
Marsh, John, 259
Marshall, John, 233–4
Mason, George, 79–80, 149, 186
Massachusetts Committee of Safety, 200
Massachusetts Constitution 1779, 219
Mather, Cotton, 25, 138
Mclane, Louis, 239
Melish, Joanne Pope, 282–3
Mercer, Gen. Hugh, 107
Mifflin, Gov. Thomas, 253
Mifflin, Warner, 38–40, 243
Mills, Charles W., 122–3
Miranda, Lin Manuel, 1–2

miscegenation
  laws, 23, 46, 125, 295–6
  white fears of, 132–4, 136, 145, 167
Missouri Crisis – see citizenship, territories
Mitchill, Samuel, 231
Monroe, James, 160–1, 234, 240
Montesquieu, Charles Louis de, 120, 123–6, 142, 163
Moore, George H., 63–64
Morgan, Cadwalader, 35
Morgan, Charles, 258–9
Morrill, Sen. David, 237
Morris, Anthony, 50
Morris, Gouverneur, 225
Mott, James, 237
Muhlenberg, Frederick, 249
Mulligan, Hercules, 2–3

Naturalization Act of 1790, 188
Negro Seaman's Act (S.C.) 234
Nelson, Gen. Thomas, 209–10
New York African Free School, 308–9
New York Manumission Society, 260, 262–3, 291, 307–310
New York Slave Revolt Panic of 1712, 50–51
Newbold, William, 291
Newby, Thomas, 55–6
Nicholas, Robert Carter, 186
Nicholson, Jacob, 57–8
Nicholson, Jupiter, 57–8
Nicholson, Thomas, 32–3, 57, 284–5
Niles, Nathaniel, 36
Non-importation Movement, 95
Northwest Ordinance, 245

Otis, James, 41, 63, 202, 213
Otis, Sen. Harrison Gray, 237

Paine, Thomas, 45, 82–3, 146, 169–70
Parrish, John, 145, 244, 287
Parsons, Theodore, 8–9
Pastorius, Francis Daniel, 26
Patriots' dilemma defined, 6
Pearson, Eliphalet, 8–9
Pendleton, Edmund, 157

Thanks to our Patreon subscriber:

Ciaran Kane

Who has shown generosity and comradeship in support of our publishing.

Check out the other perks you get by subscribing to our Patreon – visit patreon.com/plutopress.

Subscriptions start from £3 a month.

The Pluto Press Newsletter

Hello friend of Pluto!

Want to stay on top of the best radical books
we publish?

Then sign up to be the first to hear about our
new books, as well as special events,
podcasts and videos.

You'll also get 50% off your first order with us
when you sign up.

Come and join us!

Go to bit.ly/PlutoNewsletter